Lou Harrison

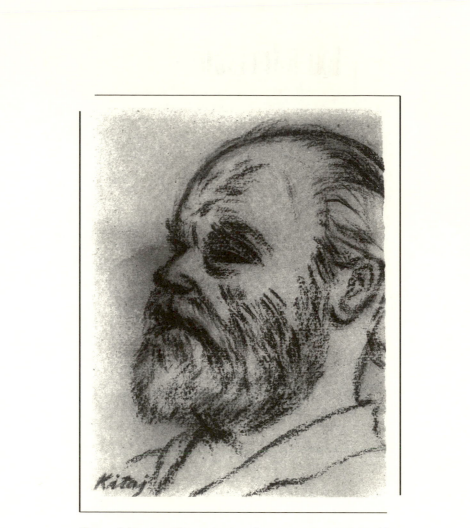

Charcoal drawing of Lou Harrison by R. B. Kitaj, 1996. Used by permission of the artist.

Lou Harrison

Composing a World

LETA E. MILLER
FREDRIC LIEBERMAN

New York • Oxford

Oxford
University
Press

1998

Oxford University Press

Oxford   New York
Athens   Auckland   Bangkok   Bogota   Bombay
Buenos Aires   Calcutta   Cape Town   Dar es Salaam
Delhi   Florence   Hong Kong   Istanbul   Karachi
Kuala Lumpur   Madras   Madrid   Melbourne
Mexico City   Nairobi   Paris   Singapore
Taipei   Tokyo   Toronto   Warsaw

and associated companies in
Berlin   Ibadan

Library of Congress Cataloging-in-Publication Data
Miller, Leta E.
    Lou Harrison : composing a world / Leta E. Miller, Fredric Lieberman.
       p. cm.
    Includes list of works: pp. 267–315
    Includes bibliographical references and index.
    ISBN 0-19-511022-6
    1. Harrison, Lou, 1917–   . 2. Composers—United States—Biography.
3. Harrison, Lou, 1917—Criticism and interpretation.   I. Lieberman, Fredric.
II. Title.
ML410.H2066M55 1998
780'.92—dc21   97-9712
[B]

Research for this book was funded in part by grants from the National
Endowment for the Humanities and the University of California, Santa Cruz.

9 8 7 6 5 4 3 2 1

Printed in the United States of America
on acid-free paper

Contents

Catalog of the Works of Lou Harrison

(By Leta E. Miller and Charles Hanson)   267

A photo gallery appears after page 174

Introduction

When Lou Harrison couldn't find the sound he imagined within the Western orchestra, he looked elsewhere for inspiration—to other cultures (China, Korea, Indonesia, Mexico), other sound sources (flower pots, brake drums, oxygen tanks), or other disciplines (dance, drama, literature). And if he still couldn't find it, he made it. Harrison's insatiable curiosity has defined his career: each artistic challenge provides the opportunity for in-depth study, whether of choreography or poetry, calligraphy or typography, new instrumental resources, tuning systems, Asian musics, or universal languages. He delights in combining disparate styles into untried syntheses: for instance, writing for Chinese instruments tuned in Just Intonation; composing concerti for Western instruments accompanied by Indonesian ensembles; using Esperanto for Buddhist texts; or requiring home-made instruments to join the standard symphony orchestra. At the age of eighty, he still bubbles with enthusiasm about musical ideas, as well as new developments in dance, visual arts, science, and literature, which he can't wait to share with friends. In fact, when moved by a remarkable book, he often orders a case from the publisher to distribute copies as gifts.

It is next to impossible to capture the full extent of Harrison's diverse artistic work but easy to identify the essence of his creativity, which is a kind of intellectual stubbornness—a drive to comprehend all aspects of a given area of inquiry from abstract conceptual issues to fundamental mechanical tools. He not only writes poetry but also explores the physical formation of the letters with which it is inscribed by mastering the art of calligraphy and even devising his own computer type fonts. For his percussion ensembles, he reached beyond the traditional battery to find new sound-sources in junkyards, hardware stores, or instruments of his own construction. He has devised his own musical modes and tuning systems—some easily realized and others more idealistic—and has designed instruments to play them.

The same insatiable curiosity drives him to constantly rethink and revise his own musical compositions, resulting in a multiplicity of versions for some works and a pattern of self-borrowing that will keep musicologists scrambling for years to come. ("Not my problem!" he quips.)

The present book began as an oral history—extended interviews with Harrison conducted by a musicologist/performer (Leta Miller) and an ethnomusicologist/composer (Fredric Lieberman). But we soon realized that we needed to cast our net further, to capture the impressions and opinions of those associated with Harrison over the past half century. Thus began a series of interviews with nearly fifty of his friends and associates, some of whom, sadly, did not live to see the publication of this book: Xenia Cage, Frank Wigglesworth, and David Tudor.[1] Others whom we would have liked to interview died before we could do so: John Cage, Bonnie Bird, Erick Hawkins, Sidney Cowell, and Minna Lederman, to name a few.

The age of many of our interviewees lent a sense of urgency to the project, prompting us to travel to remote islands off the coasts of Maine and Washington, or to meet people in less than ideal circumstances, such as noisy coffee shops or crowded restaurants. Some of those with whom we spoke were weak and fragile; others, even among Lou's immediate contemporaries, were vibrant. All, however, helped us focus the image of him at various moments in his career. Their names are listed at the end of this volume, and their voices appear in the pages to follow, interspersed with Harrison's own observations and recollections, enhancing information from our research through thousands of clippings and programs, the holdings of libraries around the country, and Harrison's personal archives, which he graciously opened to us without restriction.

Lou's name opened doors, even to those who customarily refused requests for interviews. After helping numerous graduate students with dissertation research, dancer Bella Lewitzky had resolved to curtail participation in such projects, but for a book about Lou Harrison, she told us, "How could I say no?" Alan Hovhaness and Xenia Cage, both in poor health, nevertheless invited us to interview them. Frank Wigglesworth had just been released from the hospital after surgery when we called him at his summer home in Massachusetts; he insisted that we come over immediately.

What is Harrison's secret that elicits such warm reponse? The voices of his many friends tell the story best. A sampling from our cast of characters:[2]

Mark Morris (dancer, choreographer):
You either know Lou and have been to his house and are his best friend, or you've never heard of him. To me he's like a fabulous friend who is a lot older than I am. Unlike a lot of people involved in music, Lou didn't automatically assume that I didn't know what he was talking about—or what I was talking about. A lot of musicians think that since most choreographers don't know a thing about music, that means I don't know a thing about music. The fact is I do, and Lou never thought otherwise. It's as if he said, "You're interested in what I do; what do you do?"

Daniel Schmidt (composer, instrument builder):
Lou has an inimitable generosity. After meeting him for the first time (when he learned I was building instruments), he immediately said, "Come down to Aptos; we'll show you everything we know. If you have something to show us, please show us." I came to his tiny house in the Aptos woods. The grapevines were growing all about; we had to shove them apart on the work benches to get enough space to set up our experiments. In the midst of all this, he realized that I knew about Javanese gamelan. "Would you teach me what you know about gamelan?" he asked. I'm a good deal younger than he is, but we respected each other as colleagues.

Many younger interviewees stressed Harrison's intellectual curiosity, his eagerness to treat each new stimulus as an adventure in composition. Many noted that he gave their own work a validity that allowed them to grow.

Robert Hughes (composer, Harrison's former student):
Lou taught his students the "loophole theory of existence," as he called it. "Life is a solid, big wall. We feel our way along it—and it's very dark. Suddenly an opening appears. On the other side is blinding light. There are two kinds of people. There are those who look at the light and, even though it is possible that it's hellfire, it could just as well be the brilliance of paradise. They charge through. I'm of that type," he said. "But there are those who look at the opening and back away, who carefully analyze it as it slowly shuts. They return to the wall and keep feeling along in the darkness, until another opening occurs and then begin repeating the process." Lou, of course, encouraged me to be of the first type, to leap through, to take irra-

tional chances. Many times Lou has surprised me by his new interests and ventures. He leaps forward. He never seems to back away.

Carter Scholz (composer, typographer, author):
What is most impressive about Lou is his indefatigable intellectual curiosity; his unwillingness to take anything for granted; his attempts to get at the roots of whatever he is interested in, be it music, tuning systems, or sign language; and his great gifts of synthesis, his ability to pull together varied influences and express them in different fields—music, poetry, art. He's the nearest thing to a Renaissance man I have ever met.

Older colleagues cited Harrison's energetic exuberance—part of his persona since his youth:

Merce Cunningham (dancer, choreographer):
I remember Lou at Mills [in 1938]. His energy was always extraordinary. He was always a sort of bubbling man, who seemed to be able to simply make music come out of his fingers.

Xenia Cage (artist; former wife of John Cage):
The first time I met Lou, John and I were living in San Francisco. There he was, his smiling self, and on his piano there was a little plate with a piece of half-eaten sandwich on it. He had a friend there, sitting at an easel painting, looking at his canvas while wearing a painter's cap from Sherwin Williams. That charmed me. The next time we went to his apartment, there was the same plate with the same half-eaten sandwich still there.

At the time Lou was working for the Palace Hotel in San Francisco as a flower arranger. He took us to a place called Sister Lena's, a little shacky restaurant in San Francisco, but with gorgeous bouquets of flowers on all the tables because of dear Lou. When the flowers got too tired for the Palace Hotel, he'd give them to Sister Lena.

Bella Lewitzky (dancer, choreographer):
Lou was very young when I knew him. I would go with him to nurseries where he would select terra-cotta flower pots and line them up until he got whatever harmonic structure he wanted. Anything he could get his hands onto that could make music was valid. But he differed from those who used *musique concrète*, which became a sort of semi-biblical term—something that was labeled, that was boxed. Lou had no need, ever, to say that he used this or that or the other procedure. He was after the result, not the labeling or the boxing. That's what permitted him to be so open-ended, to go in whatever direction he wanted.

That direction was always guided by a vision of sonic beauty, whether with Asian ensembles, the percussion orchestra, a chamber ensemble, or the traditional symphony:

Janice Giteck (composer):
> Lou gave me permission to be a melodist and there are very few models for that. He goes after the most beautiful sound that he can possibly get, and at the same time he loves the most primitive sounds, such as the rough, growly, deep sound of the bass drum. So one hears sound in the raw and exquisite acculturated humanness at the same time.

Dennis Russell Davies (conductor):
> [The audience's response] to Lou's music is an acceptance that comes from the directness of the language and the immediacy of the feelings and emotions that the music expresses. The audience feels as if it's being spoken to directly. There's effervescence, spontaneity, and enthusiasm. His music has passion and assuredness. There's a vulnerability as well that can be particularly touching.

Nearly everyone remarked on Harrison's integration of the arts, on his search for syntheses that capture the spirit of the model and at the same time emerge in a language all his own.

Jean Erdman (dancer, choreographer):
> [Lou was] one of the most wonderful composers to work with because he knew as much about dance as about music. He enjoyed the idea of having the music and the dance cooperate so that each was part of a whole that was different from the parts. That takes a very special kind of creativity and expertise.

Judith Malina (actress, director, writer):
> History is only a springboard for learning what works and what doesn't, what forms we can use and what forms we can't. In the kind of breakup of the arts that people like Lou were making [during the 1950s] he succeeded beautifully in creating new forms and new vocabularies sometimes out of other cultures, sometimes out of the East, but sometimes just out of his head.
> This is where the cultural has the political effect; because what is political progress except to be raised to another level of consciousness and to begin to function on a higher level in our daily commitments, whether it's the quotidian life of how we behave to each other—or whether it's creating forms to organize commerce and industry? It's functioning on that higher level—on the level of Lou's generous, open, long sweeping passages, not of

an impatient attitude of "I can't pay attention to this long line. I've got to get my work done for today. Today is so difficult; we've got so many problems. We have people to feed out there. We can't think about utopia!" Of course we've got to get this done now and there are people starving and we have to pay attention to them. But we mustn't lose the long, sweeping passages. In some way Lou's music, which is eminently playable and listenable, has this ecstatic quality.

But by far the most consistent thread that ran through the interviews was Harrison's respect for others, his cherishing of human relationships:

Vincent McDermott (composer, gamelan specialist):
Lou once told me, "What there is in life is first of all to be with people—to be as good to people as you can, to the best of your ability. Music, yes, but first, basic human relations." That goal I owe to Lou. Whether or not I have been successful at it in my own life, I consider it an ideal to work toward.

Bill Colvig (electrician, instrument builder, Lou's life-partner):
It wasn't until three or four weeks after I had met Lou [in February 1967] that I came down the first time to visit him in Aptos. I tell everybody that it was my lifelong dream to live in a little cabin out in the woods with a dirty old man. I'm kidding, of course; he wasn't dirty. The cabin was, though, and I could see that he needed somebody to help him.

By this time, the reader will no doubt have realized that this book is not a biography in the traditional sense; nor is it a dispassionate analytical treatment of the music,[3] although biography and analysis appear within its pages. We do not attempt an evaluative survey of the more than three hundred works listed in our catalog, nor do we set forth to prove a chosen critical theory. Rather, we explore the areas that have shaped Harrison's creative output—music and the dance; intonation and temperament systems; instrument construction and the percussion orchestra; the music of Asia—which along with his personal philosophy and values (described in the chapters on politics and gender) coalesce into a discussion of his compositional process and an assessment of his role in twentieth-century American music. These areas of influence lead us finally to a discussion of his related artistic activities: his writings, his poetry, and his art.

One of the major difficulties facing any writer attempting to communicate the essentials of a rich and lengthy career is the question of what must be left out. For every anecdote or letter excerpted herein, a dozen more cry out to be heard. The sheer volume of source material, both primary and secondary, could easily support a tome four or five times the length of the present one, which must, therefore, be considered as a prolegemena to the subject, and by no means the last word. While we have attempted a judicious selection, we well realize that many chapters could easily become entire books in their own right. Publishers' constraints on length, illustrations, and musical examples both force concise expression and keep the end product affordable.

Our tone throughout the book is deliberately informal, as befits our subject: no one who has met Lou would dream of calling him "Mr. Harrison" for more than five minutes. Neither of us can recall ever seeing him in a coat and tie: he typically appears, even at Davies Hall in San Francisco or at Lincoln Center in New York, in his trademark red corduroy shirt, his white beard and imposing figure evoking the image of a cross between Orson Welles and Santa Claus.

That is not to say that Lou is never angry or discouraged. On the contrary, he has at times expressed considerable annoyance and suffered periods of severe personal depression. His work has not always met with sympathetic reception, particularly from East Coast critics. (Even the most recent performances of his music in New York inspired prolonged standing ovations but several lukewarm reviews.) Harrison does not brush off such critiques lightly. They may cause him considerable pain, and they often prompt serious reassessment of his work. But through the years he has displayed admirable resilience, always finding sources of energy to embark on new studies and experiments.

In our recounting of Lou's life and work, we have attempted to the best of our abilities to document every fact and to correct errors that have appeared in previous sources, both published and unpublished.[4] Some of these errors were obvious, such as misconceptions about the birthplace of Lou's father. Others required more digging: mysteries surrounding the composition date of *Gending Vincent*, for instance, were only solved when we determined that the year given on the printed program for the premiere was wrong. Still others came to our attention almost by accident, such as Lou's offhand remark, during a discussion of his *Music for Violin and Various Instruments*, that the wrong violinist was credited on the CD recording. Nevertheless, we have doubtlessly erred ourselves at times either by omission or commission, and we welcome responses from readers.

During our research we had help from many sources to supplement the invaluable assistance of our interviewees: the initial suggestion for an oral history from musicologist Catherine Smith; a series of grants from the Committee on Research and the Arts Division of the University of California, Santa Cruz (UCSC); a Summer Stipend and Collaborative Projects Grant from the National Endowment for the Humanities; a remarkable graduate research assistant, Jonathon Grasse, who patiently transcribed the many interviews and coauthored the gamelan chapter; Lou's indefatigable archivist, Charles Hanson, who provided continuing assistance and coauthored the catalog; and the cooperation of numerous others. We especially wish to thank Todd Vunderink (Peer International), Don Gillespie (C. F. Peters),

Nancy Allison (assistant to Jean Erdman), David Vaughan (archivist for the Cunningham Dance Foundation), Don Harris (UCSC photo lab), and the library staffs at UCSC Special Collections (Rita Bottoms, Carol Champion, Paul Stubbs, and Irene Berry) and interlibrary loan, Mills College (Renee Jadushlever and Janice Braun), and Yale (Kendall Crilly). Several colleagues graciously read parts or all of the manuscript and offered helpful comments: Philip Brett, Ruth Solomon, Robert Provine, Michele Edwards, Robert Hughes, Philip Yampolsky, Sherwood Dudley, Wayne Shirley, Charles Hamm, and Steven Johnson. Others provided scores, documents, or information: Dorothy Crawford, Edith Ho, Karen Bell-Kanner, Heidi von Gunden, Susan Summerfield, Laura Kuhn, Newell Reynolds.

Most of all, however, we wish to thank Lou. He and his partner, Bill Colvig, repeatedly opened their home to us. Lou cheerfully answered our endless stream of questions and invited us to examine personal correspondence and manuscripts, to listen to tapes or view videos, or simply to browse through his library. Virtually anything we requested was expeditiously provided. Our discussions took place in an atmosphere of mutual trust. Lou talked freely to us about many personal matters, relying on our discretion to protect the privacy of anyone who might be compromised by uncomfortable revelations. After the book was drafted, Lou read and discussed its contents with us, correcting errors or misconceptions but never attempting to censor what we had written. All quotations from his letters and writings (published and unpublished) are used with his permission. We hope in turn to have been able to offer some insight into the work of this remarkable artist.

BIOGRAPHY

1 West Coast Prelude

(1917–1943)

On October 25, 1915, Calline Lillian Silver married Clarence Maindenis Harrison in Portland, Oregon. Calline, known to her friends as "Cal," was an adventurous woman, born to adventurous parents. Her father, Charles Silver, had left a prosperous family in Salem, Ohio, to seek his fortunes in the Far West. Silver and his wife, Jessie Steele, had two daughters: Lounette, born in 1882, and Cal, born in Seattle on June 18, 1890.[1] In the early 1890s Charles secured a job in Portland as head mechanic for an electric streetcar company, but he couldn't resist the promise of quick fortune in the Alaskan gold rush. About 1898, when he was offered a job erecting gold mining equipment in Dawson City, Charles, his wife, and the two girls moved to Spartan accommodations in Skagway, Alaska (see fig. 1). The gold rush was in full swing; hundreds of men and animals hazarded the harrowing three-hundred-mile journey over the mountains between the port of Skagway and the mining center of Dawson City, Charles Silver among them. When the company that had hired him refused to fulfill its obligations, Silver resigned and headed back to his family in Skagway, tackling the journey on foot in below-zero weather. Thereafter he set off alone for Portland to resume his former position, but by the time he reached Seattle, he

3

had contracted pneumonia from the long exposure to the intense cold. He died there in 1900, and Calline later moved back to Oregon with her mother and sister.[2]

Cal inherited her father's spirit of adventure. She loved cars, taking pride in having been the first woman to drive across one of the bridges in Portland.[3] Years later, after she had married Clarence and they had moved to California with their two sons, Lou and Bill, her wanderlust was partly responsible for the family's habit of moving nearly every year from one town to another.

Clarence Harrison, who disliked his given name and preferred to be called "Pop," was equally adventurous in his own way. He worked at a variety of jobs—selling automotive products, managing car dealerships, establishing an automated car wash, mining mercury in Nevada, and logging in northern California.

Clarence's father was an immigrant from Norway, who adopted the family name "Harrison" after repeated misspellings and mispronunciations of his original name, Thomas H. Nësja.[4] Lou claims that "Harrison" was randomly chosen from the phone book; Lou's brother Bill, however, says that Thomas adopted the name of a coworker in the steel or railroad shop in which he was employed. According to Bill, colleagues found Thomas's Norwegian surname so difficult to handle that they took to calling him Harrison instead; when he left the company he merely adopted the name as his own.[5] The casual suppression of the family's Norwegian ethnicity was typical of a generation eager to blend into the American mainstream—a philosophy that Pop (born in Kato Falls, Wisconsin, on May 22, 1882)[6] inherited as well. "My father was a really wide-eyed American of first generation," Lou recalls. "Progress was everything. We used to drive around on Sundays looking at new construction, farming, and bridges. He had that first generation eagerness to be an American in the full progress sense."[7]

Calline and Clarence's first child, Lou Silver Harrison, was born in Portland on May 14, 1917; three years later they had a second son, Arthur William. Cal and Pop named their firstborn after Cal's sister Lounette ("when they found that I was male, they just cut off the '-nette' and left me the Lou"),[8] but usually they simply called him "Buster."

Prior to Lou's birth, Cal worked as a beautician—she called herself a "beauty worker," a term Lou finds apt in describing his role as a composer.[9] But in 1911 her fortunes took a decided turn for the better when she inherited a sizable sum from the estate of her grandfather, Albert Silver (1823–1900). Albert had been president of the Silver Manufacturing Company in Salem, Ohio, which produced machinery for farming, woodworking, food processing, and drilling.[10] When Albert's widow Mary died in 1910, the Silver estate was divided evenly among their six children.[11] The estate was substantial: $230,044.23 after expenses (equivalent to a purchasing power of nearly four million dollars in 1997). Since Charles, their second son, had died ten years earlier, his share was split among his widow (Jessie) and the two daughters, Lounette and Calline. Cal's share was $16,670 (about $281,000 in 1997).[12]

With her inheritance Cal not only purchased a tire business for Pop but also built, soon after Lou's birth, an elegant thirty-unit apartment building: the Silver Court Apartments at NE Twenty-second and Hancock. Cal had a penchant for Asian art. The Harrison apartment was decorated with Persian carpets and Asian artworks; the walls were covered with Japanese grass paper. In contrast, the lobby of the building showed Italian Renaissance influence in its elegant simplicity and carved wooden furnishings (fig. 2). The two contrasting visual styles in the Silver Court Apartments foreshadowed Lou's cultural interests: he maintains a fascination with both the music of Asia and that of pre-Mozartean Europe.

Among Cal's acquaintances from her beautician days was the actress Verna Felton,[13] who often came into the salon. A warm-hearted and enduring friendship soon developed between the two women, and in 1920, when Felton needed a young orphan for a production of *Daddy Long Legs*, "Buster," age two-and-a-half, was selected (see fig. 3). He was the hit of the show. On February 16, 1920, Leone Cass Baer wrote about the play's "littlest orphan" in the *Oregonian*.

> Clad in his checkered rompers to match the other orphans, Buster ambles along, a roguish, pink-cheeked cherub, making eyes at Judy [played by Verna Felton], crowing over a piece of candy he finds in her pocket and making joyous remarks that do not belong in the script and have nothing to do with the play. His blasé chirrup, 'I should worry,' when Judy told him not to break a cup, brought down the house, and Buster was trotted out at the tail of a string of orphans to make his bow. The others bow gravely and gracefully, but bolshevist Buster has a monologue about the nice curtain that goes up and down . . . and almost breaks up the show.[14]

Cal even agreed to let Lou accompany Felton and her troupe on their tour of the Northwest. Despite his seemingly carefree attitude toward the theater, the experience engendered an ambivalence that was to surface in later years:

> My mother put me on the stage when I was two-and-a-half and I was a touring actor until I was three. I toured Seattle and Yakima, the whole northern route. Since my brother was born when I was three, and I'd been given away to another lady on the stage, you can imagine that there were some psychological complications! A couple of decades ago, I went up on stage at the Cabrillo Music Festival to acknowledge and commend a conductor who did a perfectly beautiful performance of my *Seven Pastorales*, and I burst into tears. I thought, "What the devil?" and came to realize that as a child I'd been frightened by the enormous amount of applause and laughter. It's frightening, even if you're hanging on to your putative mother. After I'd thought that through, though, I found I could simply milk the audience![15]

Pop's brother Harry ("H. O.") Harrison was in the car business.[16] As a major distributor for Chrysler, Hudson, and Essex, he not only owned one of the largest dealerships in the Bay Area (on Van Ness Avenue in San Francisco) but also controlled the smaller dealerships in the region. H. O. convinced Pop to move to California and become a Chrysler dealer. Lou well remembers his colorful uncle, who always carried on his person a bottle of hot sauce and who owned several ranches in California and Mexico. Lou and Bill spent delightful vacations on H. O.'s spreads in northern California.

In 1926 the Harrison family moved to Woodland, California, the first in a series of relocations every year or two: Woodland, Sacramento, Stockton, Berkeley, San Francisco, Los Gatos, Redwood City, Belmont, and finally Burlingame, where Lou graduated from high school in December 1934.[17] The moves were occasioned in part by Pop's employment, in part by Cal's wanderlust, and in part by Bill's health. (Bill had anemia, which sometimes made walking painful, and Lou would tow him around in a go-cart. Bill remembers the cause as rheumatic fever; Lou recalls that Bill had an allergic reaction to an inoculation. In any case, foggy San Francisco was a poor environment, so for a time Pop made the long commute from warmer Los Gatos to the city.) Clearly there was little opportunity for the Harrison boys to develop long-lasting friendships. Lou carted his precious mementos from place to place: "I had a little trunk of papers, photographs, all sorts of things that I carried around with me. It was my little life. Since I was moved every year and had no chance to have a peer group or any roots in any place, I made an imaginary world and carried it around in paper and books and things."[18]

He also busied himself by tinkering with electronic equipment and building instruments. During his Stockton years (ages 10–11), he dismantled the family phonograph and equipped it with a larger horn to increase its amplitude. In the same period he also tried his hand at a small violin, an early hint of the large-scale instrument-building projects to come: clavichords, Asian instruments, and, ultimately, three complete gamelan—Indonesian percussion orchestras primarily composed of various types of gongs and metallic keyed instruments.

Harrison became a voracious reader and over the years has accumulated an impressive library on a wide range of topics.

> I learned as a child in Redwood City that I could go to the city library and take out anything. And then there would be a footnote and the book wouldn't be in the City Library, so the lady would suggest, "Why don't you go around the corner to the County Library in the basement of the courthouse?" So I went there and if the book wasn't in, the librarian would say, "Well, I'll order it from the State Library." If the State Library didn't have it, there was always the Library of Congress. But when I went to New York [in 1943] and started this same process, I discovered that no book was ever in anywhere! So I started to buy and you can see the results.[19]

Cal made sure that Lou and Bill were trained in the arts, particularly music and dance. They took private piano lessons and were dutifully enrolled in ballroom dance classes; Lou also studied violin. In addition, Cal assured that her sons received an eclectic religious training by enrolling them in Sunday schools from a variety of different Protestant sects. "Church shopping," Virgil Thomson later called it when Lou told him about the frequent changes in denominations—not only when the Harrisons moved, but sometimes even more often.

Pop, for his part, was agnostic. "When you're dead, you're dead," he'd say. Nevertheless, when Lou developed an interest in Gregorian chant, stimulated by his high school studies of Latin, Pop patiently drove his son every Monday night from Burlingame to Mission Dolores in San Francisco, where Lou took a course in chant taught by two of the fathers, an experience that helped shape the sensuous wandering melodic lines so typical of his later work. His study of the structure of chant also stimulated his later fascination with manipulating brief melodic cells (which he terms "melodicles") as a compositional device.

The Harrison brothers (fig. 4) responded in radically different ways to their artistic training. Lou learned to play wind, string, and keyboard instruments, composed his first works before puberty, and was always experimenting with new sound media. Bill, on the other hand, was never much interested in the music and dance lessons. Overcoming his childhood illness, he played on the high school football team, defended his brother against anti-art bullies, and appropriated Lou's precious instrument-building supplies to make model airplanes.[20]

Cal and Pop engendered a "live and let live" attitude in the boys, not only about different Christian sects but also about politics and careers. They supported both boys in their chosen professions, although Lou's high school friend Robert Metcalf recalls Pop's less-than-enthusiastic reaction to watching his son dance in a high-profile production at San Francisco's Curran Theatre in 1937. (Clarence said it took twenty years off his life.)[21] On the other hand, when Lou became fascinated with Chinese musical instruments some years later, Pop offered to open a *cheng* (Chinese zither) factory to manufacture them. (Lou pointed out that a limited American market might not warrant the investment.)

Lou's first piano compositions date from his childhood years in California. Among them is a lament signed "Lou Silver Harrison, ten years old" dedicated to Helen Johnson, one of two sisters who owned a farm near Portland that the Harrison boys had frequented. Although Lou's heart was in the right place, it seems that his reconnaissance was faulty: it wasn't Helen, but rather her sister, who had died. Harrison now dubs this *Elegie* "subjuvenilia" and evaluates it as musically "dreadful." From this early manuscript, however, we see the unity of three arts that would occupy his attention in future years, for the music is bound by a bright cover featuring an abstract watercolor and is decorated with hand-lettered calligraphy (reproduced on the back cover).

During his high school years, Lou studied composition privately with Howard Cooper (a student of Domenico Brescia at Mills College in Oakland). He also avidly composed piano and chamber music for a circle of friends. Otis Carrington, music instructor at Sequoia High School in Redwood City, was particularly supportive, featuring Lou as soprano soloist in 1931 (his "unchanged voice . . . wandered nicely among high Gs")[22] and even giving him the opportunity to conduct the school orchestra. Burlingame High School presented one of Harrison's compositions at its commencement ceremonies on December 13, 1934, when Lou graduated: flutist Beth Bullard played "Blue Glass," with Lou accompanying at the piano. He disparagingly dismisses these early creations, including a solo violin suite that has been resurrected and performed several times in recent years: "It's awful . . . wildly Ivesian or Riegger-ish." Asked what he wants done with such juvenilia, he replied with tongue firmly in cheek: "Put PG [parental guidance] on them."

San Francisco: 1934–1942

Soon after his graduation from high school, Lou's family moved to a new home on Buena Vista Avenue in San Francisco, where he lived while attending San Francisco State University for three semesters (January 1935– May 1936).[23] There he studied French horn and clarinet, took up harpsichord and recorder in an early music consort, and sang in vocal ensembles, including a madrigal group. He soon moved into a house near Sutro Forest with several college friends, establishing a commune-type arrangement with poet and composer James Cleghorn,[24] Cleghorn's wife Fern, astronomer John Dobson, and singer and dancer Dorothy James. The period was not only one of personal readjustment but also one of civic turmoil, including major labor strikes that provided the subject for Lou's earliest dance composition (chapter 4).

Harrison soon moved from the commune into a railroad flat apartment on Telegraph Hill with boyfriend Sherman Slayback, a salesman and, later, a jukebox repairman. There they sublet the front room to a ballet "rehearser" and teacher of pantomime who was totally deaf. Lou's response to his new housemate typifies his approach to new challenges: he immediately tackled the basics of American sign language, learning finger spelling and conversational phrases so as to communicate effectively.

In keeping with the Harrison family pattern of changing residences every year or so, Lou moved twice more during his years in San Francisco: in 1940 he and Sherman found more comfortable quarters on Jackson Street (where they had a dance studio above their lodgings), and about a year later (after his relationship with Slayback fell apart), Lou rented space in the home of dancer Carol Beals and her husband Mervin Leeds; his new boyfriend William Brown joined him there in 1941.

During the eight years between his graduation from high school and his move to Los Angeles in 1942, Harrison explored the musical and cultural resources that would subsequently shape his compositions: the percussion ensemble, Chinese and Japanese music, the Indonesian gamelan, modern dance, Baroque music, and the works of Charles Ives, Henry Cowell, and Arnold Schoenberg. The only major strand in his musical personality that did not have its birth in the early San Francisco period was Just Intonation, an outgrowth of his later exposure to the theories of Harry Partch. Even here, though, the groundwork was laid by his reading of Joseph Yasser's *A Theory of Evolving Tonality* (1932).

Lou was composing actively in these years, producing numerous works that continue to be performed today. At the same time, to pay the rent he had to hold down several jobs, both musical and nonmusical: florist at the Palace Hotel, clerk at Herbert Wilson's Record Rental Library, and dance accompanist.

In 1935, soon after he began his studies at San Francisco State, Harrison met Cowell, whom he describes as a "central information booth" for two or three generations of American composers[25] and who would remain one of the most powerful influences in his life. He had already read Cowell's *New Musical Resources* (1930) and *American Composers on American Music* (1933) when, at the recommendation of Jim Cleghorn, he enrolled in Cowell's course "Music of the Peoples of the World," offered in the spring of 1935 through the University of California Extension in San Francisco.[26] Lou became "class monitor" (taking roll, etc.) and subsequently approached Cowell for private lessons in composition.[27] He vividly remembers Cowell's New Music Society concerts as well, particularly one on March 7, 1935, in which Schoenberg conducted his own music (during a preconcert lecture, Cowell called the Austrian "the most noted composer since Beethoven"), and one on April 1 of the same year featuring Japanese chamber music with koto, shamisen, voice, and shakuhachi.[28] Cowell's stepmother Olive also held a series of "house concerts" during these years, several of which Lou attended. At one such concert he met Edgard Varèse, who graciously gave him a detailed critique of his "Ricercare on Bach's Name."[29] Cowell also introduced Harrison to Irving Morrow, consulting architect of the Golden Gate Bridge,[30] who in turn exposed Lou to the late Debussy sonatas and to de Falla's puppet opera, *El retablo de maese Pedro* (1919–22), which would later inspire Harrison's own puppet opera, *Young Caesar*.

Cowell's iconoclastic challenges to conventional practices, coupled with his personal magnetism, shaped the direction of Harrison's compositional development. Due in part to a lack of conventional training,[31] Cowell's mind was open to unorthodox approaches to musical composition and performance: as early as 1913 he had called for large clusters in his piano works, requiring use of the entire hand.[32] Charles Seeger, with whom Cowell studied beginning in 1914, encouraged such experimentation and supported his later work at the Hornbostel Collection in Berlin (1931–32), which stimulated Cowell's fascination with non-Western musics.

Nearly every aspect of Harrison's work shows Cowell's influence. Lou's fascination with manipulating small melodic cells, for instance, was fueled by Cowell's composition assignments: "He would give me three- or four-tone motives and suggest that I use them to construct small model pieces . . . , transposing them . . . using the retrograde and inversions and inverted retrogrades, the melodicles either connected by a common tone or separated by a determined interval."[33] Cowell had a systematic approach to counterpoint as well: Lou's assignments included constructing various melodic lines in tertial or secundal counterpoint against a given cantus firmus. ("Tertial" and "secundal" in this context refer to the most prominent intervallic relationships on strong beats.)[34]

The rhythmic complexities of Harrison's early percussion works grew directly from his study of Cowell's piano pieces, especially *Fabric*, which calls for cross-rhythms of 3:4:5, or 5:7:8. Lou devised an ingenious tool to learn the piece: in the endless center track of a 78 rpm record he chipped the cross-rhythm patterns with a pin (using geometry to measure the appropriate distances), thereby causing the machine to reproduce the rhythms accurately when the disc was played.[35]

Cowell emphasized to Harrison that most of the world's music was comprised of "melody accompanied by some form of rhythmic behavior."[36] At the same time, however, his novel harmonic theories influenced Harrison as well. "All or any of the tones of the mode may be sounded simultaneously along the progression of the melody," Cowell taught, "and not only allow all functions within the melody to remain evident but even enforce these functions."[37] Specifically, he advocated chord complexes built from triads with closely related roots (for example, combining the triads on C, E, and G).[38]

Cowell also projected future developments in harmonic theory based on both historical models and acoustic principles. Medieval music, he noted, accepted as consonances only the first three intervals in the harmonic series: octaves, fifths, and fourths. Renaissance theorists accepted, in addition, major and minor thirds with their inversions. By extension Cowell projected harmonic complexes based on seconds, justifying tone clusters of various sizes and densities through a chronological pattern that accepted ever higher intervals in the overtone series. The concept has much in common with other compositional theories current at the time, such as those of Hindemith, who similarly sought rationalization of his harmonic experiments on historical and acoustical grounds. Lou, following Cowell's lead, explored keyboard clusters in several works from the 1930s, as well as in later compositions, such as the *Concerto for Organ with Percussion* (1973), the *Piano Concerto* (1985), the *Grand Duo* (1988), and *Rhymes with Silver* (1996). In these later works he added his own refinement, an "octave bar" (chapter 6), possibly inspired by a similar suggestion in Ives's *Concord Sonata*.

Harrison served as one of Cowell's "pedal boys" for *Banshee* and recalls the thrill of watching Cowell perform extended piano techniques: strumming the strings of the instrument or producing huge clusters of sound with his hand or forearm. "Practically anywhere Henry was, I'd ask him to play for me," Lou notes. "He'd play old favorites of mine, always with a fresh attitude and with a great deal of rubato and freedom."[39]

Cowell not only encouraged novel uses of traditional instruments but also urged Lou to seek new sound-producing media ("Henry encouraged us to forage through junkyards"). His advocacy of "found" instruments, newly invented instruments, and new uses or contexts for traditional instruments encouraged Harrison to explore the percussion ensemble and to challenge established Western instrumental practice. Cowell's promotion of automobile junkyards and floral nurseries as repositories of resonant percussion (in the form of brake drums and flower pots) was "charmingly wicked," Lou notes, "for, in effect, he offered a way of simply by-passing the establishment."[40]

But perhaps Cowell's most important influence on Lou was his advocacy of non-Western musics—both as classical traditions and as sources for new musics: specifically Asian music, Amerindian music, and Latin American music. He staunchly defended hybrids, eschewing the assertion of some ethnomusicologists "that there ought to be no interrelationship between the 'studier' and the 'studied.'"[41] In a sense, then, Cowell legitimized Lou's later experiments in mixing Western and Eastern instruments in combinations limited only by the composer's imagination. He once remarked to Lou that we are "all part of an ocean of intelligence over which there was . . . a surface tension rather like a thin rubber sheet, and that . . . one would rise up over here and another would rise up over there, and they would look across at one another as though separate, but . . . were all the time of one nature underneath."[42]

Cowell's work also set the stage for Lou's later explorations in tuning. The point of departure in *New Musical Resources* is the overtone series, from which Cowell derived harmonic extensions that create both new sonic complexes and innovative metric theories. In works such as *Fabric* or the *Quartet Euphometric* of 1919, frequency ratios from the harmonic series (3:2, 4:3, 5:4, etc.) serve as the basis for cross-rhythms. Lou experimented with the same concept in his *Fugue for Percussion* (1942). Here, the second entry of the subject, which in common-practice tradition would appear at the fifth (a harmonic ratio of 3:2), instead appears in a 3:2 *metric* relation to the opening statement. Similarly, the third entry, which normally appears at the fourth (4:3) in relation to the second entry (and at the octave—2:1—in relation to

EXAMPLE 1-1. *Fugue for Percussion* (1942), beginning.

Successive entries of the theme are lined up vertically to facilitate comparison of metric relationships.

the opening), articulates these ratios metrically instead of harmonically—example 1-1. Lou recalls that the *Fugue* presented such formidable challenges for the performers that a projected 1951 premiere at Columbia University was canceled and *Canticle #3* substituted at the last minute.[43]

The difficulty of executing complex metric ratios accurately led Cowell to visualize a mechanism for an instrument to do so. In collaboration with Léon Thérémin, he constructed the rhythmicon in 1931. Two years later Nicolas Slonimsky described its capabilities:

> The rhythmicon can play triplets against quintuplets, or any other combinations up to sixteen notes in a group. The metrical index is associated . . . with the corresponding frequence of vibrations. . . . Quintuplets are . . . sounded on the fifth harmonic, nonuplets on the ninth harmonic, and so forth. A complete chord of sixteen notes presents sixteen rhythmical figures in sixteen harmonics within the range of four octaves. All sixteen notes coincide, with the beginning of each period, thus producing a synthetic harmonic series of tones.[44]

Cowell wrote a concerto for this new instrument entitled *Rhythmicana*, which opens with a brilliant sally on the rhythmicon followed immediately by an orchestral passage in the woodwinds. "It was Henry's whimsy to open the orchestra with the woodwind section," notes Lou, "which of course sounds completely out of tune."[45]

In addition to the student-teacher relationship, Lou became close friends with the Cowell family—an association that continued until the recent death of Cowell's widow, Sidney. Thus, when Cowell was arrested in May 1936 on a morals charge, the effect on Harrison was profound both personally and professionally. (The warrant charged Cowell with violation of section 288a of the California Penal Code, which prohibited oral copulation; the particular case involved a seventeen-year-old boy.)[46] "His arrest was a real jolt," says Lou. "I knew the historical background: the troubles of Oscar Wilde, Hart Crane, Walt Whitman—and so I suspected what Cowell might be facing."[47] The previous day Lou had accompanied his teacher on a visit to Stanford, where Cowell had gathered information for a commission to write underwater music for university swimmers.[48] During Cowell's four years in San Quentin (anticipating probation, he had pleaded guilty to spare his friends the publicity of a trial), Harrison visited often and they would discuss musical composition through prison bars. On one such visit, Cowell introduced Lou to the concept of the musical "kit," a flexible performance score in which elements can be rearranged at the pleasure of the performer. (Cowell's term was "elastic form.") Dancer Marian Van Tuyl had commissioned a work from Cowell in response to which he composed—and sent to Lou—a series of single measures along with several through-composed pieces from which Lou was to assemble a complete score for the dance.[49] Harrison subsequently used a similar procedure in such works as *Jephtha's Daughter* (1963), *Ariadne* (1988), and *Rhymes with Silver* (1996).

The day after Cowell's release in 1940 Lou was invited to breakfast at his home: "We sat at a little table back of the piano. Olive served us from the kitchen. Henry didn't say anything. About halfway through breakfast he said, 'Oh, I'm sorry, we weren't allowed to talk in San Quentin.' Then, boom, he was off and away and he was the old Henry again just like that."[50]

Indeed, Lou recalls that Cowell was rarely at a loss for words. Even at a dinner with Harrison's parents in the mid-1930s, Cowell was able to discover a common interest with Clarence by describing the diesel retrofit motor car he had just driven from New York to San Francisco. He immediately won Pop's heart.

Always eclectic in his interests, Harrison also developed during this period an intense interest in early music, particularly that of the French Baroque. In 1936 he wrote to his mother that he was "working on a symphony, some songs, a piano suite, and many dances, besides giving two or three concerts at Stanford with Miss McCall. I am playing a few bass recorder solos down there next week."[51]

Indeed, well before the "early music movement" became a fixture of the American concert scene, Eileen McCall, director of a recorder ensemble at San Francisco State, piqued his interest in performing Renaissance and Baroque music on original instruments. Harrison became proficient on the recorder and performed Baroque dance music on early instruments throughout his years in San Francisco. In January 1942, a few months before he left for Los Angeles, he arranged an elaborate program for the "garden forum luncheons," a high society event in Los Gatos; his program featured music of Couperin, Rameau, and Lully, with Harrison on recorder, McCall on spinet (a small harpsichord), and period dances performed in costume by Carol Beals, Bodil Genkel, and Caroline Piatt.[52]

Lou's interest in Baroque music found voice in *Six Sonatas for Cembalo*, composed between 1934 and 1943. ("By 'cembalo' I mean the plucking string keyboards. While the two keyboards of a French classic clavecin or large German or English instrument might be very useful, I have heard these works played very beautifully and satisfyingly on tiny single manual instruments.")[53] Stimulated by French dance music and the works of Domenico Scarlatti, the sonatas are written in Baroque binary form: two sections, each repeated. Lou welcomes the addition of characteristic ornamentation on the repeats, in keeping with eighteenth-century practice.

During this time (which he calls his "mission period") he also became fascinated with eighteenth-century California culture through study of Gregorian and native American chants and their syncretism in the missions. The Franciscan fathers would "invite the Indians into the mission with their own instruments—rattles, drums, scratches, whatever they had—then gradually teach them a kind of rhythmitized Gregorian chant. . . . The fathers gradually weaned them from the percussion and introduced them to more European instruments, while expanding on the use of Gregorian chant. . . . The intermediate state . . . a kind of rhythmitized Gregorian chant accompanied with percussion, struck me as too marvelous. This I had to do."[54]

In 1939, on the day that Hitler invaded Poland, Lou began his *Mass to St. Anthony*, composing the vocal parts of the Kyrie on a cable car. The opening phrase was his "cry of anguish" about the war[55] (example 1-2). Although he completed the voice parts for the entire five movements of the mass ordinary, Harrison wrote percussion parts for only the Kyrie and Gloria before leaving San Francisco in 1942. Ten years later, at Black Mountain College, he completed the mass, abandoning the idea of percussion accompaniment and substituting trumpet, harp, and strings, which he felt would be more acceptable to the Church. Ironically, when a monk in Vermont requested the score for performance, he told Lou he would need the bishop's permission to use a trumpet. Then in 1962, when Lou visited the Immaculate Heart College in Los Angeles, Sister Theresa requested the original version with percussion. Lou was charmed by the sisters—their mosaics made from Coca-Cola bottles, their banners displaying discarded costume jewelry, and their jukebox (at the college's Folk Art Museum) that played Schoenberg and Stravinsky as well as readings of Shakespeare and Cummings. Delighted by their request but unable to accommodate it, he wrote for them instead two processionals accompanied by trombones and percussion (one solemn and one joyous) to which the sisters could set their own words.

The straightforward language of Amerindian and early mission music

EXAMPLE 1-2. *Mass to St. Anthony*, Kyrie (begun 1939; completed 1952), opening motive. (From sketchbook; courtesy of Lou Harrison.)

inspired the vocal line of an independent *Sanctus* that Harrison composed in 1940 for the dramatic contralto Radiana Pazmor; in the "Pleni sunt coeli" section he specifically used a mode found in the music of the Kwakiutl Indians of the Pacific Northwest (example 1-3). Pazmor sang the work in San Francisco concerts in 1940 and 1941, with the composer at the piano. Alfred Frankenstein noted in two reviews for the *San Francisco Chronicle*: "Lou Harrison . . . provided a brittly dynamic 'Sanctus' . . . that has dignity and individuality, and asks to be heard again. . . . [The] enormously dramatic and forceful [work] uses primitive scales treated in highly unprimitive fashion."[56] And in *Modern Music* he reported: "Harrison is a youngster who, somewhat under Cowell's influence, has been much interested in non-European music systems and in writing new music for old European instruments. You will be hearing about him in the East, if you haven't already."[57]

Others were far less impressed. In the *San Francisco Examiner* Alexander Fried wrote: "Works by 23 year old Lou Harrison indicated that he should give more reverent study to the classics. His peculiar unconventionality was more presumptuous than convincing. His 'Sanctus,' sung by Radiana Pazmor, was unfittingly barbarous and noisy."[58]

Lou avidly devoured the San Francisco Public Library's collection of music scores. Through its substantial holdings he not only educated himself in the standard repertoire but also discovered Cowell's *New Music Quarterly*, fell in love with the works of Schoenberg, read through collection after collection of sixteenth- and seventeenth-century Spanish organ music, studied the operas and ballets of Lully and Rameau, and checked out all the contemporary music he could lay his hands on. But the library's holdings were far from sufficient to satisfy him. On March 25, 1936, at the suggestion of Cowell, he ingenuously wrote to Charles Ives:

Dear Mr. Ives:

I am a student at State College in San Francisco. It seems that there are favorable opportunities to perform your works on what we have as student recitals and in theory and history classes.[59]

EXAMPLE 1-3. *Sanctus* (1940), measures 32–39. (Courtesy of Hermes Beard Press.)

He hoped to learn the two piano sonatas, he told Ives, noting that Cowell had given him "a ray of hope" that Ives might send the scores. Ives indeed sent the sonatas promptly, and Harrison performed them in the spring of 1936, later noting in a thank-you letter that Ives had touched "hundreds" of younger Americans "in some wonderful but vicarious way."[60]

Some months later, Lou wrote again, noting that "the local section of the Youth Congress wants to give a series of chamber concerts for the benefit of the youth movement." A string quartet, pianist, and vocalist were available and eager to program Ives's works. On December 17, 1936, Ives's nephew, Chester, sent the following response:

> I am writing for my uncle. He asks me to say that some chamber music pieces which were on hand were shipped to you today by express from the Quality Photo Print Company, 521 Fifth Ave., N.Y. Copies of the violin sonatas, etc. are being made and will be sent to you in a few days.
>
> Mr. Ives says that he hopes you will not feel in any way obligated to have any of his music played just because so much is being sent, or if it bothers the players too much, which is often the case. But he greatly appreciates your interest and generosity in taking the time and trouble about it.[61]

The crate of photostat scores that soon arrived included most of Ives's chamber music and all of the songs, as well as some orchestral works, including a published score of "a New England Symphony. . . . It is the only score of his which is without mistakes of the pen—that it is free from mistakes 'of the mind and heart' he won't swear to."[62] Lou devoured the music avidly, studying it daily at the piano over a period of ten years. "I'm probably the only living composer who had a ten-year access to the complete works of Ives, in effect . . . , and I absorbed them like a sponge."[63]

Next to Cowell, Ives was one of the earliest and most profound influences on Harrison's musical development. From Ives Lou acquired a license for experimentation. "Mr. Ives . . . left us the most wonderful of playgrounds, a kind of people's park in which we are all arrangers of lovely things."[64]

Years later in New York, Harrison would edit several of Ives's scores, including the second string quartet, a "war march,"[65] and the *Third Symphony*, whose premiere he conducted in 1946 (chapter 2). Although he did not meet Ives until 1947, they carried on an extensive correspondence through Ives's wife, Harmony. (Ives would prepare drafts of letters, but since his deteriorating eyesight made his handwriting difficult to read, Harmony normally recopied them.) In nearly every letter Harmony thanks Lou profusely for his efforts and hopes that "Mr. Ives's music" is not giving him too much trouble.

One day in early summer 1938, as Lou was composing at the piano in his apartment, he was interrupted by a knock at the door. Upon answering, he came face-to-face with a young man who announced, "My name is John Cage. Henry Cowell sent me."[66] Within an hour, Lou recalls, they were fast friends—and were to remain so throughout their lives (see fig. 5). More than fifty years later Cage recounted the meeting vividly:

> I was married at the time to Xenia Andreyevna Kashevaroff. We were living in the same apartment house [in Los Angeles] that my mother and father lived in. And we realized that that was not the proper way for a young married couple to begin. So we drove up to Carmel and I took the car and went up to San Francisco to meet Lou. I knew that he shared with me the love of the modern dance. And I needed a job. And through Lou in San Francisco on one day I got eight jobs![67]

Lou helped his new friend with characteristically unselfish enthusiasm, providing Cage with a long list of references, one of whom was the dancer Bonnie Bird from Seattle, who was teaching at Mills College for the first two weeks of the summer session.[68] Bird offered Cage a job at the Cornish School, an opportunity that seemed especially attractive to him when she colorfully described a closet full of 300 percussion instruments waiting to be played.[69] (Ten years later, when Lou became ill in New York, Cage would have the opportunity to reciprocate, which he did with similar generosity.)

Cage moved to Seattle to work with Bird for two years, but not before he went tam-tam shopping with Harrison in San Francisco. The two men developed enough mutual appreciation that Cage premiered Harrison's percussion works, *Counterdance in the Spring* and *Fifth Simfony*, on his Cornish ensemble concerts.[70] Lou, who had been hired by Mills College as dance accompanist in the fall of 1937 and had taught at its 1938 summer session,[71] made sure, for his part, that Cage was invited to the college for the summers of 1939 and 1940.

On July 27, 1939, Harrison and Cage staged a concert of percussion music, whose success led to annual extravaganzas that delighted the San Francisco new music community in general and critic Alfred Frankenstein in particular. Frankenstein commented, "That Western concert music has much to learn from its orchestra step-children, the percussion instruments, was suggested last night at Mills College. . . . We are still very far from the subtlety of rhythmic speech the Arabs and Indians get out of their little hand drums or the symphonic grandeur of the Balinese percussion orchestras, but such experiments as that of last night point toward interesting developments."[72]

The following year's percussion concert at Mills attracted attention in the national music press as well. "During the last two years an extraordinary interest in percussion music has developed on the Pacific coast," trumpeted Henry Cowell in *Modern Music*. "The full possibilities of percussion, whose accepted role is to provide unimportant splashes of color, have hardly been tapped in our symphonic literature."[73] Featured on the July 18 program were works by Harrison, William Russell, and José Ardévol, including Lou's *Canticle #1* (now a staple of the percussion ensemble repertory), which he had composed in a single afternoon for Marian Van Tuyl's dance ensemble.[74] Among the performers was architect Irving Morrow, to whom they assigned the siren in Ardévol's *Suite*. (Police permission was required for its use.) Frankenstein, who attended a dress rehearsal, remarked on plans to include "a . . . choreography of moving lights and projected forms," an effect that particularly impressed Esther Rosenblatt, reviewer for the *Dance Observer*.[75] The multilevel stage and the decor, designed by Bauhaus artists visiting from the Chicago School of Design, featured, at the back of the stage, knotted rope ladders with loops where the instrumentalists could hang beaters not currently in use.

The collaboration between Cage and Harrison intensified when Cage moved back to San Francisco in 1940, bringing with him several members of his Seattle ensemble. Writer Elsa Gidlow, who met Lou in those years and whose *May Rain* he later set to music, recalls their practice sessions: "I was an audience of one at many of their percussion practice sessions . . . on Jackson Street in San Francisco. Their instruments were buffalo bells, old brake drums, a variety of Japanese, Chinese, and Indian music-makers never before included in Western performance. . . . Lou and I became lifelong friends. . . . Whenever [we] come together, some new subject arises to be explored with passion."[76]

In 1941, Cage and Harrison rented performance space at the California Club in San Francisco and presented a joint percussion concert on Lou's birthday (May 14). Xenia Cage, who performed in these concerts, constructed a fanciful balsa wood and rice paper mobile to hang over the stage. "It was like a dancer," Lou recalls. "It seemed to take on the phrasing of the music as we played."[77]

Canticle #1 received a repeat performance, but there were also two new works by Lou, *Song of Quetzalcoatl*[78] and *Simfony #13*, as well as Cage's *Quartet, Third Construction,* and *Trio,* and, as a final *jeu d'esprit,* a joint composition, the now famous *Double Music.* Each composer wrote the parts for two of the four players. They agreed on compositional procedures and section lengths, then worked independently. Lou described the process:

> We agreed to use a specified number of rhythmicles [i.e., rhythmic figures] and/or rests of the same quantity, which could be put together in any combination. Then we shaped the full length of the piece in half notes. We each did our own form. We wrote separately and then put it together and never changed a note. We didn't need to. By that time I knew perfectly well what John would be doing, or what his form was likely to be. So I accommodated him. And I think he did the same to me, too, because it came out very well.[79]

The ensemble had just enough money to record one of the works on the program, so Harrison and Cage decided to let the audience vote on its choice. The winning composition was Harrison's *Simfony #13* (not #3, as Cage recalled), which they recorded at the Photo and Sound Company and issued in September 1941 for $1 apiece. (During the preparation of this book, we uncovered the score of *Simfony #13*, thought to have been lost, and have included a performance of the work on the accompanying compact disc [band 1].) Cage recalls reading

> in the magazine called *The Commonweal* an article . . . by Edgard Varèse [in which] he defined music as "organized sound." I had previously defined it as the "organization of sound" so that I saw that I had used three words whereas Varèse had used two. So it seemed to me perfectly reasonable for us to call this "the first recording of organized sound." So we did. And we sent a copy to Varèse; and we received a telegram in reply saying, "Please desist from using my term."[80]

Alfred Frankenstein, however, was delighted. He wrote in the *San Francisco Chronicle* on September 28, 1941: "Harrison shows remarkable ingenuity in developing the melodic, coloristic and rhythmic potentialities of this ensemble. There is nothing freakish or strange about the work; it is, rather, an exhilarating lyrical study and quite appealing. It is almost impressionistic compared to the annihilating roar and rage of the only other recorded piece of this type, the notorious 'Ionization' of Edgar Varèse."[81]

The Cage/Harrison percussion ensemble had its origins in dance: both composers were employed as dance accompanists. They not only found percussion sounds ideally suited to the task, but the array of new sound-media also afforded them a creative outlet for their improvisations during rehearsals. Furthermore, the "found" instruments they adopted were inexpensive and required little technical training. In fact Lou wrote *Canticle #1* for performance by the *dancers* in Marian Van Tuyl's group.

Cage had been working in dance studios in Los Angeles before he met Lou. Lou himself had been involved with the San Francisco modern dance community since he began college; had developed close friendships and working relationships with such dancers as Carol Beals and Bonnie Bird; and had even danced in several staged productions himself (chapter 4). Two of his residences had studios on the upper floor that served for both dance practice and percussion rehearsals.

Harrison traces his interest in dance back to the early social dance classes in Portland. And surely his attraction to the French Baroque, as opposed to the better known Germanic tradition, was in part motivated by the French fascination with the court dance tradition. Thus, when Mills needed a dance accompanist in the fall of 1937, Lou fit the position naturally. There he played for the classes of Tina Flade ("an elfin creature from another world")[82] and lectured from time to time on modern music and modern dance. During summer sessions, Harrison taught "musical composition for the dance" and directed a percussion orchestra. These summer workshops also provided the opportunity for him to work with such innovative choreographers as Lester Horton from Los Angeles and his young assistant, Bella Lewitzky. At Mills, Harrison and Lewitzky first met Merce Cunningham, fresh from studies in Seattle with Bonnie Bird.

Lou also wrote incidental music for Mills's drama department productions: Shakespeare's *The Winter's Tale* (fall 1937) and Euripides' *Electra* and *The Trojan Women* (June 1938 and June 1939, respectively). *The Trojan Women* played at both Mills and at the Golden Gate Exposition on Treasure Island in June 1939; its overture was later performed by Pierre Monteux and the San Francisco Symphony on a Standard Oil Broadcast on June 13, 1940.[83]

Harrison had heard 78 rpm recordings of Balinese compositions and other world music through Cowell as well as through his friend Dorothy James, who had brought a collection of gamelan records back from her stay in Indonesia in 1932–33.[84] But Lou's first exposure to a live Balinese gamelan was at the 1939 Golden Gate Exposition, in the Dutch East Indies pavilion overlooking San Francisco Bay—a formative experience that would have far-reaching influence on his own composition.

Even in the absence of such special exhibitions, San Francisco was a rich source of Asian art and theater. Lou frequented the Chinese opera (admission: 25 cents), was spellbound by a Javanese dancer's "slow and exquisite evolutions"[85] at the Curran Theatre, and secured his first recording of *gagaku* (Japanese court music) through the shakuhachi player he had met at Cowell's New Music Society concert.[86] Influenced as well by his mother's art collection, Lou felt a personal connection with Asian music and art that has ever since been a hallmark of his work.

The last in the series of Harrison's San Francisco percussion concerts took place on May 7, 1942, at the Fairmont Hotel's Holloway Playhouse. Featured were *Canticle #3* and his ballet *In Praise of Johnny Appleseed*.[87] But the novelty had begun to wear off: reviews were less enthusiastic than they had been. Even Frankenstein noted that "sometimes the lack of melodic interest gets on your nerves. Harrison, who is the romanticist among percussion composers, tried to remedy this by using the soft, melancholy hoot of the ocarina [in *Canticle #3*]. . . . [The work was] very effective, but unfortunately sounded like 'Canticles 3 to 150' before it was over."[88]

For Lou, perhaps the attraction of San Francisco had begun to wear off as well. Cage had already moved to Chicago, and Cowell, after his release from prison, had settled in New York. Harrison felt it was the right time for him to leave as well; on August 9, 1942, he and William Brown drove to Los Angeles to work with Lester Horton's dance company. (There Brown changed his surname to Weaver.) The Los Angeles residency would prove to be a short but vital conclusion to Lou's early West Coast period.

Los Angeles: 1942–1943

Although Lou's immediate objective in moving to Los Angeles was to work with Horton, he soon became immersed in the city's contemporary music scene, including the "Evenings on the Roof" concert series[89] and Arnold Schoenberg's composition classes. As an outgrowth of his previous work at Mills, he was hired by the UCLA dance department to teach Labanotation and musical form and history for dancers (mostly pre-Classical dance forms, he recalls).[90]

Melissa Blake, a dance instructor who took charge of Horton's studio for the spring of 1943, introduced Harrison to Peter Yates and his wife, the pianist Frances Mullen,[91] who in 1939 had founded Evenings on the Roof, naming it after the studio/performance space atop their house on Micheltorena Street. The series featured both familiar and little-known compositions, though Yates and Mullen were particularly committed to programming contemporary works, especially those by Los Angeles composers.[92]

The three musicians established an immediate rapport, enhanced by their common fascination with the music of Charles Ives. Mullen soon added to her repertoire Harrison's *Six Cembalo Sonatas*, which she first performed (on piano) in a Roof concert on January 24, 1944.

Yates marveled at Harrison's remarkable productivity, later commenting that when they met Lou had "already completed . . . some 450 occasional compositions, nearly all performed at least once."[93] Yates's claim may seem grossly exaggerated, but if the reader peruses the catalog at the end of this book, where we identify over 175 compositions from the period before Harrison's move to Los Angeles (including only complete or nearly complete surviving works or those recorded in programs), the claim may be well within reason.

Among these San Francisco works are a host of piano and percussion pieces as well as numerous compositions for small ensembles, many created for unique performance situations. "I wrote a lot of music because there was an occasion to do it," Harrison recalls; "it never occurred to me that it might be used later or that it was of any value other than the immediate situation."[94] As these early works resurface in recent years, however, Lou often *has* discovered their value, reworking germinal ideas within them into mature compositions. Revision, in fact, plays a major role in his compositional process (chapter 11).

While the relationship with Yates and Mullen would prove rewarding in later years, the most important element of Harrison's year in Los Angeles was his six months of study with Arnold Schoenberg. Through Schoenberg's assistant, Harold Halma, Harrison was permitted to enroll in a weekly composition seminar in the first half of 1943. "The first thing I did as a naughty young American was to present him with a neo-Classic piece. It didn't matter. No problem at all. He was only interested in structure and musicality."[95] In time, Harrison would bring Schoenberg a twelve-tone piece as well, even though Halma cautioned him that Schoenberg preferred not to critique serial works.

If Ives taught Harrison freedom, Schoenberg taught him method.[96] Lou was principally impressed by Schoenberg's ability to build large-scale structures from simple and coherent phrase relationships. "One of the major joys in [Schoenberg's *Piano Concerto*]," Lou would write a year later in *Modern Music*,

> is in the structure of the phrases. You know when you are hearing a theme, a building or answering phrase, a development or a coda. There is no swerving from the form-building nature of these classical phrases. The pleasure to be had from listening to them is the same that one has from hearing the large forms of Mozart. . . . This is a feeling too seldom communicated in contemporary music, in much of which the most obvious formal considerations are not evident at all. . . . The nature of his knowledge in this respect, perhaps more than anything else, places him in the position of torch-bearer to tradition in the vital and developing sense.[97]

Schoenberg thought highly enough of Lou's work to single him out for praise during class meetings. In one session Lou played his *Saraband* and *Prelude for Grand-piano*, already published in the *New Music Quarterly*. Schoenberg looked up at the members of the seminar and said, "Why don't *you* bring me music like this?"[98] Two years later Schoenberg included Harrison in a list of promising American composers in a letter to Roy Harris (May 17, 1945): "I used to name you, Mr. Harris, always among the first whom I considered characteristic for American music. Besides I have to mention: Aaron Copland, Roger Sessions, William Schuman, David Diamond, Louis

Gruenberg, Walter Piston, Anis Fuleihan, Henry Cowell, Adolphe Weiss, Gerald Strang. And among younger and lesser-known people I would like to mention Lou Harrison and Miss Dika Newlin."[99]

Harrison continued to compose quickly and with enormous facility, partly in response to the daily demands of the dance studio. Melissa Blake once asked him to select a minuet from one of the Bach suites for dance class practice. Instead, in less than a day (Yates says "in the fifteen minutes before class") he composed a *Gigue and Musette* "as charming in vigorous outline as it turned out to be rhythmically difficult when they tried to dance it."[100]

Inspired by Yates's and Mullen's devotion to contemporary music, Lou took only a few weeks to compose a twelve-tone suite for Mullen. ("The bargain was that I would give her a piece if she would play me Schoenberg's Opus 25 piano suite—which she did.")[101] In the third movement, however, he reached a compositional block in the manipulation of the row and, despite Schoenberg's reputed disinclination to deal with student serial compositions, boldly brought the piece to him. Schoenberg led him to the solution ("simplify," he advised) and Mullen premiered both this suite and the *Gigue and Musette* in a Roof concert on May 8, 1944.[102] By this time Lou had moved to the East Coast, but in later years he would repeatedly recall Schoenberg's advice: "Use only the essentials."

In the spring of 1943, Lester Horton moved his dance company to New York, an adventure that proved frustrating and unsuccessful. Lou and William Weaver followed Horton to New York at the end of the spring term, but not before Lou made contact with Aaron Copland, who was in Los Angeles completing a score for the MGM film *North Star*. Yates apparently paved the way. He wrote to his friend Peyton Houston in the spring of 1943: "At a quiet evening recently I met Copland and told him about Harrison."[103] The meeting was friendly and productive. Copland proved supportive, giving Harrison much practical advice for starting life in New York.

As Lou prepared to leave Los Angeles, he met with Schoenberg in his office. On the desk sat volumes of Bach on one side and Mozart on the other. Pointing to one pile, Schoenberg advised, "You don't need to study with anyone; study only Mozart"—from which Lou concluded that Schoenberg was handing him a diploma in counterpoint, honed from his years of devotion to Baroque music. Lou took Schoenberg's advice, studying Mozart's techniques of manipulating germinal material to build elaborate structures of utmost clarity. Also reminiscent of the Viennese Classical tradition were Schoenberg's exhortations to simplify, the single most important lesson Harrison retained from this apprenticeship.

With this advice and encouragement, Harrison embarked on a ten-year East Coast sojourn that would round out his musical education, exposing him to some of the most powerful musical trends of the time. Personally, however, these would be the most difficult years of his life. Like Horton, he ultimately found New York incompatible with his artistic and personal needs.

2 East Coast Fugue

(1943–1953)

Harrison's move to New York in the summer of 1943 was at first marked by his typical optimism, which was soon rewarded by welcome into the artistic circle around Virgil Thomson. Living in the big city, however, proved difficult financially and socially almost from the start, and the noise level was overwhelming. On July 9, 1943, Lou wrote to his mother: "I do not like New York *at all* and I am afraid that I will not be able to write a note in the midst of this noise and confusion." There was no work yet, he reported, and if he didn't find employment soon he would return to California. But he was reviewing for *Modern Music* "and tho it pays nothing it is a matter of great prestige & introduces me to everyone of importance in the musical life here."[1]

Lou found lodging in a series of tiny apartments, at first on the Upper East Side, later in Greenwich Village. (His friends Edward McGowan and Frank Wigglesworth particularly recall the Spartan cold-water flats in the Village.) He found odd jobs as an elevator operator at Radio City,[2] as a music copyist, and as a private composition instructor. On Sunday afternoons friends would gather in his small Bleecker Street apartment to listen to ad hoc performances of new compositions.[3]

Adding to the stress of continual financial struggle was loneliness brought on by living far from home in the midst of what seemed a vast, impersonal metropolis. Although he had moved east with Weaver, their relationship soon became strained.[4] Then in September 1943 a telegram brought the news that Sherman Slayback, whom Lou had not seen since his San Francisco days, had drowned.[5] In the same month, Lou's brother Bill was married, and Lou sent a lyrical letter: "To be without love is to be an uninhabited city or some other ghost of real living. . . . We are born utterly alone, we die utterly alone, and we had always ought to be praising God in the meantime that we are given to love and may know another as we know ourselves."[6] In February 1944 Peter Yates wrote, "Harrison is unsatisfied with New York. Believing that the future cultural centre of the world lies here on the west coast, he is planning to return."[7]

Gradually, however, Lou became integrated into New York's musical life. By November 1944 he was actively reviewing concerts for the *Herald Tribune* as one of Virgil Thomson's stable of "stringers," a group that included Paul Bowles and (later) Arthur Berger, along with regular staff members such as Francis Perkins and Jerome Bohn. Between November 1944 and May 1947, Harrison contributed nearly three hundred reviews to the *Tribune* (chapter 12).[8] The work trailed off a bit in the fall of 1945 but picked up dramatically in 1946 after Bowles decided to curtail his own involvement.[9]

By this time Harrison had found a loft on Prince Street across from a noisy bar, but his financial situation remained precarious. To heat the flat, he had to carry heavy canisters of kerosene across the street and up four flights of stairs.

Though Lou owned a piano, he also built two clavichords during his New York years so he could practice late at night without bothering neighbors. The first had a traditional box shape, with strings perpendicular to the keys. Without sufficient reinforcement of the frame, however, the string tension soon pulled the box out of alignment, making the instrument unplayable. "Then I got mad," Lou said, "and decided to find a new mechanism that would work."[10] He designed and built a second instrument in a grand piano shape with the strings beneath the sounding board, which he worked on periodically through 1953 (fig. 6). The entire instrument folded compactly for easy transport. Lou next experimented with placing a second bridge slightly behind the striking point of the tangent and discovered that the clavichord would thus imitate the sound of a celesta. Laurence Libin, curator of the department of musical instruments at the Metropolitan Museum, commented after examining photographs and a diagram of this instrument:

> Although there is a precedent for his clavichord with strings below the soundboard (a 19th-century pedal clavichord in Munich), I believe his idea is original. Certainly there is nothing in this Museum that resembles his design.

... By using lengthwise stringing rather than crosswise, he could use straight key levers all of the same length, a real convenience, as is the single (rather than paired) stringing, which halves the labor of tuning.[11]

By the time Harrison met Virgil Thomson, his compositional skills were mature and he had begun to develop a personal voice. He considered Thomson, then, not a teacher, but a senior colleague. And indeed, they found much in common: perhaps it was Harrison's love for the *French* Baroque as opposed to the German repertoire; perhaps it was his devotion to melody; or perhaps it was his gift for turning a phrase (both musically and rhetorically). In any case, the two men developed a close friendship that remained unbroken until Thomson's death in 1989. In any conversation with Lou, the only name that arises as frequently as Henry Cowell's is Virgil Thomson's (fig. 7).

Harrison worked for Thomson on a daily basis in New York. They sat together at concerts and exchanged works for each other's criticism; and through their many lively discussions, Lou refined his own compositional technique, particularly in the area of orchestration.

He also learned from Thomson to wield his pen with skill and wit, never shying away from candor, but quick to praise where it was well deserved. And nothing could compare to the education Thomson offered by assigning Lou as many as three concerts to review in a single weekend. Harrison was exposed to the full range of musical experience: from major orchestral works to synagogue compositions to Chinese music to jazz (and performance quality ranging from outstanding to dismal). For Lou, the synthesist, nothing could have been more beneficial.

He was carrying out one such assignment on June 17, 1945, when he attended a Town Hall recital of original compositions by the Armenian American composer Alan Hovhaness. Lou had brought as his guest John Cage (who had moved to New York in 1942). As the concert opened, an exquisite melody arose from the celli at the beginning of the piano concerto *Lousadzak*. Lou was at once both entranced and skeptical. "Surely," he thought, "it's going to go oompah at any minute." But it didn't. Despite rhythmic acceleration, the composition remained faithful to its opening rhetoric.

Harrison was wary. "That was lovely," he confided to Cage, "but surely the next piece won't be as good." To their surprise, it was.[12]

At intermission the New York composers were in an uproar. "The serialists were all there. And so were the Americanists, both Aaron Copland's group and Virgil's. And here was something that had come out of Boston that none of us had ever heard of and was completely different from either. There was nearly a riot in the foyer—everybody shouting. A real whoop-dee-doo."[13]

After the performance Cage went backstage to meet Hovhaness. Lou rushed off to the *Tribune* office to write a rave review. "There is almost nothing occurring most of the time but unison melodies and very lengthy drone basses, which is all very Armenian," he wrote.

It is also very modern indeed in its elegant simplicity and adamant modal integrity, being, in effect, as tight and strong in its way as a twelve-tone work of the Austrian type. There is no harmony either, and the brilliance and excitement of parts of the piano concerto were due entirely to vigor of idea. It really takes a sound musicality to invent a succession of stimulating ideas within the bounds of an unaltered mode and without shifting the home-tone.[14]

Hovhaness now recalls: "Lou gave me the first good review I ever had."[15]

Harrison had found a kindred soul—a composer as devoted to lyricism and expansive melody as he himself. Years later he would enthusiastically recommend Hovhaness's *Ardos* for a concert in Rome, calling it "20 minutes of the most shocking melodic adventure you can imagine, truly heroic & daring."[16] As for Hovhaness's rhythm, he "begins in eternity and stays there."[17] The two composers soon became close colleagues. To this day Hovhaness feels that Harrison was the only reviewer who ever truly understood what he was trying to achieve.[18]

Harrison's facility with words, which rivaled that with notes, earned him publication opportunities with other periodicals as well. For *Listen: The Guide to Good Music*, he contributed articles on dance and music, on Ives, and on the modern violin concerto. For Charles Henri Ford's avant-garde arts magazine *View*, he not only reviewed records, concerts, and literature about music but also wrote a perceptive essay on Ruggles, Ives, and Varèse. For *Modern Music*, he wrote "think pieces" on Schoenberg and Villa-Lobos, an article "On Quotation," and concert reviews.[19] Lou also completed a pamphlet, *About Carl Ruggles* (1946), which he envisioned as the fourth section of a book. Ives called the piece "strongly written & 'Ruggles-like'—& very discerning," and Ruggles wrote that it was "a masterpiece of analysis and understanding. Your insight into the 'secret places of my dwelling' is amazingly searching."[20]

Lou had known Ruggles's music long before he moved to New York. During the 1930s he had read Charles Seeger's essay on Ruggles in the October 1932 *Musical Quarterly*[21] and had discovered both *Men and Mountains* and *Portals* in Cowell's *New Music Quarterly*. "I was instantly aware," he noted in his essay, "that while this music was in the chromatic dissonant style and showed a certain resemblance to Berg and Schoenberg . . . , it also held something rare, something different from these others in its long, continuous, really vocal counterpoints."[22]

Ruggles's music skillfully linked Harrison's dual interests in contemporary experimental styles on the one hand and the intricate counterpoint of the Baroque on the other. In his essay, Lou postulated a "golden age of western music" embracing the years 1250–1750, which witnessed the evolution of "total polyphony," a style that did not reappear until the twentieth century, when it was coupled with a new consideration of consonance and dissonance. Harrison admired not only Ruggles's finely crafted counterpoint but also his ability to create a musical texture rivaling Handel's in clarity.

> Surely no other composer has had, to quite such an intense degree, the feel for the register and placement of the individual tones of a chord as Handel. In him the resonance and resilience of the tonal language were at a pitch of sensitivity seldom reached. . . . So in Ruggles one hears a resonance and texture that surprise, in view of the notes of which they are composed. . . . The sonorities give off a brilliance, they perpetuate themselves, are free-floating, connect themselves with Purcell and Handel, especially in their allegiance to material beauty of idiom.[23]

Handel has remained to this day one of Harrison's most cherished models. At a 1983 musicale at the home of music patron Betty Freeman, the musical cognoscenti were extolling Bach in reverential terms. ("Why don't they just canonize him and be done with it?" Lou thought.) After some time had passed in this vein, Lou turned to his neighbor and in a deliberately audible stage whisper remarked, "I'm a Handel man myself."[24] In Ruggles's music, Lou found an irresistible synthesis: distinctive jagged melodies, rhythmic sophistication (a trait obviously close to the heart of a percussion composer), pure secundal counterpoint, and Handel's resonant texture.

Harrison's tone in the Ruggles essay at times borders on hagiography, though he is not totally uncritical. Other contemporary composers, he notes, "have written more flexible tone relations, more exploratory instrumental combinations, more expanded forms, or more personal expressions," but none has so successfully solved the problems of "genuine and integral counterpoint."[25] Predictably, Ruggles was pleased. He sensed through Harrison's keen analysis a composer with an extraordinary ear and an ability to pinpoint the essence of style, and he encouraged Lou's work, urging him, for example, to orchestrate one of his New York compositions, *Alleluia*, which was subsequently published in the *New Music Quarterly*.[26]

And Harrison saw in Ruggles's music another resource to explore. As with each of the composing tools he encountered, Lou tried his hand at this style as well, most successfully, he feels, in a short piano work from 1945, *Triphony* (example 2-1). The following year he arranged the work as a string trio which fourteen years later served as the basis for a movement of his *Suite for Symphonic Strings*. Recently, he exhumed the original *Triphony*, which has now been performed and recorded.

Lou had met Ruggles through Henry Cowell, who introduced him to many New York musicians and dancers (e.g., Wallingford Riegger and Erick Hawkins) and who gave him work with the *New Music Quarterly*. At first Cowell had Harrison perform clerical tasks—sending out mailings and updating subscription lists—but in 1945 he appointed Lou editor. Cowell could not have found a more ill-suited replacement. "If anybody is less organized about paper than Henry," recalled Cowell's wife Sidney, "it's Lou Harrison."[27] Lou served as editor only one year, during which time the edi-

EXAMPLE 2-1. *Triphony* (1945), beginning. (Used by permission of C. F. Peters Corporation, ©
1997.)

tion published works by those contemporaries he found most inspira-
tional—Ruggles, Cowell, Thomson, Villa-Lobos, Varèse, and Hovhaness—
as well as a piece by Lou's student, Merton Brown. When Harrison became
editor, Ruggles's fourth *Evocation* for piano was already scheduled for publication. (The first three had appeared in July 1943.) Lou saw the project to
completion and encouraged Ruggles to publish two-piano versions of *Portals* and *Organum* as well.[28] He also arranged for a reception, musicale, and
exhibit of Ruggles's paintings on May 25, 1945, as part of a project to honor
composers published by the edition. Sidney Cowell, John Kirkpatrick, and
painter Jack Heliker arranged for the art. Kirkpatrick played the *Evocations*
and his own arrangements of *Angels* and *Marching Mountains*.[29]

  In time Lou developed a close circle of friends both within and outside
of music, including (besides Cage) composers Frank Wigglesworth and Ned
Rorem, painter Jack Heliker, and an African American Methodist minister

and civil rights activist, Edward McGowan, who would spend his days at his church in the Bronx and his evenings with Harrison in the Village (fig. 8). McGowan, who was New York state secretary of the American Labor Party and a close friend of W. E. B. DuBois and Paul Robeson, recalls lively gatherings at the Calypso Restaurant, a West Indian place where one could buy a full-course meal for a dollar. One of its waiters was James Baldwin. "This was a wonderful period for me," McGowan recalls; it "opened up the possibility of a life such as I had not known before; and Lou introduced me to music such as I had never heard."[30]

At lively gatherings in their crowded New York apartments, this group of friends would meet to hear, discuss, and even compose music. A favorite game was for the composers in the group—Harrison, Cage, Cowell, Wigglesworth, and Thomson—to write musical "exquisite corpses."[31] Their preferred method was for one of them to compose a measure plus two notes, then fold the paper on the bar line and pass it to his neighbor, who would complete the next measure plus two notes. Years later Lou's student Robert Hughes assembled and orchestrated twenty of these composite works as a collection of *Party Pieces*.

In his second month of reviewing for the *Tribune* (December 1944), Harrison was already confident enough to express disarmingly frank views, such as the following evaluation of a concert by New York's Little Symphony under the baton of Joseph Barone.

> The New York Little Symphony, Joseph Barone founder-director, read its way through a disheartening concert last night at Carnegie Chamber Hall. Two young vocalists appeared on the program who were obviously unready for public singing to the accompaniment of orchestra. . . . The orchestral accompaniment . . . in the Handel was especially remarkable in that it was so out of tune, and set something of a record in that its well trained constituents, chosen from the desks of the Philharmonic and N. B. C. Symphony, played wrong notes in a simple piece.[32]

Barone, perhaps questioning Lou's understanding of the difficulties under which he was forced to operate, challenged Harrison to do better by offering him the podium for half a concert in the 1945–46 season. Lou leapt at the opportunity to prepare the premiere of Ives's *Third Symphony*, adding Ruggles's *Portals* and his own newly completed *Motet for the Day of Ascension*. Despite previous correspondence with Ives and the editing work Lou had already completed for him, the two composers would not meet until ten months after the concert.[33] But they kept up a lively correspondence during this period, with Ives helping Harrison through "that old almost illegible score of the 3rd Symphony."[34] (Lou would later describe Ives's scores as "nervous and elaborate pages that resemble the paintings of Paul Klee, full of alterations and embellishments with little arrows leading from one tone to another through a maze of hazy pencil points.")[35]

A warm dialogue developed between them. Ives addressed Lou as "Lew

Harry Son";[36] Lou in turn continually bemoaned the lack of national attention to Ives's music. In November 1945 he fumed in *View*:

> Ives is gradually becoming a famous public figure without anyone having heard his major works. This smells suspiciously like the English habit; they bury their best art in total oblivion, but wouldn't think of letting the names die because it keeps up the Empire's prestige. . . . All Ives' larger works were written before 1920; it is now 1945 and not one of the major orchestra works has yet been played in full in America. . . . We seem to be mighty slow, mighty slow.[37]

He repeatedly said the same to Ives himself. After proofreading parts for the second string quartet, for example, Lou wrote to him: "I am nearly 2 generations removed from you & in any sensible society I should be able to hear your major works frequently under the most sympathetic conditions";[38] to which Ives replied: "With men of courage & independence like you, who are not afraid to think for themselves [and to] stand up & say what they believe in regardless, better times will come."[39]

As the performance of April 5, 1946, neared, Lou got a taste of Barone's frustrations. Orchestra members balked at performing under an untrained conductor, but Lou earned their respect by conducting cross-rhythms skillfully. Rehearsal time, already minimal, was further reduced by scheduling conflicts.[40] Five days before the concert, Barone tried to ease Lou's fears: "Please don't worry about the Ives for I'm certain it will go well. It is an extremely euphonious piece, and on Friday morning most of it 'sounded' even as the men were reading it."[41] But Lou had reason to worry: he prepared his half of the concert on a total of three hours of rehearsal.[42]

The performance was a resounding success, drawing rave reviews. The Ives symphony was repeated at the end of the concert for those who wished to stay. After the Ruggles, "the applause was so terrific and so long that after I had bowed a respectable number of times and the orchestra had risen . . . I finally had to turn my back on the audience and simply wait until they quieted down so we could go on."[43] Crowed the reviewer for *Musical America*,

> Ives' Third symphony, which lay neglected in a barn in Connecticut for 40 years, is an American masterpiece. It is not even Ives at his best, but this rambling, experimental score, with its quotations of old revivalist hymn tunes and deliberate awkwardness, is as unmistakably a part of our land as Huckleberry Finn or Moby Dick. . . . That a work of such profound scope and originality could be overlooked for almost half a century is a musical disgrace.[44]

Harrison was praised both for bringing Ives's symphony to light and for his masterful conducting. Noel Straus wrote in the *New York Times:* "Mr. Harrison conducted this difficult symphony in a manner that made known a real gift for the baton. . . . The young director led with an easy sense of authority, a simplicity and directness, a command of orchestral tone, and a fine rhythmic security that spoke well for his future in this field."[45]

Ives was not well enough to attend the performance, but Harmony was there and would later describe it as one of her "most pleasurable" experiences.[46] And there was a further ramification that neither Ives nor Harrison anticipated: in 1947 Ives was awarded the Pulitzer Prize for the *Third Symphony* and insisted on splitting the award with Lou. In a letter of May 1947, Ives wrote: "As you are very much to blame for getting me into that Pulitzer Prize street, and for having a bushel of letters to answer and for having a check of $500 thrown over me by the Trustees of Colum. Uni. you have got to help me by taking 1/2 of this . . . and the rest I'll send to the New Music Edition and Arrow Press."[47]

After the success of the *Third Symphony*, Lou continued to champion Ives's music, writing about him in articles for *Listen* ("The Music of Charles Ives") and *Modern Music* ("On Quotation"). In the latter he compares Ives's "imitation of life" to Chinese painting and poetry, which reflect observation of the natural surroundings.

> As opposed to Mahler, Ives no longer purposes to speak for the rest of us at the gates of heaven; rather . . . he assembles the data of his observed surroundings and tells the tale, not without tenderness, of what he and his friends were like and where they lived. . . . This . . . was also what James Joyce was up to. . . . Both artists set off from a very special, very folksy locale. Both take the road through local myth outward and across the borders towards general (personal) culture. . . . In a certain sense Ives and Joyce decompose, rather than compose their subjects.[48]

Harrison projected writing a longer essay on Ives and even assembled information from Harmony in preparation for the work.[49] Unfortunately, the project was interrupted by serious troubles in Lou's personal life.

Lou did complete other editorial projects for Ives, however, orchestrating Ives's World War I song "He Is There" on a commission from the League of Composers,[50] reconstructing the *Robert Browning Overture* from sketches, and editing the *Second String Quartet* and the *First Piano Sonata* (for performance by William Masselos). When Ives received Harrison's invoices for this work, he at times remitted more than he was billed. After Lou had completed proofreading parts for the second string quartet in October 1944, for example, Harmony wrote: "You know how to write music, Mr. Ives says, but you don't know how to write bills."[51] She enclosed $24 instead of the $6 Lou had charged.

The Ives manuscripts were in such disarray that Lou not only had to decipher marginal scrawls and follow trails of arrows around the pages but also had to reconstruct some passages, adding "a measure here or there."[52] These he would initial "LH" for Ives's attention. He had lived with Ives's music so long that he had little trouble finding the right language. In fact, he remembers that when the manuscript of the *Browning Overture* turned up in Ives's barn, the reconstructed passages matched the originals almost exactly.[53] (Long after Lou returned to California in 1953, he continued to edit Ives's music: in 1977 he orchestrated three Christmas songs discovered by Oliver Daniel, vice president of BMI, creating a three-movement suite titled *Christmas Music*.)[54]

In February 1947 Lou finally met Ives and his wife, Harmony, who had invited him for lunch at their Manhattan residence on East Seventy-fourth Street. As Lou arrived, Ives greeted him with exuberance: "He looked like Blake's drawings of God the Father," Lou recalls. "I came up the brownstone staircase of his house, and he was whirling his cane. 'My old friend! My old friend!' he shouted. . . . I had to duck the cane."[55]

After lunch Ives took Lou aside and asked if he would consent to be Ives's eyes—to prepare, in short, a definitive edition of his complete works. Reluctant to refuse outright, Lou was noncommittal and continued to shoulder additional editorial projects, though he realized that such tasks would substantially hinder his own compositional activities. He now questions whether Ives would have been satisfied with the outcome of such a project in any case: "Gradually I made the discovery that Ives never really wanted anything finished. . . . Take, for instance, the first sonata, on which Billy Masselos and I labored so intensively. . . . The minute it was published, Mr. Ives took a red pen and started rewriting."[56]

Ives's influence on Harrison was embodied primarily in a "proclamation of freedom" that allowed Ives to combine disparate elements at will, just as Lou some years later would seek his own musical hybrids. Harrison also found encouragement for his later experiments in tuning systems from Ives's quarter-tone piano pieces. "We remember the image of his father in the thunderstorm, listening to a bell and searching for its lost chord on the piano," says Lou. "Charles Ives was seeking the lost chords in 1925. . . . He was thinking about intonation as a future."[57] Lou often expresses his gratitude to mentors and friends by dedicating to them appropriate compositions or movements. In 1963 he composed a short orchestral work, *At the Tomb of Charles Ives,* that features an extended passage using his own radical tuning concept, Free Style (chapter 5).

On the surface, Lou's life in New York was improving dramatically. He was actively composing for chamber ensemble, keyboard, and orchestra, and his compositions were performed and reviewed on New York concerts: his percussion works were played at the Museum of Modern Art, for example, and harpsichordist Sylvia Marlowe performed three of the cembalo sonatas. He had established close friendships with some of the most outstanding performers in the city, such as the Ajemian sisters (Anahid and Maro), a dynamic violin and piano duo, and had expanded his contacts in the dance world as well. Barone graciously offered him a position as associate conductor of the Little Symphony,[58] and Lou eagerly began to make plans for the next season.

At the same time, however, his self-esteem had reached an all-time low. While preparing for the concert with the Little Symphony, he had written to Ruggles: "Sometimes I wish I didn't write music; life would be so much simpler. And besides, I am always so tortured and distressed during a performance of my own music that I don't really hear a note of it anyway."[59] After the concert Ives offered to fund publication of Lou's motet. "Mr. Ives says he wants so much to help in behalf of your music," wrote Harmony on June 28, "—[he] says how about publishing your 'Day of Ascension' motet?" But Lou responded: "I am very touched by Mr. Ives' kindness in offering to publish my compositions: But the truth is, that while in the past I have twice been represented in New Music I am now unsure that anything I have written is yet ready for the unblushing declaration of print. After the performance of my 'Motet for the Day of Ascension' I ripped it apart & have not yet assembled it."[60]

In fact, a crisis was fast brewing. In retrospect, it had been building for some time. As early as 1945 Lou had developed an ulcer.[61] He sought respite in trips outside the city, such as an idyllic vacation in Maine "on a charming little island with a lighthouse on the windswept white cliffs and lots of gulls, seals, coots, etc. There were eight in the party, three painters, two composers, a divine and a drone. . . . I came back with about fifteen pounds useless but pleasant fat extra, no noticeable ulcer to worry over and a vastly improved disposition and relaxed mind."[62] But as soon as he returned to New York, the stomach pain reappeared. "It has had a twinge or so . . . since I got back to this vale of toil and sin," he complained to Wallingford Riegger.[63]

In December 1945 Virgil Thomson composed a musical portrait of Lou called "Solitude" (example 2-2).[64] In seeming defiance of its title, the work's opening limns Lou's exuberance with a playful grazioso motive (a) that evolves into dissonant counterpoint against a series of long tones (b). There follows a disjunct marcato theme (c) treated in imitation (his intellectual curiosity or mercurial temper?), and a "solitary" quiet conclusion (d) in which the long tones (b) return, this time alone, suppressing both the graciousness and the harshness that preceded them. By 1947 the melancholy mode was often in evidence. Ross Parmenter, a reviewer for the *New York Times* who often sat with Lou at concerts, remembers him as quiet and introverted,[65] a description that those who have met him more recently find hard to believe. Merce Cunningham confirms that in this period Lou was "quiet— almost, in a way, unable to communicate."[66]

Lou's painter friend, Jack Heliker, remembers the last review Harrison wrote for the *Tribune* in early May. "'I can't do it,' Lou said. 'Lou, you've got to do it,' I replied and volunteered to go and sit with him in the concert. Afterwards I took him to the *Tribune* office. He didn't want to go. But he did and I sat with him while he wrote. It was a very intelligent review."[67]

A few days later Heliker was taking an evening stroll through Washington Square. "Who should I see but Lou! He was walking around as though in a daze. At first I didn't know what to do. There's an Episcopal church on lower Fifth Avenue that's always open. I thought he ought to be

EXAMPLE 2-2. Virgil Thomson, *Solitude: A Portrait of Lou Harrison* (Mercury Music, © 1948. Reprinted by permission of G. Schirmer, Inc. [ASCAP]. International copyright secured. All rights reserved.)

a. Measures 1-4

b. Measures 9-10

c. Measures 17-21

d. Measures 44-53

in a place where he could gather his wits. So we went in and sat down. We didn't talk much. But I did after I'd left him. I called John Cage. He called Virgil Thomson."[68]

The stress of big-city life had finally culminated in a nervous break-down. Harrison attributes the crisis to the noise, pressure, and hectic pace of New York City, but at the same time other factors, though more subtle, may well have exacerbated his anxiety. Despite several intimate relation-ships (e.g., Slayback, Weaver, McGowan) Lou had been unsuccessful at establishing a durable romantic partnership. And even if he could have, so-ciety at large condemned the type of partnership he craved (laws prohibit-ing homosexual behavior were on the books in every state). Furthermore, the world had just emerged from a terrifying conflagration culminating in the explosion of the atomic bomb, which, to a pacifist like Harrison, was as devastating as his private battles (chapter 9).

John Cage immediately came to Lou's aid. He drove Lou to Stony Lodge in Ossining-on-the-Hudson, where Lou stayed for several weeks until he could gain admittance to the Psychoanalytic Clinic at Presbyterian Hospi-tal in New York City. Lou, typically selfless, was primarily concerned about how he would complete his editing commitments to Ives. He urged John to find others to help.[69]

At Presbyterian Hospital treatment was free, but Stony Lodge charged nearly $11 a day.[70] Unbeknownst to Harrison, Cage sought help from Lou's friends, including Ives, who had donated generously to the *New Music Quarterly* and other contemporary music causes. Many years later Cage re-called: "It was known that Ives was very nervous and that he didn't like either the telephone or the doorbell too much. So I chose the way of mail. Then someone else was going to have to push the doorbell!"[71] John re-quested a loan (though how Lou might repay it was not at all clear). "Lou Harrison, our mutual friend," he wrote,

> has been very ill lately, and at the advice of his doctor and analyst, Richard M. Buckner . . . is at present receiving custodial care at Stony Lodge, Ossin-ing-on-the-Hudson. . . . Being one of his closest friends, I have taken the re-sponsibility of arranging for the payment of bills connected with this illness; I, myself, am not able to help, since I just manage to pay my own bills. . . . Would you be willing to assume all or any part of this expense? I am certain that Lou will want to repay as soon as he is well and working. . . . He does not know that I am asking this assistance.[72]

By the time Ives received Cage's letter, however, he had already sent Lou half of the Pulitzer Prize money—a $250 check that covered Lou's ex-penses. In his response to Cage, Ives emphasized that it was not a gift, but recognition of Lou's work on the *Third Symphony*.

During the following nine months Lou was in and out of the hospital for treatment. At first he lived there full-time; but gradually, as the treat-ment proceeded, he made the transition to independence. Some of his colleagues predicted that he would never again write significant music,[73] but they underestimated Lou's resolve and determination. The hospital's calm environment was in fact salutary not only to his mental health but also to his musical creativity. During his stay he composed the major elements of his *Symphony on G*: the opening movement; much of the slow movement; and the scherzo (a minisuite comprised of four submovements: a pair of waltzes, polka, song, and rondeau). The waltzes and polka, dedicated to two fellow patients (Leona and Janet), were inspired by the weekly dances at the hospital.[74] The song and rondeau are dedicated to the two friends who most helped and supported him during this difficult period: the "song" (a romantic long melody) to John Cage and the "rondeau" to Heliker. Lou also painted a great deal (see fig. 9) and proofread editions of Ives's first and second string quartets. Merce Cunningham visited him in the hospital as well, bringing with him a proposal for a commission for a solo dance composition, which Lou entitled *Western Dance* and Merce performed on several occasions under the designation *The Open Road*.[75] Harrison's good humor, even in this difficult time, is well illustrated by an anecdote later told by John Cage: "A composer friend of mine who spent some time in a mental rehabilitation center was encouraged to do a good deal of bridge playing. After one game, his partner was criticizing his play of an ace on a trick which had already been won. My friend stood up and said, 'If you think I came to the loony bin to learn to play bridge, you're crazy.'"[76]

Among the members of Lou's intellectual circle during this period was writer Joseph Campbell, husband of dancer Jean Erdman, with whom Lou would collaborate on several notable works in his postbreakdown period. During the time of Lou's greatest psychological struggle, Campbell was writing his masterwork, *The Hero with a Thousand Faces* (1949),[77] about the mythical struggles of the archetypal hero: the individual who sets himself apart from society and forges a unique path to achieve creative, scholarly, economic, or spiritual success. (In later years, Campbell would summarize the hero's path in the phrase "Follow your bliss, and doors will open to you.")

Campbell points out that every journey begins with a "call" —whether from outer or inner spiritual voices—that summons the hero and transforms "his spiritual center of gravity from within the pale of his society to a zone unknown."[78] As long as Lou followed his internal call, everything went well. Even when economically struggling to survive in depression-era San Francisco, Lou's life was built around an active and closely knit circle of friends, and he was incredibly productive, writing dance scores, percussion works, and other occasional pieces with apparently Mozartean effortlessness.

Campbell warns, however, that it is dangerous to contend against the force of one's calling:

> Often . . . we encounter the dull case of the call unanswered; for it is always possible to turn the ear to other interests. Refusal of the summons converts

the adventure into its negative. Walled in boredom, hard work, or "culture," the subject loses the power of significant affirmative action and becomes a victim to be saved. . . . Whatever house he builds, it will be a house of death. . . . All he can do is create new problems for himself and await the gradual approach of his disintegration.[79]

What an uncannily accurate picture of Lou's New York years—first, moving from his home to the place where, according to "society," professional composers must make their careers; next, undertaking grueling work as a stringer, writing music journalism for little pay, in thrall to Virgil Thomson, who, despite his occasional barbs to *épater les bourgeois*, subscribed thoroughly to the notion of composers as citizens of a professional establishment or community. Assaulted by noise and an alarmingly swift pace of life, and under some social pressure to conform, Lou struggled with his own lifestyle, contributing to his eventual disintegration and mental breakdown.

To his credit (and the delight of friends and family), Lou not only overcame this bout of mental illness but also used it as a catalyst for change in his compositional style. His postbreakdown period was characterized by "studies in diatonicism,"[80] although he abandoned neither dissonant counterpoint nor serialism, which he used regularly through his 1952 opera *Rapunzel* and to which he occasionally returned in later works (chapter 11).

Lou had always held a deep love of expansive melody—a lyric expressionism apparent even in his most dissonant prebreakdown works. After a 1948 Evenings on the Roof concert in Los Angeles that featured music by New York composers, reviewers remarked on this lyricism, which distinguished his string *Trio* (1946) from the other works on the program: "The first composer of the evening to indicate that a lyric impulse was not repugnant to him was Lou Harrison, the former commentator for that sincerely mourned little magazine of the musical avant-garde, 'Modern Music,' who got into this brief, nostalgic 'String Trio' a convincing sense of melodic design, with the effect of a short prose poem."[81]

Today he talks openly about his "exit from the halls of readjustment. . . . I had a second chance at life," he says, "and assembled a new person out of the remains."[82] Reflecting many years later on his transformation, Virgil Thomson remarked, "Though I called my portrait of you 'Solitude,' you haven't been alone for five minutes since!"[83]

In fact, during the period immediately following his breakdown Lou seems to have been charged with renewed energy and determination. While it took a decade for him to fully recover, the next three years saw the composition of some of his most frequently performed works: *The Perilous Chapel* and *Solstice* (premiered in 1949 and 1950 respectively), the *Air in G Minor* for flute (1947), the *Suite for Cello and Harp* (1949), two suites for strings (1948), four of his seven *Pastorales* (1949-50), *Marriage at the Eiffel Tower*, and *The Only Jealousy of Emer* (1949 and 1950).[84] In a 1950 review of the cello and harp suite, the *Suite No. 2 for Strings,* and two of the pastorales, Virgil Thomson characterized Lou's style as

> quiet poetry and intense auditory expertness. . . . Few composers now alive can fascinate the ear, as Mr. Harrison does, with simple procedures. At once plain and sophisticated, his music reflects a concentration on music's basic elements that is as expressive, surprisingly, as it is intrinsically interesting. . . . [The two] Pastorales . . . transport us to a dream world where all is music, really music, really interesting musically, really sensitive and elaborate and lovely and not about anything in the world but how beautiful the materials of music can be when handled with tenderness and with intelligence.[85]

The cello and harp duo, based in part on sketches for a film about the Lascaux cave paintings, opens and concludes with a meditative chorale depicting an "old man plowing in the ancient manner behind the immemorial ox" and portrays in the second movement "the willowed, rivered landscape of the valley of the Dordogne."[86] For the fourth movement ("Aria"), Lou adapted the "Song" from the scherzo of the *Symphony on G,* which he had begun in the hospital.

In 1948 Lou was awarded a $1,000 creative grant from the artists and writers fund of the National Institute of Arts and Letters,[87] established to "aid professional artists, composers, and writers of demonstrated ability who find themselves in financial distress owing to illness or other causes of an immediate and urgent nature." Three awards were given from the fund in 1948: to Harrison, Cowell, and Vincent Persichetti.[88] The presentation ceremony on May 21 featured a concert that included Harrison's *First Suite for Strings.*

Several of the most memorable works from this posthospital period were occasioned by Lou's strengthened ties to dance. Although he had known Graham-trained dancer/choreographer Jean Erdman for several years (chapter 4), Lou and Jean now developed a close working relationship that led to fruitful collaborations on three compositions from 1948 to 1951. The first was *The Perilous Chapel,* a psychological drama that "expresses both the individual and group experience of a shattering awakening into a larger truth."[89] The "plot," devised by Erdman, was inspired by an adventure of King Arthur's knights of the Round Table and is related to "hero's journey" motifs in the writings of her husband, Joseph Campbell. Set for six women, *The Perilous Chapel* opens in a spirit of peace, which is soon disrupted by a mysterious image in the form of a mobile that descends from above. One woman is struck by this mysterious force; meanwhile, the other five dance in frantic fear. Chaos (clearly labeled as such in the score) ensues. The individual "touched," however, ultimately reaches a new insight, "coming to understand the gift of the experience," thereby liberating the entire group.[90] The similarity of *The Perilous Chapel*'s subject to Lou's own very recent psychological drama hardly seems coincidental, though neither Lou nor Jean recall being conscious of it at the time.

Erdman's choice of six women was specifically designed to avoid any relationship between the sexes. "The dance was conceived as a spiritual experience of the individual and of the group," she says.[91]

Harrison chose an ensemble of flute, cello, harp, and drums, modeled on those pictured in Persian miniatures. The "chaos" section, which features fearsome (and fearfully difficult) scalewise passages at *molto allegro* for the three melodic instruments, gives way in the finale to an ecstatic "Alleluia" with sweeping melodic lines over a four-note ostinato, which Lou has characterized as a "dance on the floor of heaven" (example 2-3).

In 1950 Erdman and Harrison produced *Solstice*, an extended drama about struggle and rebirth set to a mixed ensemble of eight instruments (chapter 4). And in 1951 they created *Io and Prometheus* for two dancers with piano accompaniment; it was premiered by Erdman at her summer institute in Boulder, Colorado, on July 9 with David Tudor playing "the keyboard and the strings of the piano, [which he] plucked, beat and strummed sharply to punctuate the writhings of the tortured hero."[92]

In addition to working with Erdman, Lou renewed his ties to Bonnie Bird, who hired him as music director for the 1949 and 1950 Reed College summer festivals of dance and theater in Portland. During the 1949 institute he developed a new love as well: calligraphy. The Reed campus was filled with posters advertising a washing machine service ("Let Daisy do your dirty work") in beautiful lettering done by the campus's Scribe Club. Fascinated by the letterforms, Lou struck up an association with calligrapher Lloyd Reynolds, and ever since then he has written in a calligraphic script that has caused correspondents to marvel (fig. 10).[93] At the 1949 institute Lou also met the set designer, dancer, choreographer, and writer Remy Charlip, with whom he established an intimate relationship during the next five years in New York and at Black Mountain College. In Lou's copy of *The Minnesingers: Portraits from the Weingartner Manuscript*, on a blank page immediately preceding the illustration of Emperor Haenrich (1165–97), Remy drew a portrait of Lou in the guise of a Minnesinger (fig. 11). Recently Harrison and Charlip renewed their artistic collaboration when Charlip choreographed for the Oakland ballet a production entitled "Ludwig and Lou" in which he coupled Beethoven's contradances with Lou's *Suite for Cello and Harp*.

Upon his return from Reed College in 1949, Lou began teaching at the loosely organized Greenwich House Music School. He is listed in their brochure as an instructor of music history and appreciation, composition and counterpoint, and orchestration. Bird also hired him as music instructor at her own dance-drama school at 115 West Fifty-second Street.[94]

He taught a few private students in composition (e.g., Richard Miller, Mary Callentine) and even continued conducting. On February 27, 1949, Lou again conducted a Ruggles work, *Angels* (for brass ensemble), at a concert of the National Association of American Composers and Conductors.

EXAMPLE 2-3. *The Perilous Chapel* (1948–49), end of movement 5 (the "chaos" section) into the beginning of movement 6: Alleluia. (© 1990 by Peer International Corporation. International copyright secured. Reprinted by permission.)

As the work ended, "the audience started shouting 'Bis, bis.' 'What do they mean?' I whispered to Varèse. 'They mean "Repeat it, repeat it."' So I repeated it very successfully. . . . Later I found out that I had been asked to conduct because Edmund Franco Goldman refused in view of Ruggles's known anti-Semitism. Yet Franco *did* include Ruggles on the program."[95]

As early as his 1946 essay, Lou had wryly noted Ruggles's crusty side and

EXAMPLE 2-3 (*continued*)

VI. Alleluia

his love for coarse jokes. But at last Ruggles's racist outbursts became too much for Lou, who particularly recalls a luncheon at Pennsylvania Station in New York at which Ruggles blurted out antiblack and anti-Semitic slurs at the top of his lungs. Harrison, who had many black and Jewish friends, was appalled.[96] After the 1949 performance of *Angels* he gradually distanced himself from Ruggles on a personal level, while maintaining a deep respect for the music. After his breakdown, in any case, Lou had reevaluated his own compositional technique; he rejected many of the complexities of his Los Angeles and early New York periods, embracing instead a less dense and less contrapuntal style that separated him from Ruggles's idiom, though he occasionally returned to it in later years (for instance, in his *Elegiac Symphony*, 1975).

Soon an entirely different stimulus would send Lou in a new direction: in 1949 Virgil Thomson handed him a copy of a new book, Harry Partch's *Genesis of a Music*, with the counsel, "See what you can make of this." It was a recommendation that would change Lou's life. Partch's division of the octave into forty-three parts, which suggested to Harrison the potentialities of Just Intonation, launched him down a path he would never leave: a love of mathematically pure, nonbeating intervals that would thereafter influence his compositions in all genres—from the piano to the symphony orchestra to the gamelan.

Lou had already heard Partch's music several years earlier when he reviewed a 1944 concert for *Modern Music*. As he now freely admits, he "totally missed the point":[97]

> The League of Composers presented Harry Partch in a program of his own compositions for instruments of his own devising. These latter all play a forty-three-tone scale. As Mr. Partch uses them, they seem never to do much but decorate a comparatively simple basis, much in the same way that Ives uses the twelve tones to decorate a fairly simple scheme. . . . But missing is the transcendence of Ives' conceptions. The mannerisms of using the instruments were too often repeated. A chord would be struck and then suddenly swoop up to heaven via sliding tones and perhaps down again. The actual music was on the whole negligible. . . . I wondered what a composition really involving an integral use of the forty-three tones would sound like. *U.S. Highball* . . . I found several miles too long. *San Francisco* . . . was the best and shortest piece. . . . Mr. Partch has woven a spell of about the foggiest and dampest music I have ever heard. I got homesick.[98]

In 1944 Lou, fresh from his studies with Schoenberg, couldn't imagine why Partch would develop a scale of forty-three tones without using it serially. By 1949, however, he was in a far different frame of mind. Part of his hospital therapy had been to reconstruct his past. As usual, he allowed the task to take him further afield and deeper in study than the doctors ever envisioned. He embarked on an investigation of Western music theory stretching back to Boethius and the Greeks. He discovered the Greek tetrachord, centered around the pure 4:3 fourth and subdivided into various intervals reflecting mathematically pure proportions (chapter 5). When he read Partch's book, Lou suddenly realized how ancient Greek theories could be resurrected in modern practice, how pure intervals could be produced through microtonal divisions of the octave. "It meant," he says, "that there were real intervals and real relationships—not the hallucinatory ones of Equal Temperament."[99]

In retrospect it is clear that Partch's book helped facilitate Lou's recovery from the horror of his breakdown. Exposure to Partch's iconoclastic theories stimulated a change of direction that reenergized Lou both as a composer and as a human being. Within a week of reading the book, Lou had purchased a tuning hammer for his piano and was hard at work.[100] The first compositions to emerge from these studies were the *Seven Pastorales* for chamber ensemble based on a Pythagorean tuning of his piano. He composed the first (now "Pastorale 2") in October 1949 and the remainder in short spurts in 1950 and 1951.

In February 1951, one of Lou's private composition students, Richard Miller, introduced him to the actress Judith Malina and her husband Julian Beck, founders of the experimental Living Theater.[101] The Malina/Beck connection drew him into an intense circle of New York artists who, in this idealistic postwar period, set as their mission nothing short of reconceptualizing artistic form and expression. Malina characterizes them as living "on the edge," pushing against societal, cultural, and personal boundaries.

There was a movement—what we called "*the* movement"—that included that whole energetic period, whether it was levitating the Pentagon or John Cage's new sounds. We began to see that the traditional forms in the arts were to be, had to be, broken up, that the cubists had to break up the visual unity into components in order for us to understand the unity. Once the forms were shattered, some reorganization of them had to take place. So we began the search for new forms in the way that Cage sought it, the way Hovhaness sought it, or the way that Lou Harrison sought it. Asian and eastern influences were one of the places we were looking for reintegrating art from its shattered state.

[But] when you break tradition you create tradition, whether it is one's intention or not. These were times of pioneering. The problem is we had a utopian vision, but what we didn't have was any concept of how we get from where we were to that place. We had no program; we had no ideas of constructing a new world. We knew what we wanted to destroy; we didn't know what we wanted to create.

Lou's inventiveness comes from a kind of energy fostered by hopefulness, by beautiful art, by the sense that one is grasping for truth, and it's only a finger's length away. Lou's music particularly engenders this ecstatic aspect. For me, Lou Harrison's music stands for ecstasy, for what would it be like if we were already there. Lou's form of "throwing yourself into the ineffable" and coming out with the very ecstatic purity that his music breaks into is exemplary. But there's the danger: you jump into the ineffable and it's unbearable because we're not grounded enough.[102]

Although he had outwardly overcome the effects of his breakdown and was achieving increasing success, Lou never really came to terms with New York or with the psychological stress of urban life. Furthermore, the Malina/Beck crowd encouraged him to go "off the deep end, perhaps even detrimentally admiring any extension into the far out. Anything 'crazy' went over with us big," Malina recalls.

> We wanted excess. We wanted to see how far one could dare go. . . . But the courage in an artist to go far out, to break the rules, to overcome the tradition (which is somehow the ground we stand on) and then to find oneself without this ground, without the metaphor and the vocabulary that is socially acceptable—to create art out of the courage of taking those leaps and then to find that one has left the world behind— leaves us in a vulnerable, dangerous state. Lou is not the first artist to have experienced this dichotomy between what's practical and what's visionary.[103]

There were societal pressures of a more earthly nature as well, including pressure to explore heterosexual relationships, even to marry. In fact, for a few weeks in April 1951 Lou was engaged to one of his students, Mary Callentine.[104]

Black Mountain College

In the summer of 1951 Lou found a viable means of escape from New York. On a recommendation from Cage, he was offered a faculty position at Black Mountain College, a tiny institute nestled in an idyllic hideaway in North Carolina. Black Mountain was the brainchild of a disgruntled visionary, John Rice, who had been unceremoniously fired from a teaching position in classics at Rollins College in Winter Park, Florida. In 1933 Rice founded the college as an idealistic experiment in educational reform. By the early 1950s, Black Mountain had developed a reputation for special commitment to the arts, prompted in part by its summer institutes, which began in 1944.[105] Cage and Cunningham had first visited Black Mountain in the spring of 1948 and returned for the summer session, which also included as resident faculty Willem de Kooning, Richard Lippold, and Buckminster Fuller (who found the environment ideal for his early experiments on geodesic domes). The college had its share of future luminaries among the students as well: Robert Rauschenberg, Jonathan Williams, and Joel Oppenheimer, to name a few.

At first Lou found the contrast to New York a shock (the isolation could at times become almost unbearable), and the drastic change created a new emotional upheaval, which he even called, many years later, a "sort of a second breakdown."[106] In fact, outbursts of frustration were not uncommon among Black Mountain faculty and students alike. One night Lou tore up a complete score of his opera *Rapunzel*, as well as a painting by Joseph Fiore. On another occasion, he threw a bottle through a window.[107] But ultimately the move proved a blessing: he found the quiet and peace that perfectly suited his needs. As he wrote to Vladimir Ussachevsky, then editor of the *New Music Quarterly*: "The frogs sing out in Lake Eden—the air is warm and balmy and [the] outside flower-scented. In daylight the dogwood shimmers through the forests and the hills are green and soft and fuzzy. A whippoorwill has just begun its repetitive serenade. . . . Within a brief time I find that I have completed three acts of a six-act opera, and that I like it very much, and all in all astonish myself thereby."[108]

The peaceful countryside inspired him, as did the close collaboration with artists from other disciplines, as in his early years in San Francisco. David Tudor, whom Lou brought to the college on several occasions, remarked as well on the magic atmosphere of the place, where "students and performers could interact directly with creators."[109]

Wesley Huss, instructor of theater and the college's treasurer, recalls Lou's attempts to integrate his diverse interests, not only in the artistic, creative world but also in his personal relationships: "He has always had an amazing capacity to do everything—to be around, to absorb all the time, to see. And to work at relationships until they finally became integrated. His capacity for experimentalism was not restricted to music but also applied to social relationships. He would not only try to bring diverse elements together outside himself but would also seek his own relationship to those elements."[110]

Some of the excitement and exuberance that Lou rediscovered in North Carolina (as well as his sheer joy in creating music) is captured in an eight-page letter to Frank Wigglesworth that reads in part: "How wonderful that you are playing piano and guitar!! When did you take up the guitar? I'm coocoo for it! A friend of mine, a painter . . . was over during [the] Xmas holidays & played for me. . . . What a pleasure! Those dulcet tones ringing through the house. Oh, I'm delighted you've taken it up!! I'll write some pieces for it soon & send [them] to you. . . . Soon? Why not now? Here goes!"[111] There follows a complete work in binary form, the *Serenade for Guitar*, which has since been repeatedly performed and recorded.

After Lou's "seduction" by the dangerous and sexually ambiguous attraction of the Living Theater, his years at Black Mountain College were a sort of Halfway House, paving the road to recovery in a rural environment that was, at the same time, not too far removed from the New York scene to preclude frequent visits. This gentle reintroduction to the countryside convinced Harrison that he could never again live comfortably in a big city. His major work of this period, the fifty-three-minute opera *Rapunzel*, is almost tangible witness to an inner struggle that, like a hermetic seal, put paid to his New York adventure and closed off both the East Coast and urban life forever.

In the open spaces of the country, Lou composed at a prodigious pace. He finished works begun in New York or earlier: *Alma Redemptoris Mater,* the *Suite for Violin, Piano, and Small Orchestra, Seven Pastorales, Fugue for David Tudor,* and the *Mass for St. Anthony.* He continued work on the *Symphony on G,* began the four *Strict Songs* and *Songs in the Forest,* and composed works for Black Mountain dance instructor Katherine Litz. And he completed a series of new pieces as well, among them *Praise for the Beauty of Hummingbirds,* a recently rediscovered *Festival Dance* for piano four-hands, a *Nocturne* for strings, and *Rapunzel.* The opera, setting William Morris's psychological verse-drama, was "in part self-analysis," Lou remarks. It "held implicit in it some of the problems, tortures, and false rapture that I was myself experiencing in analysis and psychotherapy."[112] For most of the work, the golden-haired Rapunzel and the prince hold center stage, declaiming in jagged yet lyric serial language. The witch, who appears only intermittently, nevertheless has the final word. In the finale Rapunzel, her original name of Guendolen now restored, has married the prince (now king) and yet is haunted by the witch's cries from hell: "Woe! That any man could dare to climb the yellow stair, glorious Guendolen's golden hair!"

In a 1966 Cabrillo Music Festival performance, the opera was performed with masked actors, mimes, and dance; director Arthur Conrad portrayed the drama as a dream opera, with the witch ultimately triumphant, as her cries continue to plague Guendolen. "Rapunzel, of the golden hair, and the Prince are in a limbo; after her prayer, he reaches her momentarily across the abyss. [But] the conclusion . . . finds them unmasked, torn apart and blinded by reality or awakened from dreams. . . . She is restored to her tower and both are back in their hells."[113]

Coupling the opera with dance was one of Lou's original concepts. In 1956 he wrote to Peggy Glanville-Hicks, who had proposed mounting the opera in New York: "Both Bonnie Bird & Jean Erdman expressed an interest in choreographing [*Rapunzel*] should you elect to seat the singers in the orchestra & use dancers on stage as was one of my ideas—3 leads & perhaps 2 or 3 attendants for the Prince & Rapunzel. Also a witchling or so could be dashing in & out doing mysterious things during the Prince's long soliloquies."[114]

One reason the work has had only a limited number of performances is the difficulty of the vocal lines. The soprano (Rapunzel/Guendolen), whose lines span more than two octaves (a-flat to c"), must maintain strength sufficient to deal with some of the most difficult material at the opera's end; the baritone (prince/king), whose range is nearly as wide, sings several long soliloquies filled with dramatic but hair-raisingly difficult leaps. The opera is well worth the effort, however, for Harrison's score succeeds in capturing Morris's psychological overtones.[115]

The interactive and experimental environment of Black Mountain College also fostered Lou's excitement over his new studies in intonation. Painter Joe Fiore and his wife Mary vividly recall Lou's ebullient lectures on intonation, though "we weren't always very apt pupils," Mary notes.[116] Nevertheless, Black Mountain was the perfect place to indulge his new passion, as faculty were encouraged to offer seminars in areas they themselves were first exploring.

During these Black Mountain years Lou began to drift away from Cage philosophically. In New York, the two had continued the close collaboration and intellectual interchange they had begun in San Francisco. Lou wrote pieces for prepared piano (invented by Cage); Cage dedicated his first string quartet to Harrison (1949–50). But in the early 1950s, Lou moved toward increased control through Just Intonation systems while Cage moved toward increased freedom through chance operations. At the Black Mountain summer institute in 1952, Cage staged his first "happening," an event that has since assumed legendary status in the evolution of aleatoric composition, theater, and dance. "I organized an event," he notes, "that involved the paintings of Bob Rauschenberg, the dancing of Merce Cunningham, films, slides, phonograph records, radios, the poetries of Charles Olson and M.C. Richards recited from the tops of ladders, and the pianism of David Tudor, together with my *Julliard* lecture, which ends: 'A piece of string, a sunset, each acts.' The audience was seated in the center of all this activity."[117]

Through this initial happening, Cage established himself as a father figure of mixed media events part theatrical, part musical, part visual, part sculptural, and always antiestablishment. At the time, however, the happening seemed less momentous. "I laughed a great deal during it," Lou recalls. "John used a stopwatch to design a temporal scheme that controlled everything. There was so much going on and it all seemed so absurd."[118]

Surprisingly, given his distaste for randomness in art, it was Harrison who first introduced Cage to the *I Ching*, one of the main sources of chance operations that Cage and Cunningham would later use to dictate the arrangement of sound and movement events. An enigmatic ancient Chinese treatise on divination, the *I Ching* ("Classic of Changes") uses a method of tossing coins to select from among sixty-four predictions. Cage extracted the methodology of selecting elements by chance operations, while Lou was more interested in the philosophical underpinning. Although Cage recalled Lou showing him the *I Ching* in San Francisco during the 1930s,[119] Harrison places the event several years later.

> I read the *I Ching* at UCLA when I was working with Schoenberg and the dance department [1942–43]. My idea was to create a ballet in which there was a white backdrop. The dancers would toss for the image, and the character would be painted in broad red brush strokes on the back part of the stage. Then the dance would be done to that image. A second toss would determine the next phase. The *I Ching* would determine a set of positions and where and how to move between them. Though I had thought of the possi-

bility, I never seriously considered tossing for the actual notes and rhythms. Later in New York I introduced John to the *I Ching*. Then Merce took it up as well.[120]

Lou initially came to Black Mountain only for the summer institute of 1951, but he remained on the faculty for two years, while maintaining his New York apartment, to which he returned periodically. The brochure for the spring semester of 1952 lists his courses as harmony ("simple to complex"); counterpoint ("according to 16th century practice"); composition ("exercises in form, and tonal methods"), and ensemble—vocal and instrumental ("arrangement, interpretation and performance"). But since there were very few students (the student/faculty ratio could be as low as 3:1), most "classes" were tutorials or seminars offered on demand, leaving plenty of time for composition. Lou finished the short score of *Rapunzel* in less than two months (August 21 to October 7, 1952), although its orchestration occupied him through the following April.[121]

In the spring of 1952 Lou and one of his students founded the Black Mountain Press "to publish the smaller works of contemporary composers in as fine & inventive a way as possible."[122] Lou wrote to Ives about this new venture and immediately received a check to cover the expenses of the first two volumes, along with a note from Harmony: "I remember so well how beautifully you conducted the Third Symphony."[123]

He returned to New York for major events: to conduct the premiere of his *Suite for Violin, Piano and Small Orchestra* at Carnegie Hall with the Ajemian sisters in January 1952; for performances by Erdman's company in 1952–53; and for Stokowski's performances of the *Suite* in October 1952 and *Canticle #3* in February 1953.[124]

During his second year at Black Mountain, a Guggenheim Fellowship made his life even more comfortable. The award, announced in the spring of 1952, allowed him to reside at the college with minimal teaching duties and additional time for composing. In 1953, however, Black Mountain decided to hire Stephan Wolpe for the summer session, and though Thomson offered Harrison a regular position on the *Tribune* staff,[125] he decided that it was time to return to the West. That summer he moved back to northern California, first to his parents' home in Redwood City, later to San Francisco, and finally to the (then) very rural environment of Aptos, where he has lived ever since.

3 California Toccata

(1953–present)

In August 1953, Henry Cowell wrote to Frank Wigglesworth in Rome that Lou had picked up and moved back to California,[1] ending his ten-year East Coast sojourn and reopening his ties to the West and, ultimately, to Asia. After his return to California, four major events strongly affected Lou's compositional path, though none changed the course of his work sufficiently to delineate a new creative "period." Instead these four guideposts, summarized in the following paragraphs, plowed more deeply into furrows previously cut.

1961: Lou's first trip to Asia, the result of an invitation to the "East-West Music Encounter Conference" in Tokyo finally allowed him to study firsthand the Asian musics that had fascinated him since his early years with Cowell. The following year he returned to Korea and Taiwan for intensive private study. Soon thereafter, he began to compose both for Asian instruments and for mixed European-Asian ensembles.

1967: Lou met his life-partner, William Colvig, an electrician and amateur musician with an interest in acoustics. Together the pair set off on a decades-long career of instrument building and tuning experiments. (A biographical sketch of Colvig appears in chapter 6.)

1971: Together Lou and Bill built a set of aluminum and steel metallophones, tuned in nonbeating intervals, which they called "An American Gamelan"; this personalized orchestra integrated gamelan timbres, junk materials, Lou's old percussion ensemble experiences, and, most important, his devotion to pure intonation systems.

1975: Invited to give a class in tuning systems at the Center for World Music in Berkeley, Lou met K. R. T. Wasitodiningrat (Pak Cokro), Indonesian gamelan master and renowned teacher, who was then on the faculty of the California Institute of the Arts in Santa Clarita near Los Angeles. Thirty-six years after seeing the gamelan at the Golden Gate Exposition and four years after building his own American gamelan, Lou at last began to study traditional Indonesian techniques and repertoire with a native teacher. For years critics had remarked on "gamelan-like timbres" in Lou's music, created with both Western instruments and homemade ones. But now he began to compose for traditional Indonesian ensembles and to create hybrid works for gamelan with Western instruments.

Politically a pacifist, Lou sought ways to link East and West musically—an artistic "joining-hands-around-the-globe" for which he has become a major spokesman. His commitment to interdisciplinary cross-fertilization motivated a continuing collaboration with dancers and choreographers, and his unflagging defense of individual freedom prompted outspoken support of the gay rights movement (chapter 10).

Rome, Louisville, and Buffalo (1953–1961)

Cal and Pop welcomed their prodigy's return, providing temporary quarters in which he could compose. By the time he arrived in California, Lou had received word that he and Ben Weber had been selected as the two Americans whose works would be presented in a composition contest in Rome in April 1954. The competition, whose purpose was "to bring international acclaim to younger composers who have received a certain attention in their own countries,"[2] was sponsored by the Congress for Cultural Freedom in conjunction with the International Conference of Contemporary Music. Lou worked feverishly to prepare the prayer scene from *Rapunzel* for the event.

On March 27 he set off for Rome,[3] where he met Frank and Anne Wigglesworth, who were in Italy on Frank's *prix de Rome*. Sitting alone one day in the Coliseum bemoaning his lack of fluency in Italian, Lou made up his mind to investigate universal languages, a decision that ultimately led to his study of Esperanto (an international language invented in 1887 by Polish philologist L. L. Zamenhof). He later used Esperanto in his travels, polemical writings, and texts for compositions.

All of the Rome competition works were performed before a live audience without identification of the composer. Leontyne Price sang Rapunzel's prayer. Michael Steinberg, reviewing the competition for the *New York Times*, highlighted the work in his column: "Suddenly there was a work that achieved what only one of its competitors . . . had come close to achieving. For here was a piece of music that not only sounded well in itself, but also in which every turn of vocal melody, every rhythm or color in accompaniment was motivated by something in the text. In other words, here was a real song."[4]

When all was said and done, the *Air from Rapunzel* won for Harrison a 20th Century Masterpiece Award for the best composition for voice and chamber orchestra. The prize (2,500 Swiss francs), which came as a total surprise to Lou, was conferred by Igor Stravinsky.[5] He shared it with Jean-Louis Martinet of France in what many conferees saw as a political compromise:

> In a transparent but clumsy attempt to protect the pride of as many nationalities and individuals as possible, the jury of seven judges . . . handed out five prizes rather than the three that had been proposed. . . . That the judges could have run into some difficulty in deciding between the Klebe and Vogel overtures, or even between the Peragallo and Weber concertos, was conceivable, but that anyone could have doubted the Harrison work to be infinitely superior to Martinet's is simply beyond the realm of imagination. It had seemed, in fact, to be the consensus of the majority of conference participants that the Harrison piece would be the one sure winner of the whole dozen [works performed].[6]

The Rome prize proved to be only the first of several prestigious awards Lou received during the 1950s. In May 1954, while he was still in Italy, he received word of a second Guggenheim Fellowship,[7] and the following year he received a Fromm Foundation grant to fund a recording of his *Mass*.

Upon return from Rome, Lou again experimented with city life, renting an apartment in San Francisco, but he soon found the environment too crowded and noisy and longed instead for the peace he had discovered in North Carolina. Cal and Pop came to the rescue, locating (and ultimately purchasing) a tiny house on a property in rural Aptos, several miles south of the vacation community of Santa Cruz. When he first saw it, Lou was immediately entranced: "It reminded me of my studio at Black Mountain." (Twenty years later he and Bill Colvig bought property down the block and in 1977–78 erected the partially prefabricated house they have occupied ever since.)

Among the first people Harrison contacted in California was Harry Partch.[8] The two men soon became close friends—visiting, sharing ideas, and exchanging instruments. Lou's studies in intonation and his rejection of aleatoric composition defined for him a compositional path closely allied to West Coast eclecticism, exemplified by the highly individualized style of Partch, who did not hesitate to construct both his own sound-producing media and his own theoretical system. But Harrison's application of acoustic principles was very different from Partch's.

Harry was a nineteenth-century system builder. In the early editions of his book he reviews all the work of the great nineteenth-century theoreticians— French, English, Scandinavian. They were all attempting to build a system that would include everything. My attitude has always been practical: I use what I want to use when I want to use it. I have no interest in building a cumulative system that would include everything from Eskimo music to whatever. If I want an orchestra to play a certain tuning, I prescribe it and they play it. Or we build it.[9]

Lou would joke with Partch about the inflexibility of "systems." "Harry," he once said, "since the harp has twisters for strings and there are three positions for each which don't have to be adjusted in Equal Temperament, you could have forty-two tones by using two harps [seven strings per harp, each with three positions]. Perhaps you could just forego your forty-third tone!" "Maybe," Partch retorted, "but I don't like the harp!"[10]

A commission from the Louisville Orchestra[11] soon provided Lou the opportunity to explore his own approach to alternative tuning systems on a large scale. In the summer of 1955, he completed *Strict Songs* for eight baritones and orchestra (begun at Black Mountain), which requires retuning of the fixed pitch instruments of the orchestra—harp and piano—in Just Intonation. Each movement features a different pentatonic mode with intervals reflecting specified mathematical proportions—tunings devised by Lou expressly for this work (chapter 5; CD, band 10).

Lou extolled the beauty of nature through his own text, inspired by Navajo ritual songs (as a teenager he had wavered between careers as a poet and a composer). Each line opens with a fixed salutation, one for each four-line stanza: to "Holiness," to "Nourishment," to "Tenderness," and finally to "Splendor." Each attribute is then fleshed out by references to nature stimulated by the peace he discovered at Black Mountain College and Aptos. The first stanza is typical of the whole:

Here is Holiness—of the begonia leaf with innumerable crystalline cells.
Here is Holiness—of the Mountain's deer and the unscented fawn.
Here is Holiness—of the begonia leaf, and deer, and the star Aldebaran,
   lighting endlessness.
Here is Holiness—of the beachèd agate, wet with wave.[12]

Harrison subsequently authorized several alternative performance options for the work: traditional SATB choir and baritone solo (University of California, Santa Cruz chamber singers, 1992) and all-male chorus accompanying a highly acclaimed choreography by Mark Morris (1987).

In *Strict Songs*, Harrison also indulged his love of expansive melody— perhaps one of the best examples of Malina's "ecstatic grasp for truth." Press reaction to the January 18 premiere was as exuberant as Lou's score: "Harrison has constructed a score that is charged with spiritual expression, weaving spells and enchantments. . . . His daring is the gift to be simple. . . . He succeeds . . . in building a carpet of sounds that is serenely active. . . . The singers . . . were seated among the players. Their voices became parts of the orchestra's voices, and all the participants combined to establish a mood of quiet rejoicing."[13]

Lou's courage to be simple similarly impressed a young composer, Robert Hughes, a graduate student at the University of Buffalo (later SUNY-Buffalo) during the late 1950s. There Hughes discovered a set of twelve recordings of recent American compositions issued by the classical division of Columbia Records at the instigation of Goddard Lieberson.

> What stuck out as the freshest, most wonderful experience was the record of Lou coupled with Virgil Thomson. On Lou's side was the wonderful *Suite for Cello and Harp* and his *Suite #2 for Strings* [performed by string quartet]. It was like a breath of fresh air, particularly in an atmosphere heavily loaded with serialism; so that when you flipped from Hugo Weisgall to Lou Harrison there was a culture shock that was absolutely marvelous. It was something new. Nobody was daring to write so directly, simply, and beautifully.[14]

Hughes arranged for a Harrison residency at Buffalo in May 1959 following the New York premiere of *Rapunzel* at the 92nd Street Y.[15] Recitatives from Lou's new *Political Primer* were performed, along with older, more established works. The *Primer* (which, like *Strict Songs*, uses his own text) puts into practice a daring new tuning concept that Lou calls "Free Style": successive melodic intervals are tuned in exact proportion without relationship to a fixed tonal center or scale (chapter 5). The *Primer* was also the first of what would become a series of overtly political compositions. The University of Buffalo offered Lou a faculty position, but, happy in his Aptos hideaway, he declined.

In 1959 he also completed the *Concerto for Violin with Percussion Orchestra* on a commission from Anahid Ajemian; begun in the 1940s in New York, it has become one of his most frequently performed works.[16] The *Koncherto* (Lou prefers the Esperanto spelling) was inspired both by Alban Berg's violin concerto and by world music traditions that feature a single melodic part against rhythmic accompaniment. The violin concerto as a medium represented for Lou both the terror of solitude within an impersonal world and a vision of redemption. In an article in *Listen*, published shortly before his breakdown in New York, he likened the solo violin to a "singing person . . . pitted against or surrounded by the indefinitely large, expanded world of the modern orchestra." Noting that of all instrumental forms the violin concerto was "most representative of the spiritual course of music during the last fifteen or twenty years," he marveled at the consistently "dismal tenor" of twentieth-century works. Only Berg, he concluded, "found intuitive rebirth and the sense of continuity with things past and future."

> Berg's intimations, beyond the point of catastrophe (those dread pounding pulses of death's coming) are of rebirth and ascension. . . . Berg's Violin Con-

certo is indeed the only one that proposes a religious possibility of faith on the old terms. . . . The quoted chorale by Bach in his work seems less a Confucian observance of the ritual ordinances than a personal concordance with the impulse that drew its measures from the older composer, and a prospect, too, in Berg's own sight, of the same heavenly landscape of the spirit's hope.[17]

A credo of optimism, indeed, to guide one who had been granted "a second chance at life."

Asia, Hawaii, Mexico; Cabrillo Music Festival; the American Gamelan (1961–1975)

Meanwhile, Robert Hughes had received a Baird Foundation Fellowship to study with Luigi Dallapiccola, but after a year in Florence he became so disenchanted with the atmosphere of European serialism that he used his remaining funds to travel six thousand miles to Aptos to study with Harrison instead. He found Lou living in a tiny cluttered house among towering redwoods overlooking the Pacific. Two years later Hughes described the cottage (which at the time was empty while Lou was composer-in-residence at the University of Hawaii) in the following terms:

> Cutting . . . thru the thick foliage and underbrush which hides and protects [the] walkway and porch entrance, the visitor . . . reaches [the] door—covered mysteriously with spider webs in which are entwined a dappled splendor of vegetation. The inside of the house apparently . . . was deserted on the spur of the moment—exotic instruments, rich fabrics, wall paintings lay strewn about, food still on the table like in ancient Pompeii, wall-to-wall papering—like a cave, it is a little chilly and damp. . . . Buddha, on the distant wall, glancing sideways, at you in the half-light of evening.[18]

Still grappling with the aftereffects of his breakdown, Lou battled his way back to health, following his own "inner truth," as Campbell would have called it, rather than the dictates of society. He took only such jobs as would keep him supplied with sufficient food and shelter and allow time for composing, performing, instrument making, and in general exploring the magical worlds of music on his own terms. He worked as a forest fire fighter, for instance, or at an animal hospital ("clipping poodles," he later noted), composing at night in the ranger station or keeping himself awake with stimulant drugs after exhausting days with the dogs. "That way I could work a full eight-hour day at the hospital and a second eight-hour day afterwards at composition."[19]

On the positive side, the isolation was nearly perfect. There was no phone, no interruption, and—most important to Lou—no noise. Down the hill, an Englishman, Victor Jowers, and his wife Sidney had established a quaint cafe, the Sticky Wicket.[20] Phone messages reached Lou through the

Jowerses; in fact, when Lou's father died in July 1963, they knew before he did.

Soon Hughes and Jowers were presenting chamber music concerts at the cafe and even mounting summer open-air opera (to the annoyance of several neighbors, who instigated an unsuccessful crusade to close the productions down, complaining about lyric sopranos dying loudly late at night).[21] After a short time, Hughes was composing with self-confidence, encouraged by Harrison's catholicity, open-mindedness, and cheer: "During my study in Italy I had slowly tied myself into dark knots. I'd been staring at blackened Tintorettos and Titians high up on the walls. Everything was dark and masterpieces were obscure. In contrast here was Lou walking in Chinatown, a sort of benevolent and optimistic Diogenes, bearing a lamp, one of those southern boat gods of the Chinese and the Japanese, like Daikokusan, bouncing along and loving the golden glitter."[22]

In September 1964 the Sticky Wicket was forced out of business by the construction of a nearby highway interchange that blocked access to the cafe. By the time it closed, however, Hughes and Jowers had staged several dramatic productions (e.g., *L'Histoire du Soldat*, Gluck's *Orfeo*, Lully/Molière's *Le Bourgeois gentilhomme*), as well as thirty-three concerts of chamber music, many featuring Harrison works old and new.[23] In this rustic recital hall, Gary Beswick premiered Lou's solo violin sonata from 1936 (March 17, 1963), and Lou gave one of his first lecture/demonstrations on Chinese, Japanese, and Korean music (November 12, 1961).

Shortly after Hughes's arrival in California, Harrison was invited to the 1961 East-West Music Encounter Conference in Tokyo thanks to his mentors Cowell and Thomson. On March 25, 1961, Lou boarded a freighter for Japan, his entire trip funded by the Rockefeller Foundation. During the long sea voyage, he explored the myriad possibilities for pentatonic divisions of the octave and composed the *Concerto in Slendro* for violin, two tack pianos, celesta, and percussion. The concerto was inspired by his anticipation of this first trip to Asia not only in its combination of instruments, which suggests a gamelan, but also in its pentatonic scale, which mimics an Indonesian slendro—a five-tone mode with no semitones. Lou's slendro, of course, calls for mathematically pure intervals.

Before he left California, Harrison wrote to the fine arts representative of the International Esperanto Association in Tokyo. When the freighter docked in Japan he was greeted, to his amazement, by an entire delegation of Esperantists, who took him to the "Buddhist YMCA." A member of the association accompanied him throughout his stay in Tokyo, translating informal conversations into Esperanto. (To his chagrin, he discovered near the end of his trip that his hosts spoke serviceable English but preferred Esperanto to avoid the possible embarrassment of stumbling.)[24]

In Tokyo Lou presented a paper on April 21, "Refreshing the Auditory Perception,"[25] and met leading composers, scholars, and performers of

Asian musics. From Japan came performers Sukehiro Shiba and Shinichi Yuize, as well as composers Sadao Bekku, Makoto Moroi, and Mamoru Miyagi. Representing Indian music were performer/scholar T. Viswanathan, composer Vanraj Bhatia, and scholars Thakur J. Singh and Alain Daniélou (whose *Introduction to the Study of Musical Scales*, published in 1943, Lou had read avidly at Black Mountain College). Trân Van Khê, long regarded as the leading authority on Vietnamese music, was present, as was José Maceda, a scholar/composer from the Philippines. The United States, too, sent as delegates both ethnomusicologists and composers (Harrison, Henry Cowell, Virgil Thomson, Elliott Carter, and Colin McPhee). Indonesian music, however, was represented not by natives from that country but instead by two influential Westerners: Colin McPhee, an authority on Balinese music, and Mantle Hood, an expert on Javanese gamelan who had recently published a groundbreaking study of Javanese music.[26]

Given Harrison's long fascination with gamelan music and Mantle Hood's expertise in the area, it would have been natural for Lou to have sought out Hood as a mentor, particularly since Hood was teaching in California. That he didn't do so dramatizes Joesph Campbell's precept that when the hero follows his own instincts, "ageless guardians will appear. Having responded to his own call, and continuing to follow courageously as the consequences unfold, the hero finds all the forces of the unconscious at his side."[27] Consciously or subconsciously, Lou followed this advice and it worked. Despite the many delegates at the conference, Lou's inner voice drew him to two figures who were not presenters at the meeting but who shared an antiestablishment spirit and a missionary zeal toward their own music: Lee Hye-Ku from Seoul and Liang Tsai-Ping from Taiwan. Both men, like Lou himself, were in a sense "outsiders," coming to their musical careers from alternative paths rather than through traditional channels.

Dr. Lee Hye-Ku, president of the Korean Musicological Society since its founding in 1954 and one of the most prolific teachers and scholars of Korean traditional music (by 1969 his bibliography listed 157 publications), in many ways might seem to *be* the "establishment," but like many of Lou Harrison's "spirit guides," he is nevertheless an outsider. He majored in English literature at Seoul Imperial College[28] and was drawn to music by love, not duty, showing a degree of independence and initiative unusual in many Asian cultures.

The Rockefeller Foundation provided funds for a trip to a second Asian country following the conference, and Lou's plans were to visit Thailand until he attended a performance by the Thai Royal Ballet. He was astonished (and dismayed) to find that Thai music employs a seven-tone equal division of the octave, a sophisticated and idiosyncratic system not based on vibration ratios in the overtone series; after his intensive study of Just Intonation, Lou found such modes inharmonious and unappealing.

"During the conference in Tokyo," Lou recalls, "Dr. Lee Hye-Ku . . . gave everybody the present of a record. One Sunday morning I went to a record store and played it. I fell in love at once with Korean classical music. Just like that I knew that's where I had to go. There's been an intense connection ever since."[29]

The two men hit it off immediately, and ensuing mutual visits were arranged compliments of the Rockefeller Foundation—Lou to Korea after the conference and a return visit in 1962,[30] and Lee to Aptos during the intervening period. Together they collaborated on an English-language history of Korean music, which remains in manuscript (chapter 7).[31]

Liang Tsai-Ping's renown stems from his almost single-handedly bringing about a revival of popularity of the Chinese sixteen-string zither, the *cheng*. As is often the case among Chinese literati, Liang's work in music was a sideline. His professional training was in civil engineering, a field in which he worked in the Republic of China and continued in Taiwan after 1949. On retiring from government service, Liang established an international public relations consulting company, in which he remained active until retirement in 1985. He is also something of a cultural "outsider" in that he is a devout and active Christian. But despite his extensive professional responsibilities, he managed to maintain a career as a performer, composer, and scholar of Chinese zither music.

Liang suggested to Harrison that he visit Taiwan as a guest of honor of the Chinese Classical Music Association, an invitation Lou accepted following his second trip to Korea in 1962.[32] Through his work with Lee Hye-Ku and Liang Tsai-Ping, Lou learned to play Chinese and Korean instruments, notably the Korean *p'iri* and Chinese *kuan* (cylindrically bored double reed aerophones), the cheng, and various bamboo flutes.

After his return to California, he lectured avidly on the beauties of Korean and Chinese music to anyone willing to listen, and with typical passionate enthusiasm he taught Asian instruments to his student Richard Dee and later to his partner Bill Colvig. He even built his own p'iris. Together with Dee and Colvig (and sometimes with singer and cheng player Lily Chin) he formed an ensemble that presented hundreds of performances of Chinese and Korean music throughout California (chapter 7). Lou played cheng, *ti-tzu* (transverse flute), *hsiao* (notched vertical flute), p'iri, and bells; Bill was featured on *sheng* (mouth organ), *hsün* (globular flute), *pai hsiao* (panpipe), and *fang hsiang* (a set of tuned metal plates, although Bill built his with tubes instead). Richard played cheng, *ya cheng* (a bowed half-tube zither), and *nan hu* (two-string fiddle).

Lou also revived connections with Pauline Benton, whose Chinese shadow-puppet plays he had first watched in 1939 at Mills College. He became music director of Benton's "Red Gate Shadow Players," a theatrical ensemble that presented shadow-puppet theater, including an adaptation of a traditional Chinese opera, *White Snake Lady*.[33] The Harrison/Dee/Colvig trio provided the theater's live music, arranged by Harrison; for *White Snake*

Lady, for instance, Lou constructed "a softened, flavorsome version of Chinese theater scores."[34]

As usual, Harrison jumped into his new adventure with both feet, devoting himself to mastering Chinese and Korean instrumental techniques and compositional forms, which he transformed into his own new hybrids. The result, as Virgil Thomson was to note many years later, was a mixture executed "with infallible imagination. . . . There is nothing labored about [it]. Lou Harrison is not making plastic roses for funeral parlors. He is simply speaking in many personae and many languages. The message itself is pure Harrison. And that message is of joy, dazzling and serene."[35] Cowell would admonish purists to respect hybrids, for synthesis frequently yields new expressions of beauty. Harrison goes even further, reminding us that we have no choice but to respect hybrids, because there simply is nothing else.[36]

The first of his Asian-Western hybrid compositions was *Nova Odo* for male chorus, reciting chorus, orchestra, and p'iris, begun in 1961 and completed in 1968 (a read-through of the earliest version by the Seoul Philharmonic took place in 1962). An antiwar work with text by Harrison in both English and Esperanto, *Nova Odo* is comprised of three parts: the first, in Equal Temperament, expresses the horrors of the bomb; the second, for p'iris, male chorus, and strings, evokes the contemplative style of Korean court music; the third features Western instruments imitating Chinese sounds.

In the spring of 1963 Lou was the guest of the East-West Center of the University of Hawaii, serving as composer-in-residence for its "Festival of Music and Art of this Century" along with Filipina composer Lucretia Kasilag. During this residency he composed *Pacifika Rondo* (the spelling is Esperanto), the most eclectic of all his instrumental hybrids. Joining the Western string instruments, celesta, trombones, organ, and percussion, are numerous Korean and Chinese instruments, and even fipple flutes intended to evoke the clay flutes of Mexico (see chapter 7). Six of the seven movements celebrate the beauty and diversity of the Pacific basin: (1) Korea; (2) dolphins playing in midocean; (3) a Buddhist temple; (4) the towering sequoias of California; (5) Mexico; and (7) China. The sixth movement momentarily breaks the spell with an Equal Tempered protest (as in *Nova Odo*) of the bomb. The Asian instruments abstain from this movement in protest.

In 1967 Lou composed a third hybrid, *Music for Violin and Various Instruments European, Asian, and African* for Gary Beswick, concertmaster of the Santa Clara symphony. In the finale the solo violin is accompanied by four *mbiras* (African plucked lamellaphones—fig. 17) as well as lively foot stomping, an international extension of his earlier percussion ensemble works (example 3-1).

By the time the Sticky Wicket closed in 1964, a new musical venture was underway in the Santa Cruz area. Cabrillo Community College, which had been operating out of a high school in Watsonville, opened a campus in

EXAMPLE 3-1. *Music for Violin with Various Instruments, European, Asian, and African* (1967), movement 3, beginning. (© 1972 by Peer International Corporation. International copyright secured. Reprinted by permission.)

Aptos in 1963, providing the space and opportunity for a major summer festival.[37] The Cabrillo Music Festival, mounted annually since 1963, has maintained a dedication to new music while at the same time presenting substantial works from the classical repertory. The festival originally drew largely from the ranks of the Oakland Symphony (Robert Hughes was conductor of the symphony's youth orchestra at the time of the festival's founding). Music directors/conductors have included Gerhard Samuel (1963–68), Richard Williams (1969), Carlos Chávez (1970–73), Dennis Russell Davies (1974–90), John Adams (1991), and Marin Alsop (1992–present).

In the festival's first year, only one work by Harrison was performed: the early cembalo sonatas programmed by harpsichordist Margaret Fabrizio. Festival director Gerhard Samuel was scolded in the press both by Yates ("I have made clear by my writing that I consider [Harrison] one of the most diversely gifted and technically expert of living musicians")[38] and by Alfred Frankenstein, who, after more than twenty years of reviewing Lou Harrison concerts, remained an avid supporter. "It was a bold and interesting idea," said Frankenstein, "to open with a program of contemporary masters, but it is hard to understand why another contemporary composer, Lou Harrison, the most distinguished citizen of Aptos, is not represented on the festival programs. In Europe, a man of his standing would have been commissioned to write a dedicatory piece for the opening concert."[39]

Samuel didn't make the same mistake again. The following year he premiered Harrison's first symphony, the *Symphony on G*, begun during Lou's hospital stay in New York.[40] Thereafter the festival included works by Harrison almost every year, mounting nearly every major composition he has written, including world premieres of *Bomba* (a percussion work from 1939), the *Grand Duo* for violin and piano (1988), and the *Third Symphony*, which it commissioned in 1982. The arrival of Davies in 1974 initiated a particularly rewarding partnership that ultimately led Lou to compose his third and fourth symphonies, his piano concerto, and the *Grand Duo*, all of which Davies has performed around the world to high acclaim.[41]

Meanwhile, after his Korean trips in the early 1960s Lou returned to working as a dance accompanist. He hauled his percussion mélange around the San Francisco Bay Area, playing for dance instructors such as Chloe Scott and Lorle Kranzler, director of the Stanford Creative Dance Group. Together Harrison and Kranzler created improvisations, both musical and choreographic, not only for classes but also for films (chapter 4).[42] Once again, his own composing activities had to be relegated to the postwork hours of the night.

In 1966, however, Lou received a Phebe [*sic*] Ketchem Thorne Fellowship.[43] Funded by the National Endowment for the Arts for seven years beginning in 1966, the Thorne award provided three-year fellowships of $300 per month without conditions to composers "of mature years and recognized accomplishment." (The fellowships were disbanded when the NEA started its own composer fellowship program.) The committee that selected Lou as one of the first recipients comprised Francis Thorne, Leonard Bernstein, Aaron Copland, Douglas Moore, Peter Mennin, and Virgil Thomson. Lou used the award to travel to Mexico for an extended period beginning in September 1966.[44] During this delightful, though noisy, respite in Oaxaca he composed a number of works and wrote his *Music Primer*, a collection of compositional guidelines and general musings about music, society, and the art of composition.[45] The Mexican odyssey also provided the opportunity to renew an old friendship: Ross Parmenter, the music critic for the *New York Times* who had sat with Lou during numerous concerts in 1947, routinely spent six months of the year in Oaxaca. The two men have maintained regular correspondence ever since.

Upon his return to California, Lou began teaching world music, orchestration, and composition at San Jose State College (now San Jose State University), where he was an active member of the faculty from 1967 to 1983. In 1973 he composed a concerto for organ and percussion for his San Jose State colleagues Philip Simpson (organ) and Anthony Cirone (percussion), dedicated to music department chairman Gibson Walters, "who made it possible." The following year Lou was hired for a one-year position teaching composition at Stanford and in subsequent years he offered his world music theory course at Cabrillo College and the University of Southern California (USC).[46]

In 1973 he was elected to the National Institute of Arts and Letters, the body that had given him his first "creative grant" in 1948. The institute's membership is maintained at a constant size (250), with election initiated by member nomination.

After Lou and Bill met in 1967, they immediately began to indulge their dual interests in instrument building and intonation systems. Together they constructed harps, wind instruments, metallophones, and replicas of Asian instruments. Lou was determined to tune these instruments in pure ratios, and Bill, an electrician, immediately realized that an oscilloscope was an accurate and affordable means of doing so. "I went to Zack radio on upper Market Street in San Francisco and bought a kit for $90. I took it home and said, 'Lou, here's the oscilloscope.' Then I turned the thing upside down and all these tubes and condensers and transformers fell out on the bed in a great heap. We took the instruction book and heated up the soldering iron and went to work. And, by golly, it worked beautifully."[47]

Soon Lou, Bill, Richard Dee, and John Chalmers (who at the time was working on his extensive monograph on tetrachords)[48] were improvising on a harp in ancient Greek modes (chapter 5).

In 1969, Encounters, a Pasadena-based organization that presented concerts of new music featuring composer-audience dialogues, approached Lou about appearing on their series. "I'm currently tortured and torn," Lou responded, "because . . . I'd like to do in Pasadena a new theater piece—all kinds of puppets in a grand coordinated way . . . making use of the exhaustive text-music relations of Chinese opera."[49] Two years later, thanks to the Judith S. Thomas Foundation, Lou's dream was realized in his opera *Young Caesar,* premiered at the California Institute of Technology in November 1971. The opera commission provided the impetus for Harrison and Colvig's biggest instrument-building project to date and gave Lou an opportunity to unite many old and new passions:

- *East-West unity and homosexual love*: Julius Caesar (read "the West") meets Nicomedes, King of Bithynia (read "the East") in a union of love. This early affair of Caesar is documented in Roman histories, although some have questioned the story's veracity (about which more will be said later).[50]

- *Hybrid instrumental ensembles*: five instrumentalists play a wide array of instruments, both Western and Eastern. Caesar is accompanied by a Western ensemble, Nicomedes by an Eastern one.

- *Instrument building*: For the new opera, Colvig and Harrison set out to build their own percussion orchestra tuned in Just Intonation. Noting its similarities to the Indonesian gamelan, they later dubbed it "An American gamelan" and now fondly call it "Old Granddad." They used materials at hand or easy to procure. Aluminum slabs cut to length and meticulously filed to pitch served as keys for the large metallophone; stacked #10 tin cans created varied-length resonators. They built the smaller metallophones from conduit tubing. To this ensemble, they added larger instruments that captured the spirit of Lou's old percussion groups: bell-like cut-off oxygen tanks struck with flattened baseball bats and galvanized garbage cans (fig. 12).[51] Although Dennis Murphy had previously built a type of American gamelan, Lou and Bill worked independently, with no knowledge of Murphy's activities. Old Granddad was in fact the first full ensemble of American gamelan instruments and inspired others to follow.

- *Intonation systems*: Using their oscilloscope, Lou and Bill tuned all the hard-ware in Old Granddad to a Just Intonation D major scale that extended over more than five octaves (chapter 5).

- *Puppets*: Opera "actors" were hand and rod puppets and an occasional shadow puppet, constructed by William Jones.

Lou also used a new type of recitative, influenced by Asian vocal practices, in which the pitches but not the rhythms are notated. This degree of free-dom for the performers also reflects Lou's earlier involvement with Baroque music. Typical of his compositional practice, as we will see later, is the high value he places on interpretive insights by performers. His syntheses derive from a willingness—actually an eagerness—to learn from all sources that cross his path: students, colleagues, nonmusician acquaintances, and cer-tainly performers.

Old Granddad provided the instrumentation for two later works that have since been recorded and widely performed. *La Koro Sutro* for game-lan and chorus uses an Esperanto translation of the Buddhist "Heart Sutra."[52] The premiere, on August 11, 1972, took place during a week-long seminar at San Francisco State University following the 1972 World Es-peranto Convention in Portland. This postconference attracted 329 partici-pants from twenty-eight countries who attended lectures in Esperanto as well as programs of music and dance. The performance of *La Koro Sutro* by the Oakland Youth Symphony chorus and Lou's American gamelan was "a magical evening. The beautiful gamelans fascinated the international audi-ence. . . . The response was electric," recalls Cathy Schulze of the Esperanto Information Center.[53]

Lou composed the second work, the *Suite for Violin and American Game-lan* (1974), with his student, violinist Richard Dee, after receiving a Norman Fromm Composer's Award from the San Francisco Chamber Music Society. The suite continues his exploration of the violin concerto, a genre that had fascinated him since his early San Francisco years. His *Concerto for Violin*, begun in the early 1940s and completed in 1959, uses as its orchestra an ensemble of percussion instruments (like the *Flute Concerto* of the same pe-riod).[54] In the *Concerto in Slendro* (1961), the violin is accompanied by key-boards and percussion and employs, in addition, an Eastern scale. In *Music for Violin and Various Instruments* (1967) Harrison called for a hybrid or-chestra—reed organ, percussion, psaltery, and mbiras. In this new suite, however, he moved even further toward Asia by using an orchestra of In-donesian-inspired instruments—an American gamelan reflecting the sounds of an Asian ensemble adapted by his own imagination. By the early 1980s he would be writing concerti for Western instruments accompanied by traditional Javanese ensembles.

By the time *Young Caesar* was premiered in 1971, Peter Yates had moved to New York, where he became chairman of the music department at the State University of New York College at Buffalo. In January 1972 Yates arranged to invite Lou for a week-long festival. Harrison and friends took a twelve-day trip to the East Coast (supported by a grant from the New York State Arts Council), including performances in New York City after a five-day residency at the college.[55] Two weeks before he was due to leave, Lou was injured by a speeding bicyclist while crossing a street in San Jose. Undaunted, he headed off on schedule for Buffalo, where he was expected to teach classes, deliver lectures, perform Chinese music and excerpts from *Young Caesar*, and attend performances of his music. Neither his injuries nor logistical problems in the shipping of his instruments could stand in the way: "Well, he got here," announced John Dwyer in the local press, notwithstanding "broken rib[s] and bruises from a recent collision with a teen-age California bike rider, and a crated treasure of his esoteric musical instruments held up in Chicago."[56] Despite its inauspicious beginning, the tour went off without a hitch, though Lou still recalls the pain in his rib cage every time he inhaled to play his Chinese flutes. The uniqueness of his musical voice prompted Tom Johnson to remark in the *Village Voice*:

> I have always been impressed by rugged individuals [such as] Charles Ives . . . , Carl Ruggles, Howard Hanson, and Harry Partch. . . . Lou Harrison belongs in this category. While Harrison has never isolated himself from the musical community, none of its fashions ever seem to have had much effect on his music. . . . Many of his pieces might just as easily have been written on some other continent in some other century. . . . "Young Caesar" certainly does not sound like American music or Chinese music, nor does it have much to do with the 20th century or any other particular period. It is just music, very personal music, which transcends ethnic and historical categories.[57]

From 1975 to the Present

In the summer of 1975 the Center for World Music in Berkeley (an instructional institute sponsored by the American Society for Eastern Arts) invited Lou to teach a course on intonation in world music as part of the Second Berkeley World Music Festival. The course, which attracted composers, performers, and instrument builders, proved to be "a great confluence of forces that really put American gamelan on the map,"[58] according to composer/instrument builder Daniel Schmidt. Among the students were a group of "renegade composers," who staged a concert of new music played on Old Granddad in the face of opposition from some of the exponents of traditional gamelan.

Enrolled in the course was composer David Doty, who had come to Berkeley to study recorder with LaNoue Davenport from the well-known early music ensemble Music for Awhile. Though an avid performer on early instruments, Doty had also founded the ensemble Other Music, which specialized in "Cagian and post-Cagian improvisational music using mostly found object sound sources." They were very interested in resonant metal:

"When I saw Lou and intonation and world music on the schedule, and then I saw the [American] gamelan instruments . . . , that swept everything else off the table. The recorder and LaNoue Davenport went out the window, and resonant metal in general went toward resonant metal that could be tuned in Just Intonation."[59] Doty later founded the Just Intonation Network to open lines of communication among those interested in tuning systems; the network publishes a newsletter and has issued Doty's own manual on intonation.

Daniel Schmidt, one of the "renegade composers," clearly recalls the conflict that arose when Lou suggested to his students that they stage a concert of original compositions on Old Granddad. Like Doty, Schmidt approached the gamelan as a composer and found the idea of creating East-West hybrids both stimulating and liberating. The concert took place on August 16, using Lou and Bill's American gamelan and featuring works by Harrison, Schmidt, Barbara Benary, Peter Plonsky, and others.

Among the students of traditional gamelan, however, some reacted with alarm, startled at the notion that American composers could write for gamelan without years of lessons with an Indonesian master or traveling to Java. Lou, for his part, had determined to set out on this very path. Although he came to Berkeley as a teacher, he left as a student of the renowned gamelan master Pak Cokro (pronounced "Choke-row").

When Harrison met Pak Cokro in 1975, the Javanese musician had already completed several careers in Indonesia and was embarking on the task of transmitting his deep knowledge of Javanese gamelan music to American students. As is often the case with Javanese intellectual-mystics, Pak Cokro's names and honorifics evolved frequently—not to confuse biographers, but to mark significant changes in his life. Pak Tjokrowasito (Tjokro is his personal name, Wasito his family name), Ki Tjokrowasito (a more mature title), Ki Wasitodipuro ("Wasito, adviser to the palace"), K. R. T. Wasitodiningrat ("Wasito, adviser to the word")—though each accomplished enough for any normal lifetime—are instead stages in the evolving persona of Pak Cokro. "Pak Cokro" is a friendly shorthand, "Pak" an honorific less formal than "Ki" (roughly, "Maestro") or "K. R. T." ("Kanjeng Raden Tumenggung," literally, "most honored prince of the blood," an earned title reflecting the admiration of the prince of the Paku Alaman Palace in Yogyakarta). Complicating matters further, several systems of Indonesian orthography have had currency during his long life, so that "Pak Cokro" may be spelled "Chokro" (as it is in Harrison's titles) or "Tjokro" with equal correctness, causing considerable consternation to Western librarians and compilers of indices.

Pak Cokro was born in 1909 at the Paku Alaman Palace, one of two royal establishments in Central Java noted as centers of musical culture (the other is the palace at Surakarta, or Solo). Pak Cokro's father, R. W. Padmo Winangun, was leader of the court's gamelan. After training in gamelan performance and composition, Pak Cokro followed in his father's footsteps; in 1934 he became director of the gamelan at the radio station in Yogyakarta, a position he held during the difficult years of the Japanese occupation and on through the establishment and consolidation of the independent nation of Indonesia.

He did not shrink from using his compositional skills to write nationalistic, even propagandistic works, such as his 1952 masterpiece *Jaya Manggala Gita*, a history of Indonesia told in gamelan music and song of varying styles, lasting more than an hour in performance. Judith Becker explores Pak Cokro's contemporary compositions in her remarkable book *Traditional Music in Modern Java*,[60] including such nonclassical songs as "Family Planning" or "Village Modernization," written during the Sukarno years. He has composed well over a hundred works; some are in "classical" style, while others extend classical techniques or mix techniques from several different areas (such as Balinese drumming in a Javanese gamelan context).

When his father died in 1962, Pak Cokro was appointed his successor as director of music at the Paku Alaman palace and continued his work with the radio gamelan. He has performed and taught in many countries worldwide. In 1964 he led the delegation of Indonesian musicians to the World's Fair in New York City. When he "retired" in 1971, he moved to the United States, where he joined the faculty of the California Institute of the Arts north of Los Angeles, a position he held until July 1993, when he retired once again and returned to Java. His influence is immense, since he did not confine his teaching to CalArts but taught as a guest at many institutions. His students have gone on to lead gamelan programs at many American and foreign institutions: to cite just a few, Mantle Hood ("Pak Cokro . . . , my first rebab teacher, [was] for years recognized in the United States as the ultimate authority on the practice of Javanese gamelan"),[61] Jody Diamond, and Lou Harrison.

Pak Cokro was an ideal mentor for Lou—a formidable musician, a prolific composer, and a dedicated teacher, bringing his skills to Javanese and non-Javanese alike. Brought up in the traditional system of learning through long apprenticeship, Pak Cokro was on occasion critical of the encroaching practices of modern conservatories in Indonesia, which required, for example, codifications or exemplars of improvisation patterns. Such codification might make the learning curve easier for a student caught in a lockstep academic program but at the same time might fail to teach the essential "deep structures" that allow a professional musician to improvise freely in correct style. Pak Cokro may, therefore, have consciously adopted a cryptic teaching style; he would often quote a poem or proverb rather than give a "direct" answer of the sort one might expect from a Western teacher. And he preferred to teach by osmosis and example rather than by settled curricula and lesson plans. (It should be stressed that this persona might also be in part a deliberate "act." Pak Cokro can discourse with extensive and specific technical detail when needed.)[62]

This style of pedagogy gives maximum elbow room for a talented musician such as Lou to explore and learn; if faced with a teacher who insisted upon extraordinarily precise adherence to one specific way of doing things (typically the case, for example, with Japanese classical musicians), someone of Lou's temperament might withdraw and look elsewhere.

CMP records has recently released a compact disc devoted to Pak Cokro's compositions[63] that includes eight works spanning the years 1952–84. Though his compositions may be described as including varying degrees of internal stylistic fusion, they are evolutionary, not revolutionary; neither do they attempt to mix Western and Indonesian instruments or structures. Nevertheless, they may be felt to "license" new and experimental approaches to gamelan composition.

Typically, Lou threw himself fervently into the process of learning traditional gamelan techniques. During the following year he arranged to borrow Samuel Scripps's gamelan, Kyai Hudan Mas (most gamelan bear a personal name) for San Jose State; to bring Pak Cokro to the college for a residency; and to study intensively with Pak Cokro, Daniel Schmidt, and Pak Cokro's assistant, Jody Diamond.

Soon thereafter Lou and Bill built their own gamelan at San Jose State and named it Si Betty to honor Los Angeles music patron Betty Freeman. Unlike Old Granddad, Si Betty was designed to replicate Indonesian instruments, specifically those of Kyai Hudan Mas. Nevertheless, Harrison added elements from his own experience, including Just Intonation. Since the tuning of each Indonesian gamelan may be unique (while conforming to certain general parameters), Lou reasoned that applying pure ratios to his instruments was not only possible but also potentially appropriate culturally. Si Betty is a full gamelan; that is, it contains two complete sets of metallophones in different tuning systems: the slendro set plays a pentatonic scale without any half steps; the *pelog* instruments sound seven different pitches that include narrow seconds and wide thirds. After careful work with ratios, Lou located usable slendro and pelog scales among the pitches in the harmonic series and tuned his instruments appropriately (chapter 5).

Harrison was itching to write music for traditional gamelan and was thrilled when, after the summer session, Pak Cokro formally invited him to do so. Three works from the time honor those he wished to thank for his new composing resource: *Gending Pak Chokro* and *Bubaran Robert* were composed for the slendro instruments of Kyai Hudan Mas and are dedicated respectively to Lou's teacher and to Robert E. Brown, director of the American Society for Eastern Arts, "for his many personal favors and in homage to his beautiful dream of a true Center for World Music."[64] (For many years Mills College used *Bubaran Robert* as its graduation processional music.) The companion piece, *Gending Samuel,* calls for the pelog instruments and is dedicated to Samuel Scripps, who provided major funding for the society as well as the loan of the gamelan. Daniel Schmidt, now an active teacher of gamelan, considers *Gending Pak Chokro* "an extraordinary work. When I teach it people are always filled with joy. Though Western in nature, it can hold its own beside a traditional piece: one would think he'd been writing for gamelan for years"[65] (chapter 8).

Schmidt recalls the defining moment when Lou brought these "traditional" pieces to his ensemble to play. "Here are the pieces I've written to follow up on Pak Cokro's request," Lou told the players.

> I think several students off in the corner probably fainted. But for me it was a very important moment because I had been thinking about composing for gamelan and trying to talk to Pak Cokro [about it]. Then in came Lou, already an older established composer, almost a contemporary of Pak Cokro. He had only briefly been a student of Pak Cokro and so came blithely, as an American, into a context where the rest of us were students. I thought, "This is great."[66]

As for Pak Cokro, his most likely reaction would have been an enigmatic smile. A man who could combine archaic, nearly obsolete gamelan with contemporary ones in his *Jaya Manggala Git* or could dash off such ad hoc political ditties as "Confrontation" ("Neocolonialism, obstructor of freedom / Your suspicious ways are many / Let's go, let's go, smash them all / Kill neocolonialism, attack imperialism / Crush to bits, the English project in Malaysia"),[67] a text not far removed from Lou's outbursts in *Nova Odo* or *Homage to Pacifica*, could hardly say "You can't do that!" to Lou Harrison's American gamelan music.

The conflict between gamelan traditionalists and composers continued to gather steam after the summer session. Schmidt recalls that the following year, when he requested that his Berkeley gamelan perform some of his own compositions, many of the members participated with notable reluctance, and thereafter, several refused to play. In recent years, the rift has begun to heal, in part through such ventures as Diamond's American Gamelan Institute, its journal *Balungan*, and the availability of recordings of new gamelan compositions by Indonesian composers. "The dissonance between the students of Pak Cokro and Lou," Diamond now reflects, "was not so much a disagreement about how much he knew or could know but that he had chosen a different learning process than we had."[68]

Indeed, Lou's unique learning path led in directions the traditional gamelan students would never have considered. Having brought Asian timbres and techniques into the Western concerto by using his American gamelan as the orchestra for a violin concerto, he was now prepared to introduce Western concerto principles into gamelan compositions. There soon emerged a series of new works featuring Western solo instruments against the backdrop of the traditional gamelan: *Main Bersama-Sama* ("playing together") for French horn and gamelan (1978); *Threnody for Carlos Chávez* for viola and gamelan (1978); the *Double Concerto for Violin, Cello, and Game-*

lan (1981–82);[69] and, later, the *Cornish Lancaran* for saxophone and gamelan (1986); *Philemon and Baukis* for violin and gamelan (1987); and a concerto for piano and gamelan (1987). He also continued to compose numerous works for gamelan alone and for voices and gamelan (e.g., *Scenes from Cavafy*, 1980).

The year 1975 was indeed momentous for Lou: not only did he meet Pak Cokro, but two events of major import also took place later in the year. In October he traveled to the Philippines (again under the auspices of the Rockefeller Foundation) as the United States' representative to the Third Asian Composers' League Conference and Festival.[70] There he reported on the status of Asian music in America, reviewing pioneering work by Cowell, Colin McPhee, Charles T. Griffes, and Henry Eichheim, and noting current developments.

Soon after this trip, Denis de Coteau conducted the Oakland Symphony Youth Orchestra in the premiere of Harrison's second symphony, "The Elegiac," commissioned by the Koussevitzky Foundation. A memorial to Natalie and Serge Koussevitzky, the *Elegiac Symphony* (a "mournful but inherently upbeat" work)[71] also lamented the deaths of Lou's mother on March 21, 1974, and of Harry Partch in September of the same year. In the third movement Harrison paid special tribute to Koussevitzky, a contrabassist, by featuring an extended contrabass duet in harmonics accompanied by a trombone, two harps, and a metallophone. Originally he specified a mode using pure intervals described by Ptolemy in the third century, but eventually he abandoned this refinement, bowing to the demands of the Western orchestra—or, more precisely, to the practicalities occasioned by minimal rehearsal and musicians whose ears were steeped in Equal Temperament.

He also seized on the symphony commission to update some early works. Movements 2 and 5 are revisions of *Canticle #6*, dating from October 1942; material for other parts of the five-movement work come from a 1946 organ piece (*Praises for Michael the Archangel*) and from one of the overtures of his *Political Primer*. Because of the hectic pace of Lou's life (as well as his penchant for constant tinkering), the score was barely completed in time for the first rehearsal. A November 20 press release from the orchestra states that he was "still in the process of composing the last movement" for the December 7 concert. Nor did the composing process end with the start of rehearsals. Up to the very day of the concert, he was frantically revising, repairing, manipulating, and inserting. Paul Hertelendy wrote in the *Oakland Tribune* on the day of the concert, "When the Youth Orchestra musicians stroll in for their dress rehearsal today, a surprise lies in store: 15 additional measures will be stapled to their scores, representing Harrison's revised editing for the fourth movement. The ink will be barely dry. Harrison is like that. As if they were his children, his scores are rarely sent off into the world in final form. He reworks, rethinks and philosophizes at every encounter."[72]

Two more symphonies soon followed. The *Third*, commissioned by the Cabrillo Music Festival, was premiered by Dennis Russell Davies in 1982. A "big, opulent score" in which "the bubbly optimist wins out" over the pessimist,[73] it features an opening movement "of light and beauty,"[74] a suite of dances (a reel, a waltz, and an exuberant medieval *estampie*), a sighing largo with brass introduction and conclusion that Lou revised from an old composition of January 1937, and a bright finale. Once again, composing continued down to the wire. Hertelendy described the piece on August 23 as "a 'wet-ink' work so late in completion that some feared one or more movements might have to be omitted at the Aug. 29 premiere. [However, at the first rehearsal] not only were all four movements completed and copied, but the musicians made the rare gesture of applauding after each movement."[75] Again Lou could not resist revisions. After the premiere he reworked the finale several times before feeling fully satisfied.

The Brooklyn Philharmonic commissioned a fourth symphony, which Davies premiered with the orchestra on November 2, 1990; Lou called it *Last Symphony*. When we asked what would happen if he wrote another, he said, "I'll call it the *Very Last Symphony*." As in the *Symphony on G* and the *Third Symphony*, one movement is a set of dances, derived, Lou has pointed out, from the old minuet and trio, "which is a small suite already."[76] Yet one can't help but wonder whether his long involvement with dance, as well as the influence of the Classic symphony's pair of minuets, made it hard for him to resist the temptation to insert mini-suites into his symphonies.

Lou continued to refine the score after the premiere. In January 1995 he "unveiled the fourth, and last, version of his 'Last Symphony,'"[77] the opening movement shortened, the second and fourth movements exchanged. The work's most novel feature is a baritone declaiming Amerindian tales in chant style—three "coyote stories" describe "the creation of a multiracial world, the force of a volcano and the need to protect the environment"[78]—to a murmuring accompaniment evoking gamelan timbres. The symphony includes another high-spirited estampie, a form characterized by paired phrases with similar open and closed endings (AxAyBxByCxCy, etc.).

In 1980 Harrison was hired to teach in the music department at Mills College, thereby returning as an elder statesman to the institution that had given him his first teaching position in 1937. He was not quite ready, though, to sever ties with San Jose State. For several years he taught at both institutions, some days driving forty-five minutes to San Jose and other days ninety minutes to Mills. In January 1982, during this period of seemingly endless highway travel, his car was struck by a hit-and-run driver. He severely sprained his right wrist,[79] which ever since has hampered his ability to carry out large-scale calligraphic projects. Lou's ultimate solution was to design calligraphic computer type fonts with the help of Carter Scholz, a composer, author, graphic artist, and gamelan player.[80] Together Harrison and Scholz have created the series of fonts shown in chapter 12.

One week after his accident, Lou returned to teaching at Mills and San Jose State. A year later, however, he resigned from San Jose, fearing for his security in the face of severe fiscal cutbacks. The state university system was thrust into financial crisis by California's Proposition 13, a voter-mandated reduction in property taxes. Lou, an untenured lecturer, faced an uncertain future.

He hoped for greater security at Mills (a private institution), and the college did indeed provide a supportive environment—both philosophically and financially—for his interests in gamelan. Mills honored Harrison with two successive endowed chairs, the Milhaud chair in 1980 (a rotating position) and the Mary Woods Bennett chair in 1981–83, and gave him an honorary doctorate in 1988.[81] As one of his first projects, Harrison set out, with Bill Colvig and the able assistance of percussionist William Winant, to build a third gamelan. "I spent every day in a loft above the concert hall helping Bill make resonating boxes, cut the wood for the gambangs [xylophones], and file the bars for the metallophones," Winant recalls.[82]

Like Si Betty at San Jose State, the new Mills gamelan had both a slendro and pelog set of instruments tuned in pure ratios. They named the two sets after Darius Milhaud and his wife Madeleine (the slendro section is Si Darius, the pelog section Si Madeleine) in recognition of Milhaud's years of service on the Mills College faculty. Lou himself hammered out the gamelan's huge gong. When he thought it was quite ready, he "invited Pak Cokro to Mills to listen to it. Pak Cokro listened very intently. Finally he relaxed and turned to me and said, 'More beating, more beauty.' So I went back to beating."[83]

Lou soon formed a gamelan ensemble and recommended that Mills hire Jody Diamond to teach traditional technique. Lou taught composition, much of which focused on works for the new set of instruments. Together Harrison and Diamond staged numerous gamelan concerts with both traditional Javanese compositions and new works by themselves and other members of the East Bay gamelan community.

The years 1974–94 have been filled with travels as well: residencies and guest appearances too numerous to detail, as well as an extended stay in New Zealand on a Fulbright Fellowship, two world tours, and numerous trips to England, Europe, and Japan for performances of his music. A sampling of Lou's guest appearances and residencies shows his remarkable energy at an age when most people would be slowing down:

- Eastern Montana College (residencies, April–May 1974 and May 1975)
- Schenectady (American Composers Forum, January 1979)
- University of Texas at Austin (residency, April 1980)
- Toronto (performances by the ensemble Array, June 1980; gamelan performances, October 1993)
- Cornish School, Seattle (residencies, 1980, 1986, and 1992)
- Portland (performances and collaboration with gamelan composer Vincent McDermott, 1981; additional appearances in 1985, 1988, and 1992)

- Seattle (keynote speaker at the conference of the American Society of University Composers, 1982)
- University of Michigan (residency, February 1983)
- performance at Betty Freeman's Los Angeles musicales (1983) followed by concerts in Los Angeles and New Mexico
- six-month residency in New Zealand (June-December 1983), followed by his first trip to Indonesia and a world tour (Australia, Thailand, Jordan, Turkey, Greece, Germany, Holland, and England)
- a retrospective concert by Continuum in New York (March 1985)
- Atlantic Center for the Arts, University of New Mexico, Cincinnati Conservatory, Cheltenham International Festival, First International Gamelan Festival in Vancouver, and Saratoga Springs (all in 1986)
- Telluride Festival (1988)
- Arizona State University, University of Miami, Ravinia Festival (Chicago), and an Alaskan tour (1989)
- Interlink Festival in Japan (1990)
- University of Arizona and Cornell University (1991)
- University of Utah (1993)
- second world tour (1993, including performances of *Rapunzel* in Bonn and Budapest, of Symphonies 1, 2, and 4 in Basel, Amsterdam, and Utrecht, and concerts in St. Petersburg and Japan, at the Sapporo Festival)
- Ojai Festival (1971 and 1994)
- Djerassi Foundation (1995).

In 1983, when Lou was invited as featured composer for one of Betty Freeman's Los Angeles musicales, he decided to bring along the entire Mills gamelan, both instruments and personnel. Freeman, a fan of new music, presented five to seven musicales a year from October 25, 1981, to March 31, 1991. The invited audience, which included luminaries from the Los Angeles music community, were treated to performances and discussion with two featured composers, including one established and one emerging figure.[84] Freeman had met Harrison years earlier through Harry Partch and held his music in high esteem. As the "emerging" composer at this March 6, 1983 event, she invited Dorrance Stalvey, faculty member of Immaculate Heart College and executive director of the Monday Evening Concerts in Los Angeles.[85] The musicales were held in Freeman's living room, with space for a quartet of performers and forty to fifty audience members; overflow seating in the adjoining foyer could accommodate another thirty. Freeman recalls that at about 10 A.M. on the day of the musicale, Lou and his entourage arrived from their four-hundred-mile trip and pulled up in front of Freeman's elegant Beverly Hills home "in a huge Greyhound bus. I gulped and then said, 'Well, come in by the kitchen door' (because they had a bus full of instruments). I went to the kitchen to meet them and to shake their hands as they came in. I counted twenty-one handshakes. Lou saw me blanch; so he said, 'Well, I can see that it might not work. I can see you're upset. We'll cancel the concert. We'll go home.' I said, 'No, don't go. Let's think of something to do.'"[86]

They set up the gamelan instruments in the foyer, on the floor, and up the stairs. Typically, Lou chose to share the spotlight; in addition to the second and third movements of his *Double Concerto for Violin, Cello, and Gamelan* (with Ken Goldsmith, violin, and Terry King, cello), the ensemble performed a traditional Javanese composition and a work by Jody Diamond. Among the members of the audience were Steve Reich, Joan LaBarbara, and Morton Subotnick.

Three months later Lou and Bill traveled to New Zealand, where they spent six months at four different universities. While Lou was teaching and composing, Bill built several instruments and tuned two gamelan in Wellington. Since he found himself close to Indonesia, Lou chose to visit the country for the first time. Quite by accident his friend Vincent McDermott, a composer and gamelan expert on the faculty of Lewis and Clark College in Portland, was also in Java at the time. Harrison had met McDermott two years earlier, when Vince invited him to Portland for the first concerts of Lewis and Clark's new gamelan. Determined to present performances of both traditional and new gamelan music even in the ensemble's first year of existence, McDermott called Harrison to suggest a short residency. Characteristically, Lou's response was to bring others into the project as well: "Oh yes, of course I'd love to come up. And it's wonderful of you to play my music. Have *you* written anything for gamelan? Why don't you play that too? Oh, and I bet Alan Hovhaness, an old friend who's in Seattle now, would love to be invited too. Why don't you ask him?"[87] McDermott laughed as he recalled the conversation: "Here I'm trying to set up a big Lou Harrison extravaganza and immediately he gives parts of it away." When Lou arrived for McDermott's concerts he discovered that the players had no music stands. "Your players are putting the music on their laps," he scolded. "It's undignified to stare at one's crotch!" Thereupon he insisted that McDermott take him to a hardware store, where Lou and Bill purchased wire, cardboard, and paint and immediately seated themselves on the floor and made music stands for the entire ensemble.[88]

When McDermott discovered that Lou was in Indonesia in 1983, he immediately arranged for lectures and presentations of Harrison's compositions (both taped and live) at Surakarta's major arts academy (ASKI, now called STSI).[89] According to McDermott, the reaction from his Javanese hosts reflected the honor they felt that one of America's major composers was studying their culture and writing new works for gamelan.

McDermott was not Lou's only connection to his old home town of Portland, Oregon. On a visit there in December 1984, Harrison and Colvig heard a concert by the eighty members of the Portland Gay Men's Chorus. They found the experience overpowering, not so much in terms of the musical quality but rather in the sheer sonic power of the massed male voices and in the commitment the experience stimulated among this group of gay men. When chorus manager Richard Brown learned that Lou had been in the audience and had been favorably impressed, he determined to commission a work. He secured funding from the Metropolitan Arts Commission; though the sum was modest ($500), Lou readily agreed, perhaps as much for political as for musical reasons. Brown recalls his first impression upon meeting Lou when he arrived for the rehearsals and performance of *Three Songs*.

> Since he didn't like to fly, he and Bill came by train. I spent days dusting and polishing, making everything pristine about the house, to have them as house guests. Then I went to the station to pick them up. It was a delightful surprise, but certainly far from what I expected a renowned composer to look like. He came off the train quite rumpled wearing a sort of tent-like Indonesian shirt that looked like he had slept in it, and carrying great heavy bags. Bill loped along beside, looking like a mountain man. There was no way that you could not love them instantly.
>
> When we came through that door [indicating the front door of his elegant home] Lou said, "Oh, I love having rich friends!"
>
> I had it figured out. They were going to use the nice bedroom and I was going to produce, at the dining room table, the dinner and then the breakfast. Well, that's not what they wanted. They wanted to sit in the kitchen and raid the refrigerator. They wanted to go out and get their own special kinds of bread and natural foods. My whole, tidy plan went out the window.
>
> In the rehearsals with the chorus Lou was always encouraging. I was worried: an amateur choir always has intonation problems and that one was no exception. But Lou opened his arms and told them how wonderful it sounded and what a thrill it was to hear this many gay men together in goodwill singing his music. He won everyone's heart. I have heard him be very sharp with professional musicians who were not performing up to his standard. But never once did he make a complaint about the chorus.[90]

The *Three Songs* have remained a staple of the group's repertoire. Moreover, the goodwill generated between Lou and the chorus on this occasion led to the remaking, three years later, of *Young Caesar* for human singers and actors (rather than puppets) and an orchestra of Western instruments (chapter 10). Harrison added choruses and otherwise revised the score to make it appropriate for a large-scale production; Brown raised funds; and the opera was premiered in its revised form to sold-out audiences amid an extensive media blitz in April 1988. Unfortunately, critical response was not nearly as welcoming as it had been to the *Three Songs*. " 'Young Caesar' Fails Despite Noble Narrator, Dancers: Gay Opera First Written for Puppets Turns Dreary in the Current Version," blared the four-column headline in the *Oregonian* the morning after the premiere.[91] To be sure, the opera had drawn large crowds and audience acclaim, but the disappointment on the part of Brown, Harrison, and the members of the chorus at the *Oregonian*'s acrid review was palpable. Lou, in his typical self-critical way, is still revising the opera, trying to correct its weaknesses. "It needs arias," he has said on more than one occasion. It is the one project he is determined to complete, commission or no commission. "I'm going to get that work right before I die."

Indeed, as this book is being written, Lou shows few signs of slowing down despite repeated vows to retire. In 1989, amid all his travels, he underwent triple-bypass heart surgery. He claims to have now begun a third life (the second began after his New York breakdown). In his eightieth year, he is still hard at work on numerous composition projects, and in recent years has received more offers for commissions than he can accept. In 1991 he completed a commission for a work to inaugurate the Pacifica Foundation's new building, funded by a grant from the Gerbode Foundation. The result was *Homage to Pacifica*, a gamelan piece with a decidedly political agenda (chapter 9). In 1995 the San Francisco Symphony, which had never programmed one of Harrison's works on a regular subscription concert, commissioned *Parade for M.T.T.*, a fanfare for the opening of the season honoring its new director, Michael Tilson Thomas. Making up for lost time, the symphony played Harrison's works four times during this season. Guest conductor Dennis Russell Davies programmed the *Third Symphony*, and Thomas conducted *Canticle #3*. During the symphony's summer celebration of American music, Thomas included the *Concerto for Organ and Percussion* and featured Lou as commentator on the works of Cowell, Varèse, and others.

Dancer Mark Morris has found Lou's works ideal for his choreographic imagination. To date Morris has choreographed *Strict Songs*, the *Grand Duo* for violin and piano (composed for Davies and Romuald Tecco in 1988), movements from the *Piano Trio* (composed in 1989 on a commission from the Mirecourt Trio), and excerpts from *Homage to Pacifica*. He recently commissioned *Rhymes with Silver*, premiered in March 1997 featuring cellist Yo-Yo Ma.

Offers for other commissions are piling up in Lou's stack of mail. But he has other projects he wishes to complete first. In addition to revising *Young Caesar*, he still harbors hopes of having time for poetry, painting, and just plain relaxation. He has purchased desert property in Joshua Tree, California, and is designing a straw-bale house to which he can escape—with no phone or computer (though he expects to maintain a connection to the outside world via fax). Is he perhaps remembering (and longing for) the peace he experienced when he first moved to Aptos?

II

THE ARTIST'S WORLD

4 Music and the Dance

I believe that one can predict with assurance a good future in composition for anyone with a good head for improvisation," wrote C. P. E. Bach in 1762.[1] Bach refined his improvisatory skills at the Prussian court; Harrison refined his in the more mundane environment of the dance studio. Whether for Tina Flade or Marian Van Tuyl at Mills in the 1930s, Lester Horton or his assistant Melissa Blake in Los Angeles in the 1940s, Katherine Litz at Black Mountain College in the 1950s, or Lorle Kranzler at the Stanford Creative Dance Group in the 1960s, Lou learned to dispel the tedium of accompanying repetitious dance exercises by improvising on the keyboard or on various percussion instruments. "Improvisation . . . is a cultivated skill which is built up of years of effort and/or trial and error," he wrote in 1966. "It is good practice for young composers, too, for one may learn how to sustain Form-building Musical Functions."[2]

The demands of the dance studio could surely tax any composer's patience and imagination. Lou recalls spending an entire day at Mills improvising on the four-note motive c' a d' g, taken from the radio and stage call "We want Can-tor!" (for comedian Eddie Cantor). He constructed retrogrades, inversions, varied harmonic effects, polyphonic complexes, and diverse accompaniments. The difficulty in such situations is to avoid becoming formulaic. "That's when it becomes a 'no-no,'" he cautions, "for one loses the sense of exploration."[3]

Lou became so adept at extempore composition that Melissa Blake reported he "improvised the accompaniments for the dance exercises while he read a book propped on the piano. And then between classes he would continue reading the book while he would improvise fugues at the piano."[4] Harrison claims he actually read *between*, not *during*, improvisations, absorbing his current book in bits and pieces during the rehearsals.

Public performance, however, was quite another matter. Here Lou admitted improvisational freedom only within the bounds of predetermined structure. To be sure, "scores" for some of his early dance pieces survive only as sketches, allowing for various modes of realization. But even these were constructed from careful observation of the choreography. Harrison would watch the dance, note the "counts," then create a musical counterpoint to the visual elements.

The process could backfire with a dancer such as Tina Flade, whose choreographies themselves developed through a process of repeated improvisation. Lou recalls his first sessions with her in 1937. After composing music to fit the dance counts at one rehearsal, he was astonished to discover serious misalignments at the following session. Puzzled, he recorded Flade's choreography in Labanotation, which he had learned through a course in San Francisco. "Then I went home with confidence and wrote some music to go with what I had notated. I even made sure I could perform the dance myself. At the next session all began well until suddenly there was a big discrepancy. 'Now Tina,' I said, 'according to my notes, what you did here was this.' And I got up and demonstrated for her. 'Oh,' she said, 'I do remember something of the sort.'"[5]

With Horton, who hardly ever kept anything the same from performance to performance, much less from rehearsal to rehearsal,[6] the stimulus would flow in both directions: the music influenced the choreography as often as the dance inspired the sounds. Bella Lewitzky, Horton's brilliant lead dancer, recalls how Lou's improvisations, as well as his exuberance, could capture in sound (or even anticipate) her movements:

> As we moved, Lou was a close observer of what happened. Lester loved using ramps and platforms. I was running down a platform once in a rehearsal and suddenly I heard a wild sound. It was Lou. He had found a thunder sheet! I was so amazed and so charged that I think I could have flown at that point. It was the most wonderful sound imaginable; I had never heard a thunder sheet before. . . . He evoked the exact sound that was needed.[7]

In performance situations "controlled improvisation" was as far as Lou was willing to go. In the case of a solo dancer who has an extensive background in formal composition and a history of collaboration with the accompanying musician, Harrison admits that simultaneous improvisation can be effective. But "I'm bored by group improvisation," he wrote, "because one has to wait too long for anything interesting or beautiful to happen (when with a little planning both can be made to happen). . . . This is true of both the arts [dance and music]. Great or beautiful forms are almost impossible to create by committee—doodling is the result. The remedy is Literacy."[8] With a predetermined set of internal cues and responses, total improvisation can become "variable composition," which he has found effective.

In the majority of Lou's fully composed dance scores, the choreography preceded the music. "I only knew three composers who could do that," said Jean Erdman, "Louis Horst, John Cage, and Lou Harrison."[9] Nor does Erdman recall Lou making revisions once the score was completed. "He watched as many rehearsals as necessary to notate the form of the dance and then went away and came back with a score that fit."[10]

Lou's music does not mirror the choreography; rather, he constructs an independent composition that interacts contrapuntally with the dance. His early interest in Baroque music and in the "total polyphony" of Ruggles perhaps suggested to him that choreography was itself a form of melody, which could complement his own.

At times Lou counterbalances on-stage action with contrasting music: at a tense moment in *The Perilous Chapel*, for instance, he chose to support frantically dashing figures by a static, prolonged drone. Similarly, in music for the film *Scattered Remains of James Broughton*,[11] a scene showing Broughton's head pulsating in dizzying circles is accompanied not by wildly whirling music but by steady rhythmic regularity on three metric levels. The fastest layer is an ostinato of two parts: a seven-tone motive played four times followed by a ten-tone response also played four times (example 4-1a).[12] On the middle level is an expansive melodic line—a six-and-a-half bar phrase repeated with variation (Example 4-1b), followed by a twelve-bar phrase. The slowest layer is an irregular intermittent drumbeat. The middle ground forms a counterpoint to the whirling head, while the ostinato reflects the endlessness of the circular image. By writing a complementary rather than mimetic score, Harrison preserved the independence of the visual and the aural while capturing the message of endless repetition.

Dance and music should resemble a couple, says Jean Erdman, "two independent forms that create a third." She notes that Louis Horst taught Martha Graham's students to choreograph by adapting musical forms. The dancer might construct a theme-and-variations, for instance, by developing a visual shape through varied repetition of its components. Erdman in turn would expect the skilled composer to accompany her choreography by constructing "one counterpoint for the theme and another for the variations, rather than merely copying the choreography's rhythmic patterns. The sound form could then become a partner to the visual form."[13]

EXAMPLE 4-1. *Air for the Poet* (1987), ostinato and opening theme. (Courtesy of Hermes Beard Press.)

a. Ostinato

b. Overlying melodic line

Bella Lewitzky was attracted to Harrison's music for similar reasons:

> Music to me is danceable . . . if it permits occupancy by another art form that can move on a parallel, rather than an imitative, track so that both can flourish side by side in great honor for each other. Lou's music . . . is not dense, not overpopulated by multiple things happening at once. I personally respond to art that is inferential rather than specific, that permits one to breathe, to dream, to move; in which all the spaces aren't clamped into multiple sounds.[14]

Merce Cunningham noted this same complementary relationship of sound and motion in Lou's dance music even though he, himself, ultimately moved in a more independent direction: "The music was there with the dance, but it didn't get in the way. It was as though the two arts existed at the same time, in the way that much oriental dance and music does. They go together as though they are one entity, neither as separate identities (as with John Cage and myself) nor as one supporting the other—just two activities taking place at the same time."[15]

On rare occasions, after viewing a piece of choreography, Lou found himself at a loss for sound. Carol Beals's *Three Dances of Conflict*, for instance, were "so wonderfully rhythmic in themselves, both in space and in image, that any accompanying music was either useless or distracting."[16] After several attempts to develop a musical score that would complement the dance appropriately, Harrison and Beals settled on silence.

Lou's skill at composing for the dance stems in part from direct experience. Kinesthetic by nature, he responds physically to aural stimuli. The ears are the repository of both "musical relationships and kinetic relationships," he reminds us. "The eye [alone] is absolutely indiscriminate. It looks upon all things with an equal absence of bias—it records vision. Sound, on the other hand, is . . . connected to motion. . . . Both music and our ability to understand movement are centered in the ear."[17] Watching the dance stimulates in Lou a sympathetic reaction: "When José Limón did a leap once in San Francisco, I literally fell off my chair."[18]

During his San Francisco years, Harrison became a particularly close collaborator with Carol Beals. A student of Martha Graham, Beals taught dance classes at the Peters-Wright Dance School and the Jewish Community Center, in addition to directing her own troupe. She was instrumental in founding the Dance Council of Northern California, which in 1936 represented twenty dance groups in the Bay Area.[19] Lou approached the collaboration "the same way I do everything. I go whole hog and learn about it from the ground up. If you work with dancers, you must learn to dance."[20]

Beals not only apprised Harrison of new trends in modern dance but also provided technical instruction. He was a quick study, she recalls: "He had a dancer's body and feeling toward movement."[21] Lou even danced in several staged productions. On May 2, 1937, he appeared in *Changing World*, for which he also composed the score. The following April he danced at the War Memorial Opera House, playing the part of "Winter" in the premiere of the opera *Ming-Yi*, by Oakland composer Harvey Raab. Alfred Frankenstein, generally friendly to new music, left in disgust at 11 P.M., after the second act, and panned the opera in the following day's *Chronicle*. "Raab has talent," Frankenstein admitted, "but this is a weak and immature expression of it. . . . Of the libretto . . . one can report nothing, since it was all but completely unintelligible. . . . The place to iron out the bugs . . . is in rehearsal, not in a pretentious, presumably professional performance, at professional prices, in one of the major opera houses of the world."[22] Frankenstein reserved his compliments for the staging and costuming as well as for the "good ballet led by Lenore Peters Job."

On August 24, 1941, Lou danced at San Francisco's Stern Grove in the first presentation by the Modern Ballet Group, the brainchild of Carol Beals, Letitia Innes, and Bodil Genkel. For this event he composed the score for *Green Mansions*, played in the instrumental ensemble, and danced the role originally intended for James Lyons.[23] He recalls dancing to music by others during this period as well, particularly to Manuel de Falla's harpsichord concerto, which, on his recommendation, Beals adopted for a dance about the Spanish Civil War, *And Spain Sings*.

The first work Lou composed for Beals was decidedly political: *Waterfront — 1934* commemorated the San Francisco general strike of July 1934, which temporarily brought the city to its knees. The conflict began in May when longshoremen up and down the West Coast walked off their jobs seeking improved working conditions, higher wages, and a closed shop to prevent blacklisting. Seamen soon joined the strike, which was supported by the teamsters, who refused to move cargo from the waterfronts, thus bringing the shipping industry to a virtual standstill.[24] Attempts to resolve the dispute through negotiations proved unsuccessful. Among workers, there was a widespread perception that the union officials were far too cozy with management. The employers, for their part, would negotiate only with these officials, refusing to recognize alternative representatives chosen by the rank and file. Many workers viewed the media, the mayor of San Francisco, the governor, and the police as prejudicially allied to business interests. Conservative elements in turn played on fears of a communist revolution, painting the labor unrest as subversive political activity. After fruitless attempts at settlement, a league of business and shipping interests attempted to forcibly open the port; on July 3 they imported trucks and non-union workers, leading to rioting and street battles that culminated on July 5 in the death of two strikers at the hands of the police. Over a hundred other persons were seriously injured. The day, dubbed "Bloody Thursday," became an annual period of mourning by longshoremen.

The violence crystallized pro-union sympathy. On July 9, a funeral parade for the dead strikers drew an estimated 40,000 people. On July 12, teamsters, butchers, railway employees, and others stayed off their jobs. Additional unions followed their lead on July 16, when some 127,000 workers remained at home, marking the beginning of a three-day general strike.[25] Lou remembers well the pickets' barricades on the highway leading into San Francisco; those entering the city were obliged to explain their business.

Beals and her husband, Mervin Leeds,[26] were strike sympathizers and friends of Harry Bridges, the acknowledged leader of the union protest.[27] The premiere of her composition—which consisted of three continuous phases: Speed-up, Strike, and Bloody Thursday—took place in the boxing ring of the Longshoreman's Union headquarters, on the second floor of the ferry building. "I sat on the floor outside the ring surrounded by a whole batch of percussion," Lou recalls. "Every so often the dancers would swing out over me."[28]

Waterfront—1934 was performed on several subsequent occasions, among them the second festival of the Dance Council at the Veterans' Auditorium on May 17, 1936 (fig. 13). Two years after the general strike, the docks were far from quiet. Although the arbitrated settlement of 1934 had ironed out many of the critical disputes, several clauses were so vague that conflict between the maritime workers and their employers continued for years. When Beals presented her work at the 1936 festival, the prospect of another lengthy strike loomed.

"The dance does not attempt realism," explained the festival's program notes.

> There is no intention to represent any particular machine in the swaying movement. "Speed up" in the handling of cargo, a contributing factor leading to organization for protest, was selected by the group to begin the dance movement. The second part—Conflict between two groups—follows logically and reaches a climax in the killing of a member of the protesting group. All waterfront unions and friends join in a silent funeral march—a reminder that he must not have died in vain.[29]

For the following year's Dance Council Festival at the Curran Theatre, Lou composed music for an eight-episode cycle, *Changing World: Illusions of a Better Life*, created jointly by nine choreographers, including Carol Beals, Veronika Pataky, Bernice van Gelder, Lenore Peters Job, and Harrison himself. The program boasted: "[This project represents] a revolutionary experiment in collective choreography. The first full-length creation ever to be produced by a group of choreographers combines more than 50 dancers from seven studios in one unified production based on a crackling fresh theme as timely as newspaper headlines and American to the core."

The work again demonstrates Lou's versatility: he composed the music; performed on piano, percussion, and recorder; contributed to the choreography; and in the third scene, "All Religions Are One," left the small orchestra and joined the dancers. The score also specified voices both spoken and sung, including a vocalise in the opening scene that Lou composed for his friend Dorothy James. But at the performance, James had an attack of stage fright and could not sing a note. "I missed my big chance to sing at the Curran," she recalls, but Lou, sitting on the floor playing percussion, seemed not at all upset, responding instead with a smile of encouragement.[30] This reassuring role was one he would play often, according to many of his friends. James recalls exhausting dance practice sessions at the Beals studio after which Lou would come in wearing his ankle-length brown overcoat, looking like "a cherubic bear," and strike the large hanging gong, bringing everyone back to life."[31]

Alfred Frankenstein was unimpressed by *Changing World*, calling the performance "honorably zealous" but "not very meaningful." Though he complimented Robert Metcalf's lighting and Helen Frank's costumes, he (uncharacteristically) found the array of percussion in Harrison's score "tiresome."[32] Individual numbers from the dance were repeated later the same year, however, and Frankenstein's response was decidedly different. *Changing World*, he said at that time, is a "big, important cycle . . . [a] novel creation which should be revived in toto." As for the music, Harrison "has a particularly happy gift for writing excellent, interestingly scored and unobtrusive dance accompaniments."[33]

Among the composers who worked closely with the Dance Council was Henry Cowell, who spoke at a dinner following the organization's first festival in March 1935. Cowell had connections with Mills College in Oakland and it was at the Cowell house that Harrison first met Flade, leading to his employment in the fall of 1937 as her accompanist for classes and performances.[34]

Born in Dresden, Flade at first anticipated a career as a concert pianist but changed her focus to dance after watching a performance by Mary Wigman. Flade's work was very different from that of Graham-trained dancers, reflecting the spatial orientation of German postexpressionist dance as opposed to Graham's torso-oriented approach. Wigman's technique emphasized the relationship between dancer and physical environment; the orientation was communal, centering on movement in space. "I've never seen anyone move quite like Tina Flade," recalls Bella Lewitzky, who noted that her compositions were often "just slightly removed from recital dancing"—small in scale, with simple costumes, a restricted stage area, and minimal props and lighting.[35]

Flade came to Oakland in 1934 to develop a dance program at Mills.[36] Lou remembers her as "a lovely woman with a heart-shaped face and long hair, and an extremely thin body with very long hands and feet and toothpick connections in between. When she would push on the floor with those feet, up she would go, and fly through the air."[37]

The Mills College summer sessions brought notable artists to the campus for extended residencies. In the summer of 1938 (Flade's last months at Mills), Lester Horton came up from Los Angeles with his assistant Bella Lewitzky, and Bonnie Bird came down from Seattle with two assistants, Dorothy Herrmann[38] and a yet unknown young dancer, Mercier Cunningham. Flade and Harrison jointly taught a course in dance composition; Flade approached the topic through "analysis of movement," and Harrison offered "material in the classic dance forms of the 16th and 17th centuries in relation to modern music and dance." Harrison also taught "percussion (music in relation to the dance)" and a course dealing with "advanced problems for percussion composition."[39] Horton directed a performance workshop and convinced Cunningham to participate in *Conquest*, with music by Harrison.

Horton's approach to dance resonated sympathetically with Harrison's approach to music. In fact, the two men shared aesthetic, political, and even epicurean values (but were *not* lovers, despite a recent claim to the contrary).[40] Like Harrison, Horton explored the foundations of his craft and trained himself in related fields. He experimented with various forms of dance accompaniment, insisted that his students learn to play percussion instruments, and even accumulated a large percussion collection himself, which included some unmatched gamelan instruments. He took an interest in every detail of production, including sets, costumes, and props. Larry Warren's remark that since Horton was "not content with commercially prepared dyes, he bought the ingredients and created his own"[41] could equally fit Harrison's instrument building or typeface design.

But perhaps the most significant parallel between Horton and Harrison was their common emphasis on the artistic integration of multicultural sources. Horton was welcome in the Asian, African American, and Chicano communities in Los Angeles and in many of his dances drew together various ethnic dance styles, just as Harrison would later do with diverse musical styles. By the time Harrison met Horton, he had taken Cowell's world music course and was an aficionado of the Chinese opera. Through the *New Music Quarterly*, he was familiar with compositions by Mexican composer Carlos Chávez and Cubans Amadeo Roldán, José Ardévol, and Alejandro García Caturla. But

Horton introduced him to Mexican history and folk culture, influences that would later emerge in works such as *Song of Quetzalcoatl* and *Pacifika Rondo*.

Conquest, Horton's composition for the 1938 Mills summer session, had a political theme: the Mexican struggle against Spanish colonial rule. The final section, "Tierra y Libertad," featured contrasting dance styles representing Spanish and Mexican cultures: "Imperceptibly at first, and then with growing strength, the Mexican theme drowned out the Spanish theme, and at the climax Lewitzky, as the 'Spirit of the People,' made her entrance . . . at the top of an offstage ramp and advanced toward the audience beating a compelling foot pattern of six beats against nine."[42]

Harrison's instrumentation called for flowerpots of various sizes, piano, conch shell, thunder sheet, and some type of flute. (Horton's biographer, Larry Warren, specifies flute; Lewitzky recalls ocarina, an instrument-type found in Aztec culture; Harrison suspects it may have been recorder. No score survives to resolve the question; but during this period Harrison frequently called for recorder or ocarina.)

Horton believed that dance music should evolve simultaneously with the choreography. In a 1936 interview he asserted that through simultaneous composition "it is possible to achieve a homogeneity which is a stronger entity than either separate one."[43]

The concept fit perfectly with Harrison's work in "controlled improvisation." For some of Horton's works "I didn't have the time to write the full score," Lou recalls. "We took the metrics from the dance, selected the instruments that were appropriate for that time, and improvised whole passages. These were interspersed with Mexican folk melodies that I took from Lester or with passages I had written. We agreed on certain limits and certain usages of instruments. Passages were rehearsed so that one could improvise according to what one knew would be happening."[44]

The working relationship between the two artists was so successful that in 1940 Harrison suggested that Mills bring Horton for a return visit, which culminated on July 6 in performances of *Something to Please Everybody* and *16 to 24*. The former was a revue format into which Horton could fit his ever-evolving ideas. Like Harrison, he loved to revise, constantly reworking old compositions into new forms. (Later Horton "repeated" *Something to Please Everybody* several times with new personnel, new plots, new dances, and new music by other composers.) At the Mills performance, Lewitzky performed "Aphrodisiac," a mock "strip-tease for the tired businessman," for which Lou wrote a bluesy accompaniment. Frankenstein's review in the *Chronicle*, headlined "At Mills—Strip Tease!"[45] commended the Horton company for bringing modern dance "out of its rarefied, cultish state to meet the world around it. . . . The strip tease—a most discreet one—came in an uproarious burlesque of burlesque, while [an] alarm clock figured in a singularly effective episode called 'Surrealism.'"

In *16 to 24*, Horton turned to American political issues, particularly the frustrations of unemployed youth. In contrast to *Something to Please Every-body*, the mood was dark, the dancers evoking the longing of young people "seeking work, yearning for homes, wishing for joy but threatened by war."[46] The dance was presented over background narration in the manner of a documentary film, the dancers themselves interjecting exclamations. *16 to 24* was one of Horton's least successful pieces. Neither Lewitzky nor Harrison has any memory of it, although Frankenstein's review confirms that "the music for both [*Something to Please Everybody* and *16 to 24*] was by Lou Harrison, which means that it was ideally suited to its purpose."[47]

In 1939, the summer between the two Horton residencies, Mills hosted the Bennington School of Dance.[48] Twenty-six faculty and staff, including Martha Graham, Doris Humphrey, Charles Weidman, and Hanya Holm, moved from Vermont to Oakland for the session from July 1 to August 11. Teaching assistants were José Limón, Ethel Butler, Louise Kloepper, and Katherine Manning, who produced a joint recital at the end of the session. Merce Cunningham returned from Seattle for a second summer at Mills and was subsequently lured to New York to work with Graham. Cage came from Seattle as well and joined forces with Harrison in a concert of "modern American percussion music." Frankenstein noted in the following day's *Chronicle*,

> One might almost say that the modern dance discovered the possibilities of the battery for the Western world. . . . The modern percussion movement began with the reduction of dance accompaniment to simple, essential rhythms without melody. There followed the discovery of the delightful color of drums and gongs, and the ghostly skeleton of melody produced by varied instruments of indefinite pitch. . . . Four players handled a vast assortment of instruments. . . . The music ran a similar gamut. Sometimes it was monotonously mathematical . . . but there was grand gusto and spirit in William Russell's "Cuban Rhythms" and "Three Dance Movements," and much good color and rhythmic counterpoint in Lou Harrison's "Counterdance in the Spring."[49]

Cage returned to Mills during the summer of 1940. So did José Limón and Louise Kloepper, joining Marian Van Tuyl, a Graham- and Bennington-trained dancer who had taken over Flade's position at Mills in the fall of 1938. Lou composed a number of works for Kloepper and Van Tuyl (both at the summer session and during the regular academic year). Programs from this period list such dances as *Uneasy Rapture, Goin' to Be a Party in the Sky,* and *The Omnipotent Chair.* The last was conceived by Kloepper as a study on the plight of the abused nonconformist.[50] In this work Lou used for the first time a technique he would adopt in several later compositions: requiring the bassist to play the instrument percussively by laying it on its back and beating the strings with sticks or dowels.

Harrison's last San Francisco dance composition, *In Praise of Johnny Ap-pleseed* (a "chamber ballet" for five dancers and three musicians), was performed twice, at the Holloway Playhouse in the Fairmont Hotel on May 7, 1942, and outdoors at Stern Grove on August 9. Lou constructed a large and complex mobile for the stage, "ten or twelve feet tall, using wood and colored glass, intended to convey the concept of sparkling deity and the mysticism of Johnny Appleseed."[51] Immediately upon the conclusion of the Stern Grove performance, Lou headed off to Los Angeles with William Weaver, traveling so light that he did not even take his instruments, which were left with Beals to be reclaimed years later when Harrison returned to the West Coast.

New York and Black Mountain College
Dance Compositions

Although Lou moved to New York to maintain his association with Horton's dance company, the promise of success for the troupe on the East Coast soon soured, and Horton returned to Los Angeles. Lou, for his part, became involved in nondance activities—music criticism, editing, and conducting—and did not accompany in the studio again for several years. Nevertheless, his dance contacts in New York stimulated some of his most memorable compositions.

Soon after Harrison's arrival, John Cage introduced him to Jean Erdman, thereby bringing him into a fascinating circle of interconnected personal and intellectual relationships. Xenia Cage had previously met Erdman's husband, Joseph Campbell. Xenia's sisters, Natalya and Sasha, lived in Carmel, where they were part of a social circle that included John Steinbeck and Ed "Doc" Ricketts.[52] In 1925 Campbell met Steinbeck's wife Carol and her sister Idell, who introduced him to Steinbeck in 1932, thinking that the two writers would have much in common. Campbell subsequently moved to Carmel, where he met Ricketts, Xenia's sisters, and the marine biologist Jack Calvin (Sasha's husband). During a specimen-collecting trip on Calvin's boat in 1932, Campbell became well-acquainted with Xenia herself. In 1934 Campbell accepted a faculty position at Sarah Lawrence College, where he met Erdman; they were married in 1938. After John and Xenia Cage arrived in New York in the summer of 1942, they stayed temporarily with Max Ernst and Peggy Guggenheim, but soon had a falling out. Xenia then contacted Joseph Campbell, and the Cages stayed in the Campbell apartment before finding a place of their own.[53]

Cage arranged a performance at the Arts Club of Chicago on February 14, 1943, with Erdman and Cunningham choreographing and dancing. Meanwhile, through improvisation in the studio, Erdman had developed a solo "bird dance," inspired by her 1937 trip to Bali.[54] Since Cage had no time to write music for her new composition, "Creature on a Journey," he suggested that she use Lou's *Counterdance in the Spring*, scheduled for a concert at the Museum of Modern Art the week before the Chicago trip.[55] Erdman found

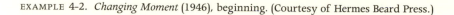

EXAMPLE 4-2. *Changing Moment* (1946), beginning. (Courtesy of Hermes Beard Press.)

Harrison's percussion trio ideal. Her choreography (fig. 14) became "another instrument, so that I was rhythmically in counterpoint" with the musicians.[56] Though Harrison and Erdman did not meet until months after the Chicago performance, the syncronicity of their aesthetic views (polyrhythm, counterpoint, attraction to Asian culture) paved the way for fruitful collaboration in the future.

After his move to New York, Harrison completed several scores for Erdman's concert dances, among them an intricate piano work, *Changing Moment*. The unpublished score, dating from the troubled period preceding his breakdown, exemplifies the dense, dissonant language of his early New York years (example 4-2). The manuscript itself is physically cramped, and Harrison's self-doubts are apparent in the extensive erasures visible beneath the final version. "It's a work I should revisit," he now says.[57] The dance starts as a pleasant duet "which is suddenly disturbed by the entrance of a powerful individual who destroys the polite world we have been experiencing," says Erdman. "It ends at the point of devastation, when even the energy of the destructive force is gone. It is about that moment-of-change before a new order is established."[58]

Composing for the dance offered financial support as well as public exposure for the young struggling composers in the Cage/Harrison circle. Ned Rorem, who moved to New York during this period, says that Lou showed him the ropes about survival as a freelance composer dependent on odd jobs and intermittent commissions:

> He would tell me about the real world of music (which of course is not real at all . . .). He believed in the practical aspects of being a composer. He thought that everyone should be able to do everything. Since he didn't have any money, he would write whatever was called for. If they wanted twelve-tone music then he'd write twelve-tone music. If they wanted percussion music, he'd write percussion music. But he would say, "I charge one hundred dollars down and then twenty-five for each additional minute." No matter who it was, whether it was Limón or Erdman or whomever.[59] [The actual fee in 1940s dollars was probably closer to $5 per minute.]

Despite such counsel, Lou didn't always heed his own advice. Cellist Seymour Barab, for whom he composed the *Suite for Cello and Harp* in 1949, recalls "in-kind" arrangements with Lou and other composers. "I was very interested in contemporary music and encouraged them to write for the cello. They would write it and I would play it. It's what we called a 'Platonic commission.'"[60]

When Erdman formed a new company in 1948, she commissioned from Lou *The Perilous Chapel*, premiered at her company's first performance on January 23 of the following year.[61] The program bore a quote from Revelation: "And I saw a new heaven and a new earth: for the first heaven and the first earth were passed away: and there was no more sea." It was indeed the dawn of a new era not only for Erdman but also for Harrison, who had only recently begun to emerge from the darkness of his breakdown. The dance, with its triumph of sanity over confusion, serenity over chaos, was in many ways representative of Lou's personal struggles. Expansive and sensuous melody replaces the dense complexities of his earlier dissonant counterpoint. Although the lyric strain had always been present, even in his most atonal works, here it breaks forth shamelessly in a rapturous concluding duet (chapter 2, example 2-3). *Dance Magazine* designated *Perilous Chapel* the best new work of the season.

Erdman, too, was finding her own voice, separating her style from that of her mentor, Martha Graham. The essential principle she developed was the independence of each composition—the adherence of the choreography to the work of art rather than to the artist. Through careful analysis of dance, Erdman identified seven physical centers in the body from which movement could originate, and explored qualities of impulse, shape, body tone, dynamics, and timing. Choosing from a range of possibilities, the choreographer could mix individual elements to create distinctive compositions, thereby avoiding personal stylization.[62]

The following year Erdman commissioned Harrison to compose music for *Solstice*, a work twice as long as *Perilous Chapel* and calling for a larger ensemble of both musicians and dancers. The thirty-minute drama, which she developed after discussions with Campbell, depicts the struggle between the old year and the new, represented by the Moon-Bull (the dark days of winter ushered in by the December solstice) and the Sun-Lion (the warmth of summer). Lou depicted the primeval fear of both solstices: "the terrifying one—is everything going to get hotter and we will all burn up?" and the "frightening one—is everything going to get darker and we will head into oblivion?"[63] In one case the fire must be rekindled; in the other, quenched. Merce Cunningham danced the part of the Sun-Lion, Donald McKayle that of the Moon-Bull.

When she approached Harrison with the completed choreography, Erdman already had another score in hand but she was dissatisfied with it.[64] Lou started from scratch; he never saw the previous music, nor does he know who composed it. His accompaniment calls for an octet including a trio of treble instruments (flute, oboe, trumpet), a trio of bass instruments (two celli, string bass), and two keyboards (tack-piano and celesta). The timbral variety and contrasting ranges allowed him to represent summer's bright days and winter's long nights, to indulge his love of a strong low register, and to imitate the gamelan by combining the keyboards with the double bass struck below the bridge with drumsticks. The reviewer for *Dance Magazine* found the new music a decided improvement. "When first done, Miss Erdman's *Solstice* was a cumbersome bore. But the dance has since acquired a luscious, oriental-sounding score by Lou Harrison. And the small orchestra under Mr. Harrison's direction gave it the sound of woven gossamer."[65]

Solstice, "a masque," opens in the Garden of the Sun, with the Sun-Lion portrayed by a languid melody in double octaves in the flute and cello, the resultant blend creating a string/wind instrument with an extraordinarily wide range. At the entrance of the Lord of the Night, this expansive line gives way to heavy rhythmic beating and harsh dissonance as the battle is joined. The Sun-Lion, temporarily the victor, carries off the Bride of Spring in a vernal dance. In part 2, the Moon-Bull returns and, in an orgiastic saturnalia, throws the world into darkness. A lone flute sings a haunting incantation as the Bride dances in desolation at the loss of both Lion and Bull. "But the Bride is life," notes Erdman, "and from a triangular point between the inert Lion and Bull, she begins a pulsation that grows in dynamics as she circles the stage. Both Lion and Bull are revived by her movement, five animal nymphs are lifted by them one by one, and she leaps into their arms."[66] The Sun-Lion and Moon-Bull face each other, now not in battle but in spiritual reconciliation.[67]

In contrast to *Solstice*, the next work Harrison created for Erdman called for minimal forces: two dancers and a pianist (who plays both the keys and the instrument's interior; see chapter 2). *Io and Prometheus* (the music was originally titled *Prometheus Bound*)[68] revisits *Perilous Chapel*'s theme of ineffable forces that control the course of human destiny. Prometheus, bound to a rock by enormous elastic bands, is free to move only his upper body. Io, who dances before him in waves of motion—now closer, now more distant—is equally restricted. She can no more end her incessant movement than he can free himself from his shackles.

In September 1985 Erdman was invited to present her troupe at a festival in the Odeon of Herodus Atticus in Athens. For this occasion she revived *Io and Prometheus* but transformed it into a group work, adding a text and a chorus of four singers/dancers. Lou composed vocal parts and orchestrated the work for chamber ensemble.

> Jean called and asked me if I could tout de suite rev up *Io and Prometheus*. She sent the text, along with a video of the current state of the work in her studio in New York. She asked each of the main characters to come before the

camera and sing their lowest and highest notes as well as a tune lying in between. Bill and I immediately bought a VCR, and I started work the next day. The result is a completely new *Io and Prometheus,* a more extended work with voices and small ensemble.[69]

Lou composed the new sections as a kit—materials that the performers may assemble in a variety of ways, as best suit the needs of the dance.

Harrison's collaborations with Bonnie Bird at the Reed College summer festivals in 1949 and 1950 resulted in three additional dance compositions of major import. During the first season, he wrote music for Jean Cocteau's *Marriage at the Eiffel Tower,* which Bird had previously choreographed at the Cornish School in Seattle using original music by Cage, Cowell, and George McKay, in imitation of the collective work created by *Les Six* in 1921. (Cowell's contributions, "Hilarious Curtain Opener" and "Ritournelle," were published in the *New Music Quarterly* during Lou's year as editor in 1945.) For the Reed College production, however, Lou composed a totally new score. Two voices portrayed as phonographs on either side of the stage provided the narration. Minor characters were "represented by hatracks, topped by silk or straw hats, with a wire coat hanger representing the essential torso."[70] Harrison's score demonstrates an uncanny ability to imitate styles very different from his own. Like the libretto and the staging, his music pokes good-natured fun at Parisian bourgeois culture. The entire production was so successful that Bird revived it for the following year's festival and presented it as well at Hunter Playhouse in New York.

In its subsequent embodiment as an orchestral suite, *Marriage at the Eiffel Tower* is one of Harrison's most frequently performed and ingratiating scores.[71] Dennis Russell Davies chose to include it (with Harrison and Virgil Thomson narrating) on the debut concert of the American Composers Orchestra in February 1977 at Alice Tully Hall. Harold Schonberg noted in the *Times:* "Harrison's score is very much in the spirit of the original . . . , French, frothy, sophisticated, peppy and lightweight . . . , a pleasant pièce d'occasion. . . . [He has] the style down pat."[72]

During the same summer institute in 1949 Lou wrote a more serious work: music for Yeats's dance-play, *The Only Jealousy of Emer.* Bird staged it with two people representing each character, one speaker and one dancer. The production was repeated at Hunter College, and recorded in the early 1950s, with Lou conducting.

During the following year's festival, Harrison composed a third work for Bird: the *Almanac for the Seasons,* which treated seasonal occupations and characters as depicted in medieval verse by Nicolas Breton. (The score is now lost.) The reviewer for the *Oregonian* found the production "pretty and matter-of-fact," with some striking dancing and excellent décor. "But what gave this ballet some of its most memorable flavor was the musical score of Lou Harrison . . . [which] evinced a 'feel' for the medieval character in line, color and harmonization."[73] The project provided an ideal outlet for Lou's long-standing love of medieval culture as well as his ability to adapt diverse styles to new contexts.

His move to Black Mountain College in 1951 brought with it a new dance associate: the whimsical Katherine Litz. Erdman recalls in Litz's style "a lyricism that was unknown in the Martha Graham days, a quality more closely associated with Humphrey-Weidman."[74] Harrison returned to improvisation, not only for Litz's classes but also for performances at the college. Litz wanted him to compose independent musical compositions that could be fitted to evolving choreographic concepts.[75] He therefore created works such as the *Adjustable Chorale* that were, like some of his San Francisco compositions, variable in performance. There were fixed compositions as well, such as the *Chorale for Spring*, which later found its way into the *Suite for Symphonic Strings*, where it was graced by a new rhapsodic middle section.

A burlesque solo dance, *The Glyph*, featured Litz wrangling with a decidedly uncooperative jersey body sock, a commentary on the absurdity of the human condition.[76] In the interdisciplinary spirit of Black Mountain, poet Charles Olson wrote a glyph poem, and Ben Shahn drew a glyph design that was realized by Litz's husband, Charles Oscar, as a screen for the backdrop of the dance. *The Glyph* became one of Litz's most popular works. A video of a New York performance in 1977, one year before her death from cancer, shows Litz becoming hopelessly entangled in the sock during the course of the six-movement, nine-minute work.[77] She writhes and crawls, disappears within it, and emerges from its clutches. Lou's score combined fixed and improvisatory sections for prepared piano, bells, claves, tuning fork, and optionally, a gong. Movement 4 consists entirely of the instruction: "improvisation on gong or piano: follow dance." Other movements are precisely notated, with all pitches, rhythms, and instruments specified. Piano preparation required pressing a 2" × 2" board firmly on the lower strings of the instrument at a nodal point. A 1952 performance of the work at New York's 92nd Street Y drew enthusiastic praise in *Musical America*: "Litz is a sensitive artist with a pronounced gift for lyricism and a vein of hilarious comedy. . . . [Her] final dance . . . was a novelty, The Glyph . . . , [with] an appropriately zany score by Lou Harrison. . . . The movement is so wonderfully senseless that it must be seen; words cannot indicate its inspired madness."[78]

David Tudor, pianist for *The Glyph* on several occasions, recalled that the title was meant to evoke an activity with multiple meanings. "The observer's mind is led in at least two different directions—the more the better," he said. The loose musical structure, partially improvisational, tried to capture in sound the remarkable quality of the visual image. The collaborators in fact strove to engender in the observer a state of confusion. "The joy of it," said Tudor, "was that I was even able to surprise myself."[79]

Black Mountain offered other forms of collaboration as well. Theater in-

structor Wes Huss produced a Noh drama, *The Pool of Sacrifice*. "I was experimenting with basic economy of movement," notes Huss. "The greatest
movement that I would allow was the shifting of weight back and forth as
if one were walking." Lou composed an accompaniment of chant and percussion using a child's toy "xylophone," the keys of which he tuned to a
scale in Just Intonation. Huss sensed, in fact, "that Lou was trying to place
in Western history an equivalent to what the Noh period was in Eastern
lore." [80]

Later Dance Works

Lou's formidable improvisatory skills and his sympathy for dance stood him
in good stead when he returned to California. Patching together a precarious livelihood through his usual mix of diverse activities, he would pile his
percussion instruments into his van twice a week during the early 1960s
and drive to dance studios in the San Francisco Bay Area. He developed a
fruitful collaboration with Lorle Kranzler, director of the Stanford Creative
Dance Group, who provided dance training as a creative outlet to over a
hundred students: "I accompanied around the clock—from the kiddies at
nine in the morning until the elderly persons about ten o'clock at night. It
was like a progression of the 'seven ages of man' through the day. I improvised the whole time—it was exciting, interesting, and exhausting."[81]

Like Lou, Kranzler was exploring the concept of improvisation within
a predetermined structure. In collaboration with KQED television, the San
Francisco PBS affiliate, she created a trilogy of dances devised through interactions with a camera-choreographer. She sought a "new medium for
dance," one dependent on the possibilities of film and thus unsuitable for
stage performance. "My job," she explained in a 1966 article, "was to organize the choreography . . . [with] a definite structure within which [the
dancers] could improvise. The structure would be like a mobile, open to
changes given through music cues."[82]

Lou, for his part, had been distressed for some time by the current fascination with aleatoric composition, which he felt often led to mediocrity.
He noted in an article in the dance magazine *Impulse* that the period following the Second World War was characterized by an exploration of the
individual, impermanent, and unreproduceable event, a reaction against the
mechanistic standardization and mass culture that had culminated in the
horrors of the Nazi era:

> Machine reproductions—the replication and dispersal of millions of "copies"
> of almost everything—has resulted in a general Bourgeois Tedium: the Re-
> peatable, then, made a common Tedium. After Hitler's War a New Effort arose
> among the Educated to avoid, and counter, this situation by producing the
> Unique event, preferably unrepeatable. Abstract Expressionism, Happenings,

Tacheism, etc., were all aimed at revivifying single states or events. I myself was miserable during that period—for it almost neglected the inter-compositional relationships that, to me, constitute Art. . . . I am happy now to notice in Society a return toward relational and/or mensurating art—Planned Art.[83]

Although Lou was uncomfortable with unstructured "happenings," he was perfectly content with controlled improvisation resulting from collaboration between musician and dancer. (His attraction to gamelan stemmed in part from the same phenomenon: not only was he entranced by the sound of the ensemble, but he was also attracted by the group interaction, creating music that was in part predetermined and in part improvisational.)

Kranzler's interaction with film and music built on a similar philosophy. She devised the overall scope of the choreography but allowed performer-camera interaction and musical cues to guide the specifics of its realization. The first work, *Mirrors*, centered on the interaction of couples, each of whom explored a theme; variations arose from mutual cross-influences. Lou similarly reacted to cues from the choreography. He recorded three tapes, one with sliding tones, one with drum motives, and a third with bells—with the intention of mixing elements from them in response to dance cues. For the final filming, however, the KQED engineer was unwilling to experiment with tape overlay as Lou envisioned.[84]

In recent years Lou's traditional interaction with dance has often been turned on its head: instead of composing a score to predesigned dance steps, he has written independent music to which the dance is later added. Such was the case with two works from the late 1980s: *New Moon* (1986), created for Erick Hawkins on a commission from Betty Freeman, and *Ariadne* (1987), written for Eva Soltes. As early as 1952 in New York, Hawkins (another connection from Henry Cowell) had choreographed Lou's six cembalo sonatas in a dance entitled "Lives of Five or Six Swords." On stage at the Hunter Playhouse was a tent that Hawkins entered after each movement, emerging with new costume and props. The result was a cultural mixture that reminded Lou "of the period in Spain in which Muslims, Christians, and the Moors all cooperated (though with some tension)."[85] For *New Moon* Hawkins and Harrison developed the overall concept through an exchange of correspondence. "One of the main reasons I wanted to write for him," Lou recalls, "is because, in these days of tape machines and computer accompaniments, he maintains a house orchestra—an absurd little band of very good soloists. The range is either way up or contrabass; as to middle, it hath none. Quite a compositional challenge!"[86] Subsequent interaction between composer and choreographer led to alterations and revisions, including a suggestion by Hawkins that Harrison include a barcarole, which Lou now feels is one of the work's most successful movements.

In the fall of 1986 Eva Soltes, who had studied the south Indian dance genre *bharata-natyam* with T. Balasaraswati, proposed that she organize a seventieth birthday celebration concert for Lou at Mills. Soltes had met Harrison during the 1970s when she was concert director for a small but influential chamber music series in Berkeley held at a private home at 1750 Arch Street. During the 1975 Center for World Music festival in Berkeley where Lou first met Pak Cokro, he also had the opportunity to enjoy Soltes's work in Indian dance. She, in turn, was fascinated by the gamelan instruments he had constructed with Bill Colvig. Soltes's training in arts management led to her employment as Lou's aide. At first she merely helped him sort and respond to correspondence and deal with paperwork. Ultimately, however, she arranged for, organized, and accompanied him on two world tours and secured several commissions for him.

When Soltes offered to arrange the Mills birthday bash (including any works, artists, or composers Lou might name), he responded with an offer to compose a piece to which she could dance in the Indian tradition. Bharata-natyam has its origins in Hindu temple dance, which is described in the *Natya-sastra* (a treatise that dates from the third century A.D. or earlier, with musical portions dating from the fourth or fifth century A.D.).[87] In this tradition dance often functions as narrative, the dancer serving both as part of the musical ensemble (keeping time with ankle bells) and as interpreter of the story.

Lou selected as his narrative the rescue of Ariadne from the island of Naxos by the god Dionysos, who was returning from a trip to India. The opening movement, "Ariadne Abandoned," portrays her despair when Theseus deserted her on Naxos after she had helped him kill the Minotaur and escape from the labyrinth on Crete (fig. 15). The musical setting, for flute and vibraphone, serves as an *alap*, an unmeasured prelude introducing the mode. The second movement, "The Triumph of Ariadne and Dionysos," is a kit, with seven lines of music for the flute and seven for percussion, which may be combined in any order, in any interrelationship, using any percussion instruments, in any octave, and repeated or omitted at will. Each line follows the basic *tala*, or rhythmic cycle—seven measures, irregular in meter: 3/2, 3/8, 4/4, 3/8, 6/8, 4/8, and 4/4. The work may range from as short as eight minutes to the limits of the dancer's endurance, depending on the number of repetitions.

Lou composed the music completely independent of any specific choreography. "The piece is very impressionistic," says Soltes. "It reflects his idea of what Indian dance does and can do in terms of rhythm. It is his memory of what he heard in Indian rhythms."[88] Her performances of *Ariadne* are in part improvisatory, in part preplanned, combining her work in bharata-natyam with previous training in ballet and modern dance. Like Lou, she has no hesitation in creating syntheses of Eastern and Western practices. The kit allows her to make each performance of the work unique, to enter the stage with 85 percent of the choreography predetermined and the rest left to the inspiration of the moment.

Harrison also used kits in parts of *Rhymes with Silver*, composed for

Mark Morris, the brilliant and controversial choreographer who served for three years as director of dance for Belgium's state opera house (the Théâtre Royal de la Monnaie) and in 1991 was awarded a prestigious five-year MacArthur Foundation fellowship. Morris first encountered Lou's music through the original Louisville Symphony LP of *Strict Songs*. He found Lou's style "rhythmically interesting; modally interesting; always surprising."[89] Furthermore, his own training in disparate national folk dance styles led him to admire Harrison's skill at utilizing diverse musical references not in a superficial way but as "an integral element in the composition. It's inclusive music," he says.

Mark Morris understands music the way Lou Harrison understands dance. Although he would never claim to be an accomplished musician, Morris has studied the musics of various eras and regions, has played the piano, and reads music fluently. "Many dancers, and even many choreographers, don't know a thing about music, which is fine if they don't deal with it. But if you're dealing with something, you should know about it," he says in words that seem to echo Harrison's comments on dance. "In that way it becomes a deeper experience for everyone." When Morris was a teenager, he listened to the music of Harry Partch and read much of *Genesis of a Music*, though he got mired in the details of temperament systems. From Partch it was a direct road to Cowell, Thomson, and Harrison.

Like Erick Hawkins, Morris is adamant about presenting his dances with live music. Nor does he necessarily use music that is well-known. Through an old recording, for instance, he became fascinated with Cowell's string quartets. Locating the scores entailed a hunt, and patrons who inquire about the music after the performance are told that they can't buy a recording because it is no longer in print. "That's why my concerts attract a music public," Morris notes. "They come to hear music they haven't heard."

In 1987 Morris was invited by the Seattle Men's Chorus to choreograph a work. "A chorus of 120 male singing enthusiasts," he calls them. "Some very good; some not so good. But the number is so fabulous." The chorus approached Harrison with the concept of transforming *Strict Songs'* ensemble of eight baritones into one of 120 men. Dubious at first, since the work was conceived for chamber orchestra, Lou was soon convinced. He traveled to Seattle and sat through every stage rehearsal, "yelling suggestions from the house." Harrison was thrilled by the result. So was Morris, who kept the dance active for several seasons and revived it in the spring of 1997.

Strict Songs marked the beginning of a close collaboration that led Morris to choreograph the *Grand Duo* for violin and piano as well as portions of the *Piano Trio* and *Homage to Pacifica*. The movement from *Grand Duo* that first attracted Morris's attention was the polka finale. Premiered on April 7, 1992, at the Manhattan Center Grand Ballroom,[90] the polka presented the entire company in "five minutes of frenzy." The dance became one of Morris's biggest hits. The following year, he uncharacteristically choreographed backward, setting the rest of the *Duo* except for the long slow fourth movement. "That made 'Polka' more desperate and exhausted," an effect he had intended but found impossible to achieve without dramatic preparation.

Morris, like Lou, is unafraid to violate taboos, in this case "music visualization." In the second movement of the *Duo*, for instance, the troupe blatantly mimics the irregular accents in the music, with angular jabs directly correlated with the piano's dissonant tone clusters. Morris taught his dancers to memorize the music to achieve aural-visual coordination. The score contains a varied repeat: a thirty-measure passage expands to thirty-three on its return. The dancers learned to sing the score during rehearsals to precisely coordinate their timing and spacing.

"Pacific," choreographed for the San Francisco Ballet, uses two movements from the piano trio. In "World Power" Morris set selections from *Homage to Pacifica* along with *Bubaran Robert*, one of Lou's early works for gamelan with Western solo instrument (trumpet). Providing live music for the premiere required more than a little effort: a full gamelan with both slendro and pelog instruments, a chorus, and a trumpet. Morris took his title from the text of *Homage to Pacifica*'s third movement, a blast against the Philippine War attributed to Mark Twain: "We have pacified some thousands of the islanders and buried them, destroyed their fields; burned their villages, and turned their widows and orphans out-of-doors; furnished heartbreak by exile to some dozens of disagreeable patriots; subjugated the remaining ten millions by Benevolent Assimilation. . . . And so, by these Providences of God . . . we are a World Power."[91] The political text resonated with Morris's own sympathies, as did the integration of Western and Eastern musics.

After these successful works, Morris offered Lou a commission for a composition specifically designed to feature Yo-Yo Ma. At a casual lunch in Aptos, Morris set almost no guidelines for the piece:

"Lou, I would like you to write a piece for me."
"How long?"
"It doesn't matter—twenty minutes maybe. I don't care."
"What's the instrumentation?"
"That's up to you. You're the composer."
"Is there text?"
"I don't know. I only want it to include a piano part and a cello part."
"But on tour, you can't take much with you."
"Don't worry about it. That's my problem. Whatever you want."
"I'm used to writing a piece after something is choreographed."
"I've never done that before. I can't imagine it. If you want, I'll start making some stuff up and send tapes to you."
"No, you don't work that way."

"Okay, fine. So let's do it my way."

"All right; I'll write a piece for you but never ask me about it again. It might be done in a week; it might be five years. I'll send it to you when it's done. "

"That's great, whenever it's done."[92]

The new work, a forty-five-minute quintet for violin, viola, cello, piano, and percussion, is now complete, and it premiered to rave reviews in March 1997. Like so many of Lou's suites, it features diverse instrumentation and compositional procedures. Harrison combined Medieval and Baroque dance forms with traditional American dances; dedicated one movement to the eighteenth-century Romanian composer and scholar Dimitrie Cantemir; and balanced strict composition with flexible kits. He left the final sequence of movements up to Morris, who determined the arrangement to a great extent by the needs of the choreography. A solo cello prelude opens the work while the curtain remains closed. Among the eleven movements that follow are three more for solo cello; a piano and percussion duet; a cello, piano, vibraphone trio; and six small dances for the entire quintet. Harrison adapted the *Gigue and Musette* from his Los Angeles days, used one of his favorite Medieval forms (a *ductia*), and introduced a fox trot and "Romantic Waltz" that echo his youthful ballroom dance lessons. Morris responded with similar eclecticism, and even mirrored the instrumental quintet with his own:

> Dancers drop out and sit on the stage with their backs to the audience. Small groups separate, creating a fugal effect. . . . In his first solo . . . Morris . . . leaps manically [sic] from the wings, only to freeze his frieze. . . . Later, [he] pushes himself across the floor in the midst of a maelstrom of movement. . . . A shoulder shrug evolves into a sinuous ensemble. A quartet of Edenic circle dances moves to a devastatingly charming waltz, in which a woman finds herself with five partners, stacked up like dominos, and the man . . . gets his own quintet, too.[93]

Lou has always found in dance the opportunity to combine his many explorations: percussion, gamelan, politics, intonation systems, theater. He is happiest creating syntheses: new links born from new associations, each new collaboration providing the opportunity to embrace an ever wider diversity. Unlike Partch, a loner, Harrison thrives on social interaction. His music is most inspired when it is born from cooperation. Bella Lewitzky summarizes: "Lou leaves room for the other arts to collaborate with his sound."[94]

This gregarious love of social interaction may stem in part from the lack of such opportunities in his youth. The Harrison family's constant peregrinations left few possibilities for establishing deep friendships. Lou now cherishes, perhaps more than those who have had such opportunities, the value of personal relationships and artistic interactions.[95]

There is no doubt, moreover, that his childhood experiences induced his love of dance. His own theatrical performances during his San Francisco years were a direct extension of his first stage appearances in *Daddy Long Legs* and the social dance classes in which Cal enrolled him. In his many dance compositions, Lou draws from this practical training, evoking forms with fixed steps that are as fresh in his consciousness today as they were during his childhood: marches, waltzes, polkas, and tangos. These he may combine with dances inspired by the Baroque suite, Medieval music, or Asian traditions.

Unlike the collaborations between Cunningham and Cage, where the relationship between sound and motion was usually independent, Harrison's music simulates the dynamic propulsion of the dance.

> John was antikinetic. When he would conduct us, the tempo would get slower and slower until we would cry, "For Christ's sake!" John was looking at the score, analyzing, aiming to hear every detail while conducting. He lacked a kinetic response. I suppose that's also why he was so fascinated with Merce's highly kinetic persona. They arrived at a kind of modus operandi through chance so that they could both do what they did best and the relationship didn't matter. I, on the other hand, am very kinetic. If I see someone moving on stage, I respond in kind.
>
> Very rarely have I liked a combination of double improvisation. My preference is for music used intentionally either in unison or in counterpoint. Cross-metrics, for example, are impossible in a chance situation.[96]

Hence his attraction for choreographers who deliberately strive to create rhythmic counterpoint to his music, such as Erdman and Lewitzky. Morris, in his recent work, is moving in the same direction. "Mark Morris in his youth would dance cross-metrics," Lou notes, "such as 5/4 to a 4/4 beat. He studied Albanian, Bulgarian, and Romanian folk dances with their patterns of seven and eleven. Such refinements of rhythmic action, both kinetically and musically, are simply destroyed by chance."[97]

Recalling Cowell's reflection that most of the world's music is based on melody and rhythm, Harrison has used dance as a cross-cultural link, coupling, for example, the Medieval European estampie with the gamelan (e.g., *Suite for Violin and American Gamelan*; *Double Concerto for Violin, Cello, and Gamelan*). Even his nontheatrical works have often been inspired by dance. The minisuites in his symphonies are excellent examples, as are the many dance movements in his chamber works and concerti. From his earliest percussion music to his most recent symphonic compositions, dance has provided a lively stimulus to Lou's imagination and given his music the rhythmic vitality audiences find so appealing.

5 Tuning and Temperament

Just intonation is the best intonation," Harrison baldly asserts in his *Music Primer*. Ever since Virgil Thomson introduced him to Harry Partch's *Genesis of a Music* in 1949, it is a tenet Lou has upheld unwaveringly. His love of acoustically pure, nonbeating intervals has found voice in all genres in which he works: from solo vocal music to full orchestra to gamelan. Neither is it an area in which he is willing to allow much room for compromise. He frequently calls upon those performing his music to hear and reproduce pure intervals, authorizing Equal Temperament either as a last resort or as a conscious political statement deriding the mechanization of modern industrial society.

Just Intonation is hardly a topic most musicians would seize upon for a crusade against an indifferent and impersonal society. But for Lou the system of twelve mathematically equidistant half steps accepted in Western music during the past two centuries represents an eradication of difference, a standardization that, by making everything equivalent, makes everything dull. Lou asserts that through such an intonation system, Western musical practice has elevated intonational expediency over acoustical purity. We have been trained, he would argue, to value standardization over diversity.

EXAMPLE 5-1. The first sixteen pitches of the overtone series.

Black notes differ significantly from the corresponding Equal Tempered pitch (see table 5-2, p. 107).

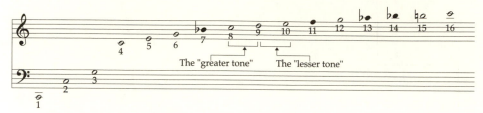

Most performing musicians throughout history have given little thought to tuning theory, although the problem of achieving a system of pure intonation has plagued musical thinkers at least as far back as ancient China. The Greeks, as well as leading Western theorists in the Medieval, Renaissance, and Baroque periods, devised a variety of ingenious systems that were for the most part abandoned in Western practice after the eighteenth century in favor of equal-sized semitones. In recent times, Harrison and many other composers and theorists have returned to earlier systems, to which some have added new solutions as well.

The problem stems from the origins of the twelve-tone division of the octave, which may be derived from a series of superimposed fifths. The pure fifth,[1] the first interval after the octave in the natural overtone series, vibrates in a 3:2 ratio. (The pure fifth above a' 440 Hz, for instance, is e" 660 Hz.) The overtones of a specific pitch, known as the "harmonic series" and given in example 5-1, yield the main intervals used in Western music: the perfect fifth, perfect fourth, and major and minor thirds. Major and minor seconds occur higher in the series as shown.

A bowed string or a column of air divided at its nodal points will produce the same series of intervals (that is, a string divided in half generates an octave; divided in thirds, it generates an octave plus a fifth, etc.). Pure intervals arise when the frequencies of the individual tones reflect the precise mathematical proportions that occur in the series: 3:2 for the fifth, 4:3 for the fourth, etc.

When a series of pure 3:2 fifths are generated one after the other (for example, c, g, d', a', e", etc.), the vibration frequency of the twelfth fifth (b-sharp) will slightly exceed that of the seventh octave. In table 5-1 two series of notes have been generated from a given frequency, the first by multiplying it repeatedly by 2 (thus generating successively higher octaves) and the second by multiplying it repeatedly by 3/2 (thus generating successive fifths). The first instance in which the two series coincide closely enough that the ear perceives the notes to be variants of the same pitch is at the twelfth fifth and the seventh octave.

The operative word here, however, is "variants," for the two series of numbers will never intersect precisely (i.e., 2/1 to any power can never

TABLE 5-1. Demonstration that twelve superimposed pure fifths are slightly greater than seven octaves

8ves (2:1)		5ths (3:2) rounded to 3 decimal places	
A_2 = 27.5	=	A_2 = 27.5	
		E_1 = 41.25	
A_1 = 55			
		B_1 = 61.875	
		F♯ = 92.812	
A = 110			
		c♯ = 139.219	
		g♯ = 208.829	
a = 220			
		d♯ = 313.242	
a' = 440			
		a♯' = 469.863	
		e♯" = 704.795	
a" = 880			
		b♯''' = 1057.192	
		f×''' = 1585.788	
a''' = 1760			
		c×'''' = 2378.683	
a'''' = 3520	<	g×'''' = 3568.023	

equal 3/2 to any power). At the point in question, the twelfth fifth exceeds the seventh octave by a small interval known as the "Pythagorean comma," corresponding to about an eighth of a tone: 23.5 cents.[2] (The cent is a convenient unit for measuring and comparing intervals; there are by definition 100 cents in an Equal Tempered half step.) Much further in the series, the two sets of figures approach each other more closely. The 359th fifth—the first point at which the variance is narrower than the minimal perceptible difference between two simultaneously sounded tones—is about 1.8 cents sharp of the octave, a fact discovered independently by the early Egyptians and Chinese. Division of the octave into 359 parts, however, is obviously impractical.

Historically, theorists have separated into two camps: those who allow nonclosure of the circle (creating in effect a spiral instead of a circle of fifths) and those who insist on closure by altering one, several, or all of the fifths in order to establish a pure octave. In some societies the debate has been linked to other natural phenomena, such as the non-coincidence of the lunar and solar years. In Chinese dynastic histories, for example, tuning theories are often treated within discussions of the calendar.[3]

In unaccompanied melody or even in a capella vocal polyphony, the problem posed by the inequality of the twelfth fifth and the seventh octave is virtually nonexistent. Pure fifths may be sung or played, resulting in a gradual migration of the starting pitch, with no ill effects. But fixed-pitch instruments operating harmonically in a dodecaphonic system require some form of "temperament"—a modification in the size of some pure intervals in order to accommodate others.

Various options are possible. In twelve-tone Equal Temperament all of the fifths are compressed slightly and equally by 1/50 of a semitone. No fifth is pure, but all are equally acceptable. Since the comma is distributed among all twelve fifths, the resulting Equal Tempered fifth diverges only minimally from its pure counterpart (2 cents); the thirds, however, differ markedly. The primacy of major and minor thirds as triad building-blocks in Western harmony suggests that their natural vibration ratios (5:4 and 6:5 respectively) should be observed as well. Yet the major third that results from twelve Equal Tempered fifths is markedly sharp: 14 cents higher than a pure third. The minor third is 16 cents flat (see table 5-2). Modern musicians and audiences have become so accustomed to the "bright" sound of wide Equal Tempered triads, particularly in keyboard music, that many perceive the pure triad to be "flat."

Many attempts at solving this essentially intractable problem in mathematics and psychoacoustics have been made. In meantone temperament, for example, some thirds and fifths are allowed to remain pure at the expense of others, which become so dissonant that they are for all practical purposes unusable. If these highly dissonant intervals are not needed in a particular composition, the unequal temperament may offer advantages not found in equal systems. Such unequal tunings not only provide a body of pure intervals to be exploited but may also be constructed so as to offer a range of increasingly dissonant (or less consonant) chordal structures. The various keys, rather than presenting a uniform picture in gray, will yield a range of tone colors from purity to stridency.

The seventh overtone has particularly troubled theorists over the centuries. As shown in table 5-2, it does not coincide closely with any pitch in the Western scale. In relation to the sixth overtone, it forms an interval 33 cents narrower than an Equal Tempered minor third; in relation to the eighth, it produces an interval 31 cents wider than a major second. To ears attuned to twelve equal subdivisions of the octave, these two intervals, the "subminor third" (7:6) and the "supermajor second" (8:7), may sound out of tune. On the other hand, they have a legitimate place in some other musics (for instance, that of the Tyrolian alp-horn).[4] Lou has called for these 7:6 and 8:7 ratios not only in his gamelan tunings but also in many of his vocal

TABLE 5-2. Vibration ratios, corresponding interval sizes, and differences between the pure interval and the corresponding Equal Tempered interval

| | | comparison (in cents) between the pure and the Equal Tempered interval | |
ratio	interval	pure interval	Equal Tempered interval
2:1	octave	1200	1200
3:2	fifth	702	700
4:3	fourth	498	500
5:4	major third	386	400
6:5	minor third	316	300
7:6	narrow minor third ("subminor third")	267	(m3): 300
8:7	wide major second ("supermajor second")	231	(M2): 200
9:8	major second ("greater tone")	204	200
10:9	smaller major second ("lesser tone")	182	200
11:10ff.	increasingly smaller seconds		
16:15	minor second	112	100
17:16ff.	increasingly smaller minor seconds		

Degree of "out-of-tuneness" of Equal Tempered intervals
octave: 0 cents
fifth: 2 cents flat
fourth: 2 cents sharp
major third: 14 cents sharp
minor third: 16 cents flat
major second: 4 cents flat (from the "greater tone")
minor second: 12 cents flat (from a 16:15 semitone)

and instrumental compositions, as have other contemporary composers who have explored Just Intonation systems.

Above the eighth pitch, the overtone series yields two sizes of whole step: 9:8, which at 204 cents is very slightly larger than the Equal Tempered tone (200 cents), and 10:9, substantially smaller (182 cents). These naturally occurring whole steps, referred to in Renaissance and Baroque theoretical treatises as the "greater" and "lesser" tones, respectively, were crucial components of many of the unequally tempered systems of those times for both keyboard and fretted instruments.

Just Intonation systems seek to create as many pure intervals as possible, relying on those that occur naturally within the overtone series. They favor intervals low in the series and with superparticular vibration ratios, that is, those in which the numerator exceeds the denominator by 1, such as the fifth 3:2, fourth 4:3, major third 5:4, and minor third 6:5.

Clearly in any Just Intonation system, the options are manifold. Lou has explored hundreds of possibilities, choosing for any particular piece whichever tuning will facilitate the instruments, scale, or affect required. Pure intervals, of course, are relatively easy to play on instruments that can produce minute pitch variations, such as the trombone and the violin family. For this reason, Lou has favored such instruments for works in which he experimented with new tuning systems (e.g., *At the Tomb of Charles Ives*).

In recent piano works, Harrison has compromised on a nearly equal temperament, using one of several such systems prevalent during the eighteenth century. In such "well-tempered" tunings the various keys remain somewhat unequal (some purer than others), while the divergence stays within a narrow range. No key is either Just or completely equal, all intervals remain acceptable, and some tonal variety is preserved. In his 1985 concerto for piano, Harrison specifies a tuning defined in 1779 by J. S. Bach's student, Johann Philipp Kirnberger (1721–83), in which all fifths are tuned pure except for two: D-A and A-E. (The single pitch A is raised.)[5] Lou found that while these two important fifths were noticeably compromised, the resulting pure thirds, C-E, G-B, and D-F♯, more than compensated for the disparity. The key of C major, he notes, is "next to heaven. It sounds like all the springtime of the world—despite the raised sixth degree."[6] Ursula Oppens, who has performed the concerto on many occasions, draws a similar analogy, likening the large C major–based chords in the concerto's slow movement to "breathing for the first time the unpolluted air of Alaska."[7] During the composition of the work Harrison discovered a delightful feature of Kirnberger's system that allowed him to play with intonation systems as a compositional element. When the opening C major theme is transposed to F minor at the development, the tuning produces a pure Pythagorean system. (In Pythagorean tuning, characteristic of some Medieval music, all of the fifths are pure except one, which is so small as to be extraordinarily harsh. In consequence, the major thirds are extremely sharp.) "The concerto thus sums up the whole history of Western tuning," Harrison notes.

The octave, of course, need not be divided into twelve parts. Increasing the number of divisions facilitates alternative combinations of pitches, thus allowing for a greater number of pure intervals within any particular key. During his high school years, before he encountered the quarter-tone piano pieces of Charles Ives, Lou composed his own quarter-tone works (among them a string chorale) inspired by a recording of the music of Alois Hába.[8] Harry Partch, undoubtedly the strongest influence on Harrison in the realm of tuning systems, devised a forty-three-tone scale, which divides the octave unequally into a series of adjacent superparticular intervals as small as 121/120 (14.4 cents). Partch's gamut allowed him to realize pure fifths, fourths, thirds, tones, and semitones, as well as a myriad of other interval combinations, but he was far from the first to explore such a possibility.[9] Joseph Sauveur, a member of the Paris *Académie des Sciences* during the early eighteenth century who coined the term *acoustique*, proposed his own forty-three-tone octave division, in this case as "a means of classifying temperaments and comparing pitches."[10] Sauveur postulated a logarithmic division of the octave into forty-three equal parts, each divided into seven units, themselves divisible into ten parts.

Naturally, any keyboard allowing for many more than twelve pitches per octave is likely to be cumbersome to construct and play, though such experiments are by no means rare. Instruments with split keys were built as early as the Renaissance, the most noteworthy example being the *arcicembalo* of Nicola Vicentino.[11] Vicentino sought to develop an instrument that could reproduce the chromatic and enharmonic genera of the Greek tetrachordal system, which was based on subdivisions of the pure fourth into various sizes of tones, semitones, quarter-tones, and thirds. Harrison's studies led him in a similar direction, as we will discuss shortly.

Fretted instruments pose a problem similar to keyboards, though even here inventors devised instruments to produce pure intervals. One novel attempt was that of the Englishman Thomas Salmon, who in 1705 presented to the Royal Society of London a viol with interchangeable fingerboards for each key on which the greater and lesser tones, as well as five sizes of semitone, ranging from 16:15 to 20:19, were properly situated for the tonality in question.[12]

Fewer divisions of the octave also allow for purer tunings. Lou has particularly favored pentatonic scale forms, which (since they require only five pitches) can be formulated to include only those with pure vibration ratios. Pentatonic scales have been attractive to Harrison from his earliest San Francisco years, stimulated by his studies with Cowell and his love of Asian music. As early as 1942, he called for a pentatonic scale in the ocarina and metallophone parts of *Canticle #3*, although he does not specify pure intervals (indeed, he does not even specify exact pitches, although he has verbally expressed a preference for an unequal slendro-type scale, with largish seconds and a third between the second and third pitches).[13]

During his 1961 freighter trip to Japan Lou spent hours devising as many pentatonic divisions of the octave with pure intervals as he could discover. He included the results of this investigation in his *Music Primer*,[14] where he describes forty-six different pentatonic scales with both their ratios and affectual qualities. The most basic, the "prime pentatonic," he labels "The Human Song" because of its widespread use globally (see table 5-3a).

The *Concerto in Slendro*, composed during this same trip, uses both the prime pentatonic and what Harrison terms "its associated 'minor'" (table 5-3b). Two tack-pianos and a celesta are tuned to these modes, which the violin can easily replicate.

To differentiate between pentatonics with and without semitones, Harrison prefers the Indonesian terms *pelog* and *slendro* to the more cumbersome

TABLE 5-3A. The "prime pentatonic" as described in Harrison's *Music Primer*, 111–12.

Ratios between adjacent pitches:		9:8 greater tone	10:9 lesser tone	6:5 minor third	10:9 lesser tone	6:5 minor third	
Pitch numbers:	1	2	3	5	6	1	
Ratios in relation to pitch 1:	1:1 unison	9:8 greater tone	5:4 major third	3:2 pure fifth	5:3 major sixth	2:1 octave	

hemitonic and *anhemitonic*. (Lou likes to describe slendro as a mode with wide seconds and narrow thirds and pelog as one with narrow seconds and wide thirds.)[15] The *Primer* presents a variety of slendro pentatonics, including several using the seventh overtone, yielding the supermajor second (8:7) and the subminor third (7:6), both foreign to the Western scale. Each set of ratios divides the octave into five unequal parts, with successive intervals in superparticular ratios. For example:

```
7:6   8:7   9:8   7:6   8:7
8:7   9:8   7:6   8:7   7:6
8:7   7:6   9:8   7:6   8:7
```

Pelog-type pentatonics listed in the *Primer* feature semitones of various sizes, that is, ratios of 16:15 or smaller. An example:

1	2♭	3♭	5	6♭	1
	16:15 semitone	9:8 greater tone	5:4 major third	16:15 semitone	5:4 major third

Using smaller semitones entails the use of some non-superparticular intervals: for instance,

```
9:8   28:27   9:7   21:20   80:63
9:8   16:15   5:4   28:27   9:7
```

TABLE 5-3B. The "associated minor" of the prime pentatonic

Ratios between adjacent pitches:		6:5 minor third	10:9 lesser tone	9:8 greater tone	6:5 minor third	10:9 lesser tone	
Pitch numbers:	1	3♭	4	5	7♭	1	
Ratios in relation to pitch 1:	1:1 unison	6:5 minor third	4:3 pure fourth	3:2 pure fifth	9:5 minor seventh	2:1 octave	

Septatonic divisions also offer intriguing interval combinations; Lou includes several of his favorites in the *Primer*.

Although he had encountered theoretical systems based on acoustical principles in his early studies with Cowell, Harrison's own investigations of tuning and temperament began in earnest only after his breakdown, when the process of exploring his personal history expanded to the history of music theory in general. Thus, Partch's book fueled an already glowing fire. For years Lou had formed the habit of beginning a new piece by setting for himself severe compositional restrictions. He would permit himself, for example, the use of only white keys, then admit one accidental, then two, and so forth. Composing with all twelve tones, therefore, became no different than composing with seven: "It was a squirrel's cage: 'round and 'round and 'round the cycle."[16] Partch's book offered an escape hatch. He discovered that he could use "real intervals," that the circle need not close after twelve pitches. Instead, the cage door opened to allow so many options that the possibilities became for all practical purposes limitless. Lou found at last, he notes, "a reason for the musicality."[17]

He immediately began to experiment with retuning his own piano. "At the same time, I was reading theoretical books on Indian music—Daniélou, for example, *Introduction to the Study of Musical Scales*. I plunged whole hog into the matter and connected it to my interests in Medieval European music as well."[18]

Indeed, Lou's tuning studies were to become one of his deepest and most wide-ranging explorations, with implications for his work in all other areas. To his friends, his enthusiasm for the subject seemed boundless. Anahid Ajemian remembers him retuning the piano in her apartment,[19] and his Black Mountain colleagues recall the missionary zeal with which he delivered lectures on intonation systems in the large meeting hall at the college.

In 1954, when he went to Rome for the International Conference of Contemporary Music, Harrison impressed Anne and Frank Wigglesworth (fig. 8) in the same way. After winning the composition prize, Lou, Frank, and Anne began a tour projected to take two weeks. In Ravenna, however, Lou tripped and broke his foot. The Wigglesworths suggested aborting the trip, but Harrison was adamant: "On to Venice," he insisted.

"There's nothing but walking in Venice, of course," Frank recalls. "When we got there Lou was in so much pain that we hired a man to carry him on his back. He looked like the illustrations of *Pilgrim's Progress* as he went across the piazza. We finally got him into a room in a hotel there. . . . And despite all his pain, he decided he had to list the partials of the bells at the San Marco church! So that's what he did!"[20]

Lou's investigations of tuning took him back to the early Hindus and Greeks (and later even to the Babylonians). He embarked on a thorough study of Greek theory, which postulates a system of interlocking tetrachords—a series of pure 4:3 fourths positioned one above the other in two possible con-

EXAMPLE 5-2. Tetrachord usage in *The Perilous Chapel* (1948–49). (© 1990 by Peer International Corporation. International copyright secured. Reprinted by permission.)

figurations: a disjunct arrangement with an intervening tone (e-a b-e) or a conjunct arrangement with a common tone (b-e e-a). The internal composition of the tetrachord was flexible. Greek theorists identified three genera of intervallic structure within the perfect fourth: diatonic (two whole steps plus a semitone), chromatic (two semitones plus a minor third), and enharmonic (two quarter tones plus a major third). The precise sizes of these intervals could vary while remaining within the boundaries prescribed by aural perception. Thus, Didymos could propose a chromatic tetrachord with two very unequal semitones and a pure minor third (16:15, 25:24, 6:5), while Eratosthenes presented one with two semitones that are nearly equal (20:19, 19:18,

TABLE 5-4. The tuning of the Mills gamelan

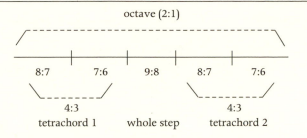

6:5). Ptolemy gave a "soft chromatic" (28:27, 15:14, 6:5) as well as an "intense chromatic" (22:21, 12:11, 7:6).[21] (Didymos's chromatic and Archytas's enharmonic—28:27, 36:35, 5:4—can be heard on the CD, bands 2-3.)

As early as 1949, Lou used tetrachords as the basis for extended compositions (example 5-2). In *The Perilous Chapel*, for instance, tetrachordal patterns appear as simple ostinati (example 5-2a, f) or as germinal melodic material (example 5-2c, d). He creates expanded forms through octave displacement (example 5-2e, g, h) and juxtaposes various internal arrangements, as in movement 1, where motive c appears with a, then d with b.[22]

Although the Greek theorists normally divided the tetrachord into three intervals, Lou also proposed the concept of a duple division. Later, to his delight, he found justification in Boethius for ancient experiments along the same lines. "Boethius' writing . . . breaks off at chapter 19 of Book Five, but the titles of chapters 20 through 30 remain, and it was at the title for chapter 21, 'How Ptolemy divided the diatesseron [i.e., the fourth] into two parts,' that my eyes widened and my jaw dropped."[23]

By dividing each tetrachord into two rather than three parts and positioning them in a disjunct arrangement, Lou established a pentatonic division of the octave mimicking slendro tunings of the Javanese gamelan (table 5-4). Since the tuning of each set of gamelan instruments may be unique, Lou felt free to apply his love of pure intervals to his own sets of instruments. His Mills gamelan slendro tuning, for example, divides each 4:3 tetrachord identically but unequally (8:7 plus 7:6), as shown in table 5-4.[24]

Long before building his gamelan instruments, Lou had called for Just Intonation tunings. His own performance of *Cinna* for tack-piano (recorded in 1957), and his demonstration of its tuning system can be heard on the accompanying CD, bands 4-9. In the *Strict Songs* (1955), each movement features a different pentatonic mode with its own unique subdivision of the octave (example 5-3). The specified modes are not an abstract exercise: piano and harp are retuned to produce the pure intervals, which are then matched by the strings, trombones, and voices. All four modes feature a pure 3:2 fifth above the *finalis*. The mode of movement 1, "Holiness," is built from the greater and lesser tones (9:8 and 10:9), along with two pure minor thirds (6:5). The adjacent unequal whole steps combine to produce a pure 5:4

EXAMPLE 5-3.

Pentatonic modes in

Strict Songs (1955).

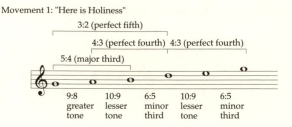

Movement 1: "Here is Holiness"

3:2 (perfect fifth)

4:3 (perfect fourth) 4:3 (perfect fourth)

5:4 (major third)

| 9:8 | 10:9 | 6:5 | 10:9 | 6:5 |
| greater tone | lesser tone | minor third | lesser tone | minor third |

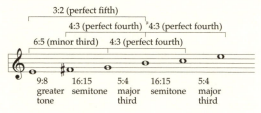

Movement 2: "Here is Nourishment"

3:2 (perfect fifth)

4:3 (perfect fourth) 4:3 (perfect fourth)

6:5 (minor third)   4:3 (perfect fourth)

| 9:8 | 16:15 | 5:4 | 16:15 | 5:4 |
| greater tone | semitone | major third | semitone | major third |

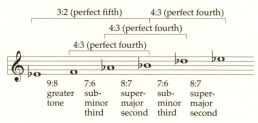

Movement 3: "Here is Tenderness"

3:2 (perfect fifth)   4:3 (perfect fourth)

4:3 (perfect fourth)

4:3 (perfect fourth)

| 9:8 | 7:6 | 8:7 | 7:6 | 8:7 |
| greater tone | sub-minor third | super-major second | sub-minor third | super-major second |

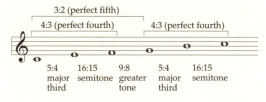

Movement 4: "Here is Splendor"

3:2 (perfect fifth)

4:3 (perfect fourth)   4:3 (perfect fourth)

| 5:4 | 16:15 | 9:8 | 5:4 | 16:15 |
| major third | semitone | greater tone | major third | semitone |

major third; tones 2−4 and 4−6 outline pure 4:3 fourths. "Tenderness" (movement 3) is expressed by the distinctive seventh overtone, creating the supermajor second and subminor third with the surrounding pitches (CD, band 10). Both of these movements feature slendro-type tunings. Movements 2 and 4, on the other hand, belong to the pelog family, with pure major thirds (5:4) and 16:15 semitones, which together divide the fourth into two unequal parts. The "Splendor" of the finale is enhanced by placing pure fourths directly above and below the *finalis*.

Lou was so taken with the diversity and variety of modes in world cultures that he wrote a proposal (in Esperanto) for a "mode room," possibly under the auspices of UNESCO, filled with drawers each containing a metallophone tuned to a particular mode. Elsewhere in the room would be tunable harps or psalteries to which one could transfer the selected tuning. Finally, the room would house a monumental reference work, a "great world-book of notated modes, their preferred tunings and both ethnic and geographic provenance, along with such history of them as we might have."[25] Lou incorporated this proposal into a manifesto, made available to participants at the 1961 East-West Music Encounter in Tokyo, in which he suggests an entire building with a mode room; a library of books, music, and recordings; a workshop in which to explore tuning theory and techniques; and a print shop.[26]

After Bill Colvig moved to Aptos in 1967, he and Lou created their own "mode room," for Bill soon began to construct extremely accurate monochords capable of measuring and sounding intervals in any chosen proportion. They registered their monochord measurements on paper or plastic scales and then transferred the tunings to a harp they built, which was equipped with both gross and fine tuning mechanisms that allowed precise pitch adjustment.

Still lacking, however, was the "monumental reference work," which did not appear until two decades later. In the early 1970s Lou met John Chalmers, a postdoctoral fellow in the Department of Genetics at the University of California, Berkeley, who had been fascinated with microtonal tunings and tetrachordal structures since high school. Chalmers started his investigations after "an unintelligible and incorrect explanation of the twelve-tone Equal Temperament in a music appreciation class."[27] By the time he met Harrison, Chalmers had built a monochord calibrated to nineteen-tone Equal Temperament, had studied the works of Partch and others, had collaborated with tuning theorist Ervin Wilson to generate Equal Temperament and Just Intonation tables, and had begun his own catalog of tetrachord types.[28] "Since the large world cultures historically have organized modes and scales by tetrachord matrix (with or without a disjunction)," Lou notes, "the tetrachord is the basic module for modal and scalar organization."[29] Harrison urged Chalmers to expand his research and compile his notes into a reference work on tetrachords.

Harrison, Colvig, Chalmers, and Richard Dee began to meet regularly, tuning the monochords and harp, and then tape-recording their own improvisations in each mode (CD, bands 2-3). "Thus the 'mode room' . . . turned into anyone's room," Lou muses, "with a good monochord and some kind of transfer instrument."[30]

It was not long before they expanded their exploration beyond the tetrachordal divisions proposed by the ancient theorists to those they devised themselves. Chalmers eventually assembled all the data into a dense monograph in which he not only describes the history and variety of tunings

EXAMPLE 5-4. *Simfony in Free Style* (1955), beginning. (Used by permission of C. F. Peters Corporation, © 1977.)

Ratios in parentheses, $\left(\frac{x}{y}\right)$, indicate Doty's calculations of the ratio of each pitch to the starting pitch.

Ratios not enclosed in parentheses, $\frac{x}{y}$, are Harrison's original ratios, specifying the melodic or harmonic relationship between adjacent pitches.

proposed by the Greeks but also lists 728 tetrachords (in ratios and cents, with proper theoretical attributions) whose internal intervals are no smaller than the syntonic comma, 81:80. Thus, the final component of Lou's "mode room" was completed, for Chalmers's *Divisions of the Tetrachord*, Harrison felt, realized his original vision of the "great book" of modes.[31]

Lou's tuning experiments were not limited to testing the theories of others. He also devised his own unique system in which he dispensed entirely with a fixed tonal center, thereby permitting all melodic intervals to be pure—a concept he calls Free Style. In Free Style intonation, individual pitches are determined solely by their proportional relationship to the preceding and following pitches. Lou began such experiments soon after his return to California, when he composed the *Simfony in Free Style* (1955), which calls for flutes, viols, harps, trombones, percussion, and tack-piano and in which he specified precise ratios linking each pitch simultaneously or successively to adjacent ones (see example 5-4). Since individual notes are related only to their immediate neighbors, their pitch may shift during the course of the work (though, for convenience, they are notated identically). For instance, the "G" in example 5-4, measure 9, is higher than the original G by a ratio of 288:275 (80 cents). The essence of this tone is not its "G-ness" but rather its "11/10-ness" from the preceding pitch and its "12/11-ness" to the succeeding one. Lou contrasts this system with what he calls Strict Style, a term he uses to define any stable system of pitches related to a fixed tonal gamut.[32]

By constructing specially tuned flutes, and viols with movable or independently placed frets, this four-minute work can be realized by human performers. Lou gives instructions in the introduction to the score:

> For the performance of this simfony will be required flutes correctly drilled, & a number of viols with frets. I have in mind that the former could simplest be made of a heat & moisture resistant plastic. . . . The roman numerals in the score indicate tonal groupings for flutes & viols up to seven tones each. Therefore, 17 flutes will be required of the kind without keys . . . , fewer with keys. The viols (treble to contrabass) should be of the European wooden kind . . . , "tutti" indicating at least four such in unison for treble, & 3 for bass, with 1 C.B. Each treble player had ought to have, perhaps, 4 to 6 instruments so that frets need not be ungainly close on any one.[33]

The performers must change instruments during the course of the work as notes shift in pitch. In the opening, for instance, the two flute lines require two different instruments (designated I and II). In measure 7, another flutist enters playing instrument III. Flute IV appears in measure 8, flute V in measure 9, and so on. Appropriately tuned tack-piano and five diatonic harps provide a stable reference for the variable instruments.

The *Simfony in Free Style* has never been performed live with correct intonation and instrumentation, but in 1992–93 David Doty realized the work using a computer program that can accurately duplicate the specified ratios from one pitch to the next (CD, band 11). Doty's first task was to calculate the ratio of each pitch not to its neighbor but rather to the starting pitch (parenthetical fractions in example 5-4). Note 2 is related to note 1 as 10/9; note 3 is $10/9 \times 9/8 = 5/4$; note 4 is $5/4 \times 8/7 = 10/7$, and so on. Having thus arrived at a ratio representing each tone's relation to the opening pitch, Doty converted the ratios into the proprietary number format required by his Yamaha synthesizer, a process similar to calculating cents.[34]

The *Simfony's* initial motive is a rising scale with gradually expanding intervals: the "lesser tone" (10:9), the "greater tone" (9:8), the supermajor second (8:7), and finally the subminor third (7:6). The fifth pitch (e") is a pure major sixth (5:3) above the starting pitch. The second player enunciates the same series of intervals beginning a pure minor third (6:5) above the starting pitch g', thus arriving, on the downbeat of measure 3, at an octave (a pure major sixth higher). Harmonically, the most prevalent interval between these two voices is the tritone (e/b-flat and g/c-sharp), which divides the octave roughly in half. The lowest voice states those pitches accented agogically by the flutes—a, c, e, g—a series of pure minor and major thirds (6:5 and 5:4). Smaller whole steps (11:10 and 12:11) as well as pure 16:15 semitones begin to appear in measure 5.

Harrison consistently specifies melodic relationships in the *Simfony.* Harmonic ones he indicates at entry points in the various voices, but otherwise he allows them to fall as dictated by the melodic relationships. The result is a harmonic complex ranging from pure intervals to extremely dissonant ones.

Clearly, in its theoretical concept the 1955 *Simfony* was far ahead of its time. "The *Simfony* is certainly the most radical piece, intonationally speaking, in Western literature before people began to write explicitly for computer controlled synthesizers," notes Doty. "It's probably still right up there in the top ten."[35]

Why, one might legitimately ask, should Lou compose a piece that had such remote possibility of performance? The answer lies both in his studies of intonation and in his history of instrument construction. Far from being theoretical, the *Simfony* was a logical extension of his studies of tuning systems. Having freed himself from the "squirrel's cage" of Equal Temperament through his discovery of "real intervals," why not move one step further and be freed entirely from the restriction of fixed pitch? His prior work in instrument building suggested that such a system might be practical as well. After building two clavichords and replicas of the Greek *aulos* (a double-reed aerophone), the construction of specially tuned flutes or viols with movable frets hardly seemed difficult. Thus, mounting a performance of the *Simfony* appeared to be not only feasible but also achievable (although even with precisely constructed flutes, the players would need to be extremely careful because intonation may vary by 25 cents or more with changes in embouchure or wind pressure). The only requirements, as Lou saw it, were dedication and money. Even now, says David Doty, "Give me $20,000 and a date a year from now and I'd get it performed."[36]

Notwithstanding its unique intonation procedure, the *Simfony in Free Style* is vintage Harrison, with short sections of imitation, sequential passages, snippets of tunes, additive meters, and instrumentation using tack-piano and harps. When it was generated by synthesizer, what Harrison missed was the human element. He asked Doty to tweak the program to add a modicum of flexibility in order to make it sound more human, even to the point of programming tiny pitch slides into the second version.

Undaunted by Free Style's difficulties, Lou continued to explore the concept in several other works from the same period. The recitatives in the *Political Primer* of 1958, for example, are notated in this manner, with an occasional drone as accompaniment. Anticipating the premiere in Buffalo, Lou wrote to the baritone, Herbert Beattie, idealistically (and with the greatest respect):

> I am most fortunate that you will sing these 4 Recitatives . . . ! Do not be frightened by the numbers—here is the explanation (which, I hasten to add, I send along only in the event that you are not already "numerate" as well as "literate"!)
>
> If you will abandon all instruments tuned in equal temperament . . . and sing a "pure" *vocal* C major scale—the result will be the following . . . :

> *Now*—so far as I remember, all the intervals you will sing in these Recitatives are included in the above. For example:

> However I do use 25/24, which is arrived at thusly—sing then and the difference is , or the small "half-tone." Now you will be stringing, or rather *singing* these intervals in free combinations all the way through—they will *not* add up to any "scale" or "gamut" at all! Therefore it would be wise to rehearse without anything but your initial tone—and *never refer to it again.*[37]

Whether Beattie's ear was keen enough to distinguish the required ratios is not known, but Lou was sufficiently satisfied with the results. Since the recitatives were never published nor the *Political Primer* completed, no one else has attempted the feat.

Lou also called for Free Style in a section of *At the Tomb of Charles Ives*, composed in 1963, premiered at the Aspen Music Festival in 1970, published by Peer in 1978, and performed and recorded by the Brooklyn Philharmonic under Lukas Foss in 1981. The central section of this four-minute work, "a cry of anguish at the tomb,"[38] calls for precise melodic tunings of intervals including the supermajor second (8:7) as well as greater and lesser tones and pure fifths, fourths, and thirds. In this case a battery of fixed-pitch instruments—two psalteries, two dulcimers, and three harps—are

EXAMPLE 5-5. *At the Tomb of Charles Ives* (1963), measures 22–27. (© 1978 by Peer International Corporation. International copyright secured. Reprinted by permission.)

first tuned using a reference tape prepared by Colvig. These fixed-pitch instruments in turn provide reference points for the strings (example 5-5). In measures 25–26, for example, the second violins and violas tune in unison with the harps. The first violins tune pure intervals above the second violins—for instance, at m. 25 beat 2 (a pure major sixth, 5:3), m. 25 beat 3 (a pure 3:2 fifth), and m. 26 last eighth note (a pure 4:3 fourth). For short periods the strings are on their own (e.g., mm. 23–24 and 27).

Lou, Bill, and Richard Dee tested Free Style themselves by recording a tiny piece Lou composed in 1974, a *Phrase for Arion's Leap*, with plucked and bowed strings, bells, and tam-tam.[39] As the legendary prize-winning singer Arion had gained his freedom from mariners who plotted to kill him by charming the dolphins with his song and then leaping into the sea to be rescued by them, so leaping into the sea of Free Style liberates each tone from its invariable position within a fixed-pitch scale system.

Even in his Strict Style works, Lou often provides tuning instructions. In the introduction to his *Suite for Symphonic Strings* (1960), for example, he lists the ratios between adjacent pitches in the scales for each of the diatonic movements. As for the chromatic ones, "certainly equal-temperament is 'wrong' here . . . but life is just too short (what with bombs and other things) for me to go through [these] movements and establish each ratio, melodically and contrapuntally. I leave it to the generosity and the good sense of my fellow musicians to make harmonious what they encounter in these compositions."

Indeed, Lou has great faith in the human ear, if properly trained. He has taught himself to tune by ear all pure consonant intervals through the seventh and, in certain cases, up to the eleventh harmonic. String orchestras easily adapt to Just Intonation, and in fact, Harrison notes that they ultimately find it both simpler and more satisfying than Equal Temperament.

He recalls, for instance, a rehearsal of the four *Strict Songs* in Louisville in preparation for the work's 1956 premiere. The harp and piano and been precisely tuned to execute the specified intervals; the percussionists had carefully adjusted their water bowls to match; and the strings and trombones had at last succeeded in duplicating the intonation of the fixed instruments. After an intense rehearsal of the new work, the conductor, Robert Whitney, turned to the other piece on the program, Brahms's violin concerto. "For some reason, known only to fate, I suppose, [he] . . . decided to start with the second movement, which . . . is entirely for woodwinds [instruments designed to perform most easily in Equal Temperament]; they . . . went on for a little while and he just tapped [the music stand] and there was silence. . . . 'Well,' he said at last, 'just do the best you can.'"[40]

The implications not only for composers and performers, but also for music education, are profound:

> The string orchestra can even adjust in a very chromatic texture. I've recently redone a passage from my *First Suite for Strings*, for example, which I heard in Portland; although it's totally chromatic it still sounds perfectly consonant with just a few rehearsals. I have great trust in musicians. As a conductor, I would love to be able to say, "Celli, you did a 9:8 there; would you mind doing a 10:9?" and get a response. There's no reason that musicians shouldn't be numerate as well as literate. I would vote that training in intervals begin when children do their fractions; they should be able to hear them as ratios. In short, we need to revive the quadrivium; we teach too damned much trivia.[41]

TABLE 5-5. The tuning of "Old Granddad"

a. The initial tuning process:

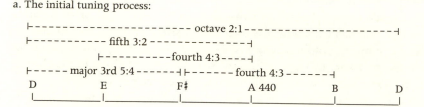

b. The full scale:

When Lou and Bill began building their own gamelan ensembles, it was logical that their instruments be tuned in pure proportions. Their objective in constructing Old Granddad in 1971 (chapter 3) was to build a percussion orchestra in Just Intonation with precisely crafted metal bars, not to imitate a gamelan. (Although similarity to the Indonesian ensemble suggested the name "American gamelan," Old Granddad's scale [D major] and range differ decidedly from Indonesian instruments; and while the sawed-off garbage cans and gas cylinders may have reminded them of gongs, Harrison and Colvig were not seeking inexpensive replacements for traditional instruments.)

They began with a pentatonic scale approximating the pitches D-E-F♯-A-B. To achieve pure intervals, they not only needed to determine the key lengths for the metallophones but also had to calculate the length and shape of the resonators (in this case, #10 tin cans). In addition, it was crucial to minimize inharmonicity of the overtones of the metal keys by finding the appropriate coupling of each resonator to its respective key.

Their starting point was A-440, from which they derived a pure 3:2 fifth with the lower D and a pure 4:3 fourth with the lower E. They then completed the pentatonic with a 5:4 major third (D-F♯) and a 4:3 fourth (F♯ to B; see table 5-5a).

The two missing pitches required for a D-major scale were then inserted by tuning G as a pure 4:3 fourth above D, and C♯ as a pure 3:2 fifth above F♯. The result is Ptolemy's Diatonic Syntonon or the "stretched diatonic" scale,[42]

TABLE 5-6. Two gamelan tunings Lou proposed to Pak Cokro

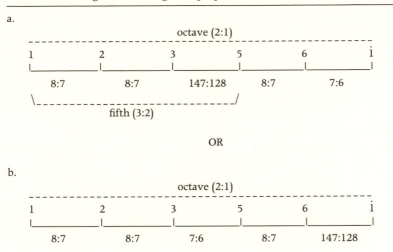

a.

		octave (2:1)			
1	2	3	5	6	i
8:7	8:7	147:128	8:7	7:6	

fifth (3:2)

OR

b.

		octave (2:1)			
1	2	3	5	6	i
8:7	8:7	7:6	8:7	147:128	

which features superparticular intervals between each of the adjacent pitches and pure fourths, fifths, and thirds between most of its tones (table 5-5b.)

Soon after Lou's studies with Pak Cokro and Jody Diamond, he and Bill began work on a set of instruments in Javanese style (Si Betty) for San Jose State. Lou tried to find an acceptable slendro within the harmonic series, finally settling on overtones 16, 19, 21, 24, and 28. Whereas the Javanese readily admit a wide variety of tunings, however, Lou sensed that this one was quite abnormal. So when he tuned the Mills gamelan (Si Darius) in the early 1980s, he chose a truly classical pentatonic scale, a balanced structure with two fourths (4:3) each divided the same way (8:7 and 7:6) and separated by a whole tone (9:8); see table 5-4 (p. 113).

During their trip to Java in January–March 1984, Lou and Bill listened to a variety of sets of gamelan instruments, which inspired them to experiment with placing identically tuned intervals between pitches 1, 2, and 3. Upon their return, they made alternative slabs for the Mills metallophones and sought Pak Cokro's opinion on two very unusual slendro tunings, shown in table 5-6.

The interval 147:128 (27 cents smaller than 7:6) is a "remainder" interval, the leftover distance after three 8:7 "supermajor seconds" and one 7:6 "subminor third" are subtracted from an octave. Pak Cokro immediately associated the two tunings with the two major Central Javanese cultural centers: the first as Yogyakarta ("Yogya") style, and the second as Surakarta ("Solo") style. When Vincent McDermott invited Lou and Bill to Portland in December 1984 to tune the gamelan at Lewis and Clark College, Lou jumped at the opportunity to use one of these new tunings. Knowing McDermott to be partial to Solo, he and Bill tuned the instruments to option b. McDermott was at first rather taken aback. "This is going to take some get-

TABLE 5-7. The tuning of Si Aptos compared to the Solo tuning and the Mills gamelan

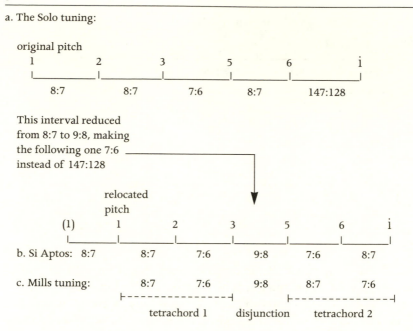

a. The Solo tuning:

original pitch

This interval reduced
from 8:7 to 9:8, making
the following one 7:6
instead of 147:128

relocated
pitch

b. Si Aptos:

c. Mills tuning:

tetrachord 1   disjunction   tetrachord 2

ting used to," he protested. But the tuning was soon endorsed by Widiyanto, a Solonese composer, gamelan director, and shadow-play performer, who called Lou personally from Portland to say, "This tuning touches my heart."[43]

Widiyanto's enthusiasm for Harrison's Solo tuning convinced Lou to try it on the iron gamelan (Si Aptos) in his home. But he soon found the "remainder" annoying. Like Ptolemy, he craved a succession of superparticular intervals. He therefore reduced the 8:7 interval between pitches 5 and 6 (table 5-7a) to a pure 9:8 tone (table 5-7b), leaving a remainder of 7:6 instead of 147:128. Lou then repositioned pitch 1 to where pitch 2 had formerly been situated and arrived at the succession of intervals shown in table 5-7b, which is similar, though not identical, to the Mills tuning (table 5-7c). Note that in the Mills tuning each tetrachord is divided identically, whereas in Si Aptos, tetrachord 2 is the mirror-image of the tetrachord 1.

Harrison also looked for a seven-tone pelog in the overtone series. Experimenting one day in his office at San Jose State, he came up with several possibilities, including one that used pitch 13: overtones 12, 13, 14, 17, 18, 19, and 21. (Like overtones 7 and 11, the thirteenth, which creates an interval smaller than a major second but larger than a minor second, sounds extremely foreign to Western ears.) Soon there was a knock on Lou's door.

When I opened it, Pak Cokro stood there.

"What are you doing?" he asked.

"I'm hunting for a pelog in the overtone series," I replied.

"That last one you did, would you please play it again?"

So I played it. He thought for a minute. "It's a good pelog," he decided. "It would be very good with voices."

I was staggered. Voices singing overtone 13?

So when we built Si Betty [for San Jose State] we tuned the pelog to that complex, courtesy of Pak Cokro. And he was right, as we found out the first time we sang with it.[44]

In recent years, as Harrison has composed more works for Western orchestra and piano, he has had to compromise in his devotion to pure intervals.

Sooner or later, in practical tuning, you must accept reality or else, like a black hole, you'll be drawn in. If you're aiming for an interval, you can tune it, within reason. Aristotelian thinking doesn't quite work in these circumstances, but fuzzy logic does. That is to say, we're not dealing in absolutes, not with any "law of the excluded middle." Fuzzy logic says that there's no such thing as white or black; there are only various degrees of gray. We must draw an average through the different shades of gray because ultimately that's the *musical* approach.[45]

At the same time Lou constantly reaches for the ideal. Although the 1985 *Piano Concerto*, for instance, is not in a Just tuning, it does contain intervals purer than those possible in Equal Temperament. In the *Concerto for Piano with Javanese Gamelan* (1987), the piano derives its intervals from the Indonesian orchestra. Given the choice, Lou prefers to write for instruments that can effect minute pitch adjustments rather than those, like the piano, that require fixed systems, for here he can request beatless intervals from his players.

In spite of his many compositions for keyboard, Harrison continues to have little patience for Equal Temperament and no hesitation expressing his dismay in the strongest terms. In July 1990 the Cabrillo Music Festival brought Philip Glass to Santa Cruz as guest composer. Following a concert filled with Glass's triadic piano music, Lou encountered a friend who innocently asked how he had enjoyed it. "If I hear one more Equal Tempered triad," he burst out, "I think I will scream." Reminded of that story several years later, he chuckled.

I still feel that way, you know. All this last week [February 1994] I was listening to Equal Temperament from Mexican composers with one exception, Mario LaVista, who wrote a movement for string quartet entirely in harmonics. It was ravishing. And, of course, it went back in his own tradition to Carlos Chávez's *Fifth Symphony for Strings*, in which the largo is entirely in harmonics.[46] They were commenting about how beautiful it was, and I shouted, "Pythagoras was right!"[47]

Temperament has become a political issue for Harrison, equal intervals often representing those aspects of Western society he most heartily rejects. "Equal Temperament (which was developed in . . . China but adopted by the Western world) is a symptom of the ossification [of Western industrialized society] — getting things a little too fixed, too invariable and unmovable — a society, if not ossified, at least arthritic."[48] Western ears, he notes, have become unaccustomed to hearing pitch as an aesthetic variable.

> We're pounded at daily by Equal Temperament advocates, by the whole industry which wants to make interchangeable instruments on a planetary basis, all in the same tuning — and an irrational one to begin with. In other places, such as Java, however, the average villager may have a greater understanding, tolerance, and interest in tuning variation than some of the most refined musicians in the West. My classic example is the young Widiyanto. He played on two gamelan whose tunings differed only in one pitch, which varied by the interval 55:54 [32 cents]. "Oh," he immediately remarked, "they are very different."[49]

Harry Partch considered Equal Temperament "a fall from grace."[50] Harrison would surely agree.

6 Instruments Foraged, Modified, or Invented

> To make an instrument is in some strong sense to summon the future.—Lou Harrison, *Music Primer*

Lou Harrison has always felt free, for reasons of timbre or tuning, to seek or construct new instruments. His ears are attuned to the musical potential of objects even in the most mundane settings, from hardware stores to junkyards. Peter Yates recalled Lou's fascination with the bell-like ring of coins dropping into a pay phone during a long-distance call. "Hello, Lou?" Pause. "Lou, are you there?" Silence. Clearly awestruck, Lou finally responded, "Wasn't that beautiful?"[1]

As a composer and instrument builder, Harrison's approach to timbre is inventive and ever wide-ranging. Particularly intriguing to him is the metallophone family, especially bells. Author David Chadwick recalls Lou's visit to the Buddhist community Tassajara in central California: "I apologized to him for the lack of music there and for the fact that there was even a rule against having musical instruments. 'Nonsense!' he said. 'This place is full of music. You have all the musical instruments and music you need. I hear your bells, that thick hanging board, and the drum going from morning to night. There's a lot of space in your music but it's all you need.'"[2]

Lou has called for cowbells, elephant bells, water buffalo bells, Chinese bells, dinner bells, cup bells, meditation bells, schoolteachers' bells, temple bells, and sleigh bells. When he wanted an Indonesian bell tree (*gentorak*), which was too expensive, he and Bill Colvig just built their own.

Old Granddad's cut-off oxygen tanks (fig. 12) are an ingenious addition to the bell family, already one of the world's most diverse classes of idiophones in terms of size-range and shape.[3] When Lou visited Korea in the early 1960s, he "noticed . . . that they had gas tanks left over from the war which they hung up and used as bells," Bill recalls.

> They'd hit them with a chunk of wood. He wondered if we could use that sort of bell in our new gamelan. I immediately got out the Yellow Pages and called the Crystal Ice Company in Watsonville. "Got any old oxygen tanks?" I asked. He had some that were defective. "How much are they?" I asked. "Three dollars apiece." I bought three or four of them. We had them cut to different lengths with a mechanical saw; it was a cheap instrument to make. I hung them in a big rack and we hit them with baseball bats.[4]

By specifying nontraditional, found, or newly invented instruments in his works, does Lou not automatically preclude frequent performance as well as acceptance into the "standard" repertory? While certainly true to some extent, his motivation is straightforward: he is unwilling to compromise the precise sound he wants in order to make his music more popular with performers.[5] A self-defeating approach, some may say—but to Lou it is a matter of principle. "You don't know a composer," he asserts, "unless you know him on the proper instruments and in the tuning he likes." That goes for Couperin and Rameau as well as Harrison.

Sometimes the question is one of sonority: "I recall once wanting a particular sound, which I called the sound of the stars coming out. I couldn't find it in any of my instruments. I finally located it in brass curtain rods resonated over what were then redwood boxes for candy. By putting bridges at the nodal points of the various-length rods, I was able to pick up enough vibrations to achieve my sound."[6]

At other times, his aim is a particular intonation system or even a political statement, such as the early percussion ensemble projects with Cage: "We were not going to write out scores, take them to the local symphony conductor, and be refused," Lou recalls. "We were going to play music with friends for those who wanted to listen—who were also friends."[7] Far from limiting the possibilities of performance, they found that their unconventional instruments attracted large audiences, stimulating more *frequent* performance of their works.

Whatever the objective, Lou would argue that locating the ideal timbre for a particular work is no less crucial than finding the best tuning, or, for that matter, the best melodic shape, rhythmic structure, form, or texture. The success of the composition, he holds, justifies the extra effort required on the part of both composer and performer. *San Francisco Chronicle* reviewer Heuwell Tircuit, commenting on a 1967 performance of *Labyrinth #3* (1941), clearly agreed:

> Eleven men with 91 [actually, 94] percussion instruments set a new standard for shake, rattle and roll Sunday afternoon as the Cabrillo Festival presented its final instrumental concert of the season. . . . What the audience gave was not so much a standing ovation as a hand-clapping bacchanal. . . .
>
> Each of [the] eleven players has a small coterie of instruments. Along with the more expected drums and scrapers, there were: brakedrums, thunder-sheet, elephant bell, saws, water gong, windbells, a bass viol (beaten with sticks . . .), and quintet groupings of flowerpots, porcelain bowls, water glasses, dragon mouths, tom-toms, and cowbells. The first sight of this bang-up menage was enough to whet everyone's curiosity.
>
> Far from being a mere charivari, Harrison offered a highly controlled and consistently fascinating texture to the ear. This was no random junk collection. The various bowls and even the drums were carefully tuned to correct pitch.
>
> The astounding movement, however, was the second, titled "Passage Thru Dreams." Harrison achieved a nearly pure electronic sound spectrum, much like the tape music of the '60s, with ordinary instruments.[8]

Lou's choice of instruments for his percussion works was never random. In an interview with Virginia Rathbun in the early 1970s, he noted that his habit was to balance long- and short-sounding instruments in each register of the ensemble.[9] By selecting high-, middle-, and low-pitched instruments that offered choices between short, sharp sounds and sustaining quieter ones, he created an orchestra with sufficient variety to serve whatever expressive purpose he chose.[10]

Over the years Harrison has found that even those compositions requiring the most arcane sound-producing media have received a reasonable number of performances and recordings. *La Koro Sutro*, for example, has been played repeatedly throughout the United States; Mark Morris shipped in a gamelan for "World Power"; and when the San Francisco Symphony commissioned a new work in 1995, Michael Tilson Thomas told Harrison that he could have "anything he wanted: a gamelan, a boys' choir, a pipe organ, two organs in fact . . . and, of course, the whole San Francisco Symphony."[11] Indeed, the percussion section for *Parade for M.T.T.* was enlarged to include four suspended oxygen tanks, a bell tree, and the large gong from the Mills gamelan.

Lou's forays in the realm of musical timbre may be subdivided into three categories: (1) "found" or "foraged" instruments: adding new sound-producing media to the existing body of traditional instruments; (2) extended usage: treating traditional instruments in nontraditional ways or combining instruments in novel ensembles to produce previously unexplored sonorities; and (3) instrument construction: inventing new instruments or modifying existing ones.

One of the tenets of the Harrison/Cage percussion ensemble was the inclusion of found instruments, stimulated by Cowell's admonitions to scour junkyards and the demands of writing for modern dance. The motivation could be economic as well, as Alfred Frankenstein suggested in 1942:

> About once each year Lou Harrison gathers together a collection of drums, rattles, gongs, bells, ratchets, Chinese blocks and old tin cans, trains a cohort of performers, and gives us the latest in the art of music for percussion instruments. . . . European art music has always neglected the battery, wherefore Harrison and his friends have set themselves to remedying that neglect. Their explorations have led them to exploit a hair-raising variety of unorthodox instruments, and to spurn a large number of the orthodox ones. This, I suspect, is partly a matter of economics. A marimba costs money and a settle of kettledrums is practically worth its weight in inner tubes, but the wooden Chinese bells called dragons' mouths don't set you back so far.[12]

"None of our pieces required timpani," Lou notes. "Who could afford timpani, and besides, how could we roll?" The solution was "good ol' Yankee practicality," says Robert Hughes. "If I don't have it, I'll go to the junkyard and get it—or I'll build it."[13]

Their financial situation allowed for neither expensive instruments nor professional performers. The Harrison/Cage ensemble was composed primarily of amateurs who rotated among the various instruments. Doris Dennison recalls, "We all had a go at everything. And we rehearsed like crazy because we loved it." Dennison had played in Cage's Seattle ensemble while teaching eurythmics at the Cornish School, and she moved to San Francisco in the summer of 1940 with Cage, his wife Xenia, and pianist Margaret Jansen.[14] Another woman in the ensemble, Brabizon Lindsay, was also trained as a pianist. No one was paid; they played for the joy of making music together. "Do you delight in doing this?" Cage asked them hopefully at one of their many rehearsals.[15]

Cage and Harrison were indeed fortunate to have found a group of friends who took delight in the experience. "Such are the problems of the union and other expenses," Lou wrote in 1940, "that performance of works for the more common combinations of instruments are not so much rendered difficult as improbable. . . . The result . . . is that there are two mediums most safe (as far as . . . probable actualization goes) for the composer: the forever present human voice or the field of percussion."[16] So Cage and Harrison took matters into their own hands. They found instruments, trained themselves and their friends, rented halls, and produced their own performances. In the process, they developed a new percussion vocabulary that permanently altered the sonic landscape.

Among the most rewarding finds in junkyards were brake drums (fig. 16). Those from prewar years were made from spun steel, and, suspended from their axle holes, afforded an extraordinary ringing sound. (The automobile industry later converted to cast iron, which is more machinable but less resonant than steel due to the presence of graphite flakes in the iron.) Laid flat and hit at the hole with mallets, the sound of the brake drums was such that "John and I considered them the trumpet section of the percussion orchestra," Lou recalls nostalgically.[17] Today, steel brake drums are a precious commodity. Lou keeps several from the 1930s, which he provides upon request. "My musical life," he notes, "has been based on a happy combination of abstruse knowledge and junk."[18] Reflecting on new developments in materials, Michael Tilson Thomas lamented that "even our junk is of inferior quality today."[19]

A very different and often raucous sound (as opposed to the decorous and surprisingly delicate timbre of the brake drums) is afforded by sheet metal. "John had an excessive love for the thundersheet," Lou recalls. "He used strips of different kinds of metal: aluminum, copper, brass, or steel. I tended to use the 'theatrical thundersheet'—a large rectangle of galvanized iron."[20] The sheet could be struck, shaken, or rolled.

Within the family of wooden idiophones, one of Lou's favorites is the crate, which yields higher- or lower-pitched sounds when struck on its various length sides. Lou called for the crate as early as *Canticle #3* (1942), and for a performance of the work in New York in 1953 he made a point of informing Stokowski that the Hiram Walker wood case had a superior tone than that used for most other brands of whiskey.[21] Twenty years later Bill built a set of "box bells," wooden instruments suspended from a rack and struck with beaters, for use in the *Concerto for Organ with Percussion* (1973). The *Fourth Symphony* (1990) requires two crates, in this case with rasps on one edge.

Retail and import stores during the 1930s and 1940s yielded other treasures as well. In hardware stores Cage and Harrison bought iron pipe of varying sizes; at nurseries they found matched sets of resonant flowerpots; and in Chinatown they purchased porcelain bowls. The pots and bowls added a delicate melodic texture to the ensemble, as did the ceramic ocarinas (globular flutes) commonly found in music stores at the time (figs. 16, 17). These instruments allowed Lou to maintain lyric melody even within the context the percussion ensemble, a feature of his music frequently cited by reviewers. A small selection from numerous examples:

1973 (*Canticle #3, Suite for Percussion, Concerto for Violin with Percussion, Concerto for Organ with Percussion*): "The music seldom indulges in those crash-bang shock effects which one finds in most contemporary percussion music. Much of it is almost lyrical, despite frequent vigorous rhythms."

1980 (*Fugue for Percussion*): "Part of the fascination lay in the absence of dynamic strain in the shifting patterns of what was essentially a rhythmic study which waxed surprisingly lyrical."

1990 (*Canticle #3*): "The hauntingly beautiful, nearly pure tones of the ocarina, cast here as soloist (possibly in the role of a shaman), have the aura of timelessness. . . . For all its reliance on percussion, Harrison's music is essentially lyrical, gentle, sanguine, uplifting, and, above all, beautiful."

1958 (*Canticle #3*): "Neither conventionality nor shock effect . . . can fully explain the emotional grip of this work. What does partially explain it is a piercingly expressive, hollow-sounding ocarina that winsomely pipes forth a plaintive folk melody upon which the percussion gadgets build shattering climaxes and desolate resolutions. In one section, accompanied by the brake drums and bells, it sounds like what can only be described as a primitive craving, crying mournfully from beneath the jazz of a mechanized civilization. It is the whimper awaiting the ultimate bang."[22]

In the performance notes for his *Fifth Simfony* for percussion quartet (1939), Lou admonishes the performers: "Above all the conductor should see that the players make the most expressive effect with their instruments in order to avoid that regrettable bang bang so often associated with the word percussion!"[23]

Harrison keeps a collection of ceramic ocarinas of various sizes (and thus various pitch ranges) for loan to anyone intending to perform his works. Even his choice of the title *Canticle* for many of his early percussion works—a word he translates as "rhapsodic song"[24]—shows his lyric orientation.

He was fascinated with other nontraditional instruments as well, such as the *teponaztli*, a multisegmented wood slit-drum from Mexico. The instrument is traditionally built from hollow log with a series of H-shaped slits that create vibrating tongues, which are struck with mallets. The first instrument Harrison used was a replica built by Cage.

Henry Cowell provided a detailed list of instruments used in Harrison and Cage's 1940 percussion extravaganza at Mills College:

Seventeen "percussors" made up the orchestra. They used the following instruments: *drums*—one snare, two bass, five black Chinese tomtoms, five small painted Chinese tomtoms, one pair of bongos; *wood*: eight Chinese wood-blocks, six dragon's mouths (temple blocks), four pair of claves; *metal*: one mariembula, two pair of finger cymbals, one pair of crash cymbals, one Turkish cymbal, four Chinese cymbals, one pair of jazz cymbals, five gongs, one tamtam, one Chinese painted gong, three Japanese temple gongs, five Japanese cup gongs, thirteen oxen bells, one set of orchestra bells, twelve cow bells, one dinner bell, one trolling bell, one turkey bell, one small Chinese bell, three loose sleigh bells, four triangles, three brake drums, eight strap irons, one pipe, three discs, ten thunder sheets, one wash tub, one washboard set; *rattles*: one quijada (jawbone), four pair maracas, one Indo-Chinese rattle, one North-Western Indian rattle, one sistrum, one tambourine, one wind bell; *miscellaneous*: one tortoise shell, one guiro, four rice bowls, three Mexican clay bowls, four slide whistles, one conch shell, one lion's roar, one string drum, one slap-stick, one piano, one xylophone, and about eighty beaters of all sorts.[25]

Xenia Cage recalls buying the ass's jawbone in an obscure music store on Market Street. "One would strike the side of it and make the teeth rattle," she said, remembering her shopping trips with Harrison and Cage. Every free moment of the day, she says, was devoted to foraging or to raising money for instrument purchase. "This ass's jaw was painted bright green with all kinds of flowers on it. We came out of the store . . . and I was holding this strange-looking jawbone. Suddenly a man came up and grabbed me and said, 'Xenia, how glad I am to see you.' Fortunately it was my brother, whom I hadn't seen in a thousand years. I had to think of a way to explain: 'Oh, I'm just carrying a musical instrument!' I said. That was embarrassing."[26]

Cowell identifies four approaches to the development of the percussion orchestra current at the time: (1) the creation of a sophisticated art form "ready-made and without gradual development," exemplified by the Italian futurists and culminating in Varèse's percussion music; (2) the expansion of the percussion section of traditional ensembles to enhance orchestration, as in the work of Percy Grainger; (3) the derivation of percussion music from folk traditions, as in pieces by Latin American composers such as Ardévol, Caturla, and Roldán; and (4) percussion music as a complement to modern dance, which he attributes to Harrison and Cage.[27] Lou's later works with percussion retain their link to dance. In the *Concerto for Violin with Percussion* of 1959, for example, the solo instrument is an analog for the solo dancer, as Alfred Frankenstein remarked after its New York premiere: "Harrison's point, if I read him right, is to contrast the long lines and soaring outpour of the violin with the strong rhythms and spangling colors of the battery. [He] used to be a dancer, and is still one of the most choreographic of modern composers."[28]

Specifying arcane instruments, however, risks misunderstandings. When Michael Tilson Thomas performed *Canticle #3* with the BBC Orchestra, for instance, he discovered that the percussionists were using wooden elephant bells instead of the brass ones Lou had found in San Francisco import stores (figs. 16, 17). Dissatisfied with "thunk" in place of "tinkle," Thomas politely requested brass bells, only to be assured first by orchestra management and then by the keeper of the elephants at the Royal Zoo himself that these were indeed the "genuine" instrument. But as Thomas persisted, a light went on in the zookeeper's head. "Ah, Mr. Thomas," he finally realized, "what you are asking for are *dress parade* Indian elephant bells!"[29]

An additional downside of "found" instruments is that at times they may yield unpredictable results in performance. Lou recalls that during the late 1960s, he, Bill, Richard Dee, and Lily Chin presented a concert of Chinese music at the Old Spaghetti Factory in San Francisco. Among the instruments they brought along were a set of porcelain bowls, which were played with thin bamboo sticks—an Indian instrument called the *jalataranga* formerly used in China. To tune the bowls precisely, they filled each with water, calibrating its pitch accurately drop by drop.

When we had them sounding quite beautiful, we put Saran Wrap over the top and went out for a nice Chinese dinner. We came back, took the Saran Wrap off, and played the piece. But the bowls went "funk" instead of "ping." None of us was aware that water standing in a bowl over time forms bubbles [from dissolved gas coming out of solution] that insulate it from the sounding body. The remedy is either to pour the water back and forth many times or to use glycerin as a wetting agent.[30]

Such problems do not deter Harrison, who has called for found objects of various types throughout his career. Among his favorite are galvanized garbage cans, which he calls "America's indigenous steel drum"[31] (see fig. 12). The *Concerto in Slendro* (1961) requires four such cans, along with six triangles and six gongs. Percussionist/composer William Kraft remembers a rehearsal of the work during which the *Concerto* acquired an unplanned olfactory component. The garbage can player apologized, "I forgot to go out and buy one this morning; so I just grabbed my own."[32]

"Passage thru Darkness" (1982), from *Tributes to Charon*, requires two alarm clocks, and the *Concerto for Violin with Percussion* (1959) includes galvanized washtubs; clock coils and coffee cans struck with beaters; wind chimes; brake drums; flowerpots; and plumber's pipes. Lou built his own "coffee-can metallophone" and "clock coil metallophone" (fig. 16). He mounted the coffee cans in a rigid stand and the clock coils onto a resonator constructed from an old guitar. Performers today can easily construct their own coffee-can instrument: Lou specifies only relative pitches and describes in the introduction to the score how to drill and mount the cans. Clock coils, on the other hand, are becoming increasingly rare in our electric age.

The *Varied Trio* (1987) includes not only water-filled rice bowls but also six baking tins, an idea that arose from a display in the window of a local kitchen supply shop. As soon as he spotted the tins, Harrison thought, "Those are musical instruments." He and Colvig stopped in, banged on a few, and purchased a set for the new trio.

Locating the appropriate paraphernalia for some of his earlier pieces is becoming increasingly difficult. As early as a 1965 performance of the *Concerto for Violin with Percussion* (only six years after the work's inception), Lou found it necessary to devote "a good part of the day chasing down metal pikes, dowels, pipe lengths and flower pots in hardware stores. You used to be able to go into a hardware store and make music with almost anything you found there. But no more; all this beautiful post-industrial stuff is soon going to be antiquarian."[33]

When there is a problem with his instruments, Lou does not hesitate to roll up his sleeves and get to work building, cleaning, tuning, or repairing. When *La Koro Sutro* was scheduled for performance in Sapporo, Japan, in 1993, for instance, Old Granddad was in bad repair. "The instruments had not been used in a long time," recalls Eva Soltes, who arranged the trip. "They were covered with cobwebs and had been chipped." There was no time to repair them before the trip. So she had the instruments crated and shipped "as is," and Lou's Japanese hosts provided paint, nails, work space, and assistants. The work space turned out to be a log cabin in an art park. "We had a ball finding our way through hardware stores in Japan. We needed baseball bats [for the oxygen tanks] because the strikers for these huge gongs weren't there. We went to art stores in search of beautiful pigment colors. In fact, we renovated the whole set of instruments in three weeks. Lou and Bill did all the tunings."[34] The experience convinced Soltes of the necessity for a second set of instruments. She subsequently raised funds for a replica of Old Granddad, which was built by Richard Cooke in Moab, Utah, and dedicated in 1996.

On traditional instruments, Lou has at times experimented with extended techniques, although he has little interest in exploring them for their own sake. That's not to imply that he was unaware of the expansion of instrumental technique taking place during the 1930s and 1940s. As early as his *Prelude for Grandpiano* (1937), a work in the Cowell idiom, he included passages strummed on the strings of the piano and small tone clusters. "King David's Lament for Jonathan," composed in 1941 and later revised and incorporated into *Three Songs* for male chorus (1985), uses tone clusters spanning a fifth as a primary compositional feature. Similar cluster writing enlivens the *Concerto for Organ with Percussion* (1973), the *Grand Duo* (1988), the *Piano Concerto* (1985), and *Rhymes with Silver* (1996).

Like the new percussion instruments, these extended techniques never become an end in themselves. Rather, they serve a more general sonic purpose—and often a percussive one. Harrison's string and keyboard techniques at times appear to be extensions of his instrument foraging. In the estampie movement of the *String Quartet Set*, for instance, two or three players form a rhythm section, beating on the bodies of their instruments with hands and fingers, while the others (sometimes the violin, sometimes the cello, and sometimes both in octaves) declaim the tune. During the "rice bowl" movement of the *Varied Trio*, the pianist is primarily occupied with knocking the instrument's frame at various locations with a yarn mallet. Lou's favorite nontraditional double bass technique—hitting the strings with dowels or drumsticks—serves the same end.

Although Lou's piano clusters certainly have a strong melodic component, their primary function often seems to be rhythmic. In order to facilitate rapid cluster movement on the keyboard, Lou and Bill developed the "octave bar," a flat wooden device approximately two inches high with a grip on top and sponge rubber on the bottom, with which the player strikes the keys. Its length spans an octave on a grand piano. The sponge rubber bottom is sculpted so that its ends are slightly lower than its center, making the outer tones of the octave sound with greater force than the intermediary pitches. The pianist can thus rush headlong through fearfully rapid passages, precisely spanning an octave at each blow—truly a visual as well as an aural treat for the audience. Lou and Bill happily make octave bars to order, although they are easy enough to construct, as the San Francisco Symphony did for its 1996 performance of the *Concerto for Organ with Percussion*.

In *Canticle #3* (1942), even the guitar functions primarily as a percussion instrument. The part includes only strummed bar chords and was intended to be played by one of the percussionists. In a recent performance of the work, the player strummed with a credit card, eliciting a bold and strident tone that complemented the struck brake drums and plumber's pipes. Lou loved the effect.[35]

Similarly, Harrison's fondness for plucked strings (harp, harpsichord, psalteries, and zithers, for instance) lies as much in their rhythmic capability as in their melodic role. The celesta, too, combines a strong percussive component with a bell-like timbre that he finds particularly attractive.

Among his favorite percussion instruments is the tack-piano—a piano in which thumb tacks have been inserted in the hammer felts. He first made its acquaintance when composer Esther Williamson Ballou took him backstage at a New York concert during the 1940s and showed him a tacked grand piano being used as a substitute for a harpsichord. In numerous works (*Solstice* is an excellent example, as is the opera *Rapunzel*), Lou calls for an ensemble of tack-piano, celesta, and sometimes harp—which he terms the "gamelan section" of the orchestra.

Indeed, it is often in the combination of instruments, rather than in their possible extended techniques, that Lou finds new timbres. Perhaps the most striking example is *Pacifika Rondo* (1963) with its mixture of *sheng* (the Chinese free-reed mouth organ), jalataranga (tuned bowls), psalteries, *fang hsiang* (tuned iron slabs hung in a decorated rack), p'iri (Korean double-reed instrument), and *pak* ("six slabs of heavy hardwood slammed together fanwise"[36]; figs. 17 and 18) along with a standard string orchestra. (The pak and p'iri can be heard on the CD, band 12.) Lou attributes his unusual instrumentations to the "me, too" phenomenon: no sooner does he see an unfamiliar instrument or a novel technique than he wants to share in the fun. These new tools he mixes with his familiar collection to create his own hybrids: French horn with Javanese gamelan, for instance, or violin and mbiras (plucked lamellaphones; fig. 17).

Lou has frequently found timbre to be the solution to compositional problems. The *Concerto for Organ with Percussion*, for instance, posed particular challenges linking abstract (nontuned) percussion with what Harrison calls the "hopelessly tonal" organ. Lou bridged the disparity with a third timbral unit: a group of pitched percussion including celesta, glockenspiel, vibraphone, piano, and tube chimes.[37]

The retuning required in many of Harrison's works is also a form of extended technique. Although in this case the "extension" is primarily on the part of the keyboard tuners, the variable instruments and the voices must clearly learn to alter ingrained pitch concepts to match an unfamiliar temperament.

When he can't find the sound he needs in foraged, found, or scavenged instruments, or in innovative uses or combinations of traditional instruments, Lou builds new ones. In fact, he considers the ability to build instruments one of the essential tools of a composer. Singer Patrice Maginnis recalls that the final requirement in Harrison's orchestration class at San Jose State was to design a new percussion instrument, develop a notation for it, and then to compose a short piece. The instrument could be as simple as rice in a Coca-Cola can, she noted, "but the student would have to specify the exact amount of rice."[38]

Lou's instrument-building history stretches back to his youth, with his dismantling and reassembling the family phonograph and his early attempts to build a violin, and reached a decided sophistication in his New York clavichords (chapter 2). By this time he was experimenting with wind instruments as well in an attempt to free them from their Equal Tempered tunings. In January 1953 he wrote to Frank and Anne Wigglesworth in Rome: "Have been glancing at my first unsuccessful flute . . . [intended] to play Pythagorean and Ptolemy intonations."[39] By May, he was working with double reeds. "I made a Phrygian Aulos the other day," he reported, after reading Kathleen Schlesinger's 1939 study of the instrument.[40]

You make the instrument either with a strong wheat stalk or oboe-reed and a tube so measured that of twelve total equal parts from tip of the double-reed to lower end of tube[,] holes bored at the lowest six measurements will sound exactly ascending 12/11 11/10 10/9 9/8 8/7 7/6. . . . [I] played [the scale], enchanted . . . on the piano, and concluded that Plato must have been an awful prude in this regard, for the accordance is most lovely and melting. Why war and Mars? . . .

I wait to sound the Dorian. . . . This has the very highest reputation of all, its heavenly body, the sun.

My Clavichord is nearly completed and sounds beautifully. It stands on its own three legs majestically and will last.[41]

Continuing to build and test his own versions of the aulos after returning to California in 1953, Lou quickly discovered that Schlesinger's tuning hypotheses were flawed because of the extensive pitch variability possible through changes in lip pressure on the large reed.

Upon his return from Korea, he built p'iri out of wood and Lucite and designed several psalteries modeled after the Chinese *cheng* (figs. 17, 18). In October 1962 he wrote to Charles Fahs at the Rockefeller Foundation:

My oriental studies continue apace: I've trained a group of 4 Piri players (who already do quite well, I must say) and am scheduled for talks and broadcasts on Korean music. I've constructed a "King-size" Piri (3 of them) in Lucite, and will make a series in other sizes so that they may be played in all keys. Yesterday I completed a Psaltery, in common "western" materials . . . that well competes with the oriental instruments, and which can be made in several sizes. I am about to tackle flutes . . . that will play in all keys. In short, my dream of a usable Sinitic orchestra in Western materials is well on the way—along with transcriptions and new works for it.[42]

In 1967, when Harrison met Bill Colvig, he found a partner who not only shared his passion for instrument construction but who also had metalworking skills and expertise with electronic tools such as the oscilloscope. Colvig could measure and tune interval ratios on fixed-pitch instruments with sufficient precision (to the nearest two cents) so that Harrison's—or, for that matter, anyone's—theoretical scales could be realized reliably in sound.

Bill, who was born in the same year as Lou (March 13, 1917) and also in Oregon (Medford), was at the time working as an electrician in San Francisco. He had been surrounded by music since childhood. His father was a bandmaster in Weed, a lumber town in northern California at the base of Mt. Shasta. "My grandfather thought Pop should go into law," Bill recalls.

It's a more hairy-chested profession than music. So he sent Pop off to law school . . . but it didn't work. Meanwhile, Pop was playing clarinet and saxophone in different groups. In Weed, [where] Pop was doing clerical work for a lumber company, there was a town band. One day the band leader couldn't come and Pop tried directing the band. Everybody liked him so much that they made him the leader. The next thing you know Pop was teaching music in the grammar and high schools.[43]

Like Lou's family, Bill's parents provided a musical education for their sons. He learned to play the piano, trombone, baritone horn, and tuba. His brother David became a professional flutist who played in the Houston Symphony, premiered Lou's *Ariadne* in 1987, and now works as a flute technician in San Francisco.

In 1934 Bill matriculated at the College (now University) of the Pacific in Stockton on a music scholarship but then decided to major in electrical engineering, much to the chagrin of the comptroller. Nevertheless, he actively participated in ensembles there and at UC Berkeley, where he transferred in 1937. He soon tired of the academic life and moved to Fairbanks, Alaska, to indulge his love of the wilderness but continued to pursue his musical interests by playing in the Fairbanks town band. ("The other baritone player didn't smell very good because his job was to empty the 'honey pots' for people who didn't have sewage systems; in winter he'd take them into his living room and thaw them out.")[44] Years later Colvig met composer Ingolf Dahl on a hiking trip in the Sierras. At a lunch stop, he sat down with Dahl, pulled out his sopranino recorder, and tootled some Couperin. Thereafter the two men became close friends and frequent hiking companions.

By the time he met Lou, Bill was satisfying his musical interests by at-

tending concerts of new and unusual music in San Francisco. He was fascinated by a program of Chinese classical music Lou presented in 1966, and
in February of the following year the two men met following a performance
at the Old Spaghetti Factory featuring Lou's musical kit, *Jephtha's Daughter*,
and William Walton's *Façade* with Lou and Ned Rorem as narrators.

Harrison and Colvig soon found that they shared not only musical but
also political and aesthetic views. A few weeks later Bill joined Lou in his
tiny cottage in Aptos, and the instrument-building side of Lou's life began
to mushroom. Together they constructed monochords and harps (chapter 5)
and began performing Chinese music with Lou's student Richard Dee.

But it was the water-bowl fiasco at the Chinese music concert that first set
Bill on the road to building the American gamelan. Determined to find a better solution to the problem of gas formation than continuously pouring
water among the vessels or using glycerin, Bill searched for a more stable
system. He ultimately chose steel conduit pipe as an alternative and built a
set of pipes tuned in Just Intonation that held its pitch permanently. "We
tuned this first little set of one-inch conduit pipes by ear—Lou's ear," Bill
recalls.

Both of them, of course, realized that a more accurate measurement tool
was required to achieve the precise interval ratios of Just Intonation, hence
Bill's use of the oscilloscope (chapter 3). He has since built numerous finely
tuned metallic instruments using both aluminum and steel, as well as string
and wind instruments such as plucked and bowed psalteries, an
Afghanistani *gitchak* (fiddle), an Indonesian *celempung* (zither), and numerous Indonesian *suling* (flutes).[45] He constructed the bowed psaltery after the
theft of a rare traditional instrument and copied the gitchak, a bowed two-
stringed spike-fiddle, from a photo on the back of a record jacket.

In a 1974 article on instrument design, Lou enumerated and described
the types of instruments that one could build at home and tune with precision: psalteries (bowed or plucked); harps with dual tuning mechanisms
(gross and fine); the double-reed aulos in which the pitch is controlled by
the player; the vertical *hsiao* or flute built from aluminum tubing; slide aerophones; fipple flutes; metallophones constructed from aluminum furniture
tubing, steel conduit tubing, or aluminum slabs, with tin can resonators
("aluminum delivers the decibels, steel the sweet tone"); xylophones constructed from various woods (particularly bamboo); and tuned porcelain
bowls. "Much is possible," he concludes. "These are a few beginnings.
Music really can be played in tune!"[46]

As they approach their thirtieth anniversary together, Lou and Bill can
point with pride to their rich legacy of found, modified, and invented instruments. Yet Lou calls less frequently these days for newly invented instruments. Bill, too, is tired from his many years of building. When they recently received a request for a new gamelan after a visit to Taliesin West
(Frank Lloyd Wright's art colony and cultural center in Scottsdale, Arizona),

Bill nearly broke into tears: the thought of undertaking still another exhausting instrument-building project was just too overwhelming. Their concern at present is consolidation, organization, and preservation to insure that proper instruments will be available for future authentic performances of Lou's works.

One timbral realm has held little interest for Lou: that of electronic sound synthesis. His music requires human executants, an issue as much political for him as aesthetic. In eschewing machine sounds, Lou protests the dehumanizing potential of technology and what he considers the excesses of modern industrialized life. Aesthetically, he finds the vibrations of "real" instruments alive in comparison to loudspeaker approximations. And on the personal level, Lou cherishes his interaction with performers, the inevitable variability in their interpretations, and, most of all, the vitality of human emotion. While he has a healthy respect for modern technology in its proper place (he uses a Macintosh computer with his own type fonts, owns DAT and CD audio equipment, and marvels at the convenience of his fax), he hears machine sounds and Equal Temperament as the aural correlates of a passionless society. His views are conditioned as well by his love for history—a striving to embrace rather than discard the past, to connect to, rather than break with, musical tradition.

7 Lou Harrison and East Asian Music

When we asked Harrison whether, in his own work, he had played with the notion of surface levels of texture and scale in Asian music as opposed to the deeper levels of rhythmic and formal organization, he responded, "No, I'm not an intellectual. I just do the best I can in my mania. Schoenberg recommended simplicity—I wonder if that admonition had some fruit in Javanese music for me. But that's as far as I go: I'm more of a craftsman than a philosopher."[1]

By the time Harrison made his two trips to Asia in the 1960s—to Japan and Korea in 1961 and to Korea and Taiwan in 1962—he was already quite familiar with many styles of Asian music. As a young student, he was a frequent visitor to San Francisco's Chinatown.

> Chinatown was in the middle of the city. In those days Chinese merchants entertained one another and there were clubs. You could walk along the street and hear a flute or a viol played by street vendors or a merchant in his lair. Then I discovered the Chinese opera, and that became a more or less steady entertainment. I would have Chinese dinner with friends from San Francisco State and then we'd go to the opera. I went to the Chinese opera very frequently. Of course I had seen many, many more Chinese operas than Western operas. One couldn't understand the dialogue, but you knew what was going on. We'd turn to each other sometimes in the pantomimes and say "It's not subtle anymore, is it?" It was very comfortable and family-oriented, with people sitting at tables.[2]

The kind of opera they saw was Cantonese, the vernacular southern Chinese theater most popular among the immigrants who populated America's Chinese communities until the 1960s "brain drain" brought large numbers of Mandarin-speaking northern Chinese to study engineering, computers, and other hard sciences. In the 1930s, however, Cantonese was the dominant tradition, which Lou learned, somewhat to his chagrin:

> My friend John Dobson's mother taught harp. That aroused my interest in the harp. Everyone [in his family] was musical. The whole family spoke Mandarin Chinese, because they had been through the Boxer Rebellion. The father was an Anglican minister and teacher and had a compound in Beijing. There were three or four sons, quite distinguished. At one point the father, who was a teacher at Lowell High School in San Francisco, decided the family ought to refresh its Chinese. And so we all gathered every so often and I learned a little Chinese. It was perfectly useless because it was Mandarin and everybody in San Francisco spoke Cantonese or some other dialect.[3]

Nevertheless, the access to Chinese music in Lou's formative years was significant and memorable. Later, when he was teaching world music at San Jose State University, he would counsel his students to take every opportunity to visit Chinatown and its myriad cultural resources.[4] "Chinatown was fascinating then. A few of the restaurants had orchestreons and they were absolutely fabulous with all these mechanical instruments bowing and drumming. They were regular entertainment during my years in San Francisco. I had a fair inkling of Asian musics, dominantly Northeast Asian: Chinese and Japanese."[5]

Harrison's memories of San Francisco's Chinese community were so vivid that they actually caused him some embarrassment when he later visited Taiwan.

> I ate every night at [Liang] Tsai-Ping's house. There I met most of the then active members of the Classic Music Association. I also made a marvelous gaffe. I was taken by taxi to a meeting of a Nanguan music club from Amoy. In order to get there we went down towards the waterfront; as you know, most of Taipei looks like less prepossessing parts of Brooklyn. All of a sudden I began to notice wedding apparel and Chinese things like I'd seen in San Francisco. I said "Oh Tsai-Ping, I'm so glad you have a Chinatown in Taipei!"[6]

Given his love of the San Francisco Chinese opera, one might suppose that Taiwan would have been Lou's choice when the Rockefeller Foundation offered him the chance to visit a second Asian country after the Tokyo East-West Encounter Conference—especially after he met cheng master Liang Tsai-Ping at the meeting (see chapter 3). Instead, Lou seized the opportunity to learn about a new culture, first planning a visit to Thailand and later substituting Korea when Dr. Lee Hye-Ku entranced him with its music.

Korea

Lou spent more time in Korea than in any other Asian country: from May 4 to July 6, 1961, and again from June 28 to October 16, 1962. During that time he studied the traditional court music repertory extensively, and under the tutelage of Maestro Kim T'aesòp he became an expert performer on the p'iri, which plays a leading part in several different court ensembles (fig. 17). Harrison's expertise on the instrument was formally recognized by his teachers at the National Classical Music Institute (now known as the National Center for Korean Traditional Performing Arts), and he was given verbal authorization to teach the instrument, which, naturally, he did upon returning to the United States. He was also honored by a scroll from the Minister of Public Information.

For his small Chinese chamber group, Lou transcribed and arranged a composition from the moribund repertory of the Korean Confucian ceremonies, called *Hyi Mun* (properly, Hùimun). Hùimun is the first of twenty-two sections in the Sacrifice to Royal Ancestors, which is composed of two suites each in eleven sections: Chòngdaeòp and Pot'aep'yòng. Of the twenty or so Confucian ceremonies that once were regularly held in royal Korea, only six or seven used music. By the turn of the twentieth century, all but two had been abolished: Sacrifice to Royal Ancestors (Chongmyo) and Sacrifice to Confucius (Munmyo). While the music played at the Munmyo is, in the strict sense, *aak* (Chinese ritual music borrowed originally from Sung Dynasty Chinese melodies), that at the Chongmyo has been heavily Koreanized since the fifteenth century, if it was not outright Korean in the first place.[7] Lou played the p'iri solo, while Dee and Colvig accompanied (CD band 12). Soon, however, the delicate Korean bamboo instruments fell victim to the vicissitudes of travel and the shifting climates of northern California, and Lou decided to create a version of the instrument that would stand up to more abuse. The result was a Lucite-bodied p'iri that the Koreans promptly dubbed the Miguk-p'iri or "American p'iri." Since audiences found the appearance of a transparent Lucite instrument disconcerting, Lou later decided to paint the tube black (fig. 17).

In this same period, he composed a major work in classical style for Korean traditional orchestra, *Moogunkwha: Sharon Rose, A New Song in the Old Style*. This work was performed by a student orchestra in Korea and sounds like a thoroughly traditional work, though somewhat stricter and more archaic, perhaps, than current Korean taste prefers. Even in his creativity, it seems, Lou was being an activist for preservation of the "tones of high antiquity."

Much of this creative work was informed by Harrison's intensive studies of the history and theory of Korean music with Lee Hye-Ku. Born in 1909, Lee completed his undergraduate degree in English literature in 1931.[8] His interest in music grew during his employment for more than ten years as a radio announcer and programmer. After World War II, Lee decided to teach music full-time. He joined the faculty of Seoul National University in 1947 and today is still an active emeritus professor. Nevertheless, it was not until 1959, at the age of fifty, that Lee was awarded a Ph.D. in literature for his work on modes in traditional Korean music—two years *after* publication of his first book of collected essays on Korean music. Three additional volumes of essays and a book on Korean musical instruments appeared by 1976; a Festschrift in his honor was published in 1969, which includes an article by Lou on the music of mouth-organs and a dedicatory poem in Lou's high-style calligraphy; and in 1981 a collection of Lee's most important essays was published in English translation by Robert Provine.

The book on Korean music history that Harrison and Lee began together during Lou's visits to Korea and Lee's to Aptos survives both in a typescript and in fifty-three folio-sized pages in Lou's calligraphic hand. It is a remarkable document, combining Dr. Lee's meticulous historical research with Harrison's grand sweeping views of human history, invention, and folly. Where else could one find such passages as these?

> Thus, in Dance Mu-ae, a monk is seen, gourd bowl in hand, dancing in the street, improvising new verses about Buddhism to the tunes of popular songs. The effect would be similar to that in Europe of a saint dancing down the street singing ecstatic words in favor of Christianity to the tune of "Frankie and Johnny."

Or:

> A word must be said here about the amazing naming system for the courtly repertoire. A goodly number of these works turn up with a variety of totally unrelated titles, & furthermore, the pieces themselves develop new progeny, & then one of them will mushroom in size & importance until one feels a little like Alice in a new Wonderland. All this makes historical tracing difficult & intricate. Bemused Korean musicologists have suggested that perhaps sometimes the Royal Ear was not too retentive & that a successful piece "by any other name" . . . [9]

Harrison and Lee skillfully interweave Korean political and cultural history with the history of the main styles of court music, including both ritual and entertainment repertories. Modern and folk genres are either omitted or only briefly mentioned. Korea's significance in the transmission of Chinese classical traditions to Japan, as a source for Japanese arts generally, and as a repository for the preservation of musical traditions long extinct in China—topics of considerable interest that are usually poorly presented in surveys of East Asian music—are all explored in detail. The final section of the manuscript as it currently exists is a rough draft of an introduction to Korean Buddhist music. One hopes for the eventual completion of this valuable work.

Taiwan

When Lou visited Taiwan in 1962, Professor Liang was president of the Chinese Classical Music Association (which he had founded). Born in 1910 in the village of Pei Tsai Kou in Hopei Province, Liang devoted extensive effort to researching cheng music of different schools and making his collections available to a broad public. According to his son, ethnomusicologist Liang Ming-yüeh, "The result of this promotion was the extraordinary development of *zheng* music in Taiwan beginning with less than six zither musicians in the early 1950's to a phenomenal some ten thousand amateur and professional *zheng* musicians by the early 1980's."[10]

In 1938, after studies in Peking with Shih Ying-mei and Wei Tze-you, Liang published his first work on the cheng, the *Ni Cheng Pu* (Peking), which, like similar texts for the scholar's zither, *ch'in*, includes information on the instrument, its history, and its music; a section describing the various finger techniques required; and a selection of fifteen tunes in a new notation system he invented. His book appears to be the first to introduce a notation system for cheng music, which had previously been transmitted in oral tradition.[11]

In 1945–46, Liang came to the United States for advanced professional studies at Yale University but did not neglect his cultural ambassadorship; he played numerous cheng recitals and made a film, *Melody of Ancient China*. On March 21, 1946, he played a concert at China House in New York, which prompted a review in *Time:* "A Yale student named Liang Tsai-Ping played centuries-old music on a Ku-Cheng that had come down to him through three generations. . . . With a faint, abstracted smile, like a man trying to remember his first girl, Liang plucked out clear notes with fingernails of his right hand; made them whine and sob with his left hand."[12]

Though Lou Harrison could have been in the audience—or could even have been reviewing the concert—he was frantically preparing for the April 5 performance of Ives's third symphony, and in any case the *Tribune* sent him to hear soprano Josephine Tooker sing French and English songs at Times Hall instead. Despite Lou's interest in things Chinese, he was not to hear or meet Liang for another fifteen years.

Soon after the civil war forced Liang's relocation to Taiwan, he established the Chinese Classical Music Association, to support and preserve traditional music. Liang edited and published articles, books, bibliographies, and collections of scores under the auspices of the association. He sought out musicians who, in the upheavals of war, had lost their instruments, regional audiences, and livelihoods, and helped them by sponsoring concerts and recordings.

Liang was recognized as the leader of the "Renovation School" (*Wei-hsin*) of cheng music, one of two contemporary schools (the other is the "Renaissance School," *Fu-ku*). Both schools aimed at preserving and reconstructing masterpieces of traditional cheng music, but Liang's school also looked toward the future, exploring potential for new developments, a posture that undoubtedly attracted Lou Harrison. Liang himself became a prolific composer of new works and an arranger of compositions from the ch'in repertoire. Liang's compositions often fuse Western and Chinese musical ideas—for example, borrowing Western notions of sequence and melodic development.

Liang's highly influential textbook for the cheng, *Ku cheng tutsou ch'ü/ Music of Cheng*, was first published in Taipei in 1961. As the double title indicates, it includes introductory material in both Western and Chinese notations and adds a series of finger exercises for development of proper technique to a collection of graded compositions for beginners and intermediate players. This book has been edited, revised, and reprinted more than eleven times. In 1971, the Four Seas Record Publishing Company in Taiwan issued a three-record set of Liang performing all of the pieces in his book, capping the more than twenty albums of music that he had recorded over the years in Taiwan, Hong Kong, and the United States (on the Lyrichord label), many of which are still in print, reissued on CD.

Liang has been one of the most active teachers of cheng, and because of his command of English (at a time when this skill was uncommon in Taiwan) as well as his prominence as a musician, he was sought after by many students, both Western and Chinese. Thus, it was natural that Harrison would choose him as a mentor. His outgoing, energetic, and friendly personality also aid his mission; Lou put it this way in a letter: "I want to say that I am personally very grateful to you for the splendid way in which you put me at ease. Perhaps you do not really know as yet how much even cultivated 'Western' musicians feel themselves 'barbarians' in contact with fine oriental musicians! (I was very frightened of meeting Sukehiro Shiba, for example, & he turned out to be a lovely man.) Your own friendliness calmed & helped me very much."[13]

Liang arranged for Harrison to take lessons on several different instruments. He himself taught Lou the cheng, and he arranged for other musicians to teach *kuan* (cylindrical double-reed aerophone, like the Korean p'iri) and *erh-hu* (Chinese two-string fiddle). Liang also took Lou to many concerts of different kinds of regional music and opera and introduced him to scholars and composers.

Among the leading composers in Taiwan is Hsu Tsoang-houei, French-trained and much interested in incorporating Chinese materials into his compositions. Lou found some of his work lovely, particularly a choral work based on the chanting of Buddhist nuns, which Hsu had recorded on Jade Mountain in southern Taiwan. One might imagine that Lou would be intrigued and influenced by Hsu Tsoang-houei's ethnomusicological approach to composition, but it is hard to hear anything in Lou's works that admits of such influence.

Rather, Lou began his study of Chinese music from the standpoint of the performer, paying special attention to instrumental techniques as he had during his previous studies of instruments in various genres—violin, piano, recorder, harpsichord, French horn, and clarinet. He now became a beginning performer on the cheng as well, and soon he began writing new compositions for it.

The cheng (fig. 18) is an ancient Chinese instrument of the zither family, which is indigenous to East Asia, unlike the lute family, which entered the region from the West in the centuries after 200 or 300 A.D.[14] The zither family consists of all instruments whose strings are parallel to a string-bearer stick, board, or box, but without the articulated neck characteristic of the lute family. Lou prefers the term "psaltery" to distinguish zithers such as the cheng, which are played entirely on open strings, from those such as the ch'in or Appalachian dulcimer, whose strings may be played either open or stopped against fingerboards.

The strings of the cheng, originally silk but replaced by metal when the technology for drawing metal was sufficiently developed, are stretched over a common, fixed bridge at the right end of the instrument (on the left in fig. 18); each then passes over an individual movable bridge on the soundboard and is attached to a tuning peg at the player's left. The player plucks with the fingers of the right hand between the movable and fixed bridges, while the left hand presses the portion of the string to the left of the movable bridge, providing vibrato, glissando, and pitches not in the gamut of open strings. Brilliant arpeggios are easily produced by stroking the fingers across the strings quickly, often using both right and left hands for water-fall-like effects.

Each string of the cheng is tuned to one pitch of the chosen scale—almost always a pentatonic mode of the slendro type (but traditionally in a Pythagorean tuning featuring pure 3:2 fifths). Rough tuning of each string is done with the tuning pegs, fine tuning by small adjustments of the movable bridges. For a composer interested in intonation systems, the cheng is a godsend—a veritable garland of potential tunings, sixteen individually adjustable "monochords" on a single body. Its strings are harder to keep in precise tune than the fixed slabs of a gamelan but much easier to work with than an instrument such as the violin, where all pitches except the four open strings must be realized by eye-hand-ear coordination.

Long zithers of the cheng type are found in all East Asian cultures: the Vietnamese *dan tranh* (also known as *dan thap-luc*), somewhat smaller than the Chinese instrument but otherwise nearly identical in structure and playing technique; the Japanese *koto*, larger than the cheng, with silk or nylon strings and a highly developed repertory and playing technique; and the Korean *kayagùm*, also generally larger than the cheng, and with silk strings. Clearly all these instruments belong to one large family, although their musics and playing techniques diverged many centuries ago. Liang Tsai-Ping has pioneered in bringing together zither players from many countries for festivals, scholarly discussions, and recordings. Lou often uses "psaltery" as a generic term and in some compositions does not specify which culture's version should be played (or indeed, whether an Asian instrument rather than a homemade one is required).

Basic instrumental technique on the cheng is not particularly difficult to acquire, and using only records and an instruction book Lou was able to find his way around the instrument with considerable facility. Even before visiting Liang in Taiwan, he had composed his first work for the instrument, the *Psalter Sonato* (dedicated to Liang), which he completed and performed after his first trip to Asia in 1961 and revised the following year after studies in Taiwan. ("You know what I do. I plunge in, play the first four pieces, and then start writing for it immediately.")[15] In this short work Lou unites the binary form of Domenico Scarlatti (which he had already explored in his *Six Cembalo Sonatas* of 1934–43), with the idiosyncratic instrumental techniques of the cheng. The work is easily playable by a traditional Chinese performer, except perhaps for Lou's specification of a Just Intonation pentatonic scale with an added sharp-7. The freely spun melody is basically Chinese in character, with a few stylistic irregularities, but shows touches of Lou's personality, particularly in the repeated melodicle making up the cadential figure of the A section and its return at the end of the B section as well (example 7-1).

Lou premiered the *Psalter Sonato* at the Sticky Wicket shortly after his first trip to Asia (November 12, 1961), and repeated it in concert at the University of Hawaii's Festival of Music and Art of This Century on May 21, 1963. His program notes for the Hawaii performance summarize its history concisely: "Resulting from many, many hours of beginner's study directly upon the strings of an East Asian psaltery, this tiny piece has been described unanimously by major Korean, Chinese, and Vietnamese musicians as 'very Chinese.' Well, of course! I wrote it for Liang Tsai Ping—perhaps China's greatest Cheng virtuoso. Still, I think of it as a straight, plain Scarlatti sonata."

Lou wrote two other pieces for cheng solo, *The Garden at One and a Quarter Moons*, and the *Wesak Sonata*. The first, dedicated to Robert Hughes, is formally less transparent than the *Psalter Sonato*; it is a series of phrases of varied length, each of which begins with the same gesture but develops differently. This style of rhetorical anaphora is found in much Chinese chamber music, allowing unity and variety within the context of a continuously developing melodic line. Harrison's performance of the work may be heard on the accompanying CD, band 13.

The *Wesak Sonata* (1964) was privately published in Lou's elegant calligraphy, and although it was played once by Margaret Fabrizio in a 1964 San Francisco concert,[16] Lou knows of no other performances. "I could play it when I was writing it," he says,

EXAMPLE 7-1. *Psalter Sonato* (1961, rev. 1962), section A. (Courtesy of Hermes Beard Press.)

(The symbol ○⌐ indicates a series of tones following a single pluck, created by pressing the string on the left side of the movable bridge.)

but I'm one of those people who can do it at the time, but can't revive it. Wesak is the celebration of the Buddha's birthday. I occasionally attended the Buddhist temple in Watsonville—we'd go to the Obon festivals, other celebrations, and regular services. I love the Obon festival system in summer. All the temples in Central California arrange their calendars so that you can go to a different one each weekend practically all summer long: Monterey, Palo Alto, Watsonville. I like that: systematic festing.[17]

In two contrasting movements (marked Grave and Allegro), the *Wesak Sonata* is both the most ambitious and the least "Chinese" of Lou's solo cheng works. Beginning with an atypical mode, specifying the sequence 1-2-4-5-♭7, the work mixes standard cheng finger techniques such as arpeggiated glissandi, ornaments made by pressing after plucking a string, alternating octaves, and others, with unusual formal structures, tempo shifts, and (particularly in the second movement) many phrases effectively in 3/8, alternating with 2/8 or 2/4. In the second movement, the prominent use of a figuration in which high pitch 1 alternates with lower melodic pitches as a kind of drone simulates the *jhālā* texture of Indian music, not out of place given the work's Buddhist referent, but not a commonly occurring melodic style in Chinese music.

Perhaps because of, rather than in spite of, these anomalies, the *Wesak Sonata* is the most musically interesting of the cheng solo works; since it relies heavily on finger techniques unique to the cheng, however, it is not easily transferable to harp or guitar, so it will have to await an enterprising psaltery player to add it to the repertory.

Psalteries are called for in several other works as well, sometimes interchangeably with harp or tack-piano, sometimes clearly a Korean instrument, sometimes Chinese. For example, *Pacifika Rondo* (1963) includes two movements scored for cheng and kayagùm, though the kayagùm part may be performed on the harp. Asian settings are specifically invoked by psalteries in *Music for Violin with Various Instruments, European, Asian, and African* (1967) and *Scenes from Cavafy* (1980), while the instrument is employed in *At the Tomb of Charles Ives* (1963) more for its flexibility in tuning to the complex requirements of Free Style intonation than for its Asian character. The psalteries specified in *Moogunkwha* (properly Mugunghwa; 1962; Korean) and *Homage to Pacifica* (1991; Javanese) are specific to those cultures.[18]

Though Lou spent only twenty days in Taiwan with Liang Tsai-Ping, he crystallized there a long-term love affair with Chinese music: "I love the sound of Chinese chamber music. I think it's exquisite, delicate, poetic. Korean music gives me a visceral experience, Chinese an imaginative and intellectual adventure and a search for ancient treasure, as in the Chinese saying 'searching amongst the dust for ancient things.' "[19]

While it is not particularly unusual for a Western composer to learn about non-Western traditions in order to access new sources of inspiration, Lou went several steps further. He was so enthused about the cheng and its music when he returned from Taiwan that he sought out potential students. Violinist Richard Dee recalls:

> He wanted me to play the cheng. I said, "Well, OK, if you can teach me." I didn't know Chinese music, but I immediately took to the cheng, the first [Chinese] instrument I learned. Lou and I played concerts at the famous Nepenthe resort hotel at Big Sur, quite a place in those days. They'd have offerings and we'd get money and a free dinner. After he taught me to play a few pieces, Lou said, "Why don't you write some music? I'll help you write some pieces for the cheng." I didn't know harmony, but Lou said, "You don't have to know harmony." So I made a little suite of pieces and we began to perform them, just Lou and I.[20]

In the early 1960s, then, Lou began to perform Chinese music regularly, forming a chamber group of friends and students and giving frequent concerts. Richard Dee's cheng piece, *The Willows*, was often included, as well as Lou's own *Psalter Sonato*. Later, Bill Colvig and Lily Chin joined the ensemble, and the instrumentation expanded:

> I gave Lily Chin, who'd just come from Beijing, cheng lessons and she became brilliant. She had studied Western opera and had a voice, and in our concerts she sang light songs for the children, nothing very fancy. She went on to teach at West Valley College, where she had twenty pupils in cheng almost every semester. Then she, with Richard Dee and Bill, did over three hundred concerts in the public schools.

Dee was my TA in World Music at San Jose State University and is still teaching there. He sort of memorized my course. He learned cheng from me and composed several pieces; in fact, I orchestrated a suite of his cheng pieces for the Santa Cruz Symphony. He was a violinist and played erh-hu very well. He was good enough to play several pieces by the eminent composer Liu T'ien-hua at our concerts. But there were things he drew the line at: he would not learn woodwinds.

Neither would Bill, except for the sheng and the *hsün*. So I was stuck with blowing the *hsiao* and the *ti-tzu* through most of our concerts.[21]

When Liang Tsai-Ping's son, Liang Ming-yüeh (a/k/a David M. Y. Liang), came to the United States for graduate study in ethnomusicology, Lou maintained a close relationship with him, and both Harrison and Colvig learned additional compositions and instruments. Lou learned transverse (ti-tzu) and end-blown (hsiao) flutes as well as Ming-yüeh's invention or re-creation of the bowed psaltery (*ya-cheng* or *ming-cheng* in Chinese, *ajaeng* in Korean), while Bill became an expert on the mouth-organ (sheng), the panpipe (*p'ai-hsiao*), and the globular flute (hsün; fig. 18). "I will never forget Bill's sheng studies with Ming-yüeh. He suddenly asked, 'What happens if I lose or break a reed?' Ming-yüeh replied, 'first you buy some bronze.'"[22]

Bill would typically play sheng and hsün solos during a concert; his rendition of the classic ch'in composition "Parting at Yang Kuan" on the hsün, which he learned from studies with Liang Ming-yüeh,[23] was particularly effective and haunting. As Richard Dee notes,

In those days it was pretty far-out for anyone to play Chinese music who wasn't Chinese. Of course that was the message: you didn't have to be a "native." You can learn to play anything if you break through the cultural armor. Lily, Bill, and I [and occasionally Lou as well] started playing Young Audience concerts. We played about eight years at every imaginable school system. We even went to NYU, and SUNY Buffalo under Peter Yates [1972; chapter 3]. It gave Bill independence, too; he sometimes gets overwhelmed by Lou.[24]

When Lou joined the ensemble, he usually acted as narrator. As he began to write more compositions using Asian instruments, he would include them in these concerts. For example, after a first half featuring Chinese music, the second half might consist of arrangements of tunes from *Young Caesar* for whatever instruments the hardy band could muster. Another element that found its way into these concerts was Chinese poetry. While Lou and Bill improvised Chinese-sounding phrases on various quiet instruments, Richard Dee would declaim the poems in a dramatically convincing style. (He also joined Lou in narrating *Marriage at the Eiffel Tower* during this period, perhaps the best performance of this work.) Soon poet Kenneth Rexroth asked to join them, reading his own translations of the texts accompanied by their improvisations on several occasions, notably at the Ojai Festival in Santa Barbara, the Mark Taper Forum in Los Angeles, and the Cabrillo Music Festival in 1971–72. While Dee was probably a better reader,

"Kenneth was fun to work with. He loved to gossip. He would tell us how he lunched in Washington and which perfume J. Edgar Hoover was wearing that day."[25]

Lou also began teaching a course on world music at San Jose State University. According to Richard Dee: "Lou was hired to teach composition, but the main thing he taught was world cultures. He claimed he took the idea from Henry Cowell's course 'Music of the World's People.' We were like Laurel and Hardy; the students got a kick out of it. Lou paid me, of course; he'd never let you do anything free. He knew what it was like not to get paid."[26]

According to former students, and judging from surviving tapes of a few lectures at San Jose State, Lou was an energetic, inspiring lecturer. His obvious love and enthusiasm for the music was infectious, and students knew that despite the professor's formidable intellect there was nothing stuffy or academic about his approach to world music. Unlike many ethnomusicologists, who approach their subject through history, theory, instruments, genres, and so on, Lou kept his tiger-eye on the music itself and made it something living, breathing, and singing.

Harrison's most recent venture into cross-cultural syntheses is a concerto for *p'i-p'a* (Chinese lute) accompanied by string orchestra, commissioned by Lincoln Center for the virtuoso Wu Man and the Stuttgart Chamber Orchestra under Dennis Russell Davies and premiered in April 1997. The concerto is a big work in four substantial movements: Allegro moderato, Bits and Pieces (a small suite: Troika; Three Sharing; Wind and Plum, an Elegy for Liu Tien Hua; and Neapolitan), Threnody to the Memory of Richard Locke, and Estampie—all newly composed, with no recycling of earlier material. In the one overtly "Chinese" movement, "Wind and Plum," Harrison portrays a Chinese landscape, evoking the remembrance of one of Liu Tien Hua's compositions for erh-hu, which Richard Dee had played in their Chinese concert series.[27] Lou studied p'i-p'a technique sufficiently to write virtuoso passages for the instrument, but except for a few idiosyncratic phrases here and there, he does not attempt to imitate Chinese compositional styles or models.

Japan

With the exception of the Japanese court music tradition of gagaku, included in the scope of *Pacifika Rondo*, Lou feels less affinity for Japanese traditional music than for that of China and Korea, primarily because of the relatively four-square rhythmic quality of the most common styles of koto and related chamber music.

In 1992, however, he wrote an unusual work, the *Suite for Four Haisho*. The *haisho* is the Japanese version of the panpipe (p'ai-hsiao in Chinese).

Though it was formerly used in court ritual music, it exists today only in parts of two instruments preserved in the Imperial Repository, the Shosoin. Thanks to the work of several generations of musicologists and organologists, many of the ancient instruments dating back to the sixth century A.D. preserved in the Shosoin—in varying states of disrepair—have been studied and "reconstructed."

As part of the large-scale effort to create historically accurate replicas of these precious fragments of antiquity, composers have been commissioned to create new works for the old instruments, not necessarily in archaic style. This project, known as *reigaku*, has attracted many contemporary composers; Lou was asked to write a piece for the retirement of Toshiro Kido, director for ancient instrument conservation and reconstruction. Since there is no extant traditional performance practice for the haisho, Lou essentially created an imaginary tradition, with some elements of old Confucian ritual music in mind.

Lou's most recent foray into things Japanese is *Suite for Sangen*, a piece for *shamisen* (a three-stringed, long-necked, unfretted lute), commissioned by the Japanese performer Akiko Nishigata and completed in 1996. In this medium-scale four-movement work, Lou does not attempt to imitate traditional Japanese forms or style. Some traditional flavors occasionally emerge through the characteristic sounds of the shamisen, which include the percussive tone of the large plectrum striking the skin head, the sympathetic buzzing of the highest string (*sawari*), and the implied drone of the open lower strings—characteristics that have analogs in Lou's compositional style and that he thus exploits. So it is not surprising to find extended drones (in the Adagio) and jhālā figurations (Prelude) among the techniques employed. The second movement is a tightly written estampie, with seven sections and complex motivic interrelationships; that this movement has some structural affinity to the Japanese *danmono* (sectional) form may just be a happy accident.

Pacifika Rondo: An Integration of Asian and Western Musics

Lou's largest and most important composition from the period following his trips to Japan, Korea, and Taiwan is *Pacifika Rondo*, written for the University of Hawaii's Festival of Music and Art of This Century which took place in May 1963. Though the festival's name consciously avoided reference to matters cross-cultural, this element was an essential motivating force throughout the many years of its existence. Cosponsored by the university's music department and the federally funded East-West Center, the festival served for several decades as a venue where leading composers from Asia and the United States could get to know each other and experiment (should they so desire) with cultural fusions. Each year, two composers were invited to spend one or two months in residence at the East-West Center, lecturing, participating in panel discussions, and most significant, composing new works for performance at the festival, crowning their residency. In 1963, the resident composers were Lucretia R. Kasilag (Philippines) and Lou Harrison. (Nicknames are common among Filipinos, and Professor Kasilag is fondly known as "King." Lou recounts that "when I met Lucretia Kasilag, and she said 'Call me King,' I very nearly responded, 'Call me Queen!'")[28] The festival has attracted notable guest composers over the years: for instance, John Cage and Toru Takemitsu in 1964, and Byongki Hwang (Korea), George Barati (United States), Gerardo Gandini (Argentina), and Burrill Phillips (United States) in 1965. Concert programs featured music not only by the guest composers but also by other contemporary Asian composers and students.

The availability of performers for many Asian instruments prompted Lou to create for *Pacifika Rondo* an orchestra perhaps as diverse as that for any work in his catalog (or, for that matter, in anyone's catalog). The score calls for organ, Western flute, piccolo, small fipple flutes, miguk p'iri, trombones, celesta, vibraphone, piano, strings, pak (Korean wooden clapper), snare drum, bass drum, *changgo* (Korean hourglass drum), *daiko* (Japanese barrel drum), elephant bells, triangles, maracas, gongs, jalataranga, cheng, sheng, kayagùm, and a male voice screaming. Only a few of the Asian instruments could be reasonably replaced with Western ones—for example, Robert Hughes's recording uses a harp instead of the kayagùm, and the lack of psaltery-specific techniques is immediately audible. Harrison could not possibly expect that such a variegated ensemble could be assembled for frequent performances of this work, yet his joy in exploring its timbral possibilities shines through the score, which remains one of his most serene and elegant large-scale compositions.

Harrison's program notes for the premiere performance give some insight into his procedures and frame of mind.

> Hawaii is very nearly central in the Pacific Basin, and I have conceived and titled this work with that in mind—for I have composed it especially for this festival, and in it I have thought, with love, around the circle of Pacifika. Indeed, the form itself is a large round, odd-numbered movements being variants of the same kind of music. Musical techniques and styles are reflected from Korean and Japanese Court Music, and Chinese chamber music; there is a light touch of Mexican, and of Spanish-colonial music, and one intrusion of common "Atlantic" modernism.
>
>   New "serial" techniques have been used in movements in which the listener is least likely to suspect them, and a new musical form was derived from the poetic rhyme-scheme "Terza Rima." I have been bold to try several of the ways in which I think classic Asian musics might of themselves, and together, evolve in the future, and have combined instruments of several ethnics directly for musical expressions. (I should add, perhaps, that Dolphins

are people, who have language, and who sensibly use their very large brains only to invent elaborate and good-natured games.)[29]

The odd-numbered movements that Harrison refers to as the "rondo" idea share a style and instrumentation that combines elements of Japanese gagaku (e.g., the sustained tone-clusters in the organ imitating the sound of the mouth-organ *sho*) and Korean aak (e.g., the melodic line in heterophonic variation between p'iri, trombone, and strings) as well as elements common to both, such as cyclic patterns in the percussion instruments. But the resulting music is something new, not a transcription or imitation of either style. By shifts of tempo, texture, and instrumentation, Harrison varies this basic sound to provide changing viewpoints around the Pacific Rim.

The first movement, for example, seems to re-create an image of magnificent Chinese T'ang court orchestras. The third movement moves from unison (heterophonic) texture to a canonic texture, the melodic instruments split into two groups in canon at the fifth, which may allude to the use of canonic technique in some parts of the Japanese gagaku repertory—though in that context it is usually three-part canons at the unison or octave. In the fifth movement the p'iri carries the main melody, with canonic imitation in the flute, while small fipple flutes add a wash of background improvisation (a textural device rare for Harrison). "All history is filled with clay flutes in Mexico," he explained, "so I simply distributed tin whistles, and everybody had notes to doodle on to give the impression of a celebratory passage."[30] The percussion parts are much more active here, and the addition of the maracas aid in making the "Aztec connection," while the overall sound retains its Asian flavor. The seventh movement returns to the style of the first, bringing the Rondo full circle.

The second and fourth movements are for small chamber groups. In the second, cheng and kayagùm are the main instruments, at first alternating, then joining together. Once their sound is established, the sheng is added, primarily for color, its melodic material following that of the psalteries. In the fourth movement, the cheng and kayagùm again start off as soli, in canon at the octave, which becomes an ostinato accompaniment to the main melodic duet, a playful combination of violin and jalataranga generally in rhythmic unison but at shifting intervals of thirds and fourths; the effect is frequently a violin solo line with a bell-like halo swirling around it. The sixth movement introduces the "intrusion of common 'Atlantic' modernism" that Lou mentions in his notes—an intentionally ugly outcry against the atomic bomb, tested on various Pacific atolls and America's western deserts, used in war only twice (at Hiroshima and Nagasaki) yet still polluting our air and water (chapter 9).

8 The Gamelan Ideal

Imagined, Imported, Invented

coauthored with Jonathon Grasse

For Lou Harrison, the gamelan tradition combines some of his most enduring interests: pitched percussion timbres; rhythmic, melodic, and contrapuntal complexity; extended yet tightly organized formal structures; a sensitivity toward subtle variations in intonation; and a communal approach to performance. By comparison to the avant-garde trends he had encountered during his formative years, gamelan music offered attractive alternatives—a definable modality, cyclic forms, and kinetic rhythm. Harrison states in no uncertain terms, "A good gamelan is the most beautiful musical ensemble on the planet."[1]

The origins of gamelan remain mysterious and multifarious, distributed among layers of tradition: from the animist religion of Indonesia's indigenous people, through successive waves of Asian and Near Eastern immigrants, to modern European colonizers. Ascending the eighth-century Buddhist temple of Borobudur near Yogyakarta[2]—the most important early monument depicting musical activities—one passes timeless images of musicians, dancers, and singers worked into dozens of stone relief sculptures. The sounds that actually emanated from the spike fiddles, transverse flutes, and double-headed barrel drums depicted here cannot be known, yet they provide pictorial evidence of ensemble contexts in which gamelan presumably developed.

Borobudur is a monument not only to Indian-born Buddhist cosmology and architecture but also to the Hindu-Buddhist culture of Central Java, which predates the temple's construction by at least four centuries. The development of gamelan traditions may also reflect the influences of Chinese, Malay, and Arab groups, each of whom introduced new religious practices.[3] The most enduring of these is the mystic Sufism of Islam, which first appeared in the fifteenth century and blended with local culture. Today Indonesia is largely an Islamic state, though Hindu culture and religion are dominant in Bali.

European influences arose from trade with the Portuguese in the sixteenth century followed in the early 1700s by competition and eventual colonial occupation by the Dutch. Further sociopolitical developments led to the mid-eighteenth-century split of the old Javanese kingdom of Mataram into the courts of Surakarta (Solo) and Yogyakarta, centers for the two primary traditions of Central Javanese performing arts.

Today the word *gamelan* describes a wide variety of ensemble types and musical styles particular to various parts of Indonesia. Perhaps the best-known of these are the musical traditions of (1) central Java; (2) western Java (Sunda); (3) north coastal Java (Cirebon); (4) eastern Java and the island of Madura; and (5) Bali. Although Harrison has written works for Sundanese, Cirebonese, and even Balinese ensembles, his primary interest is in Central Javanese gamelan. In our discussions, therefore, we use terms and concepts particular to Central Javanese practice.

Indonesians recognize gamelan as a high-prestige symbol of cultural achievement, leading to a focus on defining, representing, and preserving it as a national art form. Gamelan is at the center of the nation's performing arts conservatories and has brought out some of the best creative and scholarly efforts of Indonesian musicians and composers. As Sumarsam suggests:

> The presence of Dutch and American musicologists in Java in the twentieth century has kept Euro-American perspectives in view during the formulations of contemporary gamelan theory by Javanese musicologists. Moreover, since the middle of the century, opportunities have arisen for Javanese gamelan students to study ethnomusicology in Western countries. From the 1960s, gamelan theory has entered a new phase: the direct involvement of some Javanese musicians in formulating it. And in the 1970s, Javanese theorists often had the opportunity to exchange ideas and to work with their western counterparts.[4]

The impact of gamelan on composers such as Debussy, Messiaen, and Britten has been widely documented,[5] and its role in the development of minimalism may be heard in the works of composers such as Steve Reich. Composers James Tenney, Richard Felciano, and Pauline Oliveros have written works for gamelan that treat it as a set of pitched percussion instruments without reference to Indonesian aesthetics or formal structures. Others, such as Daniel Schmidt and Barbara Benary, though trained in traditional Javanese methods, have nevertheless pushed the limits of their ensembles by incorporating nontraditional and avant-garde techniques into their compositions.[6] Schmidt, for instance, has used minimalist processes and structured improvisation, tape-loop delay solos on the *rebab* (the two-string fiddle), through-composed linear development, and harmonic manipulations of sonorities creating sustained "chords."

Contemporary Indonesian composers have also championed the spirit of creative innovation by exploring traditional gamelan instruments as sources for new sounds or recontextualizing and juxtaposing traditional, pan-Indonesian musics. Experimentation with performance practice techniques (singing into overturned *bonang* kettles, for instance), extramusical sounds, electronic media, and newly incorporated or found instruments have all broadened the scope of gamelan music resources—sometimes challenging, expanding, or even ignoring traditional formal characteristics. As influential Sundanese composer Nano S has commented, "Even if I'm lucky enough to create something new or different, I'm really just continuing the music of my ancestors."[7]

Kreasi baru, a Javanese term for new compositions for gamelan, has its roots in the decades following Indonesian independence, when composers such as Pak Cokro, Ki Nartosabdho, and Koko Koswara ("Mang Koko") began incorporating nontraditional musical elements into their works, as summarized by Judith Becker:

> Certain aspects of their compositions indicate transition and change of a major order, not a slow, natural evolution, but a deliberate, quick turn toward a particular direction. Writing compositions in three-four meter is a basic change from the age-old structures divisible by two. The use of Western contrapuntal vocal techniques, particularly thematic development, are a substantive change. The emergence of the composer who orchestrates, conducts, and controls the total performance of a composition is a change which veers away dramatically from an oral tradition. Gamelan compositions that cannot be categorized within the traditional modal structures indicate an attempt to expand the expressive possibilities of the gamelan.[8]

Harrison has taken several approaches to composing for gamelan. He has written works in traditional Javanese forms and styles, though always with some personal elements. (In one work, *Lagu Socieseknum*, he even generated the underlying melodic structure and its ornamental realization from his social security number.) He has used Western compositional procedures and Western solo instruments in gamelan compositions and, conversely, has used Javanese procedures in compositions for Western instruments, such as the *Piano Concerto*, *Fourth Symphony*, and *Piano Trio* (chapter 11). Though Lou freely experiments with instrumental combinations and technical procedures, he remains relatively traditional in the area of gamelan performance practice. While in his Western compositions he may ask the pianist to strum on the strings or play tone clusters with fists or an octave bar, in his gamelan works he expects the instruments to be played according to their normal practice.

To this day Lou remains a student of the culture and music; at the same time, he is frequently acknowledged as the "father" of the American gamelan movement. He has encouraged others in the endeavor as well, his personal campaign having stimulated works by composers not otherwise known for writing in this genre, such as Alan Hovhaness and Virgil Thomson.

Lou's introduction to gamelan in the mid 1930s began with recordings owned by his housemate Dorothy James and by Henry Cowell, who had recently returned from studies in Berlin, where he had the opportunity for hands-on study with Indonesians visiting Erich von Hornbostel at the Berlin Phonogrammarchiv.[9] These experiences, coupled with the Balinese gamelan Harrison heard at the Golden Gate Exposition in 1939 and the Javanese dance that he saw at San Francisco's Curran Theater, planted the seeds of his future exploration of gamelan music. His seminal work with the percussion ensemble cemented his attraction to the rich sonic world offered by the Indonesian orchestra. During the 1940s and 1950s, Harrison carefully copied out examples from Colin McPhee's articles on Balinese music. "At least I had some little units of transcribed music," he recalls. "And I was fascinated."[10] By the time Bill Colvig began constructing Si Betty (the pair's first Central Javanese–style gamelan) in 1976, Lou had worked for decades with percussion instruments and had included sonic references to gamelan in many of his works for Western instruments.

Gamelan-inspired sounds first appeared in his works during the early 1950s. "Henry didn't explain any of the procedures of gamelan," Lou recalls. "It was the sound itself that attracted me. In New York, when I changed gears out of twelve tonalism, I explored this timbre. The gamelan movements in my *Suite for Violin, Piano, and Small Orchestra* [1951] are aural imitations of the generalized sounds of gamelan."[11]

Lou's studies of intonation led him not only to ancient Greece but also to the tuning practices of Indonesia and ultimately to experiments in crossing traditional gamelan techniques with Just Intonation. His first foray in this area was the *Concerto in Slendro* (1961), which requires retuning the celesta and tack-piano to an Indonesian-inspired pentatonic mode. The homemade percussion ensemble Old Granddad, loosely resembling the Indonesian ensemble, and the more traditional gamelan he and Bill later constructed for San Jose State and Mills all use pure intervals (chapter 5).

In the mid-1970s, Lou not only learned traditional Central Javanese performance techniques from Pak Cokro and others but also studied Sundanese style with Undang Sumarna, who has been teaching at the University of California, Santa Cruz, since 1976. Pak Sumarna added a tradition of West Javanese music (highly unusual in U.S. universities) to the burgeoning number of Central Javanese gamelan ensembles forming throughout the San Francisco region. Sumarna provided Harrison with a collection of some forty traditional Sundanese works and taught him instrumental patterns that included those for suling (vertical flute). Lou transcribed over thirty pieces from this repertoire. Immediately following these studies, he composed three works for Sundanese gamelan with solo instruments: *Main Bersama-sama* for French horn and gamelan, *Threnody for Carlos Chávez* for viola and gamelan, and the *Serenade for Betty Freeman and Franco Assetto* for suling and gamelan. *Main Bersama-sama* literally means "playing together," a motto for Lou's integration of West and East.

In New Zealand in 1983, Lou met the young Javanese *dhalang* (puppeteer/storyteller) Widiyanto, and worked with Allen Thomas's Cirebonese gamelan in Wellington. When he visited Java early the next year, he was also able to study Cirebonese style with Elang Yusuf Dendabrata[12] at the Kacirebonan Palace.

Meanwhile, a remarkable subculture of American gamelan had been brewing in the San Francisco region, one that would quickly spread to other regions in the United States and derive inspiration from Lou's life and his cross-cultural hybridization. This movement, in turn, set Lou on a unique course of creative discovery that has led to the composition of over fifty works for gamelan (CD, band 14).

Gamelan Instruments and the *Balungan*

The texture of gamelan music is an elaborate kind of heterophony or simultaneous variation, often called polyphonic stratification, with different instrumental types moving at various speeds to execute elaborations or abstractions of an ideal melody, the *balungan*, which may not actually be stated by any instrument of the ensemble. Unlike the surface melody of Western music, balungan is more hidden; as Jody Diamond suggests, what we often hear is the representation of "an inner melody that is referenced on the outside."[13] One way in which Lou's works differ from those of the traditional repertory is that, instead of approaching balungan as a framework whose notes may be so disguised that the listener does not even perceive them as a continuous melodic line, he treats it more like his Western melodies; that is, the balungan is closer to the surface of the gamelan texture.

The instruments of the ensemble may be divided into three general categories in terms of function: (1) colotomic instruments, which provide cyclic punctuating markers;[14] (2) slower-moving melodic instruments; and (3) elaborating instruments that add ornamentation and decoration. The drums provide cues and accents and act (along with the rebab) as a kind of aural conductor, controlling tempo and transitions between formal divisions. The Central Javanese repertory is thought to have been composed originally for two different ensembles, a loud gamelan and soft gamelan, which today have been combined into a single ensemble. In compositions for the loud gamelan, the elaborating (*panerusan*) instruments are omitted.

Melodic notes are arranged in groups of four, called *gatra*, and formed into phrases called *gongan*, which are marked by strokes on the largest gongs. Formal type in gamelan music is distinguished by the temporal relationship between the gatra and the punctuations of the colotomic instruments.

The main instruments of the Javanese gamelan are shown in line drawings in figure 19. The group of bar metallophones known as *saron* are sometimes called "balungan instruments" because their musical material is more closely related in temporal density to the skeletal melody than that of the other instrument families. The bars of the sarons (usually made of bronze, but occasionally of iron, and, in Lou's case, aluminum) are fixed over wooden trough resonators and struck with a single mallet. In Gamelan Si Betty, Lou and Bill extended the range of the balungan instruments, many of which are traditionally a single octave. To gain compositional flexibility, he and Bill built instruments with a compass of two full octaves instead.[15]

The *slenthem*, a larger instrument with tube resonators and a lower range, is the slowest moving of the balungan instruments and often plays the balungan itself.

A full gamelan will have pairs of each saron instrument. Two musicians often play on one part, either doubling each other or interlocking by alternating notes with rests, a technique called *imbal*. In addition to imbal in the saron and *peking*, Lou has been known to favor imbal in the *demung*, the lowest of the saron instruments.

The two court styles of Central Javanese gamelan, Yogyakarta (Yogya) and Surakarta (Solo), are characterized by aesthetic and sonic differences in the use of these balungan instruments: in Solo style they are generally played more softly and sparsely, while in Yogya style they are comparatively louder and sound more prominently in the texture, resulting in a more clearly defined melodic stratum. Lou's affinity for Yogyanese style is reflected (among other traits) in his sometimes aggressive, melodically independent balungan and clearly delineated orchestration, as demonstrated, for instance, in his attraction to strong imbal (interlock) in the saron instruments. At the same time, his training from Pak Cokro was syncretic. Intermarriage among Pak Cokro's Yogyanese and Solonese ancestors resulted in a mixed gamelan style, which he passed on to his students.

Sets of hanging bossed gongs (*kempul, gong suwukan,* and the largest one, *gong ageng*) provide colotomic underpinning for the ensemble, delineating the gongan and its primary divisions. The *kenong,* a set of large horizontal gong kettles, mark subdivisions of the gongan, emphasizing both pitch content (at times doubling the balungan tone) and gatra organization. Remaining structural points within the gatra are often signaled by the smaller horizontal gongs, *kethuk* and *kempyang*. While Lou frequently observes the traditional placement and function of gong strokes, he also enjoys at times dislocating and recombining these colotomic parts in nontraditional ways. Building on his approach to the percussion ensemble, for which he would carefully select a balance of instruments to represent various ranges and timbres, Lou "took a kind of census [of the] measuring-off instruments" when he began writing for gamelan, arranging them in a scale from "the most powerful and weighty up to the lightest. Then I used them in a rather traditional sense in which one weights the notes to achieve a particular tone color."[16]

Elaborating instruments (panerusan), responsible for ornamented melodic patterns, include both small gong kettles and keyed instruments. In the first class are two sets of small bossed gongs, the *bonang barung* and the *bonang panerus*, placed horizontally in double rows resting on cords within a wooden frame. They are played with two beaters and require significantly more skill than the saron instruments. Keyed panerusan instruments include the *gambang*, a xylophone with a broad trough resonator, and the *gendèr barung* and *gendèr panerus*—mellow-voiced metallophones with bamboo tube resonators. The *gendèr*, which like the bonang and the gambang is played with two mallets, contributes intricate contrapuntal patterns (two relatively distinct lines including oblique and contrary motion).

Since Solo and Yogya gendèr parts are typically virtuosic, Lou rarely had access to performers capable of playing in this style. Cirebonese gendèr parts, on the other hand, are much more straightforward, and he uses them often, thus adding yet another level of syncretism to his gamelan works.

Other panerusan instruments include the suling, a vertical bamboo flute, and the celempung, a plucked box zither, both of which Lou has studied and included in his works. As a former recorder player, he is especially attracted to the suling, which he has played both in concert and on recordings—for instance, in the *Serenade for Betty Freeman and Franco Assetto*.

The bowed rebab, a two-string spike fiddle, is sometimes known as the "prince" of the ensemble, guiding the direction of the melodic structure and relaying cues to the "minister," the *kendang*, a pair of two-headed drums played by a single performer. The leadership role of these two instruments within the ensemble demands performers of considerable skill and vast knowledge of the repertory. The performance cues given by kendang or rebab players—which are aural rather than visual—are part of a complex communication network among the members of the gamelan, an ensemble with no visually oriented conductor.[17] Though Lou has played kendang informally, he does not typically notate drum parts, allowing them instead to be realized by a musician trained in classical practice. Nor does he always require a rebab (which in any case is usually found only in soft-style pieces). While he welcomes elaborations devised by experienced performers, Harrison typically also provides verbal instructions or notational directives to guide the work's realization.

Gamelan performance may also include female and male vocalists, known as *pesindhèn* and *gèrong*, respectively. Lou's works reflect this aesthetic by frequently including vocal parts, either choral and solo: e.g., *La Koro Sutro* (large mixed chorus), *Scenes from Cavafy* (baritone and male chorus), and *Homage to Pacifica* (mixed chorus and soloist). For several of his gamelan works, such as *Ketawang Wellington* or *Gending in Honor of Aphrodite*, he supplied his own texts and carefully constructed solo vocal melodies. In the opening movement of *Homage to Pacifica*, Harrison allowed Jody Diamond to develop her own pesindhèn part;[18] and for *Gending in Honor of the Poet Virgil* he authorized director Trish Nielsen to add such a part using a text by Alfred Lord Tennyson (CD, band 14).

Over the years a host of San Francisco Bay Area gamelan enthusiasts have been key participants in the realization of Harrison's works. In addition to Daniel Schmidt and Jody Diamond, several have contributed their expertise in bringing traditional performance practices to bear on his compositions. Larry Polansky, for example, studied gendèr in Java in part to provide his American composer friends of new gamelan music with this panerusan texture. Polansky formulated appropriate elaborations for Harrison's *Aphrodite* and other works with the assistance of Javanese teachers.[19] Trish Nielson, longtime director of Si Betty at San Jose State University and of the first radio gamelan in the United States (*Kyai Tatit Ratri*), organized concerts and worked out performance versions of Lou's compositions. Daniel Kelley and Gino Robair provided kendang parts. Carter Scholz brought his study of gambang and bonang to Lou's ensembles, and ethnomusicologist Henry Spiller has played not only the gendèr and gambang but also the harp, an instrument Lou has frequently added to his gamelan not in the role of soloist but rather as a member of the ensemble. Harrison enthusiastically acknowledges these collaborative roles.

Tuning the Gamelan

A complete gamelan features two sets of fixed-pitch metallophones, one in slendro and the other in pelog, although the precise sizes of the intervals may vary from one gamelan to the next. Of the thousands of Indonesian gamelan, many with unique tunings, few would be considered "wrong" or "out-of-tune." Instead, they exemplify a musical culture that appreciates subtle differences of intonation. One of the main attractions of Javanese musical culture for Lou was its acceptance of intonational variation.

When Harrison and Colvig built their own gamelan ensembles for San Jose State and Mills, they had to make choices between many possible slendro and pelog tunings and to grapple as well with the complex vibration patterns of metallophones, which produce a rich array of inharmonic over-

tones. For their eventual solution, they sought a tuning acceptable to Javanese experts.[20]

The choice of metal was crucial as well. Lou and Bill chose aluminum,
both for its affordability and its intonational stability: "Pak Cokro . . . said
that aluminum is the best metal after bronze. . . . In many parts of the world
aluminum is still semi-precious. We are lucky that it is yet a scrap metal in
the United States. . . . [And] in slab form aluminum seems not to change
pitch, once tuned. It is a sturdy, stable metal."[21]

Inclusion of Western instruments such as violin, French horn, and piano
into his gamelan repertoire have posed additional tuning problems, requiring the Western musician to make intonation adjustments to match the
pitches of the particular accompanying ensemble.

Musical Form

The first works Lou wrote for traditional gamelan, *Bubaran Robert*, *Gending
Samuel*, and *Gending Pak Cokro*, were inspired by the Central Javanese
gamelan Kyai Hudan Mas (literally, "Venerable Golden Rain"). This famous
set of instruments was transplanted from Central Java to the West Coast of
the United States in the early 1970s by the American Society for Eastern
Arts. It was first loaned to the California Institute of the Arts in Valencia,
where Pak Cokro was teaching, and later brought to the Center for World
Music in Berkeley (chapter 3).

Bubaran, like *ladrang*, *ketawang*, and *lancaran* (terms frequently found in
Lou's gamelan works), is a distinct musical form defined by the length of the
gongan, the colotomic structure, and the drumming pattern. The term *gendhing*, on the other hand, may mean any gamelan composition (or, more
specifically, a piece with two sections—*merong* and *inggah*); *Gending Pak
Chokro* and *Gending Samuel*, however, both incorporate traditional Javanese
forms. In the former, Lou "preceded a central piece by a type of lancaran
and ended with another lancaran."[22]

> There was a period in my life when I tended to write formal Javanese forms:
> lancaran, ketawang, and ladrang as well as an occasional gendhing in a reg-
> ular form, that is to say, with from four to seven or eight gatra per line in the
> A section [merong] followed by a B section [inggah] which the players could
> elaborate in the traditional style. More recently I've been writing a combi-
> nation. My colotomy still tends to be more formal in terms of segregating the
> instruments, but their placement (though reflecting on traditional practice) is
> nevertheless untraditional.[23]

Lou has been most attracted to the shortest and least complex forms of traditional gamelan music because their comparatively fast tempi permit fore-
grounding of the melody in a way that is uncharacteristic of much gamelan

music in larger forms. Even when he uses traditional forms, he injects them with a personal flavor. An example is the opening lancaran from *Gending Pak Chokro*, discussed below.

The lancaran, a fast-paced form, contains sixteen balungan beats (four gatra) in each gongan, and anywhere from one to three or more gongan. (Forms are cyclic; sections may repeat many times at the discretion of the performers before the piece ends or continues to a new section.) The two possible types of lancaran—*lamba* and *dados*—are given in example 8-1,[24] along with the first gongan of Lou's *A Cornish Lancaran* (1986), all shown in cipher notation, a contemporary method of notating pitch used in both Indonesia and the West. In this system, the five pitches of the slendro scale are represented by the numbers 1 2 3 5 6, the seven pelog tones by 1 2 3 4 5 6 7. (Although there are seven pitches in pelog, not all are regularly used.) Rests are indicated by dots, and notes in parentheses coincide with strokes on the gong. Since the exact pitches vary from one piece to the next, zeros replace pitch numbers in the model forms shown in example 8-1. Note that the placement of the punctuating instruments is identical in both types of lancaran, but in lamba style, each balungan note alternates with a rest, in contrast to dados, in which a balungan note is played on every beat of the four-note gatra. As the example shows, *A Cornish Lancaran* is in lamba style.

EXAMPLE 8-1. The two types of lancaran and an excerpt from Harrison's *Cornish Lancaran*

+ = kethuk (small horizontal gong)
N = kenong (large horizontal gong)
P = kempul (small hanging gong)
( ) = gong (ageng or suwukan)

lancaran lamba

punctuating instruments	+ · + N	+ P + N	+ P + N	+ P + N
balungan notes	· 0 · 0	· 0 · 0	· 0 · 0	· 0 · (0)

lancaran dados

punctuating instruments	+ · + N	+ P + N	+ P + N	+ P + N
balungan notes	0 0 0 0	0 0 0 0	0 0 0 0	0 0 0 (0)

A Cornish Lancaran

balungan notes	· 5 · 7	· 5 · 7	· 5 · 7	· 5 · (4)

Among the other Javanese forms found most often in Lou's gamelan pieces, the ketawang is most like the lancaran in having sixteen beats per gongan, but the pattern in the punctuating instruments is entirely different. The ladrang, in Neil Sorrell's words, is "rather like a double ketawang,"[25] with the gong stroke occurring after eight gatra (thirty-two beats) rather than four.

In the shorter Javanese forms that Lou favors, the pitches of various gatra tend to be interrelated by sequencing, transposition, rotation, or other formal manipulation, while preserving the integrity of the four-note unit. Example 8-2 shows an excerpt from *Kebo Giro*, a traditional lancaran dados, in which the four notes of the gatra are treated as a unit that is subject to permutation.

EXAMPLE 8-2. The traditional Javanese lancaran, *Kebo Giro*, showing the interrelationship of pitches in the various gatra

punctuating instruments	+ · + N	+ P + N	+ P + N	+ P + G
balungan notes	6 5 3 2	3 2 6 (5)	6 5 3 2	3 2 6 (5)
	2 1 2 1	2 1 6 (5)	2 1 2 1	2 1 6 (5)
	1 6 3 2	3 2 6 (5)	1 6 3 2	3 2 6 (5)

(Gong suwukan is indicated by parentheses; gong ageng sounds on the final pitch of the line.)

The opening lancaran for *Gending Pak Chokro* (example 8-3) shows both Lou's debt to and deviation from the traditional Javanese lancaran form. This "type of a lancaran," as Lou puts it, retains characteristics of the traditional Javanese gendhing but at the same time shows a willful direction toward a personalization of that tradition.

EXAMPLE 8-3. The opening of Harrison's *Gending Pak Chokro* from *Music for Kyai Hudan Mas*

Colotomy	+ N + P	+ N + N	+ P + N/P	N + N/P N	+ N/P N N/P	N + P G
Balungan	2 3 2 1	2 3 2 3	2 1 2 5	3 2 5 3	2 5 3 5	3 2 5 (3)

The most obvious deviation is the addition of two extra gatra, resulting in a twenty-four-beat gongan in place of the normal sixteen beats. More important, however (and reflective of Harrison's individualized approach to the genre), is the novel, asymmetric colotomic structure, in which kempul (P) and kenong (N) sound *simultaneously*, thus adding weight to various notes of the melodic contour. (A similar technique is sometimes found in Javanese theatrical forms.) Lou's manipulation of gatra pitches also shows a Western rather than a Javanese orientation. Instead of whole gatras being transposed, sequenced, and otherwise formally manipulated as in the traditional piece, Lou's lancaran contains unusual groupings of pitches within and, idiosyncratically, across gatra—a procedure more akin to the transformations of melodic cells he learned from Henry Cowell than those in traditional Indonesian practice (see the discussion of "melodicles" in chapter 11).

This gongan contains only one gatra repetition (3 2 5 3)—a strategic one in both the Western and Javanese sense since it leads to the final gong, which is of cadential and structural importance. Otherwise, as shown in example 8-4, the groupings and their colotomic support create irregular patterns.

EXAMPLE 8-4. Demonstration of nontraditional procedures in opening of *Gending Pak Chokro*

+ N + P	+ N + N	+ P + N/P	N + N/P N	+ N/P N N/P	N + P G
2 3 2 1	2 3 2 3	2 1 2 5	3 2 5 3	2 5 3 5	3 2 5 3

The kempul (small hanging gong) emphasizes pitch 1 at the close of two 2-3-2-1 units. The first of these is a traditional gatra, but the second spans two gatra, a decidedly nontraditional procedure. Furthermore, the internal repetition of the pattern 3-2-1-2 provides a subtle syncopation, in both cases across adjacent gatra.

The combined kenong/kempul strokes (N/P), which create a distinct accent, add weight to pitch 5, three times within the pattern 5-3-2 and once with pitch 2 missing (5-3-2, 5-3-2, 5-3, 5-3-2). The metric positioning of these accents is irregular, stressing the fourth, third, second, and fourth notes of various gatra, not dissimilar to procedures found in Harrison's percussion music. The accent pattern also creates a momentary triple subdivision within the duple structure of the lancaran as well as a hint of syncopation.

Harrison's lyricism and his appropriation of balungan as a primary compositional element have resulted in similar deviations from traditional forms throughout his work. That is not to imply that Javanese models may not deviate from norms or reveal unique arrangements of balungan pitches; yet an important aesthetic aspect of gamelan music, as in many artistic sensibilities worldwide, is that of balance, the Javanese taste for *Padhang-ulihan* or, as Sorrell notes, roughly "question-answer" structures, suggesting that in certain clearly delineated gamelan forms gatra are to be arranged in an almost prosodic rhetoric of completion and repose. That Lou does not always observe this taste for balance makes his works distinctive. As in his non-gamelan music, his manipulation of melodic tension, expectation, and release plays a strong role in the compositional process.

In *Gending Paul* (for Paul Dresher), composed a year after *Gending Pak Chokro*, Lou tried a concept even further removed from tradition: five-beat gatra, an innovation that continues to confound panerusan players. Example 8-5 shows the opening of the work's B section, a twenty-four-beat gongan, in itself a nonstandard length, which Harrison subdivides into units of 5-5-5-5-4.

EXAMPLE 8-5. Excerpt from the B section of Harrison's *Gending Paul*

◯ = gong suwukan
other symbols: see Example 8-1

```
        +                              +
N   P N              N/P      N   P N/P      N   N              N
· 5 · 5  2      · 6  5  6  1      · 5 · 5  2      · 3  2  3  5      5  5  6  (5)
```

Players performing elaborating parts here face the unique challenge of forcing their knowledge of four-beat gatra patterns into a five-beat pattern.

Other gamelan works by Harrison are constructed along complex, overtly cross-cultural lines drawing from historical Western concepts, thus manifesting unique hybrid forms. In *Threnody for Carlos Chávez* (1978), for instance, Lou deliberately adapted the Medieval/Renaissance system of "prolations" to the gamelan. This metric organization, in which a given note type could contain either two (imperfect) or three (perfect) notes of the next faster time value, reminded him of the hierarchical but thoroughly duple structure of gamelan music. "I had never heard nor seen a [gamelan] piece in which every layer was triple. *Threnody for Carlos Chávez* is. The whole piece is divided into three, and each one of those units into three, and so on for eight layers. . . . I had discovered a conjunction between Javanese music and Medieval rhythmic modalities in the 'imperfect' system [that is, metric layers with entirely duple division], and so it occurred to me: why not try triple as well?"[26] The further Lou ventured from traditional Javanese musical form, the more he had to write out his elaborating parts for the players who were now reading cipher notation to create decidedly unfamiliar styles.

In addition to defining the *laras* (slendro or pelog), Lou also normally identifies the *pathet*, a complex concept that has generated controversy not only among Western ethnomusicologists but also among Indonesian theorists. The concept itself defies convenient musical definition or simple Western analogy (it literally means "constraint"). Within each laras there are three pathet, perhaps most conveniently defined here as "modes." Sorrell suggests a "melodic tonality,"[27] and Sumarsam a "gamelan modal process,"[28] defined not necessarily by the balungan but by the melodic realizations of the entire gamelan and each instrument's respective material based on the balungan. In his monumental essay on mode in the *New Grove Dictionary of Music and Musicians*, Harold S. Powers devotes six tightly spaced and tightly reasoned pages to discussing theories of pathet, and we shall not here attempt to summarize, second-guess, or enter the fray.

Nevertheless, pathet is to varying degrees manifest in every gamelan piece, highlighted by characteristic cadential patterns and colotomic structure, by hierarchical pitch relations, and by the elaboration patterns of the panerusan. In *wayang* (shadow puppet play) and large gendhing, there are specific sections known as *pathetan*: preludes, interludes, and postludes in which the panerusan instruments emphasize the pathet through their melodic material. The full title of a gendhing will typically denote laras and pathet, such as Lou's *Gending Hephaestus, laras Slendro, [pathet] Manyura* (1981).

In attempting to crack the mysteries of pathet, Lou's reliance on his intuitive musicality may have come up against an excessively hard nut, as Vincent McDermott relates regarding a 1984 encounter at the Arts University in Solo: "Some music of Lou's was played, a piece for which he had identified a pathet in the title. He said it was in manyura, one of the three pathet of slendro. During the question period afterwards, one of the most eminent of the people at that school at the time, Pak Martopangrawit, politely asked, 'Why did you say it's in that particular pathet?'"

Lou was silent for a moment. After nearly ten years of study, he had thought he understood the attributes of pathet manyura, but it now became clear that the concept was far more elusive than he had imagined. "Ignorance," he finally responded, "purely from ignorance." The problem was "politely passed over," recalls McDermott, "but it indicates that the subject of pathet is so complicated and so ultimately Javanese in its essence, that although Lou, with Pak Cokro's help, thought he had written a piece in manyura, an eminent Indonesian musician immediately wondered why it would be called so."[29] "That's the last time I ever specified a pathet in one of my pieces," Lou recalls.[30]

Garapan

An essential performance practice, both in Lou's gamelan music and in traditional Indonesian style, is the instrumentalist's derivation of elaborating parts from a given balungan, a process known as *garap* (literally, "to work out"). The most important *garapan* for the saron instruments are imbal techniques, the interlocking patterns in the parts of two players. The bonang has its own forms of elaboration, such as *sekaran* ("floral cadential phrase")[31] or *kembangan* (a form of imbal), *gembyang* (literally, "octaves"), and *mipil* (a style focusing on oscillation within pairs of notes).

In garapan processes such as mipil or gembyang, the performers on the bonang make choices within a restricted set of parameters. These choices are specifically determined by the pitches that appear at the ends of structural units such as the gatra, or by pairs of notes within the four-note group. Of the gatra's four beats, the second and the fourth are the strongest and determine the choice of patterns in the faster-moving instruments.

Given in example 8-6 are the first four gatra from Harrison's *A Cornish Lancaran*, with a typical gembyang embellishment in the bonang. Each bonang player performs two notes at once in octaves, the two parts creating an interlocking rhythm. (The lower octave of the bonang panerus is identical to the upper octave of the bonang barung so that the total range of the two sets of instruments is three octaves.) Players use their mallets to immediately dampen the notes they play in order to allow their partners' notes to be heard—easier said than done. In example 8-6, the bonang barung plays between the balungan pitches, while the bonang panerus produces a syncopation exploiting "on" and "off" balungan beat strokes.

EXAMPLE 8-6. First gongan (comprised of four gatra) from *A Cornish Lancaran*

Balungan		·	5	·	7	·	5	·	7	·	5	·	7	·	5	·	(4)

Bonang barung																
7	·	7	·	7	·	7	·	7	·	7	·	4	·	4	·
7	·	7	·	7	·	7	·	7	·	7	·	4	·	4	·

Bonang panerus																
·	7 7	7	7	·	7 7	7	7	·	7 7	7	7	·	4 4	4	4
·	7 7	7	7	·	7 7	7	7	·	7 7	7	7	·	4 4	4	4

(8ve above bonang barung)

The bonang anticipate structurally important pitches in the balungan: pitch 7, which marks the end of the first three gatra; and pitch 4, the last note of the fourth gatra as well as the gongan pitch. In this way, the last pitch of each structural unit is emphasized and anticipated in gembyang (octave) style.

The choice of elaboration style is directly related to changes in the speed of the balungan, called *irama*. There are five levels of irama, from the fastest, *irama lancar* (not numbered), to the slowest, *irama rangkep* (irama 4). In irama lancar, the fast tempo of the balungan requires a low density of elaborating pitches in the panerusan instruments. Slower movement of the balungan permits a greater number of embellishment pitches. Irama is not equivalent to tempo, and changes in balungan speed do not necessarily result in perceived changes in the tempo of the piece. As the balungan slows down, the panerusan and saron instruments typically counteract the slower underlying melody by increasing the number of notes per balungan beat. The listener may actually perceive this change as an acceleration of the ornamental parts rather than as a retardation of the melodic structure. A rough analogy in Western music might be to the relation of rhythmic densities in the fast and slow movements of a Beethoven sonata: the slow movement may have as many notes per second as the fast movement; we perceive it to be slower through the reduced pace of harmonic motion and through its character or mood.

Density ratios in the elaborating instruments double when progressing from one irama level to the next; bonang players, for instance, will perform twice as many notes per balungan pitch in level 2 as in level 1. The movement from one irama to another, signaled aurally by subtle tempo cues and deviations, is tricky, and the drummer, who guides the transition, holds great responsibility in keeping the ensemble from falling apart.

Mipil, the garapan based on oscillation within pairs of tones, is used by the bonangs for higher note-density passages—that is, "higher" irama. Irama dados, for example, requires a four-to-one ratio of notes in the bonang panerus part. Traditional stylistic modifications sometimes include more rhythmic freedom, rolled pitches, or even avoidance of the balungan tone on the beat. Example 8-7 shows a possible mipil bonang part for an excerpt from Harrison's "For Isna," from *A Soedjatmoko Set* (1989):

EXAMPLE 8-7. Sample mipil ornamentation excerpt from "For Isna"

Balungan	.	2	.	3	.	5	.	3
Bonang barung	· 2 3 2	· 2 3 2 3	· 5 2 5	· 5 3 5 3				
Bonang panerus	· 2 3 2 · 2 3 2 · 2 3 2 · 2 3 2 3	· 5 2 5 · 5 2 5 · 5 3 5 · 5 3 5 3						

Changes in irama require musicians trained not only in the particular composition but also in the general performance practice of garapan. Harrison's early works for gamelan do not include directions for irama levels. After several years of study, he began increasingly to incorporate distinctions of irama into his work, though any performance beyond irama 2 requires performers skilled on the panerusan instruments, which Lou often lacked.[32] As a result, he has frequently used a simplified notion of irama contrasting a brisk, louder sound with more subtle, slower, and lyrical moments featuring more extended melodic ideas. Harrison sometimes incorporates what he terms a "direct cut" into irama changes: the abrupt halving or doubling of a balungan rate at the end of a gongan. Lacking in his music is the highest (slowest) irama-level sound world, with its complex elaborations, super-slow balungan rate and three-minute gongan. The most common forms in Lou's gamelan works—lancaran, bubaran, and ketawang— do not require irama levels beyond 2, although he called for level 3 in *Gending Max Beckmann* (1984).

The term *cèngkok* describes longer embellishments that span one or more gatra, arriving periodically at unisons or octaves with specific "goal tones" in the balungan. Cèngkok is thus a more elaborate ornamental pattern than gembyang or mipil and is realized on instruments such as the gendèr barung and gendèr panerus. The term may derive from *cangkok*—"pruning, then planting a shrub," which evokes, as Sumarsam suggests, the "pruning" of a melody, a "process of musical delimitation which in fact prepares and fosters the new embellishing growth of each individual melodic performance."[33] Cèngkok is a process as much as a pattern: a melodic creation based on the balungan, on pathet, and on the mood of the piece.

Elaboration patterns such as mipil and cèngkok are essential elements of gamelan performance practice. Just as Lou allows performers of his cembalo sonatas to add characteristic embellishments on the repeats, so he invites the members of his gamelan to apply embellishment patterns characteristic of Javanese practice.

In his early days of writing for the gamelan, Harrison was not versed in the creation of ornamental parts of any type, whether in mipil, gembyang, or cèngkok styles. Jody Diamond recalls giving him a "how to" course, working out with him the bonang elaboration for *Bubaran Robert* shortly after the 1975 Berkeley summer course.[34]

In more recent times, he has begun to write out imaginative and creative parts for elaborating instruments as his gamelan compositions expand traditional garapan technique. Notating new elaborations, however, has also required him to coach his performers. Without specific notation or instruction to the contrary, his gamelan music should be realized according to traditional practice.

Particularly challenging to Lou's musicians are the types of divergent balungan shown earlier, which may alter the expected internal order and the phrase-length constraints of gatra or gongan. Balungan becomes in Lou's hands a finely wrought melody with distinct musical characteristics transcending traditional roles. As Virgil Thomson has stated, whatever techniques Lou absorbs and uses, the end product sounds distinctively his own.[35] Composer Vincent McDermott agrees: "Although Lou will use Javanese techniques for the instruments, the pieces come out sounding very much like Lou Harrison. . . . [He] is interested in going past what he considers some of the boundaries in Javanese music . . . for instance, by putting his chief melody directly into the balungan."[36]

Through his gamelan works Harrison completed his long-sought goal of uniting East and West both by introducing compositional processes of one culture into another and by physically combining sound-producing media from disparate musical ensembles. "It seemed perfectly natural to me," he remarks. "I don't think of it either as a problem or as a distinction. It's all part of making music as far as I'm concerned. There's no *they* and *me*."[37]

FIGURE 1. Lou's mother, Calline Lillian Silver (*left*), with her mother (Jesse Steele) and sister (Lounette) in front of their cabin in Skagway, Alaska, ca. 1898 (Courtesy of Lou Harrison; photographer unknown)

FIGURE 2. Silver Court Apartments, Portland. Photograph from the 1920s showing the front lobby (Courtesy of Lou Harrison; photographer unknown)

FIGURE 3. Lou as "Buster" in *Daddy Long Legs*, 1920 (Courtesy of Lou Harrison; photographer unknown)

FIGURE 4. Lou (*left*) and his brother Bill. Undated photographs ca. 1934 (Courtesy of Lou Harrison; photographer unknown)

FIGURE 5. Lou Harrison and John Cage, Cabrillo Music Festival, Aptos, California, 1977 (Photo by Betty Freeman; used by permission)

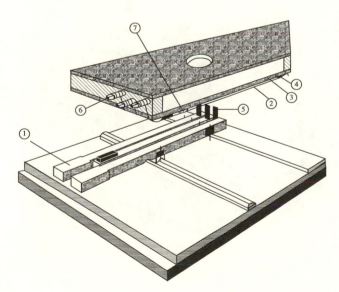

FIGURE 6. Cross section through Lou Harrison's second clavichord (completed 1953), showing representative keys and strings.

- 1: key
- 2: string
- 3: sounding board
- 4: bridge
- 5: tangent
- 6: tuning peg
- 7: hypothesized position of second bridge

(Line drawing by Alan K. Miller; used by permission)

FIGURE 7.
Virgil Thomson and
Lou Harrison,
Castroville,
California, 1979
(Photo by Betty
Freeman; used by
permission)

FIGURE 8. *Left:* Frank Wigglesworth, June 21, 1995. *Right:* Edward McGowan, November 6, 1995 (Photos by Fredric Lieberman)

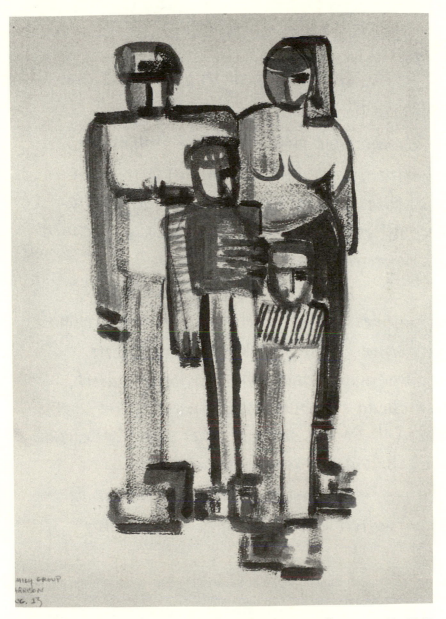

FIGURE 9. Painting by Lou Harrison, "Family Group," August 13, 1947
(Courtesy of Lou Harrison)

17 Oct. '63

Dear Fred,

Thanx for your kind letter. I am feeling a little better now & rushing to finish the Cage piece (which is simply an orchestration for full symphony orch. — the fun being in spreading a 9-tone toy piano piece all out over a large ork.) for a premiere in Monterey in spring.

I am delighted that you have an "impression of sinew-like tensile strength" from some of my melodies! I have felt the same way about some of them myself, but nobody else but you seems to have noticed! Do you suppose that some background in East Asian music is required?

You would greatly please me by a visit when you return! Can you give

FIGURE 10. One of many examples of Lou's calligraphy: a letter to Fred Lieberman, October 1963 (Courtesy of Lou Harrison)

FIGURE 11. Lou as a minnesinger, by Remy Charlip (1949). Illustration on a blank page in Harrison's copy of *The Minnesingers: Portraits from the Weingartner Manuscript*, immediately preceding Kaiser Haenrich (1165–97) (Used by permission of the artist)

FIGURE 12. "Old Granddad," Harrison and Colvig's first "American gamelan." *Upper right:* large metallophone with aluminum slab keys and stacked #10 tin cans as resonators, played by Harrison's archivist, Charles Hanson. *Upper left:* smaller metallophone with keys made of conduit tubing. *Bottom:* suspended cut-off oxygen tanks, portable organ, suspended garbage cans, ranch triangles (Photos taken in Harrison's garden by Fredric Lieberman, 1996)

FIGURE 13. *Waterfront—1934* (choreography by Carol Beals). From the souvenir program of the Dance Council of Northern California's second festival, Veterans' Auditorium, San Francisco, May 17, 1936 (Photographer unknown)

FIGURE 14. Jean Erdman in "Creature on a Journey" (Photo by Daniel Entin; used by permission)

FIGURE 15. Eva Soltes in "Ariadne" (Photo by Richard Blair; used by permission)

FIGURE 16. *Clockwise from upper left:* clock coils mounted in a guitar, which serves as a resonator; coffee-can metallophone; steel brake drums; two elephant bells; two ocarinas (globular flutes) (Photo by Fredric Lieberman)

FIGURE 17. *Clockwise from upper left:* 2 mbiras ("thumb pianos"); 2 ocarinas; a pak with 2 p'iris resting on it (the black p'iri is painted Lucite; the white one is wood); 2 p'iri reeds; 5 elephant bells in various sizes (Photo by Fredric Lieberman)

FIGURE 18. *Left to right:* Bill Colvig playing the sheng (Chinese free-reed mouth organ), Richard Dee playing the chin-han-tzu, Lou Harrison playing the ti-tzu (transverse flute). Foreground: a cheng. Undated photograph from the early 1970s (Photo by Vester Dick; used courtesy of Covello and Covello Photo-graphy, Santa Cruz)

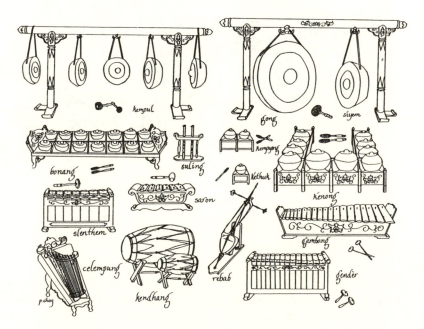

FIGURE 19. Line drawings of gamelan instruments by Peggy Choy (Used by permission)

9 Sounding Off

Music and Politics

When Lou Harrison was eighteen years old, he was already studying ancient Chinese writings on music, including the *Li Chi*, which prominently explores music's role in society. The most influential school of thought in early China, based on the political philosophy of Confucius (551–479 B.C.), held that the world—and human society—was quite literally composed by music: "Music rises from the human heart. When the emotions are touched, they are expressed in sounds, and when the sounds take definite forms, we have music. Therefore the music of a peaceful and prosperous country is quiet and joyous, and the government is orderly; the music of a country in turmoil shows dissatisfaction and anger, and the government is chaotic."[1]

Mastery of music was therefore considered an essential element in the education of anyone in public life. "From a study of the sounds, one comes to understand the tones; from a study of the tones one comes to understand music; and from the study of music, one comes to understand the principles of government and is thus fully prepared for being a ruler."[2] Thus, the politician could distinguish proper, enlightening, and safe music from that which was lewd, dissolute, and therefore dangerous in that it either led to or proclaimed political and social chaos.

Classic Greek philosophy, which Lou also studied avidly, articulated ideas remarkably similar to those of China. Plato, though denying any special theoretical expertise, devoted many pages to music and its role in human affairs: "All audible musical sound is given us for the sake of harmony, which has motions akin to the orbits in our soul, and which, as anyone who makes intelligent use of the arts knows, is not to be used . . . to give irrational pleasure, but as a heaven-sent ally in reducing to order and harmony any disharmony in the revolutions within us."[3]

An understanding of music was also considered by Plato to be requisite in a proper education for public life:

A well-educated man can both sing well and dance well. . . .

It is [in music] that error is at once most dangerous, as it encourages morally bad dispositions. . . . The Muses . . . would never commit the grave mistake of setting masculine language to an effeminate scale or tune, or wedding melody or postures worthy of free men with rhythms only fit for slaves and bondsmen, or taking the pose of a free man and combining it with an air or words of inappropriate rhythm.[4]

In our own time, popular culture has often portrayed the artist as divorced from the political arena, creating masterpieces to an individual taste, heedless of responsibility to anyone other than a personal Muse. Art created for some "ulterior" motive, whether political propaganda (the sanitized operas created by committee during China's Cultural Revolution, for example), in service of commercial interests (advertising jingles), or simply in a supporting, subservient role (film music), is often seen as either bad art or a sellout.

One major theory of art criticism (the New Criticism) holds that the work of art must be studied and understood on its own terms without reference to the biography and nonaesthetic ideas of its creator. But can we treat as artistically irrelevant the political convictions of composers such as Wagner (who was exiled for many years due to his leadership role in the Dresden revolution of 1848 and who wrote voluminous political tracts, including one that is virulently anti-Semitic); Mozart (whose mature operas do almost everything to incite revolt against tyrannical figures without actually coming out and saying so); or Verdi (who actually served in the Italian parliament and whose operas were at times so political as to excite the enthusiasm of the populace and the opprobrium of the government censors)? And should we really be surprised to learn that major artists felt comfortable supporting themselves by "day jobs" as chemists or doctors (Alexander Borodin, William Carlos Williams), or even successful insurance executives (Charles Ives, Wallace Stevens)?

The life and work of Lou Harrison reflects continuing interplay between his political ideas and his art. His composer's voice often is an extension of his political voice; and his political voice is an expression of his single-minded commitment to the preservation (and enjoyment) of life.

For Lou, societal stresses become personal stresses. While he attributes his New York breakdown to the noise and stress of the city, the war—and particularly the bombing of Hiroshima and Nagasaki—profoundly altered the course of his personal and compositional life. In the immediate wake of the bombings he found himself explaining to his circle of New York friends the extent of the potential destructiveness: during his year in Los Angeles he had read Lester del Rey's science fiction novella, *Nerves*, which described a nuclear near-disaster.[5] In the years since, he has repeatedly railed against the bomb—in his writings, in his speeches, and, most important, in his music. He divides his life into B.B. ("before bomb") and A.B. ("after bomb").[6]

Because he is unable to separate himself from the political arena, Lou has at times found his productivity directly affected by political and social upheavals. He was so upset by the 1991 Gulf War that he almost completely stopped composing for an extended period. Three years later, he was still searching for a way around his composition block. "After Bush's war in Kuwait," he told us,

> I refused a number of commissions, remunerative ones at that. I like to think of myself as writing for people who can't compose. The big works, such as the symphonies, are efforts to embody a viewpoint of the world. One doesn't assemble a large orchestra and a large audience without feeling that in some sense the composer is, if not representing, at least expressing some part of himself as the "general citizen." The composer becomes, in short, a kind of singer for others. But during this war, I no longer wanted to represent people—or even myself. It was torture.[7]

The period was indeed one of reduced output. Following a string of major works during the years 1986–90—*New Moon*, the *Mass for St. Cecilia's Day*, *A Cornish Lancaran*, the *Varied Trio*, the *Concerto for Piano with Javanese Gamelan*, *The Clays' Quintet*, *Philemon and Baukis*, *Ariadne*, *A Summerfield Set*, the revision of *Young Caesar*, the *Grand Duo*, the *Fourth Symphony*, and the *Piano Trio*—the war year saw only one major composition: *Homage to Pacifica*, a work expressing outrage at American imperialism.

During the following three years, Lou sought to regain his compositional voice by writing "only what I wanted when I wanted to." As he hoped, the strategy provided new energy and launched him into the present period of intense creativity in which he has returned to fulfilling commissions, among them *A Parade for M.T.T.*, *Rhymes with Silver*, *Suite for Sangen*, and the *Concerto for P'i-p'a with String Orchestra*.

Despite Lou's despair over U.S. military actions, he is fundamentally hopeful. "I'm a philosophical pessimist," he notes, "but a glandular optimist."

Harrison traces his political conscience to his home environment, particularly to the influence of his mother, who instilled in him a respect for divergent viewpoints and a curiosity about other cultures. He recalls the pride he felt in discovering that the home of the Silvers, his mother's ancestors from Salem, Ohio, had been a way station on the underground railroad in pre–Civil War days.[8] Historical documents support his claims: William Silver, Calline's great-grandfather, was among those active in sheltering runaway slaves during the period 1830–60, when Salem was one of the chief bases of the antislavery movement.[9]

During the 1930s, Lou chose to work with dancers whose choreographies focused on political themes: *Waterfront—1934* (labor), *Conquest* (Mexican resistance to Spanish colonization), *16 to 24* (youth alienation and unemployment), *Changing World* (featuring such movements as "Women Walk Free" and "All Religions Are One"), and *In Praise of Johnny Appleseed* (ecology). Such politically oriented dance productions were hardly unusual at the time. But Lou's involvement was more than professional: he was committed to the principle as well as the aesthetic. He also composed an antiwar instrumental work in 1937, *France 1917—Spain 1937*, prompted by the Spanish Civil War.[10]

Although in his early years Lou expressed his political views through his art rather than through overt political action (he didn't march in demonstrations until after his return to California), many of his close personal associations were based on a common political philosophy. Choreographers Lenore Peters Job and Carol Beals, as well as Beals's husband Mervin Leeds, were highly active in San Francisco politics,[11] and it was Lester Horton's politics as much as his dance that led to close ties between the two men. Similarly, in New York Lou nurtured relationships that resonated with his concerns for human rights, such as those with activist minister Edward McGowan and the intellectual circle surrounding the Living Theater.

During the 1940s and early 1950s McGowan frequently appeared at civil rights rallies in New York: "I was considered by my superiors a hot potato. I was way out in left field. So they sent me as far from New York as they could [to Frederick, Maryland; Georgetown in Washington, D.C.; and Baltimore]. I remember Lou being active intellectually; many of my ideas came from him."[12] In 1950 McGowan traveled to Poland to claim the Lenin Peace Prize for Paul Robeson (since the State Department would not issue Robeson a passport). He marched with Martin Luther King Jr., helped integrate the public schools and a concert series in Frederick, Maryland, and later encouraged his Georgetown congregation to march on the White House after Sunday services.

As for the Living Theater, it "was always pacifist and partisan," notes Judith Malina. But the "movement," which had searched for "some vocabulary to reestablish artistic form after breaking with tradition," retreated following the antiwar protests of the late 1960s and early 1970s.

> We were on an impossible path and couldn't go on; we had to go back and retrench. The movement . . . was completely debilitated by a terrible division between the people who stood by its origins from Martin Luther King and Gandhi and nonviolent resistance, and the people who felt such a strong sym-

pathy for Third World liberation that they had to agree to armed struggle. So those who felt armed struggle was an essential part of liberation and those who felt it could never be so (because it was essentially unliberating to kill people) were in a conflict that divided every group and groupiscule.[13]

Among Lou's catalog of political causes, none is stronger than his personal crusade against war. It was the news of Hitler's invasion of Poland in 1939 that triggered the opening phrase of his *Mass to Saint Anthony* (see example 1-2 in chapter 1). To the Kyrie's vocal lines, inspired by his studies of Gregorian chant and Amerindian song, he counterpoised a heavy military march with rolls on the snare drums and intermittent bass drum interruptions. But in the Gloria, his hope for world unity and sanity emerged in an outburst of church bells: "Every kind of bell I could think of," he recalls, "to make a great chime."[14]

Subsequent events reinforced Lou's pessimistic fears over his optimistic hopes. "There came a time in my life when I found myself revolted by the whole modern world. It was the atom bomb. It blew me apart. . . . The question was . . . what to retrieve from the scattered fragments. I did an about face and marched directly back through history," seeking the roots of what had gone wrong. Unable to support a "blind belief in progress," he managed to "retrieve from the fragments" a belief in "experiential, sensual, . . . intellectual realities,"[15] a faith in the commonality of human experience, and a trust in the power of art to unite diverse cultures.

Even after the war, Lou found scant cause for optimism. When he returned to California in 1953 and learned about open-air atomic testing in Nevada, he bought a Geiger counter, which he set up at his isolated Aptos cottage and, after his shift at the animal hospital, would read the meter and register flows of radiation above the normal background level. "I can count," he says, "and I knew when I was being irradiated." Finally, he decided, "Enough was enough."

> A government does not attack an individual without just cause, and irradiation is an attack on the private individual. I wrote to the IRS and said, "This is a breach of the social contract, and I'm sure that you don't want my monies this year." Within the week two men came across the mountains from San Jose to my place of work at the animal hospital and interviewed me for a number of hours. Finally they agreed that it was a breach of the social contract but said, "You have to pay anyway or suffer the consequences." So for many years I wrote under the signature on my tax form, "Signed under duress."[16]

Lou's Geiger counter also made a guest appearance in 1959 at the University of Buffalo during the premiere of the recitatives from his *Political Primer*. The text, which Lou had written the previous year in Aptos, was occasioned by the "nightmare of McCarthyism": "Its arrogant evil was backed by the notion that the United States had achieved absolute power. One saw headlines quoting Congressmen that opposition to the atom bomb was like denying God. Decent and useful citizens were harassed and liberal neighbors swept under the rug."[17]

The *Primer* describes three governmental structures differentiated by their procedures for filling offices: by birth (monarchy), by election (republic), or by lottery (democracy). "Governments are the inventions of Human Persons." As such they may be "created, altered, abandoned, or destroyed, as Human Persons wish. . . . The inventions of Human Persons do not have rights over the rights of Human Persons." Whatever the governmental structure, Lou proposed that those who enjoy the game of war be assigned designated areas in which they might pursue it at will. "Kept to weapons non-nuclear, non-gaseous, non-biologic . . . , weapons, in short, which cannot harm anyone [outside the designated areas], these zones might be a success for these persons, and at the same time financially solvent."[18]

During Herbert Beattie's performance of the *Primer*'s four recitatives in Buffalo, the small Geiger counter sat unobtrusively on the stage, its quiet ticking mildly amplified. As the work progressed, recalls Robert Hughes, the machine, "in a climactic, though understated way," gradually raised the audience's sensibilities to the possibility that they, too, were being subjected to atomic pollution in the atmosphere.[19]

During his early years in Aptos, Lou actively supported noncommercial radio KPFA in Berkeley, the first station of the visionary Pacifica Foundation. "KPFA represented a radical model for a nonprofit community-based radio station operating outside the parameters of mainstream broadcasting," notes Ralph Engelman. "On the eve of the McCarthy era, [Lewis K. Hill, the prime mover of Pacifica], envisaged KPFA as an electronic gadfly, providing access to groups and perspectives otherwise absent from the airwaves."[20] These "perspectives" were to a large degree pacifist. In a talk on the air (ca. 1959–60) which he called the "Crackpot Lecture," Lou addressed the urgent obligations of Western civilizations to combat the cold-war rush to arms and substitute ties of international understanding. The world should tolerate fools, he said, but should "encourage crackpots" (a group in which he included himself), for crackpots believe that the world's seemingly intractable problems are solvable. Civilization he likens to adult play, an extension of the "solemn play" of children, a "beautiful useful play" that he fears is gradually dying.

> I am now middle-aged. I have heard that there have been complaints against my generation. If so they are ill made. We were born during a world war and reared in the '20s. A world depression hit us in our adolescence and we were caused in our manhood to fight another world war, from which we became the "decimated generation." Then the generation of our parents spoke gaily of its willingness to blow up the world and the future. . . . We have had to spend a great deal of time and effort to restrain them. If we have done anything of individual constructive works then, anything at all, we do not merit plaints, for we have indeed been kept very busy. The "theme knowledge"

of my generation is of the exhaustibility of things. . . . We have learned that the fruits of the earth run out before mouths, that its minerals run out before machines. We have learned that a simple belief in human weakness runs out and that no one nor nature would take care of things while we were being strong, should we go in groups blood-blind to fight. Doing that, we should not "come to" in a little while with everything somehow put right, things going beautifully on the earth. Neither time nor any god would heal things. We should not wake up ever, nor any other being. We are on our own now.[21]

At the same time, Harrison championed the positive, particularly those musical elements common to diverse cultures: sonic beauty, modal structures, the continuous "solemn song" of civilization, and the alluring range of instrumental timbres ("those who love music, love instruments. . . . [And] those who love the instruments of the art, may be said to love the art.")

In 1961, at the Tokyo East-West Encounter Conference, Harrison articulated similar themes in a "Political Manifesto," in both English and Esperanto, which reads, in part:

> Our very ancient ancestors began to travel forth to visit foreign lands, foreign peoples, and other cultures: and, little by little...we began to discover one another, and to find out about our diverse beliefs, customs, pleasures, minds, and bodies. . . .
>
> But now, while we acknowledge one another, we immediately discover that we suffer ugly wrongs. . . . When each might enjoy good health, the means are used to manufacture tools of death; and when each might have a for-life, for-growth planet, the nations quarrel and . . . oppose mankind. . . .
>
> Out of cowardice, then, a few of us might kill the world by war. . . .
>
> But we are still men, and we intend to live—and while we still live we struggle to make something whatever right . . . for the beautiful art which we practice [is] an art which sings of love; we are right, being musicians, to take on one more answerability. . . .
>
> We should bring forward the good things of our separate musical cultures for the delight and help of humanity, to celebrate that man really can ennoble life, can enjoy, and value life. If the world wounds you, then strike back at the world. Don't strike at your art, embrace that as a treasure.[22]

Among Harrison's numerous political compositions from this period, *Nova Odo* (parts 1–2, 1961–63; part 3, 1968) is perhaps the most broadly representative of both his fears and his hopes. His text progresses from a diatribe about war in the first verse ("The witch who lives in the Mushroom Cloud has ashen falling hair that glitters and kills") to the comfort of nature and interpersonal relationships in the second ("Yet from Mars's Arms men turn to man. . . . They go into the original woods, that peace made, and there wake weeping from dreams") to a vision of galaxial fellowship in the third ("Then out to the flaming stars . . . From then, eventually unshackle time, and traverse galaxies.") The first movement, in Equal Temperament, denounces the horrors of the bomb. Foregrounded in the oboe (and then the woodwind section) near the beginning is a Morse code message: "Class struggle between church and state was won. Will layman win struggle against military?" (In the "Crackpot Lecture," Lou had drawn a parallel between war and religion: "I say to you on the air that I regard religion as insanity just as I regard warring as brutality. Of the two, the wise man will choose the charms of insanity, but the intelligent man will reject both insanity and brutality.") There follows a dramatic recitation of "voices of children," including the words of a San Francisco junior high school student who asks, reflecting on a ballot proposition on fluoride in the drinking water, "I consider it very confusing that the people are not able to vote on whether we put radiation in the air but we have to vote on whether we can put fluoride in the water."[23] The second movement, which combines p'iris with chorus and strings, provides a striking contrast, conjuring the solemnity of Korean court music. The finale proposes a synthesis: Western instruments imitate Chinese musical styles.

The seven movements of *Pacifika Rondo* similarly contrast the horrors of the atomic bomb with the serenity of Korean court music, the benevolent dragon of China, the peace of Buddhism, the majesty of nature, and the delightful play of animals. The bomb movement—the sixth in the series—interrupts the tour around the Pacific ("peaceful") basin with a shockingly out-of-character internal cognitive dissonance that goes well beyond Lou's typical eclecticism (CD, band 15). The Western instruments of the ensemble perform alone in Equal Temperament and strict twelve-tone serial technique—a reminder of Harrison's own "squirrel's cage" from his prebreakdown years. Near the end of the movement, the members of the ensemble cry out "Oh," and a male voice emits a scream of anguish.

Soon after Lou returned to California, the government's "breach of its social contract" came home to him in a most personal way. Victor Jowers, owner of the Sticky Wicket Cafe (chapter 3), died of aplastic anemia at the age of thirty-nine. Lou recalls that doctors ultimately traced the ailment to his observations of the Nevada nuclear tests during his years as a journalist.[24]

Jowers's death on November 15, 1967, coincided with increasingly belligerent protests against the United States' involvement in Vietnam. Campuses around the country rapidly became the focal points of peace marches, sit-ins, and antiwar demonstrations. Protest songs such as Pete Seeger's "Where Have All the Flowers Gone" and bards such as Bob Dylan and Joan Baez galvanized much of the country's youth, who in growing numbers were being drafted to fight a war in which many could not believe. The Cabrillo Music Festival, Gerhard Samuel, and Lou Harrison staged their own protest—half a concert of Harrison's antiwar music on August 17, 1968. Featured were *Nova Odo* with its new third movement; "A Hatred of the Filthy Bomb" from *Pacifika Rondo*; *France 1917—Spain 1937* (revised and retitled *About the Spanish War*); and Lou's three *Peace Pieces*.[25] Never hesitant to espouse controversial positions, Harrison chose for *Peace Piece 1* a Buddhist prayer ("Invocation for the Health of All Beings")[26] during a time when the United States was at war with a primarily Buddhist country, and for *Peace Piece 2* a shrill inflammatory antiwar poem by Robert Duncan. Duncan's "Up Rising, Passages 25," was a no-holds-barred indictment of the Vietnam War. A small extract:

> Men wake to see that they are used like things
> spent in a great potlatch, this Texas barbecue
> of Asia, Africa and all the Americas . . . ,
> the all-American boy in the cockpit
> loosing his flow of napalm, below in the jungles . . .
> and the torture of mothers and fathers and children,
> their hair aflame, screaming in agony, but
> in the line of duty, for the might and enduring fame
> of Johnson, for the victory of American will over its victims,
> releasing his store of destruction over the enemy. . . .
> The very glint of Satan's eyes from the pit of hell of America's
>   unacknowledged, unrepented crimes that I saw in Goldwater's eyes
> now shines from the eyes of the President
> in the swollen head of the nation.[27]

Lou set Duncan's tirade as a six-and-a-half-minute "fiery non-stop recitative . . . writhing in a series of impassioned crescendos."[28] As tenor Erik Townsend drew to a close, the tension in the hall became palpable. A woman in the audience broke the silence that followed with a timid "Boo"; to which a member of the bass section of the orchestra responded, "Shame." (Critics were left wondering about the source of the latter; Arthur Bloomfield wrote in the *San Francisco Examiner,* "While I interpreted this as a further bit of castigation aimed at Harrison, I'm told that someone on stage was taking a dim view of the boo.")[29] Then the audience "burst like a wave"[30] with its spirited endorsement. The outburst was headlined in all of the major San Francisco and Monterey Bay Area newspapers. "Festival Recital Stirs Storm," blared the *Oakland Tribune.* Others chimed in: "Harrison 'Peace Pieces' Stir Cabrillo Festival," "Discord at Music Festival: 'Peace Pieces' Verse Booed," " 'Texas Barbecue of Asia . . . ,' " "Harrison's 'Peace Pieces' Draw Cheers," "Doves Win Music Festival Decibel Poll."[31] Reviewers highlighted the five-minute standing ovation at the intermission ("with knots of sitting and grimly non-clapping spectators"), the enthusiastic "coat-and-tie citizens" applauding with an intensity generally reserved for "peace concerts." (This 1968 performance, including the audience response, may be heard on the CD, band 16.)

Harrison was immensely pleased. He has always "tweaked and stung the nose of almost anything and anyone worth tweaking," noted Paul Hertelendy in the *Oakland Tribune,* be it "music critics, musical tradition, heavy reliance on all things European, and plain old convention—and [he has] repeatedly gotten away with it, like a deft jouster jabbing at the hindquarters of a lugubrious dragon."[32]

Fully recognizing music's potential as propaganda, Harrison has attempted (as far as possible) to restrict performances of his works to peaceful purposes. He specifies that his *Joyous* and *Solemn* processionals may be used only for religious or civil ceremonies, explicitly proscribing military occasions—even though current copyright law does not grant him such power. Similarly, he places the following condition on performances of the *Suite for Symphonic Strings* (1960):

> Since the use of a work of art as propaganda is a use for profit; therefore: the right of any government or agency thereof, or the right of any group of governments or agency thereof, to use this work or any portion of it in any shape, form, or likeness, as propaganda, is reserved by the composer, who, in the contemplated instance of such use, will himself decide what constitutes "propaganda use," and from whom written permission must be obtained for such use.[33]

Harrison has continually bemoaned the composer's lack of control over the work. Once a musical composition is written and published, he notes, the government grants to the composer a limited right to enjoy any profit that might accrue. He has proposed two solutions over the years: the protection of authorial rights in perpetuity, or direct governmental support of the author.

Equally important to him is societal support of performing artists. In an article in the *American Composers' Alliance Bulletin* in 1957, he proposed the establishment of civic orchestras with a full schedule of duties:

> Its brass section plays at noon or evening: marches, entertainments and chorales from the city hall; the strings serenade in the evening by appointment or, in clement weather, to the public in the pleasantest park. In sections or altogether, this orchestra will entertain visiting diplomats; perhaps by rotating them, or through clerical scheduling, assist in each of the denominational Sunday worships; play at civic and religious holidays . . . , aid whatever live theatrics are taking place in the community; and last but not least, reserve some time for its members to offer instruction.
>
>   Such services are, of course, presented free and by request. . . . Any citizen with a reasonable need for music is free to ask for it and would probably get it, schedule permitting.[34]

Idealistic indeed, but hardly untried. Lou evokes the model (perhaps only imperfectly realized) of the town musician in the middle ages or the Balinese village.

In the face of the nuclear arms race and the cold war, Lou's response has been to champion simple pleasures: music in the park, the puppet theater (as a substitute for the "violence and greed" of broadcast television), and nature. His appreciation of simple pleasures may explain as well his attraction to melody: it speaks directly to the audience without requiring translation by an intellectual intermediary.

Harrison's ecological commitment is manifest in action as well as philosophy. Despite extra cost, for example, he buys kenaf paper for his photocopier and laser printer. If cannabis hemp were legal, such nontree paper would be cheaper and more efficient than the fairly expensive kenaf or "Guinea hemp" now used as a wood substitute. "The DuPonts have already made plenty of money on nylon," Lou notes. "They were the ones who got the . . . law against hemp in this country passed. . . . [Hemp paper] has a shelf life of 1,500 years, compared to 75 for tree fiber. One acre of pine forest will produce in 20 years the amount that hemp can produce five times over per year." [35]

He wages a similar battle against noise pollution, in his view an equally invidious form of environmental despoliation. He has been known to walk out of a concert in the middle of a work when the amplitude exceeded his comfort. He described his reaction to a 1993 contemporary music and dance concert when the volume became unbearable:

> We have in our ear both the apprehension of musical relationships and kinetic relationships. In this case, the volume overcame the kinetics. Bill just held his fingers in his ears the whole time. (*Colvig:* I felt attacked every minute. I didn't hear words that were spoken; they were so loud that they blasted my ears.)
>
> I concluded that people who live in cities now are deaf. We're country boys; we don't need that. The anxiety aroused by that amount of sound was such that I could no longer have the kinetic response. I could see that there were humans on the stage, and they were doing things, but my body did not respond. The ear was cut in two. Such loud-tech nonsense represents the contemporary way of impressing one with the establishment. All the corporate power is there. I don't need it. [36]

Harrison maintains a healthy skepticism about the pitfalls of overamplification and mechanical sound reproduction. As early as 1966, he noted that the "predominant practice today is for dancers to use disks and/or tapes while teaching classes, and for accompanying concerts. . . . This is Bad Practice—for it trains in lifeless (un-inter-responding) rhythm, and it increases the popular belief that Machines are Holy." [37]

Thirty years later, he continues to sound the same theme. Given the choice, Lou will favor a natural solution over a mechanical one. His current study, design, and construction of a straw-bale house in the Mojave desert, precluding the need for heat or air-conditioning and deriving its energy from solar power, is a typical example.

The same love of nature attracted him to Amerindian culture. He describes the texts of *Strict Songs*, which follow the model of certain Navajo sacred texts, as "make-things-right-and-well-again songs." The poems celebrate the relationship of humans with four aspects of nature: plant life, animal life, minerals, and the heavens.

The most important relationships for Lou, however, are those among humans—both between cultures and between individuals. The gamelan and Lou's percussion ensembles from the 1930s and 1940s elevate the group over the individual. The gamelan is first of all a collection of instruments built to operate as an ensemble, and only secondarily a group of specific players. The performers may substitute for one another or even rotate among the instruments (a practice more typical of American gamelan ensembles than of Indonesian ones), but the collection of instruments is integral: individual components cannot be moved from one gamelan to another. The contrast to the Western orchestra is striking; here emphasis is placed on the collection of players, most of whom bring a privately owned instrument. The performers are of primary concern, while (personal preferences aside) one high-quality violin can substitute for another.

The emphasis on communally produced sound over personal virtuosity was certainly one factor contributing to Lou's attraction to the gamelan. It correlated as well with the spirit of his percussion ensembles, in which professional training was not required, but all participated in the "delightful play." A similar spirit is apparent in Lou's choreographic collaborations during the 1930s and early 1940s, such as *Changing World* (with its nine choreographers) or *Green Mansions*, a product of the Modern Ballet Group, whose philosophy was to pool resources into a program that would not feature "any one person, [would] be free to the public and free from commercialism."[38]

Lou's deemphasis on the role of the individual has marked his personal conduct as well: he has expended little effort in self-promotion and has opted for the isolation of Aptos over the stress, but high visibility, of city life. The choice has worked to his disadvantage in terms of international renown but offers welcome tranquillity.

Aptos, now integrated into the larger Santa Cruz metropolitan area, still provides the freedom from noise and the connection to nature he craves. His musical hybrids, on the other hand, provide cross-cultural linkages. Examples abound in his works: from the mixing of instrumental forces to incorporating Native American "coyote stories" in his *Fourth Symphony*.

Lou's horror at the Vietnam conflict was more than a protest against war itself: it was, in addition, a response to Western armies killing Asians—the inheritors of some of the world's oldest and most highly developed cultures. When *San Francisco Chronicle* music critic Robert Commanday derided the "pitfalls of faddish and superficial involvement in Asian cultural manifestations" in April 1968, Lou responded with an angry "Letter to a Critic," in which he castigated Commanday for his "'warning' about the influence of Asian music (the source of all our music) when we are actually killing Asian musicians in an immoral war." Lou marveled that whereas "almost anywhere in Greater Asia one can obtain a full and high education in both Asian and 'Western' musics," there are "fewer than a half-dozen places in this country . . . [where one] can get a good, and accredited, education in Greater Asian music. We are the losers, of course, as informed persons know." Commanday was quick to agree, noting that Harrison was one of the few Western musicians to undertake a profound study of Asian styles as opposed to the many "faddists, dabblers and seekers of exoticism."[39]

Lou's most recent compositions continue to reflect his political views. The single large work he was able to write during the Gulf War was *Homage to Pacifica*, celebrating the opening of the new Berkeley headquarters of the Pacifica Foundation. Reflecting both his frustration with American military aggression and his long-standing love for Native American culture, the work blends sardonic commentaries on American imperialism with the vision of a united world. *Homage to Pacifica* begins and ends with Lou's "glandular optimism." For the gamelan prelude, he invited Jody Diamond to realize a vocal part in the style of the Indonesian pesindhèn. At her husband Larry Polansky's suggestion (and with Harrison's enthusiastic endorsement), Diamond chose as her text *We shall Overcome*, interlaced with the call letters of Pacifica Foundation radio stations (KPFA, KPFK, WBAI, and others). For the finale, Lou set a text attributed to Chief Seattle reflecting on the interconnectedness of all life forms:[40]

> Where is man without the beasts? If the beasts were gone, men would die from a great loneliness of spirit. For whatever happens to the beasts soon happens to man. All things are connected; this we know. The earth does not belong to man; man belongs to the earth. This we know. All things are connected like the blood which unites one family. All things are connected. Whatever befalls the earth befalls the sons of the earth. Man did not weave the web of life; he is merely a strand in it. Whatever he does to the web, he does to himself.

Between these two optimistic poles Lou inserted a condemnation of the Philippine war attributed to Mark Twain (chapter 4), followed by his own ode in the style of Horace, declaimed between expansive melodies on a plaintive solo bassoon. The narrator interrupts the bassoon's quiet monologue with a condemnation of the "untied snakes of America," who drive down

> with stinking speed-and-gleam to pierce sweet ancient things,
> To pain earth's elders' bones, to leave red poison pool—
> School buses shattered.

> The "untied snakes of America" drive down
> With speeding strike to pox earth's flesh, to bomb out birds,
> To corrupt a mountain, and to gut these sands, for
> Mad and evil men.

A speaking chorus follows with a litany of sixty-nine Amerindian tribal names and this additive refrain: "All the fine people . . . all the fine people on this original natural land . . . all the fine people on this original natural land—screwed." This angry outburst of "philosophical pessimism," however, is immediately countermanded by Chief Seattle's utopian vision.

Homage to Pacifica invokes the same themes Lou had sounded nearly forty years earlier in his "Crackpot Lecture," when he told his radio audience: "I am a vegetarian, a frank admirer of other races, and a speaker of the international language Esperanto. I am a polypolitical logician and an economic stabilitarian. . . . I am a promoter of population restraint and sexual freedom. I am a writer of letters to the editor and a reader of science fiction. . . . I'm a calligrapher and not last of all, I'm a living composer." His self-characterization has changed little in the intervening years; he has merely applied his principles and talents to new problems, continuing to condemn violence but ultimately believing in the possibilities of cross-cultural fellowship.

10 Harrison, Homosexuality, and the Gay World

In 1942, when Lou Harrison's draft board summoned him, he candidly told them that he was gay, and they classified him 4-F. "'I just answered the psychiatrist correctly,' he explains. 'They didn't want me, and I didn't want them.'"[1] It wasn't a "coming out" or a rebellion against perceived accusations of sexual "deviancy" but a political statement pure and simple: as if to say, I have no desire to be associated with a group that not only has as its primary function the killing of human beings but also practices morally indefensible discrimination against people like me. His candor required considerable courage, particularly in view of his close association with Cowell, who only two years earlier had been released from San Quentin after serving four years in prison for illegal sexual behavior with a seventeen-year-old boy (chapter 1). Though Cowell was granted a full pardon in December 1941 and his public condemnation and harsh sentence had been fueled by accusations of pedophilia, the effect on Lou was nevertheless profound. Harrison's circle of supportive friends kept him from retreating to the "closet," but Cowell's experience served as a constant reminder of potential danger.[2]

Lou's statement to his draft board followed naturally from a political philosophy that mandated respect for the rights of the

189

individual, be it the citizen's right to be free from atomic pollution, the composer's right to retain control over the work of art, the child's right to a solid education (he is fond of quoting H. G. Wells that "human history becomes more and more a race between education and catastrophe"),[3] or the right of individuals to pursue intimate relationships of their own choosing.

During our interviews, Lou was willing—even eager—to discuss his own intimate relationships and their profound effect on his musical development. We have already mentioned the most important: those with Sherman Slayback in San Francisco, William Weaver (late San Francisco period, Los Angeles, and early New York), Edward McGowan (prebreakdown New York), Remy Charlip (postbreakdown New York and Black Mountain College), and William Colvig, his companion for the past thirty years. Even a cursory examination of the catalog at the end of this book will show the large number of works dedicated to Slayback and Weaver during his San Francisco years, including the often performed song *May Rain*. During the years Lou spent with McGowan, he not only composed several ingenuous and highly melodic piano waltzes for his minister-friend but also wrote a setting of *Onward Christian Soldiers* that was performed at McGowan's Methodist church in the Bronx. The profound and enduring impact of Bill Colvig's work in instrument building and tuning has already been noted in depth.

Author Lawrence Mass remarks, "With Lou Harrison . . . being gay is something affirmative. He's proud to be a gay composer and interested in talking about what that might mean. He doesn't feel threatened that this means he won't be thought of as an American composer who is also great and timeless and universal."[4]

Lou's frank acknowledgment of his homosexuality has never led to disdain or condemnation of other modes of sexual expression, nor did he ever exhibit an "antiwoman attitude," notes Bella Lewitzky. "Lou never seemed to have any such need to validate himself [in this way] as a gay man."[5]

Whether his sexual orientation has exerted an identifiable influence on his musical style, however, is quite another matter. Although issues of sexual encoding have been explored in literature and film studies for some years, similar theoretical development in the field of musicology is still in its early stages.[6] Increasingly, in both the popular and scholarly literature, critics have been exploring the question of "gay markers" in music (compositional traits, areas of interest, or specifics of musical language that may characterize gay composers within the context of their culture and historical period, whether conscious or not) and how such markers might be discerned. While it is too early to take a definitive position on these questions, we should explore how the dialectic between theories of gender and the life of an individual plays out—to ask, in essence, how we might shed light on Lou Harrison's unique situation with the aid of current theoretical constructs.

During our interviews Lou himself consistently denied that elements of sound or expression in his music could be linked to his sexuality. Suggestions that musical "Orientalisms" may characterize the music of gay composers,[7] for instance, he finds speculative, although he is the first to acknowledge that the homosexual, as one of society's "others"—defined, and sometimes alienated, by the mainstream—may be attracted to other outsiders, to exotic cultures, and particularly to societies in which gays hold a place of honor, reverence, or simply normality. "In the mere fact of being gay," he notes, "you are automatically an outsider in your own culture."[8]

We readily acknowledge ourselves as outsiders in the field of queer theory. We chose to write about Lou Harrison not because he is gay, or a gay composer, or even an *important* gay composer—but because he is, quite simply, an important composer, one whose music, at its best, deserves a permanent place of honor in the American canon. We realize that musicologists specializing in gender theory and gay readers may perceive Lou's music, poetry, and life with an understanding that may forever elude us. Nevertheless, we hope that our perspective helps to shed light on some of these complex issues and to encourage further discussion.

Lou feels that the outsider, who is distanced from majority culture, may at times have an artistic advantage by allowing powers of observation to temper consciousness of self. He cites, for instance, as the most "breathtakingly feminine" acting he has ever witnessed that of a male Kabuki actor who, having built a career portraying female roles (*onnagata*), was able to bring out "not the normal human gestures that all of us share, but the peculiarly gender-based gestures, physical attitudes, and speech patterns that the culture tends to formalize as artworks."[9] Indeed, in Chinese opera and Kabuki theater (both of which were traditionally presented by all-male companies), male actors playing female roles so successfully abstracted the essence of femininity that they became "more female than women" and even served as positive role models for women who imitated *their* styles of dress, speech, and movement.

Although Lou is unwilling to subscribe to theories linking specific musical traits to sexual orientation, he clearly recalls speculating with friends about the orientation of historical figures.

> When I was growing up in San Francisco there was always a sub-rosa tradition as to who was gay in history. Tchaikovsky, of course, was a flaming queen who used to cruise in St. Petersburg. In short, he wasn't always in Slavic despondency.
>
> There has been speculation as well about Handel's relation with his cook and his will to an orphanage. Then there is the mysterious remark by Sir John Hawkins that Handel never married because he "had better things to do."
>
> There are reports circulating (and some scholarly evidence) that Schubert may have been part of the gay circle in Vienna. I can't imagine, however, what effect it would have had on his music. (Unless Schubert played in a gay bar, which we're fairly sure that he didn't. The concept of camp may have ex-

tended back to Vienna, but in any case, I don't find much camp in Schubert. How can you camp at heavenly length?)[10]

While Lou's preference for Handel's music over that of Bach hinges on the kinetic quality of Handel's rhythm and his melodic expressivity, might he not also have felt a personal bond to this subject of his "sub-rosa tradition," a sense that they in some way shared secrets that could only be voiced within a closed circle of colleagues?

Ned Rorem's comments on gay-related characteristics in music are even stronger than those of Harrison:

> I think the so-called homosexual sensibility is nonexistent. It's a slogan posing as an idea. I don't think there is such a thing as gay music.
>
> Conventions in music will change every generation. The minor mode did not mean "sadness" 150 years ago. And the idea of love music—violins in Wagner—changed when Shostakovich wrote "Lady Macbeth," in which the trombone blatting away meant "love," or at least "love making." Chopin, with all of his delicate roulades—is that gay music, or is that simply nineteenth-century convention? Recent theories postulate that Schubert wrote a particular kind of music because he was gay. Nobody said he wrote [in that style] because he was fat and ugly. His fat and ugliness has as much to do with his style as his sexual orientation.[11]

Despite such demurrals, the society in which Harrison and Rorem grew up has postulated certain personality traits, emotional characteristics, patterns of behavior, and artistic language as gender-related. As Rorem himself notes, television shows little girls

> as sugar and spice and everything nice. Little boys are toads. It never shows a bunch of little girls pushing each other on the sled, or a bunch of little boys having tea parties.
>
> The idea that a male homosexual is feminine inside I don't believe at all. There are too many homosexual coal miners and policemen. The idea of a woman trapped in a man's body might be true of one-tenth of one percent. There is too much arguing against it.[12]

As much as Rorem might resist such stereotypes—usually couched in bipolarizations—they are so prevalent that they cannot help but color most people's perceptions of both themselves and others. The normative metaphor for Beethoven's rhythmic intensity has become heroism and strength equals "masculinity." (Harrison likens Beethoven's codas to "an exasperated absentee landlord pounding on the door for back rent.")[13] Chopin has often been linked to the feminine, which in contemporary Western society frequently carries negative connotations such as "weak" and "short" —and by extension, "insubstantial."[14] Science and reason bear a "masculine" label, arts and emotion a "feminine" one. As for the gay male, popular image holds him to favor a "kinder, gentler" tone, an affinity for beauty, and an attraction for those traits traditionally ascribed to "feminine" sensibility—the "trope of inversion," as Eve Sedgwick notes.[15] While Rorem may object to such commonplace categorizations, they are nevertheless embedded in his and Harrison's American cultural upbringing as solidly as they are in that of heterosexuals. One can bemoan the social process of such enculturation, but neither Rorem nor anyone else can escape it any more than our ears can ignore the imprint of Equal Temperament provided by everything from elevator music and Coca-Cola commercials to Beethoven's Ninth Symphony.

In light of this cultural baggage, then, we must ask whether, despite considered denials by Harrison and Rorem, their music is not a holistic embodiment of personal and cultural traits and whether, therefore, there might be musical manifestations of "gay sensibility" of which they themselves are unaware. "I personally feel there is no artistic difference between 'gay' music . . . versus 'straight' music," says composer Robert Helps, "but who knows what affects us subliminally?"[16] As musicologist J. Michele Edwards asks: "Is it likely that such a powerful life-element as sexuality (especially when one's sexuality is outside the mainstream) would be irrelevant to one's life's work? The difficulty, however, is establishing precisely how this facet of life becomes audible in the music."[17] Lou Harrison, though indebted to manifold influences, maintains in his music a distinctive and recognizable voice, whether he writes in a serial vein, a dissonant contrapuntal style, or a lyrical melodic idiom, as more than one critic has repeatedly noted.

In spite of such subliminal influences, we must still ask whether conditioning can be encoded in specific musical markers. Gender theorists in related fields have readily postulated such codifications. Eve Sedgwick and others[18] offer as a prime example Herman Melville's *Billy Budd*, the tale of a young sailor summarily executed for unintentionally killing the ship's master-at-arms (Claggart) in a confrontation prompted by Claggart's unprovoked hatred of the young man. Although Melville never explicitly discusses homosexual desire on the part of Claggart (or anyone else in the narrative for that matter), the text is filled with codings that prompt some scholars to suggest that the roots of Claggart's hatred lie in repressed homosexual desire. Billy Budd is described in feminine-coded language: "a beauty," "the flower of the flock," "a jewel," "welkin-eyed." Melville at times even dispenses with coding, stating that Billy's face was "as yet smooth . . . , all but feminine in purity of natural complexion." He is intensely attractive to the other sailors, who "took to him like hornets to treacle." Claggart, on the other hand, is called "mysterious," "exceptional," "peculiar," "secretive," "abnormal," exhibiting a "natural depravity." Claggart's implied paranoia (in which Sedgwick sees a "terror and loathing for his own desires")[19] and Billy's panic in the face of Claggart's invented accusations (which renders him mute in his own defense) reinforce the argument. Whether or not one finds such reasoning conclusive, it is sufficiently persuasive to have affected many readers' perceptions of the story and its subtext.

Some musicologists have postulated similar codings in music, with gay stereotypes reflected by specific harmonic or melodic language; by musical references to exotic cultures; by associations with dance (a field that has attracted a heavily self-selecting gay male population); or by an affinity for delicate beauty, not in and of itself but in the context of conventions that suggest a masculine "ruggedness" as strong as that of the sailors in *Billy Budd*—the "Ruggles" style, for example, or atonal serialism.

Composer Janice Giteck finds Lou "unabashedly androgynous in his way of approaching creativity. He has a vital connection to the feminine as well as to the masculine. The female part is apparent in the sense of beingness. But at the same time, Lou is very male, too, ferociously active and assertive, rhythmic, pulsing and aggressive."[20]

Some composers have placed gender issues consciously in the foreground of their music.[21] In other cases a gay orientation may actually be manifest in a deliberate attempt to counter traditional stereotypes. "So-called 'very masculine' pieces are usually by women," says Rorem, "because they're trying to prove how manly they are."[22] Despite the frequency of words such as "lyric," "melodic," or "expressive" in descriptions of Lou's music—and flying in the face of his conscious rejection of such traditionally "masculine" influences as Beethoven—there are nevertheless a number of compositions in which Harrison seems deliberately to cultivate a posture of strength that Western society would traditionally call "masculine." ("I'm very fond of Lou when he writes twelve-tone music," says conductor Dennis Russell Davies. "There's a *virility* and a directness . . . about it—a ruggedness that I find very appealing.")[23] Many of these works (the *Symphony on G*, for example) date from Lou's turbulent New York years, when he explored dissonant counterpoint, atonality, and jagged melodic language, while at the same time seeking to come to terms with internal obstacles to the free expression of his homosexuality.

Despite Lou's candor to his draft board and the support he received from a circle of gay artists in New York, the general condemnation of homosexual practices certainly contributed to the stress he felt during the 1940s. In a postwar article in *View* he reviewed a new translation of Tchaikovsky's diaries in which his own internal conflicts are reflected in his sympathy for Tchaikovsky's tortured psychological crises. "Among the more interesting continuous patterns in Tchaikowsky's privately violent existence," Lou wrote in February 1946,

are those found in his relationships to, 1) composing, 2) liquor, 3) good-looking men, 4) his domestics, and finally 5) his own body which was in an upset state most of the time. . . .

As a confirmed homosexual his intimacies with men are rather more interesting than his frequently spiteful and vague ones with women. . . . He is attracted to a young Italian gardener, a street singer, a Russian officer, a Negro Parisian; almost all social levels and cultural types. He laments the untimely death of an erstwhile intimate, he makes a note on youths as they grow older and more attractive to him, he suffers loneliness and leaves his hotel in a strange city to "carouse." . . .

I was enchanted with the vision of him, on the occasion of a severe loneliness which lasted several days, peering over a garden wall to watch (with the aid of binoculars) his neighbors eat dinner.[24]

The parallel to Harrison's personal situation at the time, one year before his breakdown, is inescapable. He, too, experienced severe loneliness, in this case in the midst of a densely populated city. He, too, perhaps occasionally "peered over the wall" at those who seemed comfortable in a society from which he often felt estranged. Today visitors to Lou's Aptos home may chance to find Tchaikovsky in the "throne room," where Lou's painting of the disconsolate Russian, fully nude and looking rather like an Old World prophet, occupies the back of the door in place of a full-length mirror.

Though Lou now recalls postwar New York, its crowded streets swelled with returning servicemen, as "the golden years" of gay tolerance, it would be naive to suggest the absence of societal pressures to conform to majority practices. In the hospital, he was encouraged to explore heterosexual relationships, even though he had known since high school that his inclinations lay elsewhere. ("I recall my first realization of being gay. Parked at a picnic spot in the bumper seat of a car with a girl, I suddenly realized that the scene was not mine; I had another programming.")[25]

Once, after a party in New York, Harrison allowed himself to be seduced by Judith Malina, who ruefully told us that Lou's morning-after "hangover" contained more than a little element of panic. His frantic phone call to Malina's husband Julian Beck ("Judith's in my bed, Julian, what should I do?" "Don't worry, Lou, just feed her and send her home")[26] would be material for French farce save for the edge of desperation.

Even his letter of congratulation upon his brother Bill's marriage in September 1943 shows heartfelt love but also personal anxieties:

It is difficult for me yet to believe that you are "husband" and that Dot is "wife" but for so many years I have hoped you would find such happiness and now that it has happened it seems that I am in N.Y. and can't get back. I am very happy for you both and wish you a long and plentiful life together with all of the good things of the . . . outer world and inner world.

When two people live together there are suddenly many more wonderful things and many more awful things in life than one dreams. . . . There is really only *one* important fact, and that is love . . . ! Love is a strange, wild wonder in life and you can look about you and see men either made or broken by it. . . . Never let it die. Treasure it. It means the difference between real life as it was meant to be or the life of one who died inside years before it. . . .

Please don't think me dull but I am very fond of brother Bill and his bride and I want you both to be Kings and Queens. Life is so short and so little can turn the trick![27]

Musically, too, he may have sensed a need to validate himself as a "serious" and therefore "strong" (read "masculine") composer. The *Symphony on G* is tough, modernist music, filled with extroverted brass outbursts and displays of muscular strength, the product (one might think) of a man free from self-doubt (CD, band 18). We might even venture to speculate on the influence of Beethoven's heroic style if Harrison himself had not on so many occasions disavowed such indebtedness. "I listened to Beethoven day in and day out during my reviewing days in New York and realized, over my years of reporting, that he was indeed a great composer. I knew that if his pieces were on the program I could expect interesting and well-constructed works. But as to influencing my own compositions, no—in contrast to Handel, to the French baroque composers, to medieval music, etc., his influence is minimal."[28]

Rapunzel, too—a tale of masculine heroism (the prince) overcoming supernatural evil (the witch) in pursuit of the feminine ideal (Rapunzel/Guendolen)—is strong music with jagged melodies and regal trumpet calls. Even Lou's paintings from this period show ruggedness and strength (see fig. 9). But *Rapunzel* and the *Symphony on G* were not composed during a period of self-confidence. These two works—surely among his most "masculine"—are instead products of his darkest years, the bulk of the *Symphony* having taken shape during his hospital stay, and *Rapunzel* during the transitional years at Black Mountain College. In that context they seem to represent an identity crisis, perhaps fulfilling a subconscious need to validate himself in the context of American "masculinity."

Even in San Francisco—a community he remembers as embracing divergent opinion—some dissembling was unavoidable. Lou recalls the San Francisco of the 1930s and 1940s (with perhaps some rosy coloring in hindsight) as "an intellectually open-minded city. Being gay was even considered desirable and socially acceptable."[29] At the same time, laws prohibiting homosexual behavior were selectively enforced here as elsewhere in the country. Until 1962, when the state of Illinois decriminalized private consensual homosexual behavior, same-sex acts were proscribed in all fifty states;[30] California's law was not changed until 1975.[31]

During the 1950s and 1960s San Francisco's homosexual community was at the forefront of the gay rights movement and had made significant political strides well before the highly publicized New York Stonewall Riot of 1969.[32] In 1953 the Mattachine Society opened its San Francisco branch, which soon became the organization's headquarters. Daughters of Bilitis (a lesbian society) was founded in the city in 1955; the Tavern Guild (a coalition of gay bar owners seeking to thwart police raids) in 1962; and the Council on Religion and the Homosexual and the Society for Individual Rights (SIR) in 1964. The Society for Individual Rights emphasized peaceful political action, sponsoring voter registration drives, hosting "candidates nights" for politicians to meet with society members, and engaging in nonviolent picketing. The organization "was virtually alone among pre-Stonewall gay male homophile organizations in legitimating the social needs of homosexuals. . . . Its meetings often attracted more than two hundred people, and by 1968 it had a membership of almost a thousand, making it far and away the largest male homophile organization in the country."[33]

A large gay population had been drawn to San Francisco, in part because of purges from the armed forces in the Pacific during the Second World War and in part because the city's beatnik community, at the front lines of the sexual revolution, provided a hospitable atmosphere.[34] During the 1960s, however, a backlash led to periodic police raids on gay bars and a highly publicized confrontation at a New Year's Eve Ball (December 31, 1964–January 1, 1965). Although the Council on Religion and the Homosexual had met with the vice squad before the ball and were assured that there would be no trouble, riot squads appeared at the event and arrested four people for interfering with police and two others for committing lewd acts. (The former were acquitted by order of the judge, the latter found guilty of disorderly conduct.)[35]

After Lou's return to California—when he for the most part abandoned the Ruggles idiom and serialism as primary compositional tools, finding them essentially antithetical to his natural impulses—he rejected as well any attempts to deny or alter his sexual preferences. But it was McCarthyism that prompted his decision to publicly avow his homosexuality. Shortly after moving to Aptos he was asked by the minister of the local Unitarian church to "explain about being gay. . . . Some [people] were a little bit shocked; some were not," he recalls. "What happened was that I gained a great many friends and lost none."[36]

Harrison and Colvig were early members of SIR, attending social, cultural, and political events, including candidates' nights with Dianne Feinstein (later San Francisco mayor and California senator) and Willie Brown (state assembly speaker and later San Francisco mayor) and poetry readings and classes by Robert Duncan. Lou taught an Esperanto class through the organization, and SIR sponsored a concert series featuring his music. He became a kind of "Hermes" to out-of-town friends, providing "guided tours through the gay underground" to East Coast visitors. "I taught Ned Rorem the Charleston at a SIR dance. Virgil wanted a tour, as did Nicolas Nabokov and his fiancée."[37]

If Lou is unwilling to associate specific musical characteristics with his homosexuality, he is the first to acknowledge that it has influenced him in more direct ways.

> One question I have thought about a great deal is the advantage, at an intercultural level, of being gay. From my own experience, it's a very quick way into the roots of the culture without being involved in an intricate network of familial and economic relationships. A quick gay "trick," as it might be called, is often the entrance into a larger culture.

It's like what San Francisco used to be: within three days you knew every-body; you were immediately immersed in the city's cultural affairs.

One is reminded, for instance, of figures in history like Sir Roger Case-ment, who created havoc in the British foreign service by observing the treat-ment of natives in Africa. He caused an entire reform [of the Belgian gov-ernment's rule in the Congo]. It was by means of his extracurricular activities that he found out the true state of affairs.[38]

The influence of gay culture is manifest through Lou's choice of texts and his artistic associations, both within and outside of music. Among his most noteworthy nonmusical associates, we might particularly highlight poet and filmmaker James Broughton; choreographers Mark Morris and Remy Charlip; and poets Elsa Gidlow and Robert Duncan.

Lou had met Duncan soon after his move to New York. The two men shared similar interests and anxieties, and Duncan spent many hours at Lou's apartment giving poetry lessons to a small circle of interested com-posers. Duncan's anguished self-reflection over his homosexuality and his loneliness even among a group of supportive friends, which he expressed in a groundbreaking essay, "The Homosexual in Society," in 1944,[39] surely resonated with Lou's own self-deprecation and feelings of alienation.

The immediate fallout from Duncan's essay, in which he identified him-self as gay, was the cancellation of a contract by an editor who suddenly de-cided that one of his poems was "an advertisement or a notice of overt ho-mosexuality."[40] But the more lasting message was Duncan's allegiance to shared human experience over the needs of the special-interest group, or, as he stated in the late 1980s, when the essay was republished, his belief that "minority associations and identifications [including those of gay rights groups] were an evil wherever they supersede allegiance to . . . a human community good."[41]

Lou's political vision is also that of community—an international society united by common media of communication (linguistically by Esperanto, nonverbally by music and art), pursuing common political and ecological goals, and joined by bonds that are an extension of interpersonal relation-ships. When Lou was offered an opera commission in 1971, he chose a theme that highlighted homosexual love in the context of international community. The affair between Julius Caesar and Nicomedes, King of Bithy-nia, which had been part of Harrison's "sub-rosa tradition," offered the op-portunity to combine historically documented gay content with cross-cul-tural synthesis. *Young Caesar* appears to be the first opera centered on an overtly gay subject: though opera as a genre presents a fascinating field for the study of gender issues (from castrati to trouser roles to the occasional gay or lesbian character), the plots of earlier works did not turn on the issue of homosexuality.[42] Despite the controversial topic, the opera's sponsors greeted the proposed libretto with enthusiasm and "doubled my commis-sion," notes Lou.

Harrison's choice of puppets for the first version (chapter 3) was in no sense an attempt to suppress the human element. Rather, it was inspired by de Falla's puppet opera, *El retablo de maese Pedro*; by Lou's vision of the opera as an intimate chamber piece; and by his need to portray lavish court, banquet, and military scenes on a limited budget.

This original version was small in scale: "It started out being for five friends who played half the instruments in the world," Lou recalls. Other friends constructed the puppets, and Lou himself painted the scenic backdrop on a scroll that could be rolled smoothly during the course of the production.

He indulged his interests in diverse tuning systems as well. Caesar's music used the syntonic diatonic mode of "Western" Rome; Nicomedes's mode included the unusual seventh and eleventh overtones to evoke faraway, "Eastern" Bithynia. "Nicomedes was a known Orientalist," Lou notes, "suggesting Persian culture and Mithraic religion."[43]

In transforming the opera for human actors and standard orchestra in 1988 (chapter 3), much of the narration natural to a puppet opera suddenly seemed extraneous, the contrast of instrumental timbres was significantly reduced, and the modal differences between the music of Caesar and that of Nicomedes was suppressed. On the other hand, the opera was enlivened by new and compelling choral numbers, contrasts between choral and solo song, colorful costuming, and imaginative staging.

Lou's decision to transform *Young Caesar* from an intimate puppet opera to a full-scale Western opera grew from his association with the Portland Gay Men's Chorus and its manager, Richard Brown. The Portland chorus had been founded in 1980 by Steven Fulmer and Gary Coleman on the model of the San Francisco Gay Men's Chorus, established two years earlier.[44] About a year after its inception, Brown, a former newspaperman, critic, and novelist who had moved to Oregon from Kansas City, saw a tiny notice in the *Oregonian* announcing the chorus's third concert. Fascinated by this small listing in a large urban paper, he and his partner attended the performance and found themselves carried away, particularly by the spirit of fellowship evident among the group's members. Brown, an amateur musician, immediately joined the chorus and before long was serving on its executive committee and as chairman of the music committee.

When Harrison and Colvig visited Portland to tune Vince McDermott's gamelan in 1984 (chapter 5), they attended the chorus's Christmas concert. Brown suspects that Lou's excitement about the performance stemmed from the same roots as his own.

> What came across to him and to later audiences was the commitment that those amateurs brought. When we walked onto the stage for any concert, it was partly the usual exhilaration of walking before an audience, but even more, it was a public declaration of who we were in a time when that still wasn't done. Many people used the chorus as a way of telling their friends

and families about themselves, by inviting them to come to a concert. Before each performance, we would gather in a circle and people would be given a chance to speak. "Tonight my parents are here for the first time"; or "I just told my boss"; or "I invited my boss to come to this concert and he's not known about me before."[45]

As a former journalist, Brown knew the political power of publicity. He saw in the chorus a means to make an affirmative statement about homosexuality, a way of "projecting a positive image onto a group that had previously been a taboo subject in public discourse." In fact, the chorus had faced open opposition, including antigay banners; a picket line and massive telephone protest to the school board when they hired high school auditoriums; and, on two occasions, bomb threats. (In both instances, they proceeded nonetheless.)

But the positive responses far outweighed the negative. Brown had already successfully secured a grant from the Metropolitan Arts Commission for a performance of the Liszt *Requiem*, which, as far as he can determine, was the first instance of government support of an openly gay arts organization anywhere in the country. Now he had a new plan in mind.

> I began to feel that the chorus could not only make a difference in the lives of its members (which was important) and make a social statement (which was at least as important) but that it could also leave real tracks on music history by commissioning music. I remember standing up in front of the chorus during one of the business meetings and reflecting on a piece by Bruckner, commissioned by an Austrian chorus, which we were working on at the time. I said, "The members of that chorus are forgotten. The chorus itself would probably be forgotten if it weren't for this piece. But this piece is going to be performed and enjoyed and loved and move people for centuries. If we can cause music of lasting value to be created, we will have done something marvelous, far beyond what might be expected of an amateur group of gay men getting together because they thought that they needed to be doing something better than going to the bars." In my mind it would turn the chorus into a real force, both social and musical.[46]

The result was the commission for *Three Songs*, premiered on September 28, 1985 (chapter 3). For the first, Lou revised a setting of *David's Lament for Jonathan* (II Samuel), composed in San Francisco in October 1941 (CD, band 17). He included with the score two English versions (King James and the Revised Standard version), as well as the Hebrew, and suggested that the chorus experiment with using all three to create vivid changes in tone color.[47] Songs 2 and 3 feature texts from Walt Whitman's *Calamus* cycle from *Leaves of Grass*. "Oh You Whom I Often and Silently Come" is a revision of a baritone solo from 1946; "When I Heard at the Close of Day" uses entirely new material.

The *Songs* were an instant success, and the group featured them again in a joint performance with the San Francisco chorus on July 1, 1986. During the intermission of this concert Harrison approached Brown with the concept of rescoring *Young Caesar* for the ensemble of massed male voices. Despite the size of the chorus (programs from 1985–96 list 69–83 members), Lou still envisioned the work as a small understated production. "It could be done simply with shadow images," he suggested.

But Brown developed his own vision of the opera. He encouraged Lou to compose new choral numbers and secured external funding to hire costumers and stage managers. He reserved Portland's new Intermediate Theater in the Center for the Performing Arts (around nine hundred seats) and mounted an extraordinary publicity campaign. Lou did indeed compose new dramatic choruses and, in collaboration with Robert Hughes, altered and expanded the orchestration. Meanwhile, the chorus was awarded grants from the Metropolitan Arts Commission, the Oregon Arts Commission, the Whitelight Foundation, and the L. J. and Mary C. Skaggs Foundation. The group brought Hughes from Oakland to conduct and hired as the orchestra the Virtuosi Della Rosa, which called on musicians from both the Portland Opera and the Oregon Symphony. Ric Young, director of the Storefront Theater, created fanciful costumes that "struck a bohemian attitude" on a tiny budget. "I need you to bring me every piece of ribbon and glitter and gaudy material you can find," Brown recalls him telling the members.

Eventually the production's budget reached $40,000; Lou himself was amazed at its scope. "This achievement of the Portland Gay Men's Chorus," he wrote to Brown after the performances on April 9 and 10, 1988, "exceeded any of my expectations—I was, in fact, a little embarrassed and awe-struck during my first visit to realize the grand scale and theatrical genius that was being brought to bear on my work."[48] Brown summarized the outcome of their efforts: "Two performances, full costumes, seventy singers on the stage, some absolutely wonderful musical and stage effects. . . . And some long dry spells. Some of the audience loved it, and some didn't, including the *Oregonian*'s reviewer."[49]

After the exceptional effort, the intense fund-raising, and the widespread publicity that had been invested in the production, David Stabler's strongly negative review of the first performance (chapter 3), which appeared on the front page of the Sunday morning *Oregonian*'s Lively Arts section, was, at best, disheartening. " 'Young Caesar' may have worked with puppets, but it definitely does not with people," Stabler wrote. "A drearier work would be difficult to imagine. . . . The narrator was the most exciting thing about the production. . . . He had a magnificent voice. He spoke slowly and loudly; we could understand his words. He smoked a cigarette nicely, too."[50] But perhaps most discouraging was the paragraph in which Stabler subtly questioned the historical validity of the plot. " 'Young Caesar' is the story, supposedly true, of Julius Caesar and his exploits as a teenager avoiding one marriage and one beheading before falling in love with a Turkish king, Nicomedes."

That night Hughes gave the chorus a pep talk and they staged an inspired second performance, perhaps more so in defiance of the critic's caustic pen. The theater was sold out both nights.

Although the production resulted from intensive effort by many musicians and theatrical experts, Brown felt a measure of personal responsibility for any perceived failure. "I had to work out, over a period of time, whether I had made a mistake or whether I had indulged in any hubris of the bad kind," he reflects. "I now think not." Neither did the chorus. They wrote to Lou after the performance, "'Young Caesar' was an extraordinary event in our lives and in the life of the Portland Gay Men's Chorus. . . . Other productions of the opera may be more professional than ours, but none will be done more lovingly, nor with greater respect for the composer."[51]

Press response did not cease with Stabler's review. Articles and letters pro and con appeared in Oregon papers and in the gay press,[52] and the question of historical accuracy was debated in several letters to the editor. "In a way, we were delighted [by the questioning]. We all agreed that it was good to be noticed and to ruffle some feathers," said Brown.

In 1995 Lou, Bill, and Richard Brown were honored by life membership in the chorus. The organization noted their contribution to the musical life of the city and the positive image they helped create for Portland's gay community.

Lou's work with the Portland chorus piqued his interest in large all-male singing groups. He therefore responded positively when, soon after the premiere of *Three Songs,* Mark Morris suggested choreographing *Strict Songs,* with the Seattle Men's Chorus replacing the original eight baritones. Though Morris's 1987 choreography lacks the explicit gender-bending ambiguities of some of his later works (*Dido and Aeneas,* for example, or even *The Hard Nut*), the chorus of one hundred men suggests an agenda both aesthetic and political.

Harrison, too, along with Colvig, had become increasingly active politically in support of gay rights. The pair allowed their photos to be featured on a 1978 bus poster opposing the so-called Briggs Initiative, a California ballot measure that would have required school boards to fire or deny employment to anyone whose homosexuality became publicly known or who supported homosexual conduct. The poster, which appeared prominently on public buses in Santa Cruz County, featured the two men among a group of diverse individuals, with the simple slogan: "Somebody in your life is gay." (Colvig recalls seating himself prominently beneath the poster on a bus in Watsonville and was deeply disappointed that no one noticed.)[53]

By the time of Morris's production of *Strict Songs,* Lou and Bill had marched in numerous demonstrations, including one in San Francisco in the mid-1980s in which Harrison left the marchers to express his personal gratitude to the police posted along the route. "It dawned on me . . . that here were these patient policemen, hundreds of them along the route, and they were helping all around. . . . I went over [to one of them] and said . . . 'I want to thank you; you've been terrific through all of this.' He looked at me with such surprise. The officer next to him said, 'What did he say?' and it went on down the line that somebody had thought to thank them."[54]

Their open activism in recent years does not mark a change of direction but rather a more public extension of their long-term support of gay issues through such organizations as SIR and KPFA (one of the first stations to broadcast programs on homosexual issues). Lou has been equally outspoken in the press. As early as May 1963, during his residency at the University of Hawaii, he penned a letter of protest to the editor of the student newspaper:

> I encountered Carol Jay's letter in your columns of May 3. Haoles [Caucasians] have long called Negroes inferior & dirty. Headlines daily inform us that Negroes no longer accept the Haole view of them.
>
> Homosexuals have also been called inferior & dirty—& sick as well. This, one of the world's largest minorities, increasingly no longer accepts such views; neither does the state of Illinois. Several national organizations, among them the Mattachine Society, in San Francisco, & One Incorporated, in Los Angeles provide educational material on the subject for scholars & laymen.
>
> In the present population explosion, . . . calling homosexuals sick strikes this reader as a case of pots & kettles.[55]

To Harrison's credit, he did not allow societal condemnations of homosexuality to thrust him into the closet, to discourage the expression of his own sexuality, or to foster a bitterness toward the heterosexual majority. While it is impossible to assess the effect of such subtle pressures on his New York breakdown, he nevertheless was able to come to terms with his own sexuality without pretense or dissembling and to do so while retaining a respect for contrary viewpoints. He speaks to his society not as a representative of gay culture or Asian culture or Western American culture but as Lou Harrison, synthesizer of cultures, "composing a world."

11 Assembling the Pieces

The Compositional Process

For Harrison, the art of composition turns on the balance between spontaneity and craft. Never having comfortably settled into a single method or style, he is forever searching for new ones to try out. Lou rarely lacks ideas; instead, his task is more often to weed out enough of them to render his material manageable. He has absorbed one musical influence after another: Handel, Rameau, Cowell, Ives, Ruggles, Schoenberg, Thomson, Partch; percussion, tuning systems, Gregorian chant, Amerindian song, Korean court music, gagaku, gamelan, Chinese opera; Medieval, Baroque, modern, Indian, Turkish, and Javanese dance styles. As we have seen, he dives headfirst into an in-depth study of each new discovery; learns to imitate it; and then shapes the technique to fit his personal language—exemplifying his oft-stated motto: "Cherish, conserve, consider, create."[1]

Virgil Thomson noted in an essay in honor of Lou's seventieth birthday:

> It was Mozart's boast that he could master any musical style within a week and by the end of that time compose in it adeptly enough to deceive experts.
>
> Lou Harrison has something of that virtuosity himself. Eva Gauthier, who had spent some years in Java, told me that a symphony of Lou's for percussion orchestra was the only Western music she had ever heard that both felt and sounded like Indonesia. There is also a Mass that not only looks Elizabethan on the page

but that when performed with Elizabethan tunings takes on a harmoniousness both surprising and convincing. And there are twelve-tone orchestral works which might well be taken for the music of some hitherto unknown contemporary of Arnold Schoenberg. . . .[2]

With a mind constantly open to new sounds, and an easy facility to absorb and understand them, the problem for Harrison becomes one of sifting through the vast array of possibilities to arrive at a coherent and integral work of art. He often starts the compositional process by imposing on himself severe restrictions, which he calls "controls." These controls may take the form of a limited selection of intervals, melodic shapes, or rhythmic figures; or a tightly regulated organization of the material by extramusical factors (such as Cage's "square root" system, which defines a fixed mathematical relationship among the various subdivisions of the composition, from the length of the smallest phrase to that of the overall work). Controls may also be dictated by the technique of a particular instrument or by the restrictions of a specific tuning or mode. The effect, in any case, is to exclude enough possibilities so that those remaining provide a set of choices limited enough to be manageable. Bob Hughes notes that

> Lou seldom starts out with a gut, sensual idea. Rather, he begins with the scaffolding, which is usually some kind of logically rational preconceived formula that turns loose, as he manipulates the materials, into wonderfully sensuous, forward-flowing music. Although he may sometimes be motivated by an image or some lines of verse, as in the quote from the angel Israfel in the *Elegiac Symphony*, he begins composing by determining his structural basis.[3]

A second and perhaps equally important motivation for setting severe limitations is the challenge of solving an intricate puzzle. Lou "wins," so to speak, if he can create an inspired work evoking a sense of spontaneity while at the same time adhering strictly to a rigorous set of rules. The challenge is reminiscent of the hidden compositional restrictions in much Renaissance and Baroque music: proportional relationships in the repetition of a cantus firmus buried in the tenor of a Renaissance mass or motet, for instance, or complex canonic structures in Bach. Lou likens the process of composition to a delightful game in which he follows his own rules: "One does not usually cheat at solitaire";[4] when the artist loses his sense of play, "his art goes out the window."[5]

Among Lou's most common compositional restrictions is "interval control": he permits only a limited number of intervals either melodically or harmonically. He has used the technique since his earliest San Francisco compositions, such as the *Concerto for Flute and Percussion* (1939), in which the first and third movements contain only the intervals of a M2, m3, and M7 ascending or descending (example 11-1a). In the intervening slow movement, the m2 replaces the M2, an alteration appropriate for the change of mood from joyful to "slow and poignant" (example 11-1b).

EXAMPLE 11-1. *First Concerto for Flute and Percussion* (1939), showing "interval control." (Used by permission of C. F. Peters Corporation, © 1964.)

a. Movement 1. Permitted intervals: M2, m3, M7 ascending or descending (inversions not allowed).

Earnest, fresh, and fastish

b. Movement 2. The m2 replaces the M2.

Slow and poignant

In several early piano works (e.g., *Saraband* and *Prelude for Grandpiano*, from 1937, and *Third Piano Sonata*, from 1938) certain intervals are admitted for melodic motion, others for harmonies. In the *Prelude*, for instance, melodic intervals include the m2/M7, M3/m6, P4/P5, and tritone; harmonies are built from those remaining: the M2 and m3. Example 11-2 shows the opening of the *Third Piano Sonata*, with melodic motion restricted to the m2, M3, m7, and tritone (ascending or descending), and harmonic simultaneities built from superimposed perfect fifths and/or major seconds in each hand. Interval control, though particularly characteristic of early works, appears in compositions throughout Harrison's career, from the *Concerto for Violin with Percussion* (1959: m2, M3, and M6 in the violin part) to *New Moon* (1986; melodic M2, m3, and m6).

On the motivic level, Lou often chooses to limit his melodic material by preselecting specific figures, which he then transforms or rearranges by a kaleidoscopic process that continuously varies the composite picture. This fascination with manipulating small melodic cells was no doubt stimulated both by his study of Gregorian chant and by his work with Henry Cowell. He finds the technique so useful that he highlights it as the first item in his *Music Primer*.

The initial step is to select a few so-called melodicles, each comprising a small number of tones (the examples in the *Primer* range from two to four). These motives may be altered through transposition, inversion, or retrograde; combined in various ways; and placed either in successive or over-

EXAMPLE 11-2. *Third Piano Sonata* (1938), movement 1, beginning. (Courtesy of Hermes Beard Press and Peter Garland, ed., *Lou Harrison Reader*.)

(Grace notes are treated as harmonic intervals.)

lapping positions. Like interval control, restrictions on melodic figuration challenge the imagination. Example 11-3 shows a section from his *Suite for Symphonic Strings*, movement 6 (1960), in which every note can be related to one of three melodicles.

Rhythmic motives ("rhythmicles") can undergo similar transformation, or a rhythmic repetition can evoke the memory of a melodic motive. Such rhythmic manipulations date back to Harrison's early percussion works, many of which are built from the mutation of a simple motive with a distinct melodic and/or rhythmic shape. In *Canticle #3* (1942), for instance, Lou structured a fifteen-minute work around an opening figure in the ocarina, given as a melodic shape with unspecified pitches but with a distinctive rhythmic character (example 11-4). Pitched and unpitched percussion recall the motive in various forms throughout the composition.

This type of compositional process foreshadows the principles of minimalism, a connection cited by numerous commentators. "There's nothing Philip Glass has done that Lou hasn't done better," asserts Ned Rorem.[6] Daniel Cariaga, reviewing the Los Angeles premiere of the *Varied Trio* in 1988, notes: "Deceptively accessible, [the *Trio*] flaunts the elegance of simplicity. . . . Minimal in its materials—Harrison was a minimalist 40 years ago, when today's composers of that persuasion were children— it utilizes them with a thoroughness and rhetoric that make the total irresistible."[7]

The term *minimalism*, however, connotes decidedly different aesthetics in different contexts. In Lou's case, it implies a compositional process aimed at deriving maximum effect from a limited range of components: a materials-limiting device with which he can build on his attraction to the melodic and rhythmic surface to create both momentum and variety. The result is very different from the minimalism of Philip Glass, for example, where small amounts of material are repeated for such an extended period

EXAMPLE 11-3. *Suite for Symphonic Strings* (1960), movement 6, showing "melodicle" usage.

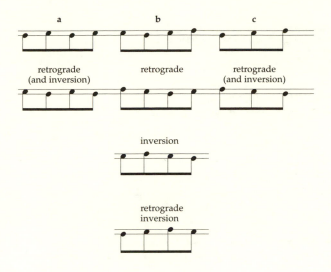

Measures 76-88. In the introduction to the score, Harrison remarks that the thirty-second notes are written-out ornaments and therefore should not be taken into account in the melodicle structure. These ornaments appear here in small notes within parentheses.

EXAMPLE 11-4. *Canticle #3* (1942). "Rhythmicle" manipulation. (© 1960 by Music for Percussion, Inc. Used by permission.)

(Although precise pitches for the ocarina are not given, Harrison prefers the following series, reading from lowest to highest: M2 m3 M2 M2. Interval sizes are approximate. Pitched percussion follow the same pattern.)

a. Opening figure in the ocarina

b. Measures 92-100. Development of the motive

EXAMPLE 11-4 (*continued*)

c. Measures 122-27. Motive treated in imitation

that the listener is forced away from the melodic surface to a meditative state in which change occurs in slow motion. In Glass's style, there is no momentum, no "getting to the point," no striving for diversity, as in the music of Harrison. Steve Reich, La Monte Young, and Terry Riley have also used the principle of material-limitation to further individual aesthetic aims: Reich providing subtle alterations in an established pattern through phase shifts, Riley and Young building on the traditional Hindu concept of a cosmic music, always present, to which we can "tune in." Of these younger composers, Harrison has a particular affinity for the music of Riley: he finds the Indian influences compelling and admires the diversity of his output.

Twelve-tone serialism imposes compositional restrictions potentially even tighter than interval control or melodicle/rhythmicle restraints, particularly since Lou finds that "the last three, and sometimes four, tones more often than not don't want to be there" (example 11-5a).[8]

EXAMPLE 11-4 (*continued*)

d. Measures 363-73. Gradual expansion of the rhythmic shape

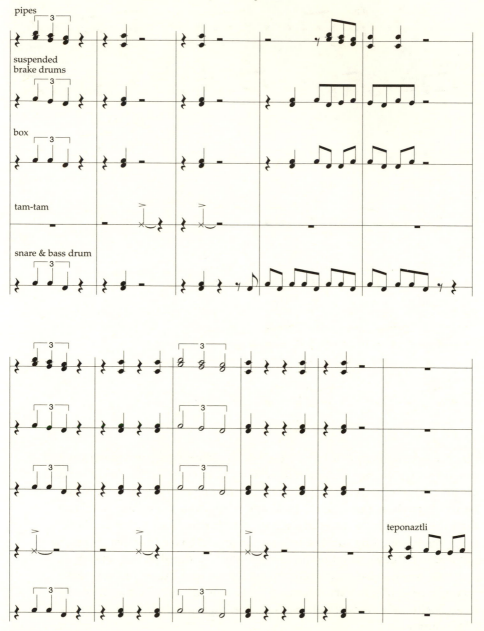

EXAMPLE 11-5. Tone row usage.

a. Examples of rows in which some notes fail to fit the predominant pattern:

1. *Rapunzel* (1952):

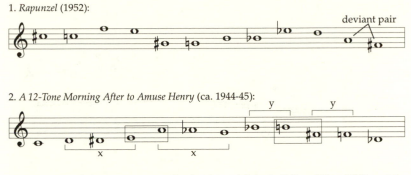

2. *A 12-Tone Morning After to Amuse Henry* (ca. 1944-45):

3. *Symphony on G* (begun 1947; completed 1964) and *Suite for Cello and Harp* (1949; revision of mvt. 3c of *Symphony*):

Tone rows, like any other restriction, can be manipulated to serve specific aims: in Lou's case, often lyricism. The "Aria" from the *Suite for Cello and Harp* (example 11-5b)[9] features a singing, chromatically based melodic line over an ostinato with tonal references—creating an impressionistic play of triads during the first four measures and an arrival on F in measure 5. It is easy to hear the triadic implications of this opening passage: the perfect fourth in the opening ostinato, the prominent major third at the entrance of the cello, the third-fifth-sixth complex on the downbeat of measure 4, and the major triad with added tone in measure 5. "Lou has always been a 'tonalist' even when he wrote serial music," notes conductor Dennis Russell Davies.[10]

A similar lyric impulse is found in many other compositions, such as the "Aria" from the twelve-tone *Suite for Piano* or the Ruggles-inspired *Trio* for strings. Reviewers admired Lou's bent for melodic expression even in an atonal context,[11] and the *Trio* prompted Virgil Thomson to compliment his skills in both counterpoint and expressivity: "Lou Harrison's *Trio* is . . . both consistently dissonant and deeply felt. It has clear phraseology, spontaneity of gesture, a humane discourse. Except for the Webern pieces . . . it is the real news of the week end. Few composers anywhere in the world are writing integral counterpoint . . . with either Mr. Harrison's skill or his intense and straightforward expressivity."[12]

Harrison's row usage is based on a principle of permutation: rather than always starting on pitch 1, he may begin anywhere within any of the row's

EXAMPLE 11-5 (*continued*)

b. *Suite for Cello and Harp,* movement 4, beginning (© 1954 by Peer International Corporation. International copyright secured. Reprinted by permission.) Intervals notated by Harrison for the convenience of the harpist are interpreted in our analysis as they are perceived aurally.

forms, cycling back to the beginning to encompass all twelve notes in order. At times he extracts one or two pitches as drones or ostinatos, allowing him to skip those notes and in effect work with a shorter series. Such variations on strict serial technique came in handy while he was writing *Rapunzel*, whose series is a "trick row" with only half the possibilities of a normal row—a feature Harrison did not discover until he was partway through the composition.[13] *Rapunzel*'s row is limited in two ways: (1) it is nearly semi-combinatorial: combining halves of two different versions yields eleven of the twelve pitches; and (2) the first ten notes of P_0 are identical to the first ten notes of I_1 in retrograde (example 11-6a). The row itself, then, becomes self-limiting, making the compositional game that much more difficult.

For the opening theme of the opera (introduced in imitation), Lou built a melody from the row minus tones 2 and 3 (F and C), which form an ostinato throughout Act 1 (example 11-6b). Extracting the same tones (F and C) from P_{11}, he then used the inner ten pitches to create a dramatic, descending line in the strings that recurs as an ominous reminder of the witch's power (example 11-6c). The witch herself frequently interjects a chilling leitmotif—"Rapunzel, Rapunzel, let down your hair"—derived from P_0 by beginning with its third pitch and cycling back to pitch 1 (omitting the drone tone c; example 11-6d).

While Harrison became enormously skilled at manipulating twelve-tone rows and unearthing hidden possibilities within them, he was often more comfortable with a shorter series, which he could create not only by extracting tones as ostinati or drones but also by using freer procedures such as the "Ruggles style," in which "a particular tone does not usually return until seven or eight have intervened."[14] Lou was attracted both to Ruggles's ability to avoid excessive pitch repetition and to the "total polyphony" of his music—"a community of singing lines." Using quasi-serial procedures, Lou could avoid the perception of tonal center while at the same time being freed from the strict "rules" of row usage, thus creating an internally consistent dissonant polyphonic style that was at the same time unique to the individual work. He has experimented with the Ruggles style periodically throughout his life, in works as disparate as the *Saraband* for piano (1937), the fourth movement of the *Elegiac Symphony* (1975), and the *Double Canon for Carl Ruggles* (1951), later revised as movement 2 of the *Concerto for Organ with Percussion* (1973; example 11-7).

In the 1950s, when American composers young and old increasingly embraced serialism as the new postwar credo (Copland, for example, wrote his first serial piece in 1950,[15] and Stravinsky gradually slid into serial practice after Schoenberg died in 1951), Harrison did the opposite. He had been writing twelve-tone works since his San Francisco years and was ready for a new direction. "The cyclic nature of 12-tone music," notes composer Janice Giteck, "made an interesting transition for Lou out of Western music into Asian musics, which are also based on cyclical principles. But the irony is

EXAMPLE 11-6. Tone row use in *Rapunzel* (1952).

a. Row forms

b. Opening of Act 1: row with F and C
   (tones 2-3) extracted as a drone

c. Violin/viola motive: P_{11} with F and C (tones 1 and 12) extracted as a drone

d. Witch's theme: row beginning on pitch 3 and cycling back to beginning with drone
   tone C extracted

Ra - pun - zel,_____ Ra - pun - zel,_____ Let down your hair_____

Orchestra:

EXAMPLE 11-7. *Double Canon for Carl Ruggles* (1951), later revised for *Concerto for Organ with Percussion Orchestra,* movement 2 (1973). (Courtesy of Hermes Beard Press.)

Avoiding excessive pitch repetition without using strict serial procedures. Most pitch repetitions in a single voice recur only after seven or more intervening notes.

that Lou went from twelve-tone music, which was a door out of big tonal development in Western music, to something that was so modal that the suspension of the tonic is allowed because the tonic is ever-present."[16]

After *Rapunzel* (1952), Lou for the most part reserved serialism (often in conjunction with Equal Temperament) for representations of the evils of Western society, as in the bomb movement of *Pacifika Rondo* (1963), whose row features historical musical symbols of tragedy: half steps (a traditional "lament" signature in Renaissance and Baroque music); two tritones (the old "devil in music"); and, at the row's center, an augmented triad (example 11-8a). Occasionally he turned to tone rows purely for the joy of method that Schoenberg had instilled in him, as in the triumphal trumpet fanfare in the last movement of *The Clays' Quintet* (1987; example 11-8b).

Other types of compositional controls often govern phrase or movement structures. The form of the odd-numbered movements of *Pacifika Rondo,* for example, is determined by the permutation of prime-number beat sequences. Large phrases are comprised of seventeen primary quarter-note beats subdivided into discrete subphrases of 2, 3, 5, and 7 (in any order), yielding twenty-four possible arrangements. Movement 1 opens with the cycle 7-3-5-2, followed by its retrograde, 2-5-3-7 (example 11-9). The four subphrases are always separated by an extra quarter-note rest or tied note, thus clearly marking the end of one subphrase and the beginning of the next, perhaps an attempt to notate the "breath rhythm" of gagaku (boxed elements in example 11-9). At the same time, Harrison disguises the structure by allowing for expansion of any quarter-note beat by interpolating an extra eighth note, yielding measures of 3/8 or 5/8 (interpolated notes are shown in brackets). The process resembles a compositional technique of expanding phrases by interpolation described as early as 1787 by H. C. Koch and apparent in many late-eighteenth-century works.[17] In *Pacifika Rondo,* however, the beat pattern is further masked by marking individual tones at

EXAMPLE 11-8. Later twelve-tone works. (ST = semitone; TT = tritone.)

a. *Pacifika Rondo* (1963), movement 6

b. *The Clays' Quintet* (1987), movement 4

regular or irregular intervals with ornaments (written-out ornaments are enclosed in parenthesis in example 11-9).

Lou thus disguises the prime number sequence while retaining it as the deep structural basis for his composition. The listener senses a recurring pattern whose details are not transparent; in the Asian styles that inspired *Pacifika Rondo*, the pattern would have been not only recurring but also regular and isometric. In Lou's reimagining of the style, the phrase length itself—seventeen beats—mandates an irregular subdivision, and the ordering of the subphrases is subjected to constant permutation.

EXAMPLE 11-9. *Pacifika Rondo* (1963), movement 1 melody. (© 1976 by Peer International Corporation. International copyright secured. Reprinted by permission.)

In order to clarify the structure, the example below shows the melody in its simplest form. Other instruments may be simultaneously ornamenting the same melody as shown in small notes above the main staff. Celesta chords have been simplified to their essential notes; examples of the actual pitches are shown above the staff.

Interpolated eighth notes are shown in brackets [♪].
Quarter-note beats separating sub-phrases are enclosed in boxes ♩.

Pacifika Rondo gives the impression of regularity despite asymmetric controls; at other times (such as variation works like the *Air in G Minor*), the immediate effect is one of freedom, while in fact the structure is surprisingly rigid. Again, the eighteenth-century parallel is striking. C. P. E. Bach, in his influential manual on keyboard playing,[18] instructs the performer to begin the process of creating a free fantasia by fashioning a coherent bass line from a simple scale into which chromatic tones have been interpolated or whose pitches have been rearranged. Harrison similarly delights in such hidden controls. "It's part of the game of writing music," he notes. "I don't want to be taking the listener on a guided tour of my compositional technique."[19]

Lou's ability to devise a tight framework but then clothe this skeleton with elegant attire makes the final result at once accessible and coherent. "He doesn't write music for which one has to read three journal articles before listening," notes David Doty.

> Sonic beauty is always his primary consideration. Many composers [today] don't consider it quite decent to make sonic beauty a consideration—perhaps not even a secondary one. People working with computers and artificial intelligence, for instance, come up with arcane algorithmic schemes that are fascinating to read about. But when you hear the pieces you think, "Maybe I'd better stick to reading the articles and not have to listen to the final results."[20]

Those who have studied composition with Lou often highlight his emphasis on freedom supported by structure. Robert Hughes's decision to move to California to study with Harrison resulted in part from his learning (from Lou himself) about restrictive controls underlying the apparently unfettered *Suite for Cello and Harp*. Hughes, Richard Dee, Seymour Barab, and others report that Lou teaches composition by assigning exercises that seem at first so restrictive as to stifle individuality. By learning to find the expressive possibilities within the rules, however, the student gains exceptional control of the compositional process. Hughes describes his exposure to the method when he arrived in California, "tied up in knots" from his studies with Dallapiccola:

> I arrived thinking the only way to make great art is to furl your brow and follow the European model. Lou immediately said, "Oh, you've got yourself constipated now, haven't you? Well, we need a cathartic for musical constipation. Let's give you a dose of John Cage's square root theory. Pick a number from 1 to 9." I picked seven. "Now you're going to use a series of melodicles, little groups of notes, seven each. Seven times seven will give you your first phrase. Seven times the first phrase will give you the number of strophes in the piece." I sat down with enormous admiration for Lou and absolutely no faith in what he was telling me. I knew artistic creation was something other than this type of mathematical exercise. But the composition that emerged ended up being about the best thing I'd ever written. I realized that by letting the natural playfulness of my intuition dominate the elaborate constipations of the twelve-tone serial technique, he had freed me from the knots. I eventually orchestrated that little piece as part of a suite which, of all my orchestral work, has been played more than any other.[21]

The movement that emerged from this exercise was an estampie, a lively melody with complex rhythm and straightforward organization. For Lou, melody and rhythm have always held primary importance: "Music," he has often said, "is basically a song and a dance." The simultaneities in most of his music are governed primarily by contrapuntal rather than harmonic considerations. Lou's attraction to Ruggles was above all to the integrity of the counterpoint: no filler lines, each voice "a real melody."[22] A brief item in the *Music Primer* outlines types of counterpoint found in the world's various musics. Lou separates formal counterpoint into imitative and nonimitative, each subdivided into diatonic or chromatic; these four categories he defines further according to the prevalence of simultaneously sounding intervals on strong beats: octaval, quintal, tertial, or secundal. "Informal counterpoint," whether imitative or nonimitative, diatonic or chromatic, is based on heterophonic structures. Finally, counterpoint may be "differentiated" or "nondifferentiated" (in Virgil Thomson's terminology) by the rhythmic character and style of its component voices.[23]

At times Lou has dispensed with both harmony and counterpoint, preferring to let his melodic/rhythmic invention stand alone accompanied either by rhythmic figuration or a drone. Obvious examples are the concerti with percussion (the *First Concerto for Flute and Percussion* [1939], the *Concerto for Violin with Percussion* [1959], the *Concerto in Slendro* [1961], etc.), but the technique also appears within other works, such as the *String Quartet Set* and the *Varied Trio*, or in his many estampie movements.

Harrison has found the estampie one of the most attractive and practical forms of musical composition. He has used it in at least a dozen compositions, ranging from solos to full orchestra, including the *String Quartet Set* (1979), the *Suite for Symphonic Strings* (1960), the *Suite for Violin and American Gamelan* (1974), the *Double Concerto for Violin, Cello, and Gamelan* (1982), the third and fourth symphonies (1982 and 1990), the *Piano Concerto* (1985), the *Grand Duo* (1988), and his new *Concerto for P'i-P'a with String Orchestra* (1997). In recent years he has taken to calling these lively movements "stampedes," a delightful cognate of the medieval French word that he seized on after an off-hand comment by percussionist William Winant. Unfamiliar with the term *estampie*, Winant ingenuously blurted out "stampede" during a rehearsal, immediately sending Lou to the dictionary to trace the word origins. There he discovered a reference to noise, or as he says, "a general brouhaha."[24] His estampies often feature whirling melodic lines in octaves or double octaves supported by irregularly accented rhythmic figures.

Melodies supported by drones are another favorite technique. Examples abound in Lou's works: in the recitative passages of *Rapunzel*, in the *Suite for Symphonic Strings* (movement 1), and in *La Koro Sutro*, to cite but a few. For many years Harrison sought a contrapuntal line that would complement a sensuous four-minute flute air composed near the end of his hospitalization in 1947.[25] Nothing worked to his satisfaction until he tried the single tone d' sustained during the entire piece, which lent a shimmering background to his expressive plaint. A similar rhapsodic song with drone appears in the *Music for Violin with Various Instruments* (1967, movement 2), during which the violinist imitates Asian psaltery techniques with pitch slides.

Still another support for many of Lou's melodies is the ostinato, which can be as basic as an expanded drone or as complex as a multimeasure melodic line treated in canon, as in *Pacifika Rondo*, movement 4 (example 11-10a). A similar technique, jhālā, borrowed from North Indian practice, involves the intermittent reiteration of a single tone between the notes of the main melody—in essence, an interrupted drone or, as Lou likes to call it, "India's answer to the Alberti bass."[26] The *Suite for Violin and American Gamelan* contains three "jahlas" (Lou's orthography); he wrote another for harp (or guitar) "to pleasure Leopold Stokowski on his ninetieth birthday" in 1972 (example 11-10b).

The importance Harrison places on melody explains the immediate affinity he felt for the music of Hovhaness (chapter 2)—another composer unafraid to indulge in pure melodic expression during a period (and among a community of composers) attracted to complex harmonic and contrapuntal structures. Lou's *Herald Tribune* review of Hovhaness's concert highlighted the "clean, decorative . . . melodic lines, frequently of a highly ornamented nature," supported by extended drones. "For the listener, such music is a sure test of the degradation of his ear," Lou wrote. "If he can hear ideas without the aid of modulations and the like he is yet of sound listening abilities."[27] Hovhaness remembers himself as "a lone voice for melody" during the 1940s: "I expected people to make fun of me." He admires in Lou's music "the strength of pure melody; strong, empty, often chordless harmonies; pure, free and clear textures; melodies often sounding against single tones; clashing melodic, moving sounds."[28]

Harrison's breakdown in a sense freed him from forces urging him to compose in a style antithetical to his inclinations and encouraged him to explore more fully diatonicism and melody. Shortly after his hospitalization, he traveled to Canada (his first trip outside the United States) where he became acquainted with Quebecois art, architecture, and music, and purchased volumes of folk songs. "That proved to be very important in my melodic evolution," he notes, "because it constituted my first real study of a folk music, except for a brief early encounter with Appalachian music."[29]

In 1952, he wrote:

I . . . think of [melody] as melos riding on the crest of kinesis. I believe in . . . traditional formations, on the grounds that form and expression are accidents of assemblage, and not possible without the first essential, traditional choice. . . .

I am quite opposed to Frank Lloyd Wright's remark that just as modern architecture has done away with unnecessary cornice adornment of buildings, so has modern music done away with melody. On the contrary, I feel that essentially and necessarily, music is an adventure in time awareness and that the singlest, most simple route to this beauty is through melody; for herein is form, shape, "recollection," surprise, architecture, and the "take-home-pay" of memorable tune.[30]

EXAMPLE 11-10. Ostinati.

a. *Pacifika Rondo* (1963), movement 4: a six-measure ostinato figure treated in canon. (© 1976 by
Peer International Corporation. International copyright secured. Reprinted by permission.)

EXAMPLE 11-10 (*continued*)

b. *Jahla in the Form of a Ductia to Pleasure Leopold Stokowski on his Ninetieth Birthday* (1972),
showing an "interrupted drone" on d'. Quoted from the transcription by David Tanenbaum
(*The Lou Harrison Guitar Book,* 1994. Used by permission of Lyon and Healy Harps, Inc.;
guitar arrangement used by permission of Columbia Music Company, Inc.)

Lou's trips to Asia reinforced his appreciation of the manifold possibilities of intricate melody, downplayed by Western music since the late Renaissance in favor of harmonic complexity. During his second trip to Korea, in 1962, he delivered a lecture titled "Creative Ideas in Classical Korean Music" (subsequently published in the *Korea Journal*), in which he extolled the value of melody as a form-building technique.

> First in importance to the western mind is the revelation that . . . the form of a piece can be one giant melody, evolving as melodies beautifully do, and accumulating body decorations as it goes. Since the middle ages, European music has broken . . . further down into minuscule two-tone "motives" . . . which are the end of the matter. Suddenly one realizes that, to classic Korean ears, the first movement of Beethoven's *Fifth Symphony* must sound like a fairly uninteresting melody ornamented by a persistent little repeated grace-note. Personally, I feel that young composers . . . should begin to learn to compose just such giant basic melodies, and, repeating the methods of history, learn also to enrich and ornament these into full compositions. . . .
>
> The importance of Melody (as musical form) in opposition to motive cannot be overemphasized—it is of capital importance to the future of music. . . .
>
> The concept of "octave" music . . . results in a beautiful kind of simultaneous variation, for each instrumental group varies the melody in a way appropriate to itself. What is more, each of the variations is a true melodic variation, related perpetually to the giant melody. Europe knew this technique as late as the seventeenth century in the English "Divisions on a Ground." This was before Variations deteriorated into fiddling around on a chord succession.

The classic pieces of Korean music are already contrapuntal in style. All the lovely variations being played at once presents a fascinating and intricate counterpoint which is very real. Some have expressed an urge to simplify all this luxury into triads. It would be folly. . . . Some have a wish to hear thorough-going imitative polyphony in the classic style. I see nothing much wrong with this whimsy and can offer that the best way to do it is simply to find out at what beat distant and at what interval . . . the giant melody will make a good total Canon. . . . Almost every good melody has at least one or two fine canons inherently possible to it; one does not at all need to compose a melody especially for canon.[31]

Lou's awareness of the uniqueness of melody arose from his early San Francisco experiences, such as those with the deaf roommate who shared his apartment on Telegraph Hill. "I would play music for him, and he could get some sense of the rhythm and dynamics . . . by feeling the vibrations. But the one thing I could never get across to him was what melody is. . . . I concluded that melody is something special."[32] Another early influence was his study of Gregorian chant and Amerindian song, which have found more recent voice in works such as his chant mass for the feast of St. Cecilia set for unison choir with optional organ and percussion (1986).

Intellectual circles in contemporary music may at first distrust the ingenuousness of forthright melodic expression. The concert-going public, however, has a very different response—at times almost a relief that it's OK to delight in simple pleasures and indulge in melodic sensuousness. Cowell, for one, consistently supported Harrison's emphasis on melody. After the 1939 concerto for flute and percussion was published in 1953, he wrote: "The [flute] line is so interesting—your pieces are always a peg more exciting and more musical than those of others!"[33]

The role of melody was one of the main attractions of Asian music. But Lou's study of the musics of various cultures ultimately led him to integrate diverse compositional procedures as well. On the most obvious level, we have noted the intermingling of instrumental forces, from his earliest experiments at introducing Chinese and Korean instruments into a Western string ensemble (*Nova Odo, Pacifika Rondo*) to his concertolike settings for violin, viola, cello, saxophone, trumpet, French horn, and piano against the background of the Javanese gamelan (1978–87). On a more subtle level, the process may involve transference of melodic, rhythmic, or harmonic language from one style into another, such as the two "gamelan" movements in the *Suite for Violin, Piano, and Small Orchestra* (1951) or the Indonesian mode in the *Concerto in Slendro* (1961). One reviewer even called his *Concerto for Violin with Percussion* "Alban Berg on an Indonesian jaunt."[34] The transfer has also occurred in reverse: tuning gamelan in Just Intonation systems, for instance.

Pacifika Rondo is a personalization of Japanese and Korean musics. In essence Harrison presents his own vision of the music of ninth- and tenth-century China by creatively extrapolating back from surviving forms of gagaku and Korean court music, which preserve many Chinese practices. During the Tang and Sung Dynasties (618–1279 A.D.), many Japanese and Korean students traveled to China to study. The Chinese works from that period have all changed or been lost, and the few surviving manuscript sources are difficult or impossible to interpret today. Thus, the best contemporary evidence of early Chinese musical style survives in those Chinese elements preserved in Japanese or Korean court musics. Unlike the work of musicologists such as Laurence Picken and his students at Cambridge, however, Lou is not attempting historical reconstruction but rather is sharing a Harrisonian vision of the past.

Similarly, the recitatives in *Young Caesar* were inspired in part by the Chinese theater.

> I love the Chinese system of punctuating vocal melodies with woodblocks and cymbals. . . . It makes everything more vivid. . . . I wondered, when I was hearing Chinese operas as a young man, whether [it] would be distracting if you understood what they were saying. . . . And then at the University of Hawaii [in 1963] I heard a Chinese opera in English . . . and, no! It . . . works very well, and so I adopted it. You can vary [the punctuation depending on] the importance of the sentence, or herald the new sentence . . . , or vary the points in between.[35]

These recitatives are an example of creative adaptation of a musical technique for its functional value without any attempt at directly imitating the model. There is no use of Chinese instruments or rhythmic patterns, nor any attempt to evoke the sound of Chinese opera; rather, where Western recitatives might use harmonic punctuation, Lou has substituted rhythmic punctuation (example 11-11).

In recent years Lou has used Javanese compositional techniques in otherwise Western works, notably in the *Fourth Symphony* and the *Piano Trio* (both composed in 1990), where he adopts embellishment procedures commonly heard in the faster-moving instruments of the gamelan to a chromatic harmonic language. Example 11-12 shows the opening of the second movement of the *Trio*, in which Lou imitates mipil (embellishment by oscillation between pairs of pitches; see chapter 8). Each pair of balungan pitches in the cello is played twice in diminution by the violin, which anticipates the first pitch and arrives in unison with the second (example 11-12a). In typical Javanese fashion, the gatra pitches cross the beat. Beginning in measure 15, Lou introduces cèngkok procedures in the piano: an ornamental figure eight times faster than the skeletal melody is repeated with small variations in succeeding measures, while intersecting it at the unison on the "goal tones" at downbeats (example 11-12b). The change from a 2:1 to an 8:1 ratio also suggests a shift of irama. As with his other controls, Lou has here adopted a strict set of rules that provides a basis for the movement's organization without wearing his compositional technique on his sleeve. "I'm

EXAMPLE 11-11. *Young Caesar* (revised version, 1988), scene 11. (Courtesy of Hermes Beard Press.)

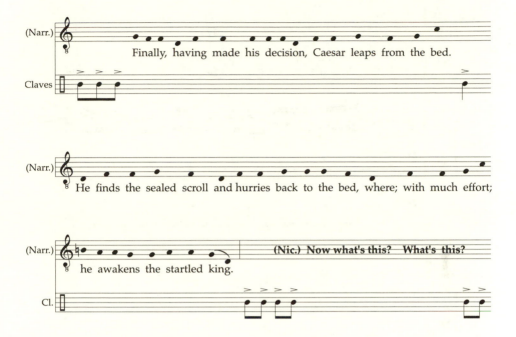

EXAMPLE 11-12. Demonstration of *mipil* and *cèngkok* procedures in the *Piano Trio* (1990), movement 2. (Courtesy of Hermes Beard Press.)

a. Opening of the movement

EXAMPLE 11-12 (*continued*)

b. Measures 15-19

Piano ornamentation reaches unison with melody on each downbeat.

quite proud of this movement because using the mipil and cèngkok behaviors works well and one wouldn't know what I had done. If I pointed it out, of course, you'd say, 'Oh yes.' "[36]

Lou is also currently exploring a complementary idea: specifically, using the Western concerto grosso form in a gamelan composition. The concept is a logical extension from the *Concerto in Slendro* (1961), which was "just planned as a simple Vivaldi concerto" even though its mode evokes Java, as do the washtubs and garbage cans, which "were a convenient way of imitating the sounds of Indonesian gongs."[37] As Lou notes, "The gamelan has [the concerto grosso] possibility within it since it's divided into the loud instruments and the delicate chamber textures of the panerusan instruments."[38]

Such synchronic integrations of East and West are a natural development from the diachronic integrations Lou had employed for years: his adoption, for instance, of Medieval forms such as the estampie, ductia, or *conductus*, or of Elizabethan variation forms.[39]

He has also derived musical forms from poetic forms. (One of his working tools, Lewis Turco's little encyclopedia of poetic forms,[40] has stimulated a number of structural concepts.) As early as the 1940s, Lou based a movement of his *Labyrinth #3* on terza rima, Dante's structure in the *Divine Comedy*: three-line units with an interlocking rhyme scheme, ABA-BCB-CDC-DED, and so on. (The dolphin movement of *Pacifika Rondo* uses the same form.) In this and other compositions, Harrison translates the poetic rhyme scheme into a series of musical phrases that repeat verbatim according to the defined pattern.[41]

Harrison (unlike Cage) has maintained and defended the authority of the creator over the work of art in the detailed manipulation of motives, rhythms, textures, and timbres. "I would rather chance a choice than choose a chance," he has often stated.[42] Not that Lou has in any way eschewed improvisation; on the contrary, he had been improvising since the age of two-and-a-half when he recited ex tempore dialogue in *Daddy Long Legs*, and, as we have already shown, he became highly skilled at musical improvisation through his work with dancers. But when it came to a completed composition made ready for public presentation, he could not help but feel that the inspiration of the moment was nearly always less successful than choices considered in advance. He is fond of quoting Stravinsky that an inspired composition is the reward of hard work. "When I find myself inspired, I enjoy it—but I try to lay the pencil down, for, if I continue, I know that I shall have to use the eraser in the morning. The 'inspiration' here meant is as in the story of God taking Sunday off to find his work good."[43] While the idea may be considered old-fashioned in light of the postmodern reaction to the restrictions of serialism, Lou still holds firm to his belief in "planned art. The world is very full of chaos," he notes. "The world of chemistry and physics . . . simply [boils down to] entropy—it all grinds down to nothing. . . . But . . . I still believe that life and its activities are for the creation and maintenance of form. . . . I'm still on that side—planning, making, creating and maintaining form."[44]

How, in this context, can one explain Lou's musical kits, which authorize the performer to create new compositions by ordering, repeating, or selecting materials in ways not controlled by the composer? We have already cited one such work, *Ariadne* (1987), in which seven phrases for percussion and seven for flute may be joined in any combination, played on various instruments or in different octaves, repeated, or omitted entirely. The movement's length can thus range from five minutes to fifteen or more, subject to control not by the composer but by the musicians or the dancer, who also determine the simultaneous or successive interactions between slow-moving or rapid passages and hence the prevailing emotional affect. Over the years Harrison has used the kit concept in about a half dozen works, including two very recent ones: the second movement of his 1992 *Suite for Four Haisho* and portions of *Rhymes with Silver*, premiered to great acclaim in 1997.

In most cases, Harrison's kits have been prompted by an attempt to meet the elastic needs of other artforms, such as dance or film. As early as 1942, he provided such performance flexibility in his eight-movement dance, *In Praise of Johnny Appleseed*. In this work performers and choreographer are free to assemble pre-composed phrases within each movement in various orders and to repeat or omit them at will. By skillful composition of the building blocks, Harrison retains his personal voice while allowing for appropriate contextual use by dancers or filmmakers. In such works he followed the lead of his mentor Henry Cowell, who spent years seeking a successful interaction of dance and music that would respect both arts as equal partners in a composite work.[45]

Harrison's most flexible composition is the loosely organized theater kit *Jephtha's Daughter*, begun in 1941 and expanded in 1963, which contains dramatic readings, three melodies for flute, four patterns for percussion, suggested drones, and other elements. He authorizes any combination of these melodies, rhythms, drones, and even color schemes, to be interspersed with the spoken text.

Such extensive compositional freedom, however, is highly unusual for Harrison. In general, he makes the compositional choices and the performer executes them. That is not to say that he restricts the performer's freedom of interpretation. On the contrary, Lou is not only tolerant of varied interpretations of his works; he welcomes them so long as they remain within the work's intent and style. Many of his instrumental scores provide minimal instructions on slurring or phrasing. Keith Jarrett and Ursula Oppens, the two pianists who have most often played his *Piano Concerto*, emphasize different phrases within each movement and different notes within each phrase, divergencies that Lou cherishes. "I was stunned when I heard [Oppens play the *Concerto*]," he recalls. "She found secret places different from the ones Keith found. It felt like another first performance."[46]

Unlike many composers who hold rigid ideas about the interpretation of their scores, Harrison allows performers to find in his music the interpretation most natural to their personal style. During a recording session of the *Concerto for Flute and Percussion*, for example, Leta Miller (the flutist) inquired about his preferred interpretation of a motive in the slow movement: should the quarter-note ending the phrase be played as a release from the previous half-note or as a pick-up to the next phrase—that is, as a sigh or as a dynamic thrust? "Whichever you wish," he replied, later explaining that by leaving such decisions to the performer, he increased the likelihood of a convincing interpretation. "I've learned a great deal from performers," Lou has told us on more than one occasion.

And from conductors as well. Robert Hughes recalls Lou telling him about Stokowski's recording of the *Suite for Violin, Piano, and Small Orchestra*.[47]

> Lou was already in California when the recording was made and was sent the vinyl LP master. He played it, and when he got to the end of the last movement the recording kept going. Stokowski had added an extra bar and a half. Lou was outraged. How had Stokowski felt the liberty to do this? He went to a friend who lived nearby and played the recording. The audacity, you know, of these conductors and what they do! Still outraged, he went to another and slowly let off steam. By the time he had played the record for three or four people, however, he realized that Stokowski was right; the movement needed those extra few beats. Stokowski had come to the work fresh and saw what was needed. Lou decided to accept Stokowski's revision and simply allow the bars to be added.[48]

On the other hand, notes conductor Dennis Russell Davies, Harrison is very particular about tempi. "Generally he wants the slow tempos very, very slow, and the fast tempos very, very fast. That gray area that so many musicians like to be in doesn't interest him."[49]

Lou's eagerness to learn from performers, conductors, and critics and his seemingly continuous series of investigations into unfamiliar styles has led him to constantly tinker with his older compositions—revising, repairing, reevaluating, rescoring. Even a cursory examination of the catalog at the end of this book shows the large number of cross-references and revisions. Here Lou is in good company. His beloved Handel was a master at using old material in new guises; so were Bach, Ives, Mahler, and many others.

There are, of course, several motivations for revision or alteration, the most obvious being a dissatisfaction with the original. A critic once asked Lou how he knew when a work was finished. "When it stops itching," he replied.[50] Some works have itched for years. In 1937, for example, Harrison composed *Passacaglia* for piano. Five years later he revised it, coupled it with the *Ricercare on Bach's Name*, which he had begun in the same year, and orchestrated the two pieces for strings to form his *Canticle #2*. Still dissatisfied with the *Passacaglia* in 1946, he reworked it once again, creating a new work, *Ground for Strings*, that then became movement 3 of the *First Suite for Strings*, premiered in May 1948. Peer International published the *Suite* in 1978 and republished it again in 1991, with some alterations to the second movement. Even then the old *Passacaglia*, now in its third metamorphosis, still itched, as did several of the other movements. In 1995 Harrison completely revised his *Suite* once again. In so doing, he threw out the old *Passacaglia/Canticle #2/Ground for Strings*—one of his longest-lasting and most persistently annoying dissatisfactions—and replaced it by an entirely new movement. The *Suite*, now titled *New First Suite for Strings*, is finally complete . . . at least for the time being.

In other cases a work remains incomplete for lack of a performance opportunity; when it is finished many years later, new considerations demand revision. Such was the case with the *Symphony on G*, much of which Lou composed in the hospital in 1947. He put the symphony aside until the prospect of performance materialized with the founding of the Cabrillo Music Festival. After the work's 1964 premiere, however, he found that he didn't care for the finale. Neither did Alexander Fried, who reviewed the concert for the *San Francisco Examiner:* "The symphony is in great part a striking, absorbing score, written on a big scale and marked with forceful, various expressive personality," wrote Fried. "The one weak part is its Finale. . . . The movement sounded laborious and ended pointlessly. He ought to rewrite it."[51] He did.

All of his symphonies have undergone some reworking following their initial performances. Some, such as the *Third* and the *Fourth*, have been revised several times. Carlos Chávez told Lou, after the premiere of portions of *Young Caesar* at the Cabrillo Music Festival: "This is only the first performance; now you can get to work."[52] The issue is particularly critical in the case of large symphonic works in which the composer has little opportunity to hear a realization of the score before the premiere; and it may be particularly acute in Lou's case, since he frequently avoids standard orchestration practices, instead preferring to invent new sounds and experiment with unusual instrumental usage. He advised composer Janice Giteck, as she began to prepare a commission for the San Francisco Symphony, "Don't start with brand-new material; start instead with material you already feel good about, and orchestrate it. In that way, you can spend your time making the orchestra sound wonderful."[53]

Harrison grabs eagerly at every opportunity to perfect his work before its performance, assiduously attending rehearsals with score in hand. Nor does he hesitate to revise even at the last minute. After the first rehearsal of *Parade for M.T.T.* (1995) he immediately began a series of alterations. "I could hear exactly where the problems lay and knew how to fix them before the weekend performance," he noted.[54] He omitted one repeated section and altered the orchestration, adding an organ to the ensemble.

Revisions and alterations may also be occasioned by a commission that provides the incentive to gather unpublished and rarely performed short works into a longer, more substantial composition. Inevitably, some alteration of these old works becomes part of the excavation process. Perhaps the most extensive example of such a compilation is the *Suite for Symphonic Strings*, commissioned by BMI for its twentieth anniversary in 1960. Movements 1, 4, and 6 of this nine-movement suite were newly composed. For the rest, Lou drew upon earlier pieces that, though promising, he felt could stand revision. For the *Suite*'s second movement, he used a lovely *Chorale for Spring* written for dancer Katherine Litz but expanded it with a new central section. A "Double Fugue in Honor of Heracles" from 1936, which he liked so much that all it required was orchestration, became the third movement. *Triphony*, a piano work already transcribed as a string trio, served for the fifth movement, "Lament": too short to stand alone, the four-and-a-half-minute trio made a fine slow movement for center of the new suite. For movement 7, Harrison arranged a fugue composed for David Tudor in 1952; and for movement 8, he selected a section from the *Almanac of the Seasons*, which he had written for Bonnie Bird in 1950. As a finale he appended the first movement of a nocturne from 1951. Lou had little reason to hope that any of these short pieces would be published, or performed more than very rarely. Some, such as the *Chorale for Spring*, were truly occasional works, written for a specific event to accommodate a particular need. Together, however, they formed the backbone of a major string orchestra work, which he fleshed out and graced with three new movements.

Such gatherings of older compositions often create eclectic works with a great deal of internal contrast. Stylistic variety characterizes many of Harrison's compositions, whether they were assembled from older works or newly composed. In the *Elegiac Symphony*, for instance, the first, third, and fifth movements, in gentle Asian-influenced language, contrast sharply with the second and fourth, in a strong Ruggles-inspired idiom. Such stylistic contrast has won him praise not only for his facility for writing in various styles but also for his success in making the combination work. One reviewer noted in regard to the *Piano Concerto*:

[He is] a defiantly anti-establishment (which is to say non-academic) composer. . . . Some people, notably Dennis Russell Davies, have begun to look at Harrison all over again. To judge from the Piano Concerto, it is high time and then some. . . . The Concerto contains a lot of music that ordinarily would not go together in the same work. After a first movement . . . that sounds a little like the ubiquitously rolling "open spaces" prairie music of Roy Harris . . . , there is a drum-dominated scherzo . . . , a wildly stomping, jazzy, highly dissonant piece that seems never to stop and never to be boring. . . . The third movement seems almost timelessly still. . . . The postlude fourth movement returns to continual motion in its most gentle permutation yet, and with the solo part reduced to a repetitive chant-like formula. . . . It takes courage . . .

EXAMPLE 11-13. *Canticle #3* (1942), revisions to the ocarina part, measures 232–240. (Courtesy of Lou Harrison.)

a. 1942 version

b. 1989 ornamented version

to compose music like this in 1983, but then Harrison has listened to few if any "other drummers" throughout his underrated career.[55]

Revision or alteration of an older work is not always a result of dissatisfaction with the original. Sometimes the purpose is to create alternative performance options either with new instrumentation or reflecting different stylistic influences. Examples of alternative instrumentation include *Strict Songs* (original for eight baritones, authorized version for male chorus in 1987, and rewritten for baritone solo and SATB chorus in 1992); a series of compositions for either harp or guitar; and several works for gamelan and Western instruments in which the gamelan parts can be performed alone.

Canticle #3 offers an intriguing example of an alternative version reflecting a new stylistic influence. During a 1989 recording of this 1942 composition, Lou decided that the ocarina's melody in the central section was too plain. In light of his varied experiences during the intervening forty-seven years, he decided to add a host of ornamental grace notes, drawing both upon his love of Baroque music (in which the performer was free to ornament the composer's score) and upon the inflections of Asian melody types (example 11-13). Not that he rejected his original version; both forms of the work are perfectly acceptable to him. The ornamented one, however, reflects a maturation in his style coupled with his mastery of East-West syntheses.

In this chapter we have explored compositional processes shaping Harrison's musical style without assessing the quality of individual works. For the most part, the pieces we have highlighted are those we find most compelling. In instances such as *Young Caesar*, where further revision is clearly still warranted (a task Harrison considers urgent), we have taken pains to say so. Such opinions, of course, in part reflect our personal preferences: Harrison might well disagree with us. Lou acknowledges that his compositions vary in quality, and, as his preoccupation with revision shows, he is constantly involved in the evaluative process. Though he may take issue with critics, he has frequently reconsidered his work in the light of intelligent suggestions.

The quality of particular works seems to have little to do with speed of composition. Some of Harrison's occasional works (many written in haste) are among his most memorable. A case in point is *Canticle #1*, composed in four hours and now among the staples of the percussion ensemble literature. The *Suite for Cello and Harp* was also a rush job. Before leaving for Reed College in the summer of 1949, Lou had agreed to one of Seymour Barab's "Platonic commissions" (chapter 4) but then completely forgot about the project. When Harrison returned from Oregon in the late summer, Barab reminded him of his promise, and Lou produced the score in a few weeks. In the years since, the *Suite* has had only minor revision and has proven to be one of his most felicitous compositions.

Harrison has come to dislike a number of his earlier works—even some published ones (e.g., the *Alleluia for Small Orchestra*, 1945)—and prefers that they not be performed. Lou specifically requested that we publicize his opinions, which we have done in our catalog by adding a special sign for unpublished works and a note for published ones (since composers have extremely limited control over works that have appeared in print). Whether critical opinion will concur with his assessment remains to be seen.

12 Not Just Music

Criticism, Poetry, Art, and Typography

During the course of this book we have quoted often from Harrison's writings, not only from his *Music Primer* but also from articles in *View, Modern Music, Listen, Impulse,* the *Dance Observer,* the *American Composers' Alliance Bulletin,* the *Korea Journal,* and other periodicals. We have not yet, however, examined his criticism—specifically, the nearly three hundred short pieces he produced for the *New York Herald Tribune* from 1944 to 1947 (a complete listing is given in appendix 2). Scholars often dismiss music criticism as the superficial product of tight deadlines, leading to instant analysis and hackneyed turns of phrase. Though Lou certainly had to make quick analyses under time pressure, his reviews are rarely clichéd or jaded. In reading them—or even just perusing a list of them—one not only grasps the frantic pace of his life and the diversity of cultural experiences that shaped his education in the mid-1940s but one also completes the picture of Lou as a multitalented artist who could toss off elegant prose with the same ease that he could imitate diverse compositional styles.

Harrison holds the critic in high esteem, a partner in a triumvirate of musical life: the composer, who "designs the piece," the performer, who "makes it public," and the critic, who "gives a totality to the project."[1] Harrison has acted as all three. He discovered to his surprise that people actually read (and took seriously) what he wrote. He recalls Aaron Copland stopping him on a street corner one day after his review of some twelve-tone music had appeared in the *Tribune*. "He quoted me literally and then followed up by asking: 'Doesn't it restrict you too much to write using all twelve tones?' I remember my 'stomping-the-feet' reply: I looked at him and said, 'Aaron, you're old enough to know better.' Later he wrote his first twelve-tone piece."

The philosophy of music reviewing for the *Tribune* differed markedly from that of its closest rival, the *New York Times*. "Virgil Thomson was made top man at the *Tribune* in the same year I joined the *Times* staff as the bottom man," recalls Ross Parmenter. "Olin Downes, who was the top man at the *Times*, had totally different tastes from Thomson. Downes didn't have much use for modern music, and he was crazy about Sibelius; Virgil Thomson couldn't stand Sibelius. Thomson liked French music; Downes preferred German symphonic music. Downes had a sense of humor as a person, but when he got on his critical cap, he wrote in a formal way. Thomson liked to be witty."[2]

A striking example of these differences is their contrasting opinions of a 1953 Museum of Modern Art concert conducted by Stokowski.

Downes:

This program could be called . . . a "laboratory" program of music by the avant garde of our native composers. . . . Most of the evening, one devoutly wished that the compositions had stayed in the laboratory where they belonged. . . .

Lou Harrison's Canticle No. III, composed evidently with the Far East in mind, does have a quality of oriental meditation and that objectivity of style, with endless repetitions of rhythmic, sonorous and melodic patterns, that is interesting for three minutes, soporific in five minutes and trying to the nerves and patience thereafter.

Mr. Harrison has let us know that his scoring calls for plumbing pipes, sixty-seven wood blocks, a Korean dragon mouth, marimba, an ocarina, a guitar, whisk broom, tire rims and brakedrums of assorted sizes, etc. That is all right with us. He does achieve interesting tone color and rhythmical combinations, so far as these in themselves go.

Thomson:

A funny thing about the concert of American music that Leopold Stokowski conducted last night . . . was that the conservative works sounded tentative, insecure and experimental, while those of more outlandish cast all sounded serene and normal. . . .

Lou Harrison's "Canticle No. III" . . . is one of those delicate and delicious symphonies masterfully sustained that are a unique achievement of the composer. The most instantaneously recognizable effects come from the Far East, but one can not call it a piece about Java or Bali or India. It is Western in its drama and structure, though many of its rhythmic and instrumental devices have been learned from the lands where percussive orchestration is the norm of music. Many of them have been invented also by the composer. The work is subtle, lovely to listen to and powerful in expression, a memorable experience.[3]

Thomson wanted music reviewed by composers, who could comment in depth on new music. He therefore hired a group of stringers, among them Paul Bowles and Lou Harrison. The *Times* operated on a different premise, employing noncomposers in regular staff positions. Parmenter notes, "[Downes] didn't want people who would have personal axes to grind. We were taught to make no entangling alliances. When Bernard Shaw was once accused of being too friendly to certain people, he replied, 'To be friendly does not mean to be corrupt.' Thomson had the same philosophy, although he certainly was not above playing favorites. He was not impartial, but then he never claimed to be."[4]

During the late 1940s, Downes had first pick among the scheduled productions; Howard Taubman and Noel Straus came next; and at the bottom of the heap was Parmenter: "I got the musical milk after it had been skimmed three times. As the junior man, I got the debutantes and the unknowns; but in addition, nobody else liked modern music. I didn't know enough to know whether I liked it or not, but I was open-minded and became interested because none of the others wanted to bother with it. So I got a lot of modern music pieces to cover."[5]

At these concerts by debutantes and unknowns, and at the performances of contemporary music, Parmenter grew to know Lou Harrison: "He was tall, slender, dark-eyed, and very handsome. He had a high-pitched voice and spoke rapidly. Lou was extraordinarily articulate and seemed to have no problem expressing anything he wanted to—a natural gift of gab."[6]

Nor was Lou hesitant to write precisely what he thought of a performance, despite the option, used by some of his colleagues, of resorting to positivistic description. (He recalls that Francis Perkins, one of the longtime members of the *Tribune* staff, would take a stopwatch to the concert to get precise timings.) Singers provoked some of Lou's most cutting reviews (one of which even prompted a threatening letter from an angry husband).[7] Some examples:

Miss Lorenne has a tiny piping voice, which is weaker than a flute in all but the topmost register. It also is more crystalline and less human sounding than a flute and sounds for all the world like an overwound mechanical nightingale. It wabbles and trills on every note except those that go by too quickly to be wabbled upon. (March 2, 1946)

Billy Rose should find Miss Kosta, for she is very good indeed as an entertainer, and has a large, well controlled voice that could be heard in the largest place. . . . On this occasion she swooped in covered from head to foot in brilliant silver reflecting sequins, with a dash of white and frigid blue crepe here and there. Though looking like an illuminated juke box in action, she really has a fine deep contralto . . . and is always truly on pitch. (December 30, 1946)

Mr. Melzer has no need to overplay the powerful basso role . . . for he was created a large man and with a loud voice. . . . [However, his voice] changes color on every note, sometimes oftener than that, and is loath to stay on the correct pitch with wabbling. (February 4, 1946)

Mr. Marcellos effects some strange sounds, particularly in tones of high volume. Here he sounds as though he had momentarily submerged and the vocal result resembles bubbling. . . . He commits many peculiarities of phrasing by the separation of words usually sung continuously. . . . And last, but not least, he audibly and grandly clears his throat in every song, between phrases. (May 13, 1946)

Ill-behaved and nondiscriminating audiences were also subjected to castigation: "Miss Grey is probably at her best in the situation of a homey gathering of cultivated persons. . . . Such a situation on a slightly more public scale was suggested by the audience of the evening, which came late, indulged in conversation when it so chose, and which sported . . . a fantastic array of the maddest spring bonnets worn as though one went around that way all the time" (March 26, 1946). Or the following: "The youngsters gave out with the 'hottest' style, were slick and loud in instrumental technique and acted, physically, exactly like players performing in cabaret. The young usually emulate their elders, and since a large number of the latter were present . . . and applauded vigorously it is to be presumed that the citizenry finds it proper for children to behave in this way" (June 6, 1946).

Flashy instrumental technique and whirlwind performance tempi rarely impressed him.

For the busy modern person, Joan Slessiner, whose New York piano debut was heard at Town Hall Sunday night, has thought up a new idea. By programming an organ prelude and fugue in D major by Bach . . . , twelve etudes of Chopin . . . , Herbert Haufrecht's Sicilian Suite, a "Mouvement" from Debussy's "Image[s]," and the Prokofieff "Suggestion Diabolique," and performing them at a nearly dead level of prestissimo, she is able to present for one's money's worth the same number of tones in an hour and fifteen minutes including intermission that are in the usual concert spread out over nearly two hours. In this way commuters are enabled to catch trains and at the same time not lack for culture. Performed with such superb finesse and accuracy that credulity was strained, Miss Slessiner set at Town Hall last night a new high in public tributes to the marvelous double escapement action of the modern grand pianoforte. (October 29, 1946)

Lou looked for depth of interpretation, sensitivity to style or text, control of tempo and dynamics, and an ability to relate emotionally to the audience. He was more apt to praise the beauty of a slow movement than facile technical flourishes. When Artur Schnabel suffered a serious memory lapse during the performance of Mozart's D-minor *Piano Concerto* (K. 488), for instance, Harrison found that it caused only a mild disruption of the magic the pianist had woven during the slow movement.

> Mr. Schnabel gave a superb performance. . . . It was serene, elevated, pellucid and convincing throughout. His touching reading of the beautiful second movement was in every way finely thought and tenderly presented. He was playing in a relaxed and delicate way yesterday [that] for some reason suggested to this reporter the image of a classically cultured Chinese gentleman at the age of leisure from noble public duties sitting down to an instrument to convey to those attentive a few choicely turned phrases of counsel and reflection.
>
> The entire presentation was instructive and edifying, again reminding one that the greatest performance on an instrument always takes place at a lower decibel level than a mediocre performance. For Schnabel played almost throughout at the average volume of medium soft. . . .
>
> The calm accompanying his performance was unbroken by a lapse of memory in the final movement, which precipitated the composition into a number of bars of fascinating, if inappropriate, polytonality. A glance at Dr. Rodzinski's score by the soloist, and the movement was resumed a few bars before the point of the mishap. All forces, by reason of the shock, played nearly half again as fast and brilliantly on to the end. The final movement was then repeated in response to vigorous applause. (March 4, 1946)

On the same page in the *Tribune* appears Lou's review of Marisa Regules's performance of Rachmaninoff's third piano concerto (D minor) with the same orchestra under the same conductor the evening before Schnabel's appearance.

> Miss Regules . . . has the glittery technique which makes the ear giddy and she plays almost entirely with a hard, sun-baked tone. . . .
>
> Her reading of the . . . concerto was not very gratifying. . . . Nearly every phrase was accorded a new tempo by the soloist and the joints, though Dr. Rodzinski labored valiantly to heal them over, stood out with loose notes and stray ends much in evidence. (March 4, 1946)

He had even less tolerance for Witold Malcuzynski's performance of the same concerto a year later: "[He] presented a rather brutal reading of the Rachmaninoff Concerto. Though having a whirligig ability at the keyboard, and enough force to dull the orchestra, he seemed incapable of reserve. His loudest passages, at which he lunged with full impetus, rang with a disagreeably piercing sound, and he varied his tone but little in the more lyric parts" (March 3, 1947).

When it came to performances by young people and minorities, however, Lou's reviews are an early example of affirmative action: even in cases when he found the quality substandard, he nearly always moderated his tone, giving the performers the benefit of the doubt. In spite of his uncanny control of the written word, one at times senses his struggle to express honestly what he heard while at the same time providing encouragement:

Miss Grudeff . . . has few manual difficulties for one of eighteen years and seems to have polished off all but a few of the major problems of piano playing. She did play too loud in the lower register when anything dashing was encountered in that range, and made a bit of a muddle of some Chopin passages, which she essayed too rapidly. But she elicited the most beautiful tone imaginable from the instrument in all less extreme moments. . . .

This reporter would like to express the hope that Miss Grudeff does not get caught up in a dizzy and premature whirl of engagements . . . and is able to mature a while longer in comparative peace, for she has remarkable potentialities. (March 6, 1946)

Miss Thompson can be termed a soprano only by grace of the falsetto which she makes use of in producing every tone that lies beyond her limited range. Her voice is rich and a bit heavy, actually more like a contralto in texture. It is, however, of firm body in a small central register and she has made a happy adjustment in this range to the beautiful natural sound of the Negro voice. . . .

It would be pointless to deny that there is a special and lovely tone that is beyond the power of Caucasians to produce and that is the special privilege of Negro artists to cultivate. It is to Miss Thompson's credit that she has discovered this. (March 5, 1945)

The concert fare, though dominated by routine voice, piano, and string recitals, was at times enlivened by more remarkable events. Possibly because of an expressed interest in Baroque music, Lou was frequently assigned "early music" concerts. His reviews reflect his experience performing on (and composing for) old instruments and show a historian's interest in informed performance practices as well. His 1946 review of a performance of Bach's *Mass in B Minor* is tactful, yet we detect his impatience with grandiose "romanticized" productions of Baroque works:

The Bach Mass is rather like a national park to most of us. Sooner or later every one who can goes to hear it. . . .

We play the B-minor Mass today on instruments which are the common ones to our day, but are not at all what Bach himself had in mind. We also double or quadruple their number. And we employ a style of vocal production which fits our new instruments and was probably unknown to the elderly organist. (March 27, 1946)

He goes on to remark on violins equipped with steel strings, trumpeters pushing "their range up to the very top of their modern instruments," voices with "the full and rounded tone customary to the last century's grander effects," and ("as a concession to modern scholarship") the sound of the harpsichord imitated by a piano equipped with tacks in its hammers.[8] Harrison nevertheless enjoyed the performance and commended the production.

He was much less tolerant of a recital featuring Bach's harpsichord and organ works on the piano. "This reporter never had heard the Aria with Thirty Variations, also known as the Goldberg Variations, on any other than the instrument for which they were written, the harpsichord, and finds that they turn up in a shocking state of disguise when done on the piano" (January 10, 1947). He found "equality of tonal tension" lacking, "at least a half dozen tone colors" absent, as well as a "general blurring" and a lack of the "range of octave registration and couplings."

Yet he was not rigid in his opposition to such modernization and was quick to compliment musically sensitive performances even when they made no pretense at historical veresimilitude. A case in point is his review of a performance of the *St. Matthew Passion* under Stokowski with Robert Shaw's Collegiate Chorale, which Harrison called "rich and moving" despite "the omission of the organ continuo, as well as the employment of so large a choir . . . [that there was] a tendency to befog the tense counterpoint" (March 20, 1945).

More to his liking were performances evoking the characteristics of the era in which the works were composed. He was taken with a boys' choir from Texas singing Lassus and Byrd (April 7, 1945), a concert of the music of Heinrich Schütz (January 30, 1946), a performance on early instruments ranging from the works of Dufay to those of Handel (May 7, 1947), and, most of all, with Arthur Mendel's Cantata Singers. He reviewed three of Mendel's concerts, including such performers as Paul Hindemith on viola d'amore and Ralph Kirkpatrick on harpsichord. After the first, Harrison remarked that hearing the viola d'amore, lute, and viola da gamba with reduced string tension made "for a sweetness of sound and hovering warmth that are unknown to modern instruments." Combined with "a reasonably sized chorus and expert soloists" and "amplified and enriched" by an appropriate acoustic space, he found the concert "in every way beautiful" (April 19, 1945). Even in less ideal circumstances, such as a performance by a contralto whose voice "though of large range . . . very much resembles the French horn," Lou was supportive of the effort, complimenting the singer's "devotion to the music of the Renaissance and baroque periods," her "serious and frequently affecting" delivery, and the "excellent" group of performers on harpsichord, recorder, and strings (January 20, 1947).

His reviews of new music concerts are less frequent than one might expect, although with Thomson's staff of composer-reviewers, one supposes that the *Tribune* staff vied for opportunities to review them, in contrast to the attitude at the *Times*. Even if he did not attend such concerts in the employ of the *Tribune*, Harrison was often present, as his (unpaid) essays in *Modern Music* affirm. On those occasions when he did review them for the paper, he turned his attention more to the music than to the performance, and in his writing one detects both an intense excitement and an astute ear. In addition to the reviews of Hovhaness and Partch cited earlier (chapter 2), he offered insightful commentary on the music of Stravinsky, Krenek, Dello Joio, and Bartók (whose second violin sonata "depends on a static contemplative tonal scheme," in which "phrases frequently drop away rather surprisingly. . . . Interest lies in the details that come and go, sometimes catching hold in a longer portion of working out, but frequently never coming back at all" [February 26, 1946]).

Harrison's reviews are typically embellished by clever Thomsonian bons mots as well: Moravia, as evoked by Janáček's *Sinfonietta*, for instance, is "New Jersey with peasants added" (February 8, 1946). His descriptions of new works are analytical enough to be meaningful but still comprehensible to the nonspecialist. Composer Norman Lockwood, for example, "is capable of inventing specific and strongly characterized sections of material . . . imbued with a . . . romantic turn of expression. But he seems to have difficulty in disentangling the firm structures he starts out with into sufficient fluidity so that he can design large forms without a blocked-out effect." On the same concert, by contrast, Norman Dello Joio's second piano sonata "bounced along on a strong rhythmic foundation [which] gave a close and rewarding unity to both the fast outer movements. . . . Nary a moment is dull" (May 1, 1947). Lou reviewed music by Kodály (April 7, 1947), new music for the synagogue (May 11, 1946), a lecture on modern French music (November 9, 1946), and a performance of theremin music (December 2, 1946). In *Modern Music* he summarized the contemporary music offerings of the New York season, detailing those works he found most novel and listing many others with little editorial comment.

Reviews of ethnic concerts, though not numerous, clearly constituted one of the most pleasant aspects of his job. Even when Harrison found the performances wanting, he was invariably supportive and encouraging of the endeavor. Early in his work for the paper, he wrote about a concert of Arabic music (January 29, 1945), and later he evaluated performances of music from Armenia, the Caribbean, and Czechoslovakia. Among his most revealing pieces are the reviews of Chinese music, which foreshadow the excitement that would emerge later after his trips to Asia. Reviewing a lecture-recital of Chinese classical music for the p'i-p'a (Chinese lute), erh-hu (two-stringed bowed chordophone), and flutes, Lou concluded with a foreshadowing of his political writings (and his musical style) of the next two decades: "It is a refreshment (and a shock), what with the increasing degradation of our own art into an industry pure and simple, to realize that most of the world (and the Orient is most of the world) considers music a gentle pursuit of the spirit finding its own poetic integration, in religious terms, with the rest of creation" (May 2, 1946).

His West Coast experiences with Asian music most likely made Harrison one of the few New York critics knowledgeable enough to evaluate such performances. He was particularly enamored by the p'i-p'a, piquing an interest that culminated in his 1997 concerto for the instrument commissioned by Lincoln Center. In a review early in 1947, he noted that the technique of this ancient instrument could rival any athletics on modern plucked strings:

[After Yue-tuh Sung's performance of] "The Downfall of Chu," he drew excited applause from the members of the large audience for his manipulation and mastery of every conceivable thing an instrument of this sort can do. Indeed the piece is difficult, involving stretching of the strings, elaborate plucking tricks, multiple chordal slides and a number of other devices usually thought of in the West as being the special province of experimentally minded modern composers. (March 3, 1947)

Harrison was occasionally assigned concerts of folk music or jazz, though they were outside his area of primary interest. (Nevertheless, he was by no means a novice in the field of jazz, having transcribed twenty-four pages of recorded examples for Rudi Blesh's 1946 history, *Shining Trumpets*.) He thoroughly enjoyed performances by Burl Ives, Pete Seeger, Woody Guthrie, and Duke Ellington, whom he dubbed "the Couperin of the jazz band" for his whimsical titles and distinctive style (November 25, 1946). He was less taken with Dinah Shore, who "wavered in pitch a great deal and attacked many tones like a paratrooper in action, but since this reporter had never heard her before, he carefully watched his surrounding audience members, observed that no one showed signs of thinking anything amiss, and concluded that such mannerisms must be what in popular music is termed 'style'" (July 4, 1945).

Poetry

Harrison's facility with the written word had caused him to vacillate, during his youth, between careers as a composer and a poet. At the age of eighteen, he wrote to his mother: "The old inner war about music versus poetry has arisen again. . . . I am in a perpetual state of alternation between doubt and belief in everything I do in either poetry or music. When in either art I become absolutely sure that I am on the right track, that will be the sign and that the art. I wish you would help me; you can you know, a very great deal."[9] Lou would devour an average of two books a night during this period, scouring the public libraries in pursuit of obscure footnote references. The letter to Calline provides an interesting glimpse into his eclectic reading activity, for he requests that she renew some library books, including "Cecil Forsythe's [*sic*] Orchestration book . . . , 'Earlier French Musicians' by Hargrave . . . , and the Chinese treatise on music, 'Yok-Kyi'"[10] (chapter 9).

"My interest and impulse for poetry," he now reflects, "is largely oral. It's the sound of the verse and its rhythm that matter to me."[11] He is particularly attracted to the stress-based rhythms of Latin poetry and to isosyllabic forms common to many world cultures. Many of his own poetic texts are tributes: "Nines to John Cage on his 65th Birthday," "Lines of 11 and 8 on Harry Partch," "Elevens from Reading Pope," "Fourteens to Honor Claude Lorraine," "Tens on Remembering Henry Cowell." Playfully humorous, these tributes may even gently chide the subject, as in this excerpt from his "Fours on Kenneth Rexroth's Reading":

He always paused
just a breath-pause
at the end of
lines, thus making
meaning's own line
often doubtful;
so we were left
to bridge the gaps,
collect context;
and restore his
flow of writing.
(August 1991)[12]

Lou delights in poetic controls that resemble his compositional controls. The tribute to Cage, for instance, uses nine lines of nine syllables, derived from a simple count of letters and spaces (John Cage: 9) and an application of Cage's square root form.

The cinquain form of the American poet Adelaide Crapsey, with its fixed syllabification of 2, 4, 6, 8, 2, provided a similar restriction. To his surprise Harrison found in Crapsey a link to his personal history as well: she had maintained a close friendship with Jean Webster, author of *Daddy Long Legs,* Lou's 1920 stage debut.[13] On more than one occasion, Harrison himself tried the cinquain form, which creates "a working up to and falling away from a climax."[14]

Weary,
but light of pack,
the mountaineer comes back,
with air & light & stars upon
his face.
(July 8, 1967)

The sun—
which burns our eyes—
in tomorrow's eclipse
will shadow bright little crescents
through trees.
(July 10, 1991)

Mythological topics have frequently inspired his poetic texts. In "The Four Patrons of the Palaestra," Harrison pays tribute to Apollo, Eros, Heracles, and Hermes; and on several occasions, he wrote praises to Aphrodite (Venus), "the goddess of all things having to do with sexuality,"[15] as well as to her sons, Eros (Cupid) and Priapos. A few lines from "Gending in Honor of Aphrodite":

Persuasion's queen, concede her.
Foam-born, her carriage lofted
by sparrows, Aphrodite
lights the world, amid her doves,
her myrtle, quince, and roses.
(May 28–30, 1989)

And "To Aphrodite":

Bright lady—bird-drawn in the sky of light,
Oh move us all to unstrict affection.
Oh love of the great and broken smithy,
Send the full strength of your beautiful son
Against this suiciding, kill-worn world.

On numerous occasions, Harrison set his own texts; among the most effective are the *Strict Songs*, modeled on Navaho Blessing Way songs (quoted in part in chapter 3). He set "To Aphrodite" for chorus accompanied by harp and gamelan and found a musical voice for his protest poetry in *Nova Odo* and *Homage to Pacifica* (chapter 9). For *Scenes from Cavafy* (1980), he paraphrased selections from the Alexandrian poet, which he then set for male chorus, baritone solo, gamelan, psalteries, and harp in a celebration of homosexual love. The work reads in part:

At the table next
  in the lines of limbs unclothed—
    He sees all youth of twenty-two
    in the man before him.
  Remembered or forgot, drunk or not,
    the poet sees the lines of the limbs
    of a lad he loved.

The poet remembers the two of them
    in the empty tavern,
    almost unlit and much past midnight,
    in their light clothing,
    in the soft summer heat,
    in their great intensity.
He remembers the hasty flesh,
    the pressured flesh
    revealed that summer night,
    and that sight and sense
    savored in older years
    and in his very lines of verse.

Lou's extensive personal library of poetic collections attests to his eclectic influences: from Blake, Whitman, Keats, Shelley, Browning, and Wordsworth to Robert Bridges, Elsa Gidlow, and Gerard Manley Hopkins; from Horace and Ovid to E. E. Cummings; from Goliard songs to Chinese verse. An examination of the catalog at the end of this book aptly demonstrates the breadth of poetic sources on which he has drawn for musical settings. He studied poetic writing with Robert Duncan in New York and after returning to California would attend Duncan's poetry group at SIR in San Francisco as often as he could. Duncan used a pedagogical device that resembles Cowell's method of teaching about melodicles (chapter 1): "He would give us a set number of words," Harrison recalls, "and we would have to arrange them as poems."

In 1992, the Jargon Society, in collaboration with the University of California, Santa Cruz, library and the Cabrillo Music Festival, published *Joys and Perplexities*, a collection of eighty-eight poems by Harrison graced by eighteen of his black-and-white drawings. The poetry is set in a typeface designed by Lou and transformed into a Macintosh computer font by Carter Scholz. By now the reader will hardly be surprised to learn that after Harrison's 1982 automobile accident left his right hand too unsteady for extensive calligraphic work, he jumped into the project with passion, investigating the history of typography and designing typefaces to represent several historical letterforms:

THE FONT HARRISON AND SCHOLZ CALL "APTOS UNCIAL" IS DERIVED FROM LETTERING DATING FROM THE 4TH TO 8TH CENTURIES. THIS FONT WAS USED FOR THE SUPPLEMENTARY MATERIAL IN THE 1993 EDITION OF HARRISON'S MUSIC PRIMER.

Rotunda is modelled on a 14th century Gothic type from northern Italy. Its majuscules are Lombardic: 7th-13th century Italian.

Pluma is the font used in *Joys and Perplexities*. Like most book faces, it appears to stem from Carolingian minuscules that superceded the Gothic letterforms.

Inspired by the work of the 16th-century Russian printer, Ivan Feberov, Lou designed a "Feberov" font, using the Cyrillic letterforms as a model. As they had for Rotunda, Harrison and Scholz combined Lou's lower-case letters with Lombardic majuscules

SCHOLZ ALSO DEVELOPED "LOU CASUAL," BASED ON HARRISON'S EVERYDAY HANDWRITING, AND

LOU TITLING, DERIVED FROM AN AFTER-DINNER IMPROVISATION.

To round out the historical picture, a "Rustica" font based on pre-fourth-century writing is presently under development.[16]

Painting

Lou has been active in the visual arts as well: he has accumulated an impressive collection of art objects, paintings, and books; and he himself has painted, designed sets, and even constructed puppets, a passion that dates back to 1933, when he made a marionette modeled on the "Pierrot" described in a poem by Edna St. Vincent Millay.[17]

German Expressionism, with its intense black-and-white relationships on the one hand and vivid color on the other, has formed a particularly important visual substratum that resonates with the rhythmic and textural contrasts Harrison loves to explore in his music. "German Expressionism includes a wide variety of formal usage within any one canvas," he notes.

> I am also attracted to the connection between the German Expressionists and world art, which was much stronger than that of the French. We hear, of course, of Picasso and African art, and also of the influence of the Japanese prints on certain French artists. But the Germans actually went there, to the Islands of Palau, for example. (Gauguin, of course, was an exception and was always treated as such.) The Germans more thoroughly incorporated their new discovery of the world, realizing that East and West cannot just be combined but that they are essentially similar.
>
> That's why, for example, I still think of Munakata and [Max] Beckmann, with some caveats, in the same breath. They have certain things in common: an intense black and whiteness, and vivid color treated separately from it. It's as though the structure is basically dark and light, and the color is more brilliant by being separated from it. It's a quite different approach than that of impressionism, which mixes colors to make form.[18]

And then, of course, there is the question of proportions. Lou's exhaustive investigations into tuning systems sensitized him to the role of proportion in painting and architecture as well. He was fascinated by the proportional schemes of Egyptian and Greek statuary and by the work of Corbusier and Palladio, whose writings he has read in detail. The page sizes and text layout in *Joys and Perplexities* are designed proportionally, and several of the drawings in the volume reflect the interval ratios in modes Lou has used in musical compositions.

Over the years, Harrison often turned to painting during times of personal stress. After his long days accompanying dance in the early 1960s, for example, he would find himself too exhausted to compose music. But painting provided a wonderful release. Fred Lieberman, viewing some of Lou's works at that time, recalls exclaiming, "Oh, fake Mondrians!" "No," responded Lou, "*echt* Harrisons." His works have appeared in public exhibitions including one organized by John Cage, the Rolywholyover, which was mounted in Los Angeles, New York, Philadelphia, and Japan. He vows soon to retire from musical composition to devote more time to painting.

Harrison's most recent area of study has been American Sign Language, which he and Bill began to learn after Bill started to experience some loss of hearing. Though Colvig soon gave up the project, Harrison organized a signing group that continues to meet weekly. He has built a sizable library of source materials and has become proficient enough to strike up sign conversations with total strangers. The study creates a link to his early San Francisco years, when he learned the basics of sign language to communicate with his deaf housemate. But a significant part of its attraction stems from the expressive use of the hands, so vital a component of dance, and particularly of the Indian and Indonesian styles he loves (fig. 15). In the fullness of his eighties, he may no longer dance with the grace of the sylph he was in his twenties, but he still dances through life with his hands.

Conclusion

Critics seeking to classify and describe Harrison's diverse output have often resorted to labeling it "typically West Coast"—a discursive strategy that seems, on the surface, more of a sound-bite than a basis for rational analysis. At the same time, the East-West polarity has been evoked so frequently and in relation to such diverse artists that, like "masculine-feminine," or "Republican-Democrat," it raises enculturated images in the minds of many Americans, whether or not such traits fully (or even adequately) characterize specific individuals. Thus, while composers such as Harrison, Partch, and Riley are unequivocally "West Coast" in the easy parlance of media critics, so are Hovhaness and Cowell, both of whom spent many years—indeed, major portions—of their lives in New York or Boston. Conversely, the West Coast has had its share of "Eastern" composers: Schoenberg, Stravinsky, Ernst Toch, Ingolf Dahl, Conlon Nancarrow, Gerald Strang, Ursula Mamlok. East and West, it seems, are states more of mind than of residence.

Is there, then, any meaning in this bifurcation, any rational association of stylistic traits with the regions they have come to represent? In short, what (if anything) does it mean to be a "West Coast composer"?

Indigenous resources stemming from historical patterns of immigration are obvious: the strong Asian presence in California, the inheritance of Spanish mission culture, the proximity to Mexico—all of which, we have seen, played a strong part in shaping the musical language of Lou Harrison. But the popular image of "West Coast" goes beyond these traits to characteristic attitudes and modes of expression.

Lou himself provides a starting point for this discussion. In a 1946 review for the *Herald Tribune* describing the New York debut of a Seattle violinist, he wrote, "Mr. Rosen has brought with him from Seattle some of the size, frankness and psychological space that surrounds persons living on the west coast."[1]

Size is one of the first images of the West to come to the minds of many easterners: vast tracts of open space; miles of empty (and uncultivated) land between cities, rather than continuous urban sprawl; valleys and mountainous regions apparently uninhabited. These images have frequently become analogous to prototypical East-West contrasts in musical texture: dense vs. transparent; intricate vs. uncomplicated; exploration of depth vs. fascination with a slowly evolving surface.

The impression of "space" in Harrison's music frequently results from such open textures, as composer Janice Giteck notes: "There's a feeling of big space even in his little pieces. He can use unisons (a whole chorus, for example, or group of instruments doing the same thing) and just drop one other sound into it—one gong or one chord. The effect will be bigger than a chorus singing in ten parts. It takes up more space, yet the procedure is very simple."[2] Such textures are congenial to dance, says Bella Lewitzky: "Lou's music has open spaces you can move into."[3]

West Coast spaciousness is embodied in a relaxed attitude toward time as well, enhanced by fascination with the contemplative in Asian artistic expression. A 1985 concert in New York featuring the music of Harrison and the late San Diego composer Robert Erickson prompted K. Robert Schwarz to comment:

> Despite the homogenization of American culture, the new music emanating from California has possessed a consistently different outlook from the more rationalist, determinedly modernist East Coast products. It was that special California aesthetic—far more relaxed, reveling in sonic beauty, inspired by non-Western sources—that this evening's program celebrated. . . .
>
> Despite the rhythmic animation of Harrison's music, it shared with Erickson's quieter work a sense of timelessness, a static, almost motionless presence that hovered in air, creating a fragile beauty before dissolving as it began. This Zen-like rapture and non-directionality is a far cry from East Coast academia's rigidity and Expressionist *Angst*.[4]

New York Times reviewer Will Crutchfield had a similar reaction but less sympathy: he couldn't muster sufficient patience to enjoy the experience. He described Harrison's compositions, which in this performance spanned forty years, from *Canticle #3* (1942) to the *Double Concerto for Violin, Cello, and Gamelan* (1982), as "prettily tonal, approachable, mostly nondirectional, and never severe, forbidding or astringent. . . . [But] my uptight Eastern academic intellectualism, if that's what it is, positively welled up, like an allergic reaction. The mellower the music got, the antsier I got. A biased response—but after all, East is East."[5]

Lou's reference to frankness and psychological space in his 1946 review reflected his longing for San Francisco's reputed open-mindedness, perhaps the most important factor that drew him back to California in 1953. He was uncomfortable dissembling either artistically or personally, whether this meant composing dissonant counterpoint or discretion regarding homosexuality. In California he felt more at ease expressing his social, political, and sexual views. He found greater tolerance for diverse musical styles as well, possibly resulting (as Andrew Imbrie has suggested) simply from the smaller number of composers, who found greater profit in supporting each other than in cultivating individual "schools" that would have lacked the critical mass to survive.[6] In northern California Harrison found the "psychological space" to pursue eclectic pathways. "Lou is free to go wherever he wants," says Lewitzky. "Whatever he thinks comes from his very center . . . and not from comparison with another West Coast composer. They coexist peaceably in separation."[7]

Those pathways have frequently led to expressive melody, whether in the context of his percussion works, his chamber music, or his gamelan compositions. "Lou has given us a prolific body of music that has validated the West Coast openness to sheer uninhibited beauty," notes Robert Hughes, "pouring forth melodies—at a time when length of melody was frowned upon. Hanson could do it for a certain length of time, but even here there was a self-consciousness if it went on for too long. Lou saw (and praised it immediately) when Hovhaness started to do it—a length of melodic line that just spins on and on."[8]

Many critics, both East and West, are skeptical of such accessibility, as Alan Rich notes:

There's strange and wonderful stuff in this lifetime of Lou's music. Much of it is so damned beautiful, so open-handed and eager to please, that a first impression can be to mistrust it. It's easy to make the distinction, in dealing with new music, that diatonic harmonies plus recognizable tunes equals conservative and that abstruse harmonies plus bristling melodic lines equals progressive. But those equations break down constantly in the real world, and they do with Lou.

In the best known of his music [Harrison] comes up with an ingenious kind of transcultural music. . . . In [some] pieces he will start with the ravishing orchestrations of Indonesian gamelan music, its array of bright percussion . . . and patterned rhythms. . . . Then he'll set against this the sinuous shapes of Western melody—real song tunes of the sort nobody else writes anymore, at least not as well.[9]

Hughes found that Harrison's nonjudgmental approach to compositional styles removed compositional roadblocks: "Growing up in the East, when I was a student and composing, one either looked to the Europeanism of Stravinsky or the serial system of Schoenberg. . . . What was so incredibly opening about Lou was that nothing was forbidden."[10]

In Harrison's music, divergent styles coexist peaceably even within single compositions—a musical analogue, in some sense, to his political philosophy. Listen, for example, to such works as the *Suite for Symphonic Strings*, the *Piano Concerto*, or the *Elegiac Symphony*. Serialism finds reconciliation with melodicism, the symphony and concerto with the gamelan, the monophonic estampie with dissonant counterpoint. Harrison finds no awkwardness in this kind of juxtaposition. On the contrary, works like the *Suite* take the listener on a tour of compositional styles just as *Pacifika Rondo* tours the Pacific basin.

In March 1973, as Lou was racing toward a deadline to complete his *Concerto for Organ with Percussion*, he welcomed a local newspaper reporter, Wally Trabing, to his tiny house, "comfortably cluttered with books, several harps, paintings, jewelry, Oriental instruments and strange looking drums." On the stove was a pot of Lou's legendary soup, dubbed by a neighbor "cream of garbage. . . . The pot was set on the stove in 1968. It is never emptied. All left-overs except meat go thereinto—even stale beer once—but mostly vegetables and sauces. . . . There is a constant taking out (to eat) and a constant putting in, and although there are those who would wince at this practice, the soup was superior."[11]

Harrison's musical pot was set on the stove many years earlier. Into it he threw whatever ingredients intrigued him at the moment. The Indonesian gamelan appeared early as did the Chinese theater and modern dance. Schoenberg and modernist New York added a different seasoning, soon to be peppered by the cross-disciplinary influences of Black Mountain College and studies in Korea and Taiwan. Like the culinary process, there has been a constant taking out to taste and a constant putting in to modify. But whatever ingredients dominated the musical soup at a particular time, the resulting brew assumed a distinctive flavor, reflecting the aromas of its component parts but carrying a unique taste of its own.

The eclecticism of many of Harrison's works makes stylistic classification of his output difficult, if not impossible. At the same time, the music's diversity is its most defining characteristic: the musical-cultural mosaic is precisely its essence.

Harrison's limited international recognition until quite recently has also resulted in part from this eclecticism. His major contributions to twentieth-century music are spread among disparate areas normally treated separately in musical writings: the development of the percussion orchestra (in relation to modern dance), the construction of new musical instruments, theories of tuning and temperament, and Asian-American-European hybrids. Composer Charles Amirkhanian notes:

> Having been so focused on what he wanted to do and doing it in his own way, Lou became a paradigm of inventiveness and an inspiration to people in many different areas. You'll meet a percussionist in Kansas who'll be familiar with Lou's music because he is an innovator in percussion music. You'll meet a person studying gamelan music who'll have Lou as an icon. Then you'll find someone in the field of intonation who knows Lou as one who is not only interested in intonation but has worked with it musically to the best of anybody's ability.
>
> For sixty-plus years, he has been an innovator in these many areas and has synthesized them beautifully. And what's wonderful is that he does it not in a superficial way but from a very deep experience of each thing that he treats, whether it's gardening or type fonts.[12]

Recognizing the risk of spreading his energies too broadly, Harrison nevertheless prefers diversity to the potential recognition he might gain by focusing on one area alone. When asked: "Do you see any continuum in the progress of Western music and, if so, where would you place your own work?" he retorted (with characteristic good humor), "As to the first question, I haven't the faintest idea, and in answer to the second, I can only say, 'Lou Harrison is an old man who's had a lot of fun.'"[13]

Appendix 1

List of Interviews

Interviews with Lou Harrison

1. Dec. 29, 1993. Dance
2. Jan. 13, 1994. Instrument construction
3. Feb. 10, 1994. Tuning and temperament
4. Feb. 23, 1994. Literary work
5. Mar. 8, 1994. Gamelan
6. Mar. 31, 1994. Interactions with other composers
7. Apr. 19, 1994. Gender issues
8. May 16, 1994. Chinese, Korean music
9. May 26, 1994. Compositional process
10. June 10, 1994. Art and calligraphy
11. Sept. 30, 1994. Music criticism
12. Oct. 21, 1994. Miscellaneous
13. Apr. 3, 1995. Miscellaneous
14. May 20, 1995. Public interview following concert at Lick Observatory
15. Nov. 21, 1995. Miscellaneous

Interviews with Others

Anahid Ajemian (violinist), June 28, 1995

Charles Amirkhanian (composer, radio commentator), June 15, 1995

Seymour Barab (cellist, composer), June 27, 1995

Carol Beals (dancer, choreographer), June 11, 1996

James Broughton (poet, filmmaker), Aug. 31, 1995

Richard Brown (writer; manager, Portland Gay Men's Chorus), Aug. 30, 1995

Xenia Cage (artist, former wife of John Cage), June 30, 1995

John Chalmers (tuning theorist), Sept.–Oct. 1995 (by e-mail) and Feb. 25, 1996

Remy Charlip (dancer, choreographer, artist), Jan. 15, 1995

Bill Colvig (engineer, instrument builder, Harrison's life-partner), Apr. 3, 1995

Merce Cunningham (dancer, choreographer), Nov. 7, 1995

Dennis Russell Davies (conductor), Oct. 9, 1995

Richard Dee (violinist, instructor), Feb. 20, 1995

Doris Dennison (instructor, Mills College; colleague from San Francisco), Dec. 5, 1995

Jody Diamond (gamelan specialist; founder, American Gamelan Institute), June 18, 1995

David Doty (composer), July 25, 1995

Paul Dresher (composer, tuning theorist), Dec. 11, 1995

Jean Erdman (dancer, choreographer), Sept. 6, 1995, and Nov. 7, 1995

Joseph Fiore (painter), June 19, 1995

Mary Fiore (writer), June 19, 1995

Betty Freeman (photographer, arts patron), June 8, 1995

Robert Garfias (ethnomusicologist), Feb. 25, 1996

Janice Giteck (composer), Aug. 30, 1995

William Harrison (business administrator, Lou's younger brother), Jan. 12, 1996

Jack Heliker (artist), June 20, 1995

Alan Hovhaness (composer), Sept. 1, 1995

Robert Hughes (composer, conductor), Dec. 12, 1994, and Jan. 14, 1996

Wesley Huss (instructor of theater), July 25, 1995

William Kraft (composer, percussionist), Sept. 15, 1995

Bella Lewitzky (dancer, choreographer), June 8, 1995

Judith Malina (actress, director, writer), June 29, 1995

Vincent McDermott (composer, gamelan specialist), Aug. 15, 1995

Edward McGowan (minister), Nov. 6, 1995

Robert Metcalf (stage designer), June 1, 1996

Richard Miller (former student), Dec. 24, 1996

Mark Morris (dancer, choreographer), Nov. 6, 1995

Ursula Oppens (pianist), Oct. 15, 1995 (brief interview with Jonathon Grasse)

Ross Parmenter (writer, music reviewer), June 27, 1995

Larry Polansky (composer), June 18, 1995

Jarrad Powell (composer, gamelan specialist), Sept. 1, 1995

Ned Rorem (composer, writer), Nov. 8, 1995

Dorothy James Russell (colleague from San Francisco), Apr. 4, 1996 (by telephone)

Daniel Schmidt (composer, gamelan specialist), Nov. 28, 1995

Carter Scholtz (composer, author, graphic artist), May 23, 1995

Eudice Shapiro (violinist), Sept. 16, 1995

Eva Soltes (dancer, arts administrator), Nov. 3, 1994

David Tudor (pianist, composer), Dec. 20, 1995 (by telephone)

Frank Wigglesworth (composer), June 21, 1995, and Nov. 5, 1995

William Winant (percussionist), Aug. 21, 1996

Appendix 2

Lou Harrison's Reviews in the New York Herald Tribune *(1944–1947)*

Subtitles are omitted unless they provide essential information. Articles listed as appearing on two days were published in different editions of the paper on different days. * = Articles not present on the standard microfilm of the *Tribune* but found among Harrison's personal papers or in an album of clippings compiled by Calline Harrison. Apparently these articles appeared in editions of the paper that were not filmed.

1944

Nov. 6: Alice Blengsli, Pianist, Heard in Recital Here
Nov. 7 and 8: Hilde Somers Is Heard in Haydn C Major Sonata
[Nov. 9, 1944?]: Selma Kramer Gives Carnegie Hall Recital (unsigned)
Nov. 18: Karina-Achron Concert Presented at Town Hall
Nov. 20: Helen Snow Is Heard in Times Hall Recital
Nov. 20 and 21: Elizabeth Bolek, Soprano, Sings Old French Songs
Nov. 30: Charlotte Martin Recital at Carnegie Chamber Hall

Dec. 2: Barone Conducts Concert by N.Y. Little Symphony
Dec. 4 and 5: Margit Kormendy Gives Times Hall Song Recital
Dec. 5: Alton Jones Plays: Pianist Is Heard in Concert at Town Hall
Dec. 6 and 7: Robert Kitain [violinist] Gives Concert
Dec. 11: Cellist and Pianist Heard in Recital at Town Hall: Nikolai and Joanna
    Graudan Play Mendelssohn Sonata
Dec. 11: Nana Lewis [soprano] Gives Recital
Dec. 14: [Jakob] Gimpel, in Piano Recital, Plays 3 Modern Works
Dec. 15: Norma Andre, Soprano, Makes New York Debut
Dec. 16: Marian Kalayjian [pianist] in Debut
Dec. 18: Youth Orchestra Makes Debut at Carnegie Hall
Dec. 19 and 20: City Symphony Offers Yule Concert at Center: Stokowski Interprets Religious and "Sleigh-Bell" Music

1945

Jan. 4: Jose Echaniz Presents Town Hall Piano Recital
Jan. 8: Ruth Luty [pianist] Gives Recital
Jan. 8 and 9: Pruth McPharlin Sings Program at Times Hall

Jan. 9: Harry Davis Is Heard in Concert at Town Hall

Jan. 15: Mathew Carnan [baritone] in Recital

Jan. 17: Rose Raymond [pianist] in Recital

Jan. 19: Doda Conrad [bass] Presents Recital in Times Hall

Jan. 20: Edmund Kurtz, Cellist, Appears at Town Hall

Jan. 22: New Music Is Presented by League of Composers

Jan. 24 and 25: Elly Kassman, Pianist, Makes Town Hall Debut

Jan. 29: Wadeeha Atiyeh Offers Arabian Music Program

Jan. 30 and 31: Heida Hermanns Heard at Piano in Town Hall

Feb. 15: Gordon Richards [baritone] Concert

Feb. 1: Doris Stockton at Town Hall: Marimbist Heard in Concert with Members of
   Philharmonic

Feb. 5: Myrtle Day, Soprano, Heard

Feb. 12 and 13: David Pokotilow Heard in Recital of Violin Music

Feb. 13 and 14: Fredell Lack [violinist] Presents Concert at Town Hall

Feb. 16: Coreania Hayman Heard in Town Hall Song Recital

Feb. 16 and 17: Latta-Ancher-Sandor Joint Recital Is Heard: Soprano, Cellist and
   Pianist Perform in Times Hall

Feb. 19 and 20: League of Composers Concert at City Center

Feb. 23: Jeanne Therrien Presents Town Hall Piano Recital

Feb. 28: Alice Sirooni Is Heard in Debut at Town Hall

Mar. 3: Michael Zadora [pianist] Heard in Town Hall Recital

Mar. 5: Geneva Thomson [soprano] in Recital

Mar. 8 and 9: Julius Goldstein-Herford Plays Hindemith Work

Mar. 16: Stokowski Gives Concert for Students at Center

Mar. 17: [Anton] Maaskoff Heard in Violin Recital at Town Hall

Mar. 19: Annette Royak [soprano] Heard in Recital at Town Hall

Mar. 20 and 21: Stokowski Interprets St. Matthew's Passion

Mar. 21 and 22: Bernard Kundell [violinist] Gives a Concert at Town Hall

Mar. 27: Gypsy Markoff (accordionist) Heard in Concert at Town Hall

Mar. 28: Oratorio Society gives B Minor Mass of Bach

Apr. 3: Choral and Dance Recital given by Sarah Lawrence [William Schuman,
   conductor]

Apr. 7: Old Music Is Presented by Apollo Boys Choir

Apr. 16: Strauss's "Gypsy Baron" Presented at City Center; Production Features
   Sets by Condell; Rudel Conducts [New York City opera]

Apr. 16: Joseph Lockett [pianist] Gives Recital

Apr. 19 and 20: Cantata Singers Present Bach's St. John Passion: Arthur Mendel
   conducts at All Souls Church [Paul Hindemith, viola d'amore, Ralph Kirkpatrick, keyboard]

Apr. 23: Soprano and Pianist Give Joint Town Hall Recital: Mayme Richardson
   and Bruce Wendell Offer Programs

Apr. 24: William Hacker, Pianist, in Debut at Town Hall

Apr. 27: Nadia Cortez [soprano] in Recital with Alexander Zaroff [bass-baritone]

June 18: Alan Hovhaness Offers Original Compositions

June 26: Mozart Work Heard at Lewisohn Stadium [Smallens, conductor]

June 26: Philharmonic Plays Sibelius at Stadium [Smallens, conductor; Josef Hofmann, pianist]

July 4: Dinah Shore at Stadium in Philharmonic Concert

July 9: Alec Templeton Is Piano Soloist at the Stadium [Bernstein, conductor]

July 13: Philharmonic Plays Gershwin at the Stadium [Smallens, conductor; Levant, pianist]

July 24: Ania Dorfmann, Pianist, Plays in Stadium Concert [Sevitzky, conductor]

July 31: Duo-Pianists [Luboshutz and Nemenoff] at Stadium as Goossens Conducts

Aug. 13: All-French Program Led by Smallens at Stadium [John Corigliano, violin]

Oct. 15: Song Recital Presented by Devora Nedworney

[Nov. 13?]: Harpsichord and Organ Heard in Church Recital [Edith Weiss-Mann and Ernest White] (signed "LB" but traced to LH)

Dec. 18 and 19: Miss Appleton and [Michael] Field Give Two-Piano Recital

1946

Jan. 11: Elizabeth Hipple [pianist] Heard in Recital at Times Hall

Jan. 21 and 22: Henryk Szeryng: Violinist Is Heard at Town Hall with Artur Balsam

Jan. 23 and 24: Ruth Kisch-Arndt: Contralto Aided at Town Hall by Ancient Instruments Group

Jan. 24: Rudolph Bochco: Violinist Gives Recital at the Town Hall

Jan. 26: Duo-Pianists Heard: Pierre Luboshutz and Genia Nemenoff at Town Hall

Jan. 28: Debut and Encore: Final Concert of Series Given at Times Hall

Jan. 29: Floyd Worthington [baritone] Heard in Concert at Town Hall

Jan. 30: Dessoff Choirs: Works of Heinrich Schutz Sung at Hunter College

Feb. 1 and 2: Mildah Polia [mezzo-soprano] Presents Recital at Times Hall

Feb. 4: Hans Mezzer [recte: Melzer; bass baritone] Is Heard in Recital at Town Hall

Feb. 4: Collegiate Chorale: Shaw Conducts in a Concert of New Friends

Feb. 6: Marcel Hubert: Cellist Is Heard in a Concert at Town Hall

Feb. 7 and 8: Jan Cherniavsky, Pianist, in a Recital at Town Hall

Feb. 8 and 9: The Philharmonic: Serkin Is Soloist in Brahms's D Minor Concerto

Feb. 14 and 15: Pa[i]siello's "Barber": 18th Century Opera Revived at Columbia University

Feb. 18 and 19: Chajes Program: Pianist and Schola Cantorum among Town Hall Artists

Feb. 18 and 19: New Friends of Music Present Brahms Works

Feb. 19 and 20: Debut as Colline: Giacomo Vaghi in La Boheme Role at the Metropolitan

Feb. 20: Ozan Marsh: Chopin and Liszt on Pianist's Times Hall Program

Feb. 23: Olga Coelho: Brazilian Guitarist and Soprano Heard in Town Hall

Feb 25: Charlotte Bergen: Cellist Presents Her Second Town Hall Recital

Feb. 26 and 27: Bartok Program: League of Composers Offers Concert in His Memory

Feb. 28 and Mar. 1: Bruce Barbour, Pianist, Heard in Town Hall Debut

Mar. 1: Debut of James Mitchell [baritone]

Mar. 2: Etelle Lorenne Recital: Coloratura Soprano Makes Debut in Town Hall

Mar. 4: Budapest Quartet Concert: Bensar Heifetz Joins with Group at Town Hall

Mar. 4: Marisa Regules Is Soloist: Plays Rachmaninoff D Minor Concerto with the Philharmonic

Mar. 4: Schnabel Plays Mozart in Philharmonic Concert: Lapse of Memory Interrupts a Major Concerto

Mar. 4: Carmelina Delfin [composer-pianist] in Recital

Mar. 5: Edison Harris, Tenor: His Widely Selected Program Is Heard at Town Hall

Mar. 6: Marion Grudeff, Pianist, Heard in Her U.S. Debut

Mar. 7: Joseph Wagner [pianist] Is Heard in Debut at Town Hall

Mar. 11: Olyve Hopkins, Soprano, in a Recital at Town Hall

Mar. 12 and 13: Arlie Furman: Violinist Plays Mozart, Ravel, Stravinsky and Brahms

Mar. 13: Samuel Dushkin: Violinist Plays Classical and Modern Music at Town Hall

Mar. 18: Armenian Music Is Led by Alexander Aslanoff

Mar. 20 and 21: Kopeikine Recital: Pianist Is Heard in Concert at Town Hall

Mar. 22 and 23: Josephine Tooker [soprano] Heard in a Recital at Times Hall

Mar. 25: Lida Brodenova [soprano] in Recital

Mar. 26 and 27: Jenny Grey [soprano] Recital

Mar. 27 and 28: Bach B-Minor Mass: Oratorio Society Gives Its 20th Rendition of the Work

Mar. 30: 3 Choir Festival: New Works Are Presented at Temple Emanu-el

Apr. 1: Contemporary Music Is Heard at Times Hall: Composers and Conductors Association Gives Concert

Apr. 2: Harold Kohon, Violinist, Gives Town Hall Concert

Apr. 8: William Hacker, Pianist, Gives Town Hall Concert

Apr. 12: Maurice Wilk [violinist] Heard with Lydia Edwards [soprano]

Apr. 15: Frances Dutton [mezzo-soprano] Recital Offers Elizabethan Air

Apr. 16: Emerson Conzelman, Tenor, Presents Recital

Apr. 17 and 18: Forum Group Music: Contemporary Music Society Concert at Times Hall

Apr. 19: Muriel Spector, Soprano, Is Heard in Song Recital

Apr. 22: Novella McGhee Heard in Town Hall Song Recital

Apr. 25: Centre Symphony Heard in Concert at Town Hall

Apr. 29: Arrangers Concert: Composers Aid in Conducting Music at Town Hall

May 1 and 2: Alice Howland Presents Times Hall Song Recital

May 2: Chinese Music: Iranian Institute Presents Concert and Lecture

May 3: [Dean] Dixon Conducts: Program Features Works by American Composers

May 6: Workmen's Circle Choir Gives Town Hall Recital

May 6: Teachers College Choir Sings American Music

May 10: A "Hootenanny" Is Given by People's Songs, Inc.: Labor-Union Pieces Featured on Town Hall Program

May 11: Jewish Liturgical Music by Modern Composers

May 13: John Marcellos [bass] Recital

May 14: Pia Igy [soprano] Presents Concert to Benefit Greek Relief

May 15 and 16: Harms Chorus Heard in Haydn's "Creation"
May 20: Artists' Concert Service Quartet at Town Hall: Four Vocalists Are
    Heard . . .
May 20: "The Soldier's Tale": Stage Version Is Given by the International Society
May 22: Lois Jordan, Soprano, Is Heard at Times Hall
May 24: Alonzo Estrada [bass-baritone] Is Heard at Carnegie Chamber Hall
May 27: "Pop" Concert Orchestra Conducted by Callimicos
May 29: Welfare Bureau Chorus Give[s] Recital at Town Hall
May 30 and 31: Two Riccis Are Heard at Carnegie "Pop" Concert: George Plays
    Cello Concerto, Ruggerio a Violin Work
May 31 and June 1: Carnegie "Pop" Concert: Irene Farrell and Conrad Mayo Are
    Vocal Soloists

June 6: High School Musicians Play Jazz in Town Hall
June 27 and 28: Welch Chorale Presents Marquette League Benefit
June 29: Goldman Band: Schoenberg's Variations Has Manhattan Premiere

July 17: "Caribbean Night" Given in Barbizon-Plaza Series: Moune, Smith Kids
    and Daville Are Featured
July 26: Lily Pons at Stadium; Monteux Is Conductor

Aug. 6 and 7: Claudio Arrau Soloist with N.Y. Philharmonic [Kurtz, conductor]
Aug. 8: All-Russian Program Presented at Stadium: Teresa Sterne Piano Soloist . . .
Aug. 13: Goldman Band Heard in Final Concert on Mall

Sept. 4 and 5: Saratoga Springs Music Series On
Sept. 24: City Symphony Gives Season's First Concert [Bernstein, conductor]
Sept. 28: Two Singers in New Roles in City Opera "Pagliacci"
Sept. 30 and Oct. 1: City Center Operas: Smetana and Puccini Works . . .

Oct. 5: Lois Jordan [soprano] Presents Town Hall Song Recital
Oct. 7: Two Soviet Singers: Miss Haidai, Patorzhinsky Are Heard at Town Hall
Oct. 7: All-Girl Orchestra Gives Program at Town Hall
Oct. 8 and 9: Arnold Eidus [violinist] Presents Recital at Carnegie Hall
Oct. 11 and 12: Harvey Shapiro, Cellist, Is Heard at Town Hall
Oct. 12: Carrillo Concert: Argentine Pianist Is Heard at Carnegie Hall
Oct. 14 and 15: Harold Haugh, Tenor, in Town Hall Recital
Oct. 14: Eddie Condon: Improvised Jazz Concert Heard at Town Hall
Oct. 14: Leona Vanni, Soprano, Sings in Town Hall Debut
Oct. 16 and 17: Oscar Shumsky [violin] Is Heard in Carnegie Hall Recital
Oct. 19: Bernice Reaser Presents Program of Piano Pieces
Oct. 21: Iceland Pianist [Rognvaldur Sigurjonsson] Is Heard in Recital at Town Hall
Oct. 21 and 22: Max Pollikoff: Violinist Heard in Town Hall Recital
Oct. 22: Stanley Hummel, Pianist, Plays at Carnegie Hall
Oct. 26: Leonid Bolotine [violinist] Heard in Town Hall Recital
Oct. 28: [Dean] Dixon Conducts: American Youth Orchestra in Concert at Hunter
    College
Oct. 28: Szeryng [violin] Plays as Soloist at Philharmonic Concert
Oct. 28 and 29: [Edward Lee] Tyler Song Recital
Oct. 28 and 29: Joan Slessiner Makes Piano Debut at Town Hall
Oct. 29 and 30: Bernstein Conducts the New York City Symphony

Oct. 30: Music of Czechoslovakia Heard at Hunter College
Oct. 31 and Nov. 1: [Alexander] Schneider Plays Recital of 3 Numbers by Bach

Nov. 4: Carlos Alexander: Bass-Barytone Is Heard in Recital at Town Hall
Nov. 9: Yves Baudrier Lectures on Modern French Music
Nov. 11: Guiomar Novaes Heard in Recital with Corigliano
Nov. 11: Nora Norman, Pianist
Nov. 11: Alton Jones, Pianist, in Town Hall Recital
Nov. 14 and 15: Edith Schiller, Pianist, Is Heard in N.Y. Debut
Nov. 16: Vladimir Elin, Barytone, Heard at Carnegie Hall
Nov. 18 and 19: Grant Johannesen Plays Casadesus' "Third Sonata"
Nov. 18 and 19: Betty Sanders Song Recital: Ballads of Many Nations Are Heard . . .
Nov. 19: [J. Kremer] Neumann Piano Recital
Nov. 20 and 21: Paul Drozdoff [piano] Recital
Nov. 21: Sara Sokolsky-Fried in Times Hall [piano] Recital
Nov. 25: Susan Reed Gives Recital of Ballads at Town Hall
Nov. 25: Ellington Festival at Carnegie Hall
Nov. 26 and 27: Kensley Rosen, Violinist, Heard in His Debut Here
Nov. 27 and 28: Dorothy Averell [violinist] Is Heard in a Recital at Town Hall
Nov. 30: Hilda Banks [pianist] Is Heard in Carnegie Hall Recital

Dec. 2: The New Friends: Bach, Bartok Works Heard at Town Hall Concert
Dec. 2: Lucie Rosen Recital: Performer on Theremin Appears at Town Hall
Dec. 2: American Ballad Concert
Dec. 3: Jeanne Rosenblum Gives Town Hall Piano Recital
Dec. 3 and 4: Genevieve Pitot, Pianist, Is Heard at Times Hall
Dec. 7: Welch Chorale Is Heard in Yule Season Concert
Dec. 9: Irene Beamer [contralto] Is Heard in Recital at Times Hall
Dec. 9: Dorothy Eustis, Pianist, in Concert at Town Hall
Dec. 11: Ajemian-Masselos: 2 Pianists Play Works of Cage at Carnegie Concert
Dec. 14: Raymond Duncan Concert Introduces Two Artists: Cellist and Pianist . . .
Dec. 16: Burl Ives at Town Hall
Dec. 16: Fritz Reiner Conducts N.B.C. Symphony Here
Dec. 16: Song Recital Presented by Josephine Brewster
Dec. 21: American Works Played at Memorial to [Henry] Hadley
Dec. 23: Calypso Musicians Give Concert at Town Hall
Dec. 23: Pearl Percival, Soprano, Gives Town Hall Recital
Dec. 30: Hilda Kosta (contralto) Is Heard in Town Hall Recital

1947

Jan. 6: Leah Effenbach [pianist] Is Heard in Recital at Town Hall
Jan. 6: Budapest Quartet Heard at New Friends Concert
Jan. 7: Geraldine Smith [soprano] Recital
Jan. 8 and 9: Fern Hammers [mezzo-soprano] in Recital
Jan. 10: Friskin Recital: Bach Works Make up Pianist's Town Hall Program
Jan. 13: Eugene Szenkar, Brazil, Leads N.B.C. Symphony
Jan. 13: Ingrid Robertson [soprano] Heard in Recital at Times Hall

Jan. 14 and 15: Katja Andy, Pianist, Gives Her First Recital Here

Jan. 14: Bernardo Segall, Pianist, Heard at Carnegie Hall

*Jan. 14: Ingrid Robertson [soprano] Heard in Recital at Times Hall

*Jan. 20: Stokowski Is Conductor at Philharmonic Concert

Jan. 20: Viana Bey, Pianist, Gives Her First Recital Here

Jan. 20: Ruth Kisch-Arndt: Contralto, Instrumentalists in Program of Old Music

Jan. 21 and 22: Cantata Singers: Heard at Church in Bach's Christmas Oratorio

Jan. 23: New Works Heard: 3 First Performances Here on Times Hall Program

Jan. 25: Little Symphony: Barone and Lorin Conduct in First Concert of Year

Jan. 27: Marion Kerby Presents Recital at Times Hall: Character Actress Heard in Song-Story Program

*Jan. 27: Harold Kohon Conducts Chamber Music Concert: Carmen de la Plaza, Soprano, Soloist at Town Hall

Jan. 29 and 30: Beata Malkin: Dramatic Soprano Is Heard at Times Hall

Feb. 1: Betty Muscart, Contralto, Gives First Concert Here

Feb. 3: Muench Directs in Concert at Carnegie Hall

Feb. 3: Szigeti Is Soloist: Violinist with Philharmonic Plays Mozart Concerto

Feb. 3 and 4: Harry Adaskin [violinist] Presents Recital at Times Hall

Feb. 6: Maria Mendoza [soprano] Recital

Feb. 8: Alice Eaton Gives Recital on Piano at Town Hall

Feb. 10 and 11: Harry Davis Presents Town Hall Piano Recital

Feb. 11 and 12: Bernard Greenhouse [cellist] Is Heard at Town Hall

Feb. 15: Festival Concert: Susan Reed and Dodd Chorus Heard at Town Hall

Feb. 17: Sevitzky Conducts: Indianapolis Symphony at Carnegie Hall

Feb. 17 and 18: John Feeney, Irish Tenor, Is Heard at Carnegie Hall

Feb. 20: Joseph Raieff: Pianist Gives Third Recital in Town Hall

Feb. 22: American Program: National Association [for American Composers and Conductors, Inc.] Presents Concert in Times Hall

Feb. 24: New Friends: Gordon String Quartet at Town Hall

Feb. 24: Maurice Wilk: Violinist Is Heard in Recital at Town Hall

Feb. 26 and 27: Bertha Melnik: Pianist Is Heard in Her Debut at Town Hall

Mar. 3: Walter Hendl Conducts: [Witold] Malcuzynski Is Philharmonic's Soloist at Carnegie Hall

Mar. 3 and 4: Music of China: Cultural Group Also Presents Dancing and Drama

Mar. 3: Edith Campbell [soprano] in Recital

Mar. 4: David Hollander: Pianist Heard in First of Two Concerts at Times Hall

Mar. 5: Mildred Milford, Pianist, Gives First N.Y. Concert

Mar. 10: Roesch Symphony: Lois Wann Appears as Oboe Soloist at Town Hall

Mar. 10: Society of Classic Guitar Presents Blain in Recital

Mar. 12: Wyangco-Rivera Concert: Philippine-Born Pianist and Soprano at Times Hall

Mar. 17: Kerttu Wanne, Violinist, in Recital at Town Hall

Mar. 17: Julia Bennett, Soprano, in Her New York Debut

Mar. 17 and 18: Pauline Leslie Recital: Dramatic Soprano Is Heard at Times Hall

Mar. 19: Leslie Frick Concert: Soprano Appears in Recital at Carnegie Chamber Hall

Mar. 21 and 22: Robert Stevenson Gives Program of Own Pieces

*Mar. 24. [Peter] Jarrett Piano Recital
Mar. 24: Gertrude Bonime Gives Town Hall Piano Recital
Mar. 25: Harry Neidell, Violinist, Gives Times Hall Recital
Mar. 2 and 27: Helen Kwalwasser: Violinist Heard in Her Debut at Town Hall
Mar. 29: Three Choirs: 11th Annual Festival Held at Emanu-El Hall
*Mar. 31: Doris Pape Is Presented in Town Hall Song Recital
Mar. 31: Enesco Concert: Violinist Plays in Times Hall to Aid Romanian Fund

Apr. 1 and 2: Gershwin Concert: Third Annual Memorial Held by B'nai B'rith
Apr. 2 and 3: Trio Concert: John Wummer, Eva Heinitz, Ernst Woff Heard
Apr. 3: Schola Cantorum Sings Bach's St. John's Passion
Apr. 4 and 5: Edna Iles, Pianist, Heard in a Recital at Town Hall
*Apr. 7: [Thaddeus] Kozuch, Pianist, Heard in Recital at Town Hall
Apr. 7: Myrtle Phillips Heard in Song Recital Here
Apr. 7: Kodaly Music [Missa Brevis] Celebrates the Resurrection
Apr. 10 and 11: Inez Bertail, Soprano, in Times Hall Recital
Apr. 11: Cantata Singers Present Three Bach Works at Church of Heavenly Rest
Apr. 12: Walden Quartet: String Concert Presented at Hunter Playhouse
Apr. 14: Bach Choir: B Minor Mass Is Given Here by Bethlehem Group
Apr. 15 and 16: Juilliard Chorus: Robert Shaw Leads Bryan's "Bell Witch" Cantata
Apr. 16 and 17: Morris Neiberg, Violinist, in New York Debut at 17
*Apr. 21: Clara Shen, Pianist, Plays Program at Town Hall
Apr. 21: Armenians Sing: Mixed Chous at Town Hall; Roseville Group Heard
Apr. 21: Sunday Afternoon Program [NYC Opera: "Cavalleria Rusticana" and
    "Pagliacci"; appears at the end of a review of "Rigoletto" by Arthur Berger]
Apr. 21: N.Y.U. Presents Concert by All of Its Glee Clubs
Apr. 24: Contest Winners: Janet Bloom [piano], Richard Browning [tenor] in Con-
    cert as Award
Apr. 25: "Madame Butterfly": Opera Staged at City Center and at Center Theater
Apr. 28 and 29: Oscar Griffin, Tenor, Is Heard at Town Hall
Apr. 28: Town Hall Concert: Frances Lehnerts, Jay Karlin, Anthony Palazzo Heard
Apr. 28: Mariko Mukai, Soprano, Gives Town Hall Recital

May 1: Composers' Forum: Works of Dello Joio and Lockwood Performed
*May 4, 1947: Veterans Orchestra: Small Organization Presents Town Hall Program
May 5: Octavia Morris [contralto] Is Heard in Recital at Times Hall
May 7: Renaissance Music: Judith Leigner Is Director at Carnegie Chamber Hall

Catalog of the Works of Lou Harrison

by Leta E. Miller and Charles Hanson

Editorial Procedures

The following catalog reflects the state of Lou Harrison's oeuvre as of November 1997. The information contained herein will necessarily continue to evolve as new recordings are made, as new manuscripts are unearthed, and as Harrison continues to compose new pieces and revise earlier ones. We are continuing to update our information, and, at such time as it is clear that his compositional work is complete, we anticipate reissuing this catalog as a separate publication.

Composition dates derive primarily from indications on autograph manuscripts. Unless otherwise stated, the date given is the completion date. Premiere dates normally come from programs or reviews. Works are listed chronologically within each year. Those for which a month/day are unknown or whose chronology cannot be determined by other factors (e.g., premiere date or correlative events) are listed alphabetically at the end of the year.

Undated early manuscripts have been assigned to one of three groupings by extramusical factors (handwriting, instrumentation, etc.): 1933–34, 1934–36, and 1936–40. These groups appear at the end of the listings for 1934, 1936, and 1940, respectively. Only complete or nearly complete works are included; none is authorized for performance.

To show compositional history without numbering the same work twice, pieces completed many years after their inception are listed without catalog number at the time they were begun and cross-referenced to the full (numbered) listing at the date of completion.

Complete works later used as movements of larger works are numbered separately because (1) they were complete compositions at the earlier date and remain as separate viable compositions on their own; and (2) new material was added when they were incorporated into the later composition. Cross-references are given in all such instances.

Numerous tiny "gift" pieces (e.g., birthday gifts, lullabies, going-away presents, etc.) have not been listed. Example: *A Thought on the Anniversary of Katherine Litz and Charles Oscar*, July 26, 1951, and a *Walking Tune for the Family Shahn*, both included in the Litz Collection at the New York Public

Library (and given in some works lists), are each a few measures in length and were never intended for public performance.

Titles are given as they appear on manuscripts or printed editions, even when that policy leads to inconsistencies (e.g., *Ritual #3, Prelude in C no. 2, Psalm Sonata no. IV*).

Choreographers are listed for works specifically composed for dance. In the case of nondance works that later were choreographed, references are provided only when they pertain to discussions in the present book.

Symbols and Abbreviations

† = Juvenilia or manuscript scores not authorized for performance at this time. Fragments and sketches not listed.

∫ = Score presently lost or improvisatory work for which no score exists.

I	instrumentation	**S**	score availability (publisher, etc.)
M	movements	**L**	approximate length, where
D	composition date, filed by date of completion		available, derived from recordings and rounded to the nearest half minute
P	premiere date, location, performer, if known	**R**	selected recordings
C	choreographer	**X-R**	cross references to other works
F	filmmaker	**N**	note
T	author of the text		

AmGam   American gamelan (a specific set of instruments built by Harrison and Colvig. Two sets of instruments are available for performances.)

appr   approved

arr   arranged, arrangement: same work with different instrumentation; no substantive variants

BFBM   *Beyond the Far Blue Mountains*, film by Molly Davies

BMC   Black Mountain College

CMF   Cabrillo Music Festival

cmpr   composer

comm   commissioned

comp   composed

compl   completed

Crys   Crystal Records

CRI   Composers Recordings, Inc.

Etc   Etcetera

FLPh   Free Library of Philadelphia

gam   gamelan

GGC   *Gending-Gending California*, 1981

HBP   Hermes Beard Press (distributed by Frog Peak Music, Box 1052, Lebanon, N.H. 03766)

JP   *Joys and Perplexities: Selected Poems of Lou Harrison* (Winston-Salem, N.C.: Jargon Society, 1992)

LHCAW   *Lou Harrison: Composing a World*

LHGB   *Lou Harrison Guitar Book* (D. Tanenbaum, ed., Columbia Music, 1994)

LHR   Peter Garland, ed., *A Lou Harrison Reader* (Santa Fe: Soundings Press, 1987).

MC   Mills College

MGWI   Lou Harrison, *Music for Gamelan with Western Instruments* (Hermes Beard Press, distributed by American Gamelan Institute, 1989)

Alphabetical Index by Title

Index by Medium and Genre

Numbers in italics = juvenilia, works not yet authorized for performance, or score
lost

Single instrument

115, 117, 119, 122–24, *126*, 127, 132, 136, 142, 145, 146, *147*, 151, 153, 157, *160*, 170 (tack-pf), 219, 274, 288, 290

hpsch: *35.16, 59*, 112

clavichord: *35.9*

org: *5, 35.8, 35.25, 41, 42, 58*, 131, 232, 277

keybd: *155*, 274

perc: *21*

psaltery or cheng: 177, 186, 189

Chamber music for Western instruments

Duos

fl, pf: *10, 58*

fl, org (or str): *34*

fl, harmonium: *35.36*

fl, 1 perc: *106*, 269

fl, drone: 133

rec, perc: *80*

2 rec, opt perc: 176

cl (or Eng hn), pf (or hp): 197

tpt, pf: *107*

tbn, vibraphone: *155*

vn, vla: *17*

vn, vc: *90.22*

vn, perc: 72

vn, pf: *35.37, 55, 90.23*, 276

vla, perc: *90.24*

vc, hp: 141

vc, pf: 297

viol, pf: *20*

hp or psaltery, perc: 190, 196, 204

guit, perc: 196, 204, 220

2 pf or pf 4-hands: *35.11, 35.24, 66, 90.20, 96*, 128, 154

pf, perc: *74, 85*, 148

org, pf: *19*

Trios

fl, clar, bn: *54*

fl, clar, pf: *53*

fl, vn, guit: *35.28*

fl, vla, vc: *35.39*

fl, 2 perc: 73

rec, pf, perc: *84, 96*

2 rec, viol: *35.22*

3 rec: 113

tpt, pf, perc: *35.38*

2 vn, vc: *12.1*

vn, vla, vc: 129

vn, vc, pf: 280

vn, pf, perc: 268

2 vn, tack-pf: *150*

vc, 2 perc: *90.6*

3 perc: 71, 101, 241, 291

solo instr w 2 ostinati: 273

Quartets

picc, tpt, harmonium, vc: *35.34*

fl, vc, hp, 1 perc: 138

fl, vn, pf, vibraphone: 286

vn, bn, hp, perc: *90.2*

2 vn, vla, vc: *18, 27, 30, 90.5, 90.10*, 116, 137, 224

4 perc: 70, 92, 93, 95, 105

Quintets

fl, 2 vn, cel, perc: 161

fl, 2 mandolins, guit, vc: *35.2*

fl, cl, vn, vc, pf: *206*

fl, ob, cl, bn, hn: 117

fl, cl, hn, bn, pf: 118

fl, vc, cb, tack-pf, cel: 140

3 tpts, 2 perc: 182

tpt, hn, mandolin, hp, perc: 272

vn, vla, vc, pf, perc: 300

str qt, pf: *35.10*, 290

5 str: *90.3*

5 perc: 77, 83, 100, 103, 104, *168*

Sextets

fl, cl, bn, vn, vla, vc: *36*
fl, bn, tpt, pf, vn, vc: 132
2 fl, ob, cl, bn, hn: 116
vn, 5 perc: 172

vn, 2 tack-pf, cel, 2 perc: 174
str qt, 2 perc: 48
6 perc: *81*

Septets

fl, cl, tpt, tbn, vn, cb, perc: 264
ocarina, guit, 5 perc: 100

Octets

fl, cl, tpt, vn, vc, cb, pf, 1 perc: 139
fl, ob, tpt, 2 vc, cb, tack-pf, cel: 143
vn, org, 1 perc, psaltery (or tack-pf, hpsch), 4 mbiras (or hp, marimba):
    195
str qt, 4 perc: *35.40*

Percussion works

Percussion ensemble

3 perc: 71, 101, 241, 291
4 perc: 70, 92, 93, 95, 105
5 perc: 77, 83, 100 (incl
    ocarina/guit), 103, 104, *168*

6 perc: *81*
11 perc: 91
12 perc: *228*

Percussion ens plus solo instrument

fl, 2 perc: 73
vn, perc: *72*
vn, 5 perc: 172

vn, 2 tack-pf, cel, 2 perc: 174
vla, perc: *90.24*
org, 8 perc, pf, celeste: 207

Orchestra

Full orch: symphonies: 187, 211, 243, 281; other: *78, 89, 109,* 139, *171,* 273,
    298
Str orch: *35.13, 49, 50, 99,* 135, 137, *150,* 173, 296
Cham orch: *16, 24, 35.1, 35.19, 35.35, 51, 64, 65,* 120, *121,* 149, *162,* 185, 244,
    295
short scores, orch undecided: *32, 33, 35.15, 37, 40, 47, 90.1, 90.7, 90.17, 90.18,
    114, 134, 155, 188*

Orchestra with one or two soloists

vn: 209
vn w cham orch: *90.11*
vn, pf: 156, 209

vc: 141, 297
pf: *12.2, 35.7, 90.12,* 262
p'i-p'a: 301

Opera

163, 203, 275

Voice

w pf: *35.33*, 88, 97, 130
w pf, perc: 98
w vc, 1 perc: 87
w gamelan: *246*, 250, 252, *292*
w perc: *90.13*, 171

w cham ens: *25, 35.30, 35.31, 35.33,
   39, 44, 144,* 152, *155,* 165, 166,
   180, 293
w orch or cham orch: 199, 281
8 bar, cham orch: 167

Chorus without soloists

a capella: *102*
w keybd: *35.17,* 287
w 2 pf, perc: *285*
w org, tpt: *125*
w opt org/hp: 266
w tbns, perc: 181

w perc: *35.42*
w orch or cham orch: *15, 35.6,* 159,
   167, 179, 198, 200, 205, 261
w AmGam, hp: 205
w gamelan, hp: *263*
w Asian instr, perc: 194, 201

Chorus and soloists

w gamelan, bn, 1 perc, hp, psaltery:
   283
w gamelan: 278
w gamelan, hp: 227

w cham orch: 167, 191, 226A
w cham orch, gamelan: 260
w metallophone: *164*
w perc: 202

Works for American gamelan
(Harrison's own instruments)

w hp, org, chor: 205
w vn: 209
puppet opera: 203

Other gamelan works (without voice or solo instrument)

Balinese: 284
Cirebonese: 248, 249, 251, 256
Sundanese: 222, 259, 279
Javanese: 212–14, 216–18, 229–31, 233–39, 242, 245, 247, 252–55, 257, 258,
   265, 302

Gamelan and Western solo instrument

vn: 209, 271
vn, vc: 240
vla: 223
pf: 270

sop sax: 267
tpt: 212
hn: 221

Asian instruments (other than gamelan)

4 haisho, perc: 289
p'iri, org: 178
2 Korean fl, opt changgo: 176
shamisen: 299
psaltery or cheng: 177, 186, 189

psaltery, perc: 190
p'i-p'a and orch: 301
Korean ct orch: 175
East Asian instr: 225
Filippine kulintang: 201

Western and non-Western instruments: 184, 185, 195, 203, 210, *226*, 301
Renaissance instruments: *35.22, 215*
Specially built instruments: 169
Miscellaneous: *11, 35.32, 35.43, 52*, 183, 192, 273, *294*
Film music: 201, 225, 242, 247, 273
Incidental music for dramatic productions: *51, 65, 78, 80, 107, 139, 140, 144*, 170, 246, 260, 295
Music composed for dance: *21, 44, 56, 61A, 66*, 67, *74, 82, 84–86, 90.8, 95A, 96*, 101, 110, 127, 132, *138–40, 143–46*, 148, *160, 162*, 183, *192*, 264, 269, 288, 300

Chronological List of Works

1927

1. † *Elégie*
   I pf D 1927 S Unpub N Signed "Lou Harrison, ten years old." For Helen Johnson

1931

2. † *Sonatina in G Minor*
   I pf D Nov. 11, 1931 S Unpub

1932

3. † *Sonata no. 1 in C*
   I pf D Jan. 25, 1932 S Unpub
4. † *Sonatina no. IV in A Major*
   I pf D May 6, 1932 S Unpub
5. † *Organ Sonata no. 1*
   I org D Begun May 12, 1932; finished May 1932 S Unpub
6. † *Pianoforte Sonata no. 7*
   I pf D May 14, 1932 S Unpub
7. † *Prelude in C no. 2*
   I pf D May 23, 1932 S Unpub
8. † *Sonata for Piano*
   I pf D May 30, 1932 S Unpub

9. † *Psalm Sonata no. IV*
    I pf D 1932 S Unpub

1934

Binary Variations on "O Sinner Man" (Renaissance instr ens; begun 1934, compl 1977). See 1977 listing

10. ∫ *Blue Glass*
     I fl, pf D 1934 P Dec. 13, 1934, Burlingame H.S. grad: Beth Bullard, fl, and Harrison

11. † *Detail of Adoration of the Lamb*
     I fiddles, harmonium, harp (short score) D 1934 S Unpub N incompl

12. † Undated compositions, ca. 1933–34 (scores unpub)
     12.1 *Allegro for 2 Violins and Cello* (incompl)
     12.2 *Variations*: pf, str

1935

13. † *American Pastoral with Byzantine Furnishings*
     I pf D 1935 S Unpub

14. † *The Censor* (recte: *Censer*) *Swingers*
     I pf D 1935 (Burlingame) S Unpub

15. † *The Geography of Heaven*
     I chor, 2 harmoniums, 2 pf, str D 1935 (Burlingame) S Unpub N incompl quarter-tone piece

16. † *Movement for 2 Horns, Strings, and Piano*
     D 1935 S Unpub

17. † *Music for Handel in Heaven*
     I vn, vla D 1935 S Unpub

18. † *Sonata*
     I str qt D 1935 (Burlingame) S Unpub

19. † *Sonata 4th*
     I reed org, pf D Undated but on same folio as *Waterfront—1934* S Unpub

20. † *Song for Tenor Violin and Pianoforte*
     D 1935 (San Francisco) S Unpub

21. † *Waterfront—1934*
     I perc M Three "phases": speed-up, strike, Bloody Thursday D 1935 or early 1936 P Boxing ring, Longshoreman's union hqtrs, S.F., date unclear; subsequent perf: May 17, 1936, Veterans' Aud, S.F. C Carol Beals S partial ms score in cmpr's archives

1936

22. † *Sonata #1*
     I pf M (1) Ostinato (2) Discussion (3) Jubilation D Mar. 1936 P Mar. 26, 1936, Calif. Sch of Fine Arts, S.F.: Douglas Thompson S Unpub

23. † *Hill-Rise*
    I pf **D** Apr. 1936 **S** Unpub
24. † *Midnoon*
    I str, hp **D** Apr. 1936 **S** Unpub
25. † *Song*
    I ten, 2 pf, str qt **D** Apr. 1936 **S** Unpub
26. † *Project no. 2 for Piano*
    D May 1936 **S** Unpub
27. † *Fugue for String Foursome*
    I str qt **D** Aug. 7, 1936 **S** Unpub
28. † *Double Fugue*
    I unspecified **D** Sept. 4, 1936 **S** Unpub **X-R** Rev and used in *Suite for Sym Str*, mvt 3 (1960)
29. *Ground in E Minor*
    I pf **D** Sept. 5, 1936; rev 1970 **S** Unpub **L** 2 min. **X-R** Rev again for *A Summerfield Set*, mvt 2 (1988)
30. † *Suite*
    I str qt **M** Two mvts **D** Nov.–Dec. 1936 **S** Unpub
31. † *Sonata for Unaccompanied Violin*
    M (1) Largo maestoso (2) Allegro vigoroso (3) Largo **D** Dec. 4, 1936 **P** Mar. 17, 1963, Sticky Wicket, Aptos: Gary Beswick **S** Unpub **L** 11 min
32. † Untitled
    I orch (short score) **D** Dec. 23, 1936 **S** Unpub **N** Incompl; for John Dobson
33. † *Overture for a Tragic, Heroic Drama*
    I orch (short score) **D** 1936 **S** Unpub
34. † *Sonata for Edward MacDowell*
    I fl, org; or str **M** Only mvt 2 extant **D** 1936 **S** Unpub
35. † Undated compositions, ca. 1934–36 (scores unpub)
    35.1 *Adagio*: fl, harmonium, str, pf (incompl: mvt 2 only)
    35.2 *Adagio*: fl, 2 mandolins, guit, vc (incompl)
    35.3 *Adagio*: pf
    35.4 *Allegro Maestoso*: pf (incompl)
    35.5 *Antiphon*: pf
    35.6 *Aubade for Gabriel*: chor, str, perc (2 versions)
    35.7 *Autumn*: pf, str
    35.8 *Choral*: org
    35.9 *Choral Preludes*: clavichord
    35.10 *Concerto for Piano and Str Qt* (incompl; 1935–36 while working with H. Cowell)
    35.11 *Dance*: I—"Cum Laude," II—"Exit et Adit," III—"Veni, Vidi, Vici": 2 pf; #3 for 1 pf
    35.12 *Dance for a Little Girl*: pf (incompl)
    35.13 *Discussion*: str
    35.14 *Feelingly*: pf
    35.15 *Fore-Piece to St. George; or, After the Dragon*: orch short score
    35.16 *Gothic Piece*: hpsch
    35.17 *Mass*—Kyrie, Sanctus: 2 pf, chor (incomplete)

35.18 *Minuet*: pf

35.19 *Moderato espressif*: str, org

35.20 *Moderato espressivo*: pf (quarter-tone)

35.21 *Pastoral and Minuet*: pf

35.22 *Pavan for Two Recorders and Bass Viol* (1935–36)

35.23 *Piece for Cello: Green Trees in a Field*

35.24 *Piece for Two Players at a Piano*: pf 4-hands

35.25 *Prelude for an Organ Toccata*

35.26 *Rondeau*: pf

35.27 *Rondeau for Pianoforte*

35.28 *Serenade*: fl, vn, guit

35.29 *A Small Fugue to be Crooned*: pf

35.30 *Song: Pastoral Night Piece; or a Request*: fiddles, male vo (1935–36)

35.31 *Song*: low vo, fl, cl, hn, str (short score). For John Dobson

35.32 *Song*: str qt, pf, unident mel instr (2 mvts, second incompl)

35.33 *Three Songs* from *The Geography of the Soul*: "Excursion in other Land-scapes"—vo, pf; "Unity in Strength"—vo, str qt; "A Little Girl Walked"—vo, harmonium

35.34 *Two Pieces for John Dobson*: "Apples"— pf; "Slowish"—picc, tpt, harmonium, vc (1935–36)

35.35 Untitled cham wk: fl (?), cl, cornet, tbn, 2 vn, vla, vc (parts)

35.36 Untitled (4 mvts): fl, harmonium (1935–36)

35.37 Untitled (Slowish and Serene): vn (?), pf

35.38 Untitled mvt: pf, tpt, drums

35.39 Untitled mvt: fl, vla, vc

35.40 Untitled: str qt, 4 perc

35.41 Untitled (Very fast): pf

35.42 *We are Always Winter*: 3 perc, speaking chor

35.43 *A Whatnot for Harpsichord and Other Things*: hpsch, violins, flutes, guitars

1937

36. †*Overture*

   I fl, cl, bn, vn, vla, vc **D** Dec. 1936–Jan. 1937 **S** Unpub

37. † *Overture*

   I pf or orch **D** Jan. 8, 1937 **S** Unpub **N** For Douglas Thompson

38. *Largo Ostinato*

   I pf **D** Jan. 15, 1937; rev 1970 **S** HBP **L** 4.5 min **X-R** Rev and orch for *Third Sym,* mvt 3 (1982) **N** Orig ms says "piano or orchestra" but there is no or-chestration from this period. For John Dobson

39. † *Last Music*

   I alto or bar, fl, cl, hp, str, org ad lib (short score) **D** Jan. 23, 1937 **S** Unpub

40. † *Fugue for Orchestra or Piano*

   D Jan. 1937 **S** Unpub

41. † *Slow (Symphony for Organ)*

   I org solo **D** Feb. 10, 1937 **S** Unpub **N** Early 12-tone wk

42. † *Simfony for Organ*
    I org solo D Feb. 23, 1937 S Unpub
43. † *A Bit of Rotten Chopin on Order of J. Cleghorn*
    I pf D Feb. 27, 1937 S Unpub
44. ∫ *Changing World*
    I 2 pf, perc, vo, recorder (from program) M (1) City Pull (City; Country)
    (2) Women Walk Free (3) All Religions are One (4) Seeding Time—1776
    (5) Sudden Showers—1864 (6) Reapers—1929 D 1937 P May 2, 1937 C 12
    choreogr, incl Harrison N Incompl ms of pt (3) survives.
45. *Saraband*
    I pf D May 24, 1937 S *NMQ* 11, no. 4 (July 1938) L 4 min R NewpCl NPD-
    85606: M. Boriskin
46. † *Saraband*
    I pf D May 25, 1937 S Unpub
47. † *Symphony #1*
    I Orch (short score) M 1 mvt only ("slow") D June 11, 1937 S Unpub
48. *France 1917–Spain 1937 (About the Spanish War)*
    I str qt, 2 perc D June 16, 1937; rev 1968 P Aug. 17, 1968, CMF, Aptos
    (rev vers w additional title) S *Soundings* 3/4, (1972); *MUSA* L 3 min N
    The title *Ritual #5* also appears on the 1937 ms (not the same work as #55).
49. † Untitled: allegro moderato
    I str D June 17, 1937 S Unpub N Part of this work used in rev vers of
    France 1917–Spain 1937.
50. † *3 Runes for Strings*: no. 1, "Oracle"
    I str orch D July 1937 S Unpub N Titles and yr of compl for mvts 2–3:
    Monolith, Atav (1939) appear at end of "Oracle"; scores for these mvts lost
51. † *[The] Winter's Tale*
    I fl, tpt, 2 vn, vla, vc, perc M Incid music for drama D Sept. 1937 P Oct.
    15–16, 1937, MC T Shakespeare S Unpub
52. † *Ritual #2: Dance*
    I hp (or pf or ww or marimbas) D Sept. 12, 1937 S Unpub
53. † *Ritual #3*
    I fl, cl, pf D Sept. 13, 1937 S Unpub
54. † *Ritual #4*
    I fl, cl, bn D Sept. 13, 1937 S Unpub
55. † *Ritual #5*
    I vn, pf D Sept. 14, 1937 S Unpub, incompl
56. *Prelude for Grandpiano*
    I pf D Sept. 16, 1937 P Nov. 16, 1937, Community Playhouse, SF: Lou Harri-
    son C Tina Flade S *NMQ* 11, no. 4 (July 1938) L 6.5 min R NewpCl NPD-
    85606: M. Boriskin N For Henry Cowell
57. † *Piece for Pianokeys*
    I pf D Sept. 20, 1937 S Unpub
58. † *Ritual #6*
    I org or pf or fl/pf D Sept. 21, 1937 S Unpub
59. † *Pieces for Harpsichord or Piano*
    I hpsch or pf M 1 mvt only D Oct. 5, 1937 S Unpub

60. † *Passacaglia* (also titled *Consort 5* and *Ritual #8*)

    I pf **D** 1937 **S** Unpub **X-R** Rev and used as *Canticle #2*, mvt 1 (1942); 2d rev for *First Suite for Str,* mvt 3 (1948; see listing there for history). Abandoned 1995

61. † *Ritual #7*

    I unspecified **D** 1937 **S** Unpub

61A. † *Three Dances of Conflict*

    I pf **D** 1937 **C** Carol Beals **S** Unpub

62. † *Threnody and Chaconne*

    I vn solo **D** 1937 **S** Unpub

63. † Untitled piano sonata

    I pf **M** (1) Moderato (2) Largo **D** 1937 **S** Unpub **N** Early 12-tone work. Title "Third Piano Sonata" crossed out (wk is unrelated to item 69)

1938

64. † *Concerto Grosso*

    I Baroque-style orch (str, dbl reeds) **M** (1) Slowish and intense (2) Brisk and sprinting (3) Very slow **D** Jan. 3, 1938 **S** Unpub

65. † *Electra*

    I cham orch (fl, hp, vns, vc, cornet, pf) **M** Incid music for drama **D** Spr 1938 **P** June 10–11, 1938, MC **T** Euripides **S** Unpub

66. † *Tribunal*

    I pf 4-hands **D** Spr 1938 **C** Marian Van Tuyl **S** Unpub

67. ∫ *Conquest*

    I fl or ocarina or rec, pf, conch shell, perc **D** Aug. 1938 **P** Aug. 5, 1938, MC **C** Lester Horton and Bella Lewitzky **N** Controlled improv for dance; Horton later renamed the work *Tierra y Libertad* (title of final section) and perf it in L.A. with music by Gerhard Dorn.

68. † *Rondo*

    I vn solo **D** Nov. 1938 **S** Unpub

69. *Third Piano Sonata*

    I pf **M** (1) Slowish and singing (2) Fast and rugged (3) Very slow, very singing and solemn **D** 1938; edited Dec. 3, 1970 **P** Radio perf, 1938: L. Harrison **S** HBP; *LHR* **L** 10.5 min **N** For Douglas Thompson

1939

70. *Fifth Simfony*

    I 4 perc **M** (1) Vigoroso (2) Slow and dramatic (3) Brisk **D** Feb. 22–Mar. 8, 1939 **P** May 19, 1939, Cornish School, Seattle: John Cage, cond **S** WB; Fleisher Coll, FLPh **L** 14 min **N** For Sherman Slayback

71. *Counterdance in the Spring*

    I 3 perc **D** Mar. 29, 1939 **P** May 19, 1939, Cornish School, Seattle: John Cage, cond **S** *MUSA* **L** 3.5 min. **X-R** Later incorporated into *Tributes to Charon* (1982) **N** Subsequently choreogr by Jean Erdman as "Creature on a Journey" (1943)

72. † *Fourth Violin Concerto*
I vn, perc **M** (1) Brisk and Brite (2) Free and tense and slow (3) Swinging and sure **D** Apr. 12, 1939 **S** Unpub **N** For Marian van Tuyl

73. *First Concerto for Flute and Percussion*
I fl, 2 perc **M** (1) Earnest, fresh, and fastish (2) Slow and poignant (3) Strong, swinging, and fastish **D** Apr. 15, 1939 **P** Aug. 10, 1941, Bennington Coll: Otto Luening (fl), Henry Cowell, Frank Wigglesworth (perc) **S** Peters (cmpr prefers fl pt in mvt 1 transposed up a 4th; in mvt 3, up an 8ve) **L** 9 min **R** *CD*: MHS 513616L: L. Miller, W. Winant, H. Sloan; CRI CD-568: R. Rudich, K. Grossman, W. Trigg; Bis 272: M. Wiesler, Kroumata Perc Ens **N** For Henry Cowell

74. ∫ *Uneasy Rapture*
I pf, perc (from program) **D** 1939 (appears on programs from May 2 and later) **C** Marian van Tuyl

75. † *Usonian Set*
I pf **M** (1) Reel (2) Range Song (3) Jig **D** 1939: (1) May 2; (2) Apr. 30; (3) Apr. 28 **P** May 23, 1939 **S** Unpub (MC library)

76. † *Canon: Langorously Latin*
I pf **D** May 11, 1939 **S** Unpub

77. *Bomba*
I 5 perc **D** May 15, 1939 **P** Aug. 14, 1976, CMF, Aptos, CA: CalArts Perc Ens **S** WB; Fleisher Coll, FLPh **L** 4 min

78. † *The Trojan Women*
I Orch (fl, cl, pf, hp, str) **M** Incid music for drama (3 mvts survive: Prelude, Ground, Chaconne) **D** 1939 ("Ground": May 23; "Prelude": May 26) **P** June 9, 1939, MC; June 10, Golden Gate Expo, Treasure Is **T** Euripides **S** Unpub **L** 4.5 min **N** Prelude [Overture] perf by S.F. Sym, Pierre Monteux, cond, Standard Oil Broadcast, June 13, 1940

Mass to St. Anthony (unis chor and perc, later changed to tpt, hp, str. Begun Sept. 1, 1939; compl 1952). See 1952 listing

79. *Reel: Homage to Henry Cowell*
I pf **D** 1939 **S** PMTCA **L** 4 min **X-R** Rev and orch for *Third Sym,* mvt 2a (1982). Also related to "Polka" from *Grand Duo* (1988) **N** Von Gunden, *Music of Lou Harrison,* gives 1936 for this work, based on N. Rutman's thesis. However, the date 1939 appears on the ms and is also given in L. Celso's SJSU master's thesis on Harrison's pf music, prepared under the cmpr's supervision.

1940

80. ∫ *Processional from the Choephoroe of Aeschylus*
I recorder, perc **D** 1939–40 **L** 2.5 min **N** Recorded on a noncommercial 78rpm disc that has Prelude to *The Trojan Women* on the other side. Dated 1939–40 on the basis of comp, perf, and broadcast date of *The Trojan Women* (recording presumably from 1940 radio broadcast)

81. † *Rune*
I 6 perc **D** Jan. 15, 1940 **S** Unpub **N** possibly incompl or a kit

82. † *Goin' to be a Party in the Sky (Skyparty)*
   I pf, str D Before Apr. 1940 (perf Apr. and Aug. 1940) C Marian van Tuyl S
   Unpub (MC library)

83. *Canticle #1*
   I 5 perc D June 21, 1940 (1:30–5:30) P First concert perf: July 18, 1940, MC.
   Perf earlier in yr by dancers during L.A. tour S MP, 1965; WPA score photo-
   stat: Fleisher Coll, FLPh L 5.5 min R *LP:* Time S-8000: Manhattan Perc Ens,
   P. Price, cond; Mainstream MS-5011

84. ∫ *Something to Please Everybody*
   I rec, pf, perc (acc to Harrison's memory) D Summer 1940 P July 6, 1940, MC
   C Lester Horton

85. ∫ *16 to 24*
   I pf, perc (?) D Summer 1940 P July 6, 1940, MC C Lester Horton

86. † *Omnipotent Chair*
   I cb, xyl, drums, bells, zither (instr from review) D Aug. 1940 P Aug. 2,
   1940, MC C Louise Kloepper S An untitled ms in 5 mvts in the cmpr's
   archives may be this wk.

87. *Pied Beauty*
   I bar, vc, 1 perc D Oct. 28, 1940 P Oct. 6, 1963, Old Spaghetti Factory, S.F.:
   Robert Hughes et al. T Gerard Manley Hopkins S HBP L 2.5 min N For
   William Brown (later Weaver)

88. *Sanctus*
   I contralto, pf D 1940 P Nov. 14, 1940, S.F. Mus of Art: Radiana Pazmor T
   Cath mass ordinary S HBP L 5.5 min R MusicMasters: E. Golden, mezzo,
   D.R. Davies, pf (forthcoming)

89. † *Labyrinth*
   I orch (fl, ob, tpt, 4 hn, pf, hp, perc, str) M (1) Slowish (2) Fastish (3) Slowish
   D 1940 S Unpub N Spelled "Labrynth" on orig ms

Concerto #5 (vn, perc; 1940 or 1941—appears undated in notebk of wks from
   these two yrs. Becomes *Concerto for Violin and Percussion Orchestra.*) See 1959
   listing

90. † Undated compositions, ca. 1936–40 (scores unpub)
   90.1 *Antipodes*: short score (str and brass?; late 1930s?)
   90.2 *Chorus for the Eumenides*: solo vn, bn, hp, perc
   90.3 *Implicity for 5 Strings* (unspecified)
   90.4 *Minnesingers*: pf
   90.5 *Movement for String Foursome*: str qt
   90.6 *Prelude*: vc, 2 perc
   90.7 *Processionals*: pf (probably short score for orch; 2 mvts, second
       incompl)
   90.8 *R.A.H.*: pf (ms at MC library)
   90.9 *Second Suite for Solo Violin* (to Sherman Slayback; perc ostinato opt)
   90.10 *Second Usonian Set*: str qt (after May 2, 1939, date of "first" Usonian
       Set)
   90.11 *Set of Fragments—"Lovesong"*: solo vn, muted str (1936–37)
   90.12 *Song of Joy: "We beat upon gold gongs"*: pf, str; short score (Mills period)
   90.13 *Song Project #2*: vo, perc (1936–39)

90.14 *Suite for Solo Violin* (to Mervin Levy [=Mervin Leeds]; perc ostinato opt)

90.15 *Suite of Pieces for Martha Hill* (Prelude, Saraband, March): pf

90.16 *Theme and Variations*: pf

90.17 *Tragic Pantomime* (short score for orch)

90.18 Untitled (Allegro moderato, Slow and legendary; mvts 2, 3 of a short score for orch)

90.19 Untitled (Andante): pf, str

90.20 Untitled (Fastish): 2 pf; incompl

90.21 Untitled (three mvts): pf (1937 or 1938)

90.22 Untitled (two mvts): vn, vc (1938?)

90.23 *Variations*: vn, pf

90.24 *Viola Concerto*: vla, perc (1936–38)

1941

91. *Labyrinth #3*
I 11 perc M (1) Ode (2) Passage thru [sic] dreams (3) Seed (4) Image in the soil D Begun 1940, compl 1941 P Jan. 16, 1961, Town Hall, N.Y.: Manhattan Perc Ens, P. Price, cond S MP, 1961; WPA copy (pts only): Fleisher Coll, FLPh L 20 min R Pan Classics 510103: P. Sacher, cond X-R Rev for use in *Orpheus*, mvts 2, 3, 5, and 8 (1969) N Originally projected w nine mvts. Spelled "Labrynth" on orig ms

92. *Song of Quetzalcoatl*
I 4 perc D Feb. 6, 1941 P May 14, 1941, Calif Club, S.F.: Harrison, Cage, et al. S MP, 1962 L 6.5 min R *LP*: Orion ORS-7276: P. Price, cond; *CD*: NA 055: S.F. Contemp Mus Players N Published as "Quetzecoatl"

Jephtha's Daughter (kit for perc, reader, dance. 1st vers: Feb. 26, 1941; expanded: 1963) See 1963 listing

93. *Simfony #13*
I 4 perc D Mar. 25, 1941 P May 14, 1941, Calif Club, S.F.: Harrison, Cage, et al. S WB; ms copy in Paul Price Coll, U of Illinois L 9 min R *CD*: LHCAW: UCSC Perc. Ens, W. Winant, cond N Title from program: *Thirteenth Simfony*

94. † *Suite for Flute*
I unacc fl M (1) Fast (2) Slow (3) Fast D Apr. 8–9, 1941 S Unpub

95. *Double Music* (joint comp with John Cage)
I 4 perc D Apr. 1941 P May 14, 1941, Calif Club, S.F.: Harrison, Cage, et al. S Peters, 1961 L 5 min R *LP*: Time S-8000: Manhattan Perc Ens, P. Price, cond; *LP* and *CD*: NewW 330 and 80405-2: New Mus Cons; *CD*: Hungaroton HCD12991: Amadinda Perc Grp; Wergo 6203: Quatuor Helios; Decca/Argo 455 590-2: Calif Sym

95A. † *Exposition of a Cause*
I pf M 5 untitled mvts D May 18, 1941 S Unpub (MC library) N Dance work: choreographer unidentified.

96. † *Green Mansions*
I rec, pf, perc (alternate: 2 pf) D Aug. 1941 P Aug. 24, 1941, Stern Grove, S.F.: Harrison et al. and the Modern Ballet Grp C Letitia Innes S Unpub N

Based on W. H. Hudson novel. Harrison danced as well as perf music at premiere.

97. *King David's Lament*
I ten, pf **D** Oct. 8, 1941 **T** Samuel II; alt text/title: *Lycidas' Lament* (Milton) **S** Unpub **X-R** Rev June 18, 1985, for *Three Songs*, mvt 1

98. *May Rain*
I vo, pf, perc **D** Oct. 30, 1941 **P** Feb. 17, 1963, Sticky Wicket, Aptos **T** Elsa Gidlow, "From Alba Hill" #3 **S** HBP; *LHR*; *Soundings* 1 (Jan. 1972) **L** 3 min **R** *LP*: MHS 4187: J. La Barbara, R. Bunger; *CD*: NA 055: J. Duykers, J. Steinberg, W. Winant **N** For William Weaver

1942

99. † *Canticle #2*
I str orch **M** (1) Rich and singing (2) Ricercare on Bach's Name **D** (1) Begun 1937, compl 1942 (see X-R) (2) Begun Aug.–Oct. 1937, compl 1942 **S** Unpub **X-R** Mvt 1: rev vers of *Passacaglia* (1937); 2d rev becomes *Ground for Strings: Version for two pianos*, May 14, 1946, which is pf vers of *First Suite for Str*, mvt 3 (1948)

100. *Canticle #3*
I Ocarina, 5 perc, guit (guit, ocarina pts may be played by two of the percussionists) **D** Jan.–Feb. 1942, rev 1989 (ocarina pt ornamented) **P** May 7, 1942, Holloway Playhouse (Fairmont Hotel), S.F.: L. Harrison, cond **S** MP, 1960 **L** 15 min **R** *LP*: Urania UX 106: Am Perc Soc, P. Price, cond; *CD*: MusM 60241X: Ens Nova, D. R. Davies, cond; Etc KTC1071: CalArts Perc Ens, J. Bergamo, cond **N** MP score (and many subsequent sources) erroneously cite date as 1941. Cmpr prefers ocarina's 5-note scale to be slendro type: intervals, lowest to highest, approximately M2 m3 M2 M2.

101. *In Praise of Johnny Appleseed*
I 3 perc (one pt incl wooden fl). Cmpr also appr perf with 4 or more players per part **M** (1) The Trumpets of Heaven (2) Seed (3) Coronation (4) The Battle with Bunyan (5) Fruition (6) Meeting with the Ancient of Days (7) Ode (8) Whoops for Johnny **D** 1942 **P** May 7, 1942, Holloway Playhouse (Fairmont Hotel), S.F.: Harrison, Cage, and ens **C** Carol Beals **S** HBP **L** Variable (see notes) **N** A kit with various options for the order and repetition of phrases

102. † *Canticle #4*
I SATB chor **M** 7 mvts with various versions of mvts 1–2 **D** ND, but betw *Canticles 3* (Feb.) and *5* (June) **S** Unpub

103. *Suite for Percussion*
I 5 perc **M** (1) Moderato (2) Slow (3) Recitative—Moderato allegro **D** June 2, 1942 **P** Feb. 28, 1963, Museum of Modern Art, N.Y.: Manhattan Perc Ens, P. Price, dir **S** MP, 1969 **L** 9.5 min **R** *LP* and *CD*: CRI SD-252 and CD-613: Manhattan Perc Ens

104. *Canticle #5*
I 5 perc **D** June 10, 1942 **S** Unpub **X-R** Rev for *Canticle and Round for Gerhard Samuel's Birthday*, mvt 1 (1993)

105. *Fugue for Percussion*
I 4 perc **D** 1942 (before move to L.A. in Aug.) **S** MP, 1962; repub 1982 w cor-

rections by G. Kvistad **L** 4 min **R** *LP*: Opus 1 #22, Blackearth Perc Grp; *CD*:
NA 055: S.F. Contemp Mus Players **N** Harrison, *Music Primer*, and other
sources erroneously give date as 1941. Listed on program for New Music Society concert, N.Y., May 10, 1951, but replaced by *Canticle #3* at the last
minute (review in *N.Y. Herald Tribune*, May 12, 1951)

106. † *Canticle #6[a]*
    I perc, fl **M** 21 mvts projected **D** Five mvts compl, Oct. 3, 1942 **S** Unpub **N** A
    different wk from *Canticle #6*

107. † *The Beautiful People*
    I tpt, pf **M** Incid music to drama **D** Fall 1942 **P** Nov. 3–7, 1942, Royce Hall,
    UCLA **T** William Saroyan **S** Unpub

108. † *Music for the River-Merchant's Wife*
    I pf **D** 1942 (Los Angeles) **S** Unpub

109. † *Canticle #6*
    I orch (2-2-2 alto sax–ten sax–bar sax; 2-1-1; perc; hp; str) **M** (1) Allegro (2)
    Passacaglia (3) Rondo **D** Sept.–Dec. 1942 (mvt 3: Oct. 23) **S** Unpub **X-R** Mvt 1
    rev and used as *Elegiac Sym*, mvt 2 (1975). Mvt 2 rev and used as *Elegiac
    Sym*, mvt 5 **N** A different, incompl wk (perc and fl, Oct. 3, 1942) is also enti-
    tled *Canticle #6*.

1943

110. *Gigue and Musette*
    I pf **D** 1943 (before move to N.Y. in summer) **P** May 8, 1944, Evenings on the
    Roof, L.A.: Frances Mullen **C** Melissa Blake **S** HBP **X-R** Orch and used in
    Rhymes with Silver, mvt 5 (1996)

111. *Suite for Piano*
    I pf **M** (1) Prelude (2) Aria (3) Conductus (4) Interlude (5) Rondo **D** May 1943
    P May 8, 1944: Evenings on the Roof, L.A.: Frances Mullen **S** Peters, 1964 **L**
    16.5 min **R** *CD*: NewpCl NPD-85606: M. Boriskin **N** For Frances Mullen Yates

112. *Six Sonatas for Cembalo*
    I hpsch (cmpr also appr pf) **M** (1) Moderato (2) Allegro (3) Moderato (4) Alle-
    gro (5) Moderato (6) Allegro **D** Begun 1934, completed 1943 (before October)
    P Entire set: Jan. 24, 1944, Evenings on the Roof, L.A.: Frances Mullen **S**
    NMQ 17, no. 1 (Oct. 1943); new edition (w suggested ornamentation by S.
    Summerfield): Peer, 1990 **L** 29 min **R** *CD*: MHS 513988A: L. Burman-Hall,
    hpsch; NewpCl NPD-85606: M. Boriskin, pf (#3, 5, 6 only); Bridge BCD-
    9041: arr guit/hp, J. Schneider, A. Shulman **N** Sonata 1 used by Esther Bal-
    lou, *Variations, Scherzo and Fugue on a Theme by Lou Harrison*, 1959

Easter Cantata (contr, chor, cham orch; begun summer or fall 1943, compl 1966).
    See 1966 listing

113. *Serenade for Three Recorders*
    I S, A, T rec **M** (1) Allegro moderato (2) Largo (3) Gigue and Rondeau **D**
    Dec. 25, 1943 **S** Laureate Music Press, 1997 **L** 7 min **N** For Henry and Sidney
    Cowell

114. † *Untitled symphony*
    I short score **M** 2 mvts **D** ND (1943–44: on same page with *Serenade for
    3 Rec*) **S** Unpub

1944

115. *Waltz in A*
    I pf **D** Sept. 14, 1944 **S** HBP **L** 1.5 min **R** NewpCl NPD-85606: M. Boriskin
    X-R Absorbed into *New York Waltzes*; see compl listing, 1951 **N** For Edward
    McGowan
116. *Schoenbergiana*
    I (a) str qt (b) arr for 2 fl, ob, cl, bn, hn by Robert Hughes **M** Vers a: (1) Alle-
    gro (2) Siciliana (3) Theme and Variations. Vers b: mvts 1−2 reversed **D** (a)
    Begun May 1944; compl Nov. 17, 1944 (b) 1962 **P** (a) Never perf; (b) Apr. 1,
    1962, Sticky Wicket, Aptos: Robert Hughes and ens **S** (b) only: HBP **N**
    Sketches list title as *Second String Quartet*.
117. *Serenade in C*
    I (a) pf (b) arr for ww qnt by Robert Hughes **D** (a) 1944 (b) 1962 **P** (a) Never
    perf (b) Apr. 15, 1962, Sticky Wicket, Aptos: Robert Hughes and ens **S** (b)
    only: HBP

1945

118. *Party Pieces* (joint comp with John Cage, Virgil Thomson, Henry Cowell)
    Orig title: *Sonorous or Exquisite Corpses*
    I fl, cl, hn, bn, pf (Orig short score w unspecified instrumentation orch by
    Robert Hughes, 1963) **M** 20 short mvts comp at social gatherings in N.Y. **D**
    Various occasions in 1944−45 **P** Oct. 12, 1964, S.F. Tape Music Ctr: West
    Coast Wind Qnt **S** Peters, 1982 **L** 10 min **R** *LP*: Gramavision 7006, L. Foss,
    cond **N** Composers: Cage and Harrison: 1, 7 "for V.T. [Virgil Thomson] in ab-
    sentia (et amoroso)." Thomson, Cage, and Harrison: 2, 4, 5, 6, 8, 11; Cowell,
    Cage, and Harrison: 3, 9, 10, 12, 13, 14, 15, 16, 17, 18, 19, 20. One additional
    piece not orchestrated.
119. *A 12-Tone Morning After to Amuse Henry*
    I pf **D** ca. 1944−45 **P** Mar. 25, 1997, 92nd St Y, N.Y.: Michael Barrett **S** HBP
    L ca. 2 min **N** For Henry Cowell
120. *Alleluia for Small Orchestra*
    I cham orch (2 fl, 2 ob, cl, bcl, 2 hn, hp, str) **D** Begun Aug. 1943, compl Jan.
    1945 **P** May 8, 1951, McMillin Th, Columbia U: Manhattan Sch Cham Orch,
    Harris Danziger, cond **S** *NMQ* 21, no. 2 (Jan. 1948) **N** Cmpr prefers that this
    piece no longer be performed.
121. † *Motet for the Day of Ascension*
    I cham orch (4 vn, 2 vc, cb, hp) **D** Begun Feb. 1945, compl May 16, 1945 **P**
    Apr. 5, 1946, N.Y. Little Sym: L. Harrison, cond **S** Unpub
122. *Waltz in C*
    I pf **D** Sept. 16, 1945 **S** HBP **L** 1 min **R** NewpCl NPD-85606: M. Boriskin
    X-R Absorbed into *New York Waltzes*; see compl listing in 1951 **N** For
    Edward McGowan
123. *Triphony*
    I pf **D** Dec. 6, 1945 **P** William Masselos, date unknown **S** Peters **L** 4.5 min **R**
    CD: NewpCl NPD-85606: M. Boriskin **X-R** Arr as string *Trio* (1946). Rev and
    used in *Suite for Symph Str*, mvt 5 (1960) **N** For Oscar Baradinsky

124. *Two Unused Pieces for Jose Limón*
    I pf **M** (1) Polka (2) Allegro alla Jarabe **D** Dec. 6, 1945 **P** Apr. 28, 1997, Lincoln Ctr, N.Y.: Michael Boriskin **S** HBP **L** 5 min **N** These 2 mvts were originally mvts 5–6 of a longer composition; other mvts are lost.

125. † *Onward Christian Soldiers*
    I unis chor, tpt, org **D** ca. 1945 **P** United Methodist Church, Bronx, N.Y., ca. 1945 **T** Protestant hymn **S** Unpub **N** For Edward McGowan, minister, United Meth Ch

1946

126. † *Sonata in D*
    I pf **M** 2 mvts **D** ca. 1945–46 **S** Unpub **N** Incompl

127. *Changing Moment*
    I pf **D** Feb. 13/15, 1946 **P** 1946, N.Y. (Jean Erdman, Helaine Blok, Elizabeth Sherbon, dancers) **C** Jean Erdman **S** HBP **L** 3.5 min

128. †*Ground for Strings: Version for two pianos*
    I 2 pf **D** May 14, 1946 **S** Unpub **X-R** Rev vers of *Canticle #2*, mvt 1 (1942), which in turn was a rev of *Passacaglia* (1937). Orch and used as *First Suite for Str*, mvt 3 (1948). Subsequently abandoned. See *First Suite for Str*, 1948

129. *Trio*
    I vn, vla, vc **M** Single mvt **D** 1946 **P** Jan. 26, 1947, New Sch for Soc Research, N.Y.: New Music Str Qt **S** Peters, 1961 **L** 4.5 min **R** *LP* and *CD*: NewW 319 and 382-2: New Mus Cons **X-R** Arr of *Triphony* (1945). Rev and used in *Suite for Symph Str*, mvt 5 (1960)

130. *Fragment from Calamus*
    I bar, pf (originally bar, str qt) **D** 1946 **T** Walt Whitman, *Calamus* #43 **S** Bomart 1950; *LHR* **L** 1 min **X-R** Rev and orch for *Three Songs*, mvt 2 (1985)

1947

131. *Praises for Michael the Archangel*
    I org **D** Begun Jan. 1946; compl Jan. 15, 1947 **P** 1966, Honolulu: Fred Tulan **S** *MUSA* **L** 7 min **X-R** Orch and rev for *Elegiac Sym*, mvt 4 (1975)

132. *Western Dance* (dance title: *The Open Road*)
    I (a) pf (b) fl, bn, tpt, pf, vn, vc **D** Fall 1947 **P** Vers (b): Dec. 14, 1947, Hunter College, N.Y. **C** Merce Cunningham **S** HBP **L** 4 min **R** *CD*: BMG 9026-68751-2: Eos Ens (vers b)

133. *Air in G Minor*
    I fl, drone **D** 1947; rev 1970 **S** HBP **L** 4.5 min **R** *LP*: Opus 1 #129: L. Miller; Carlston 101: A. Koregelos; *CD*: NA 093: L. Miller (newly recorded) **X-R** Unused sketch material for this piece later incorp into *Suite for Cello and Piano* (1995) **N** Orig for recorder; written for yacht designer Olin Stevens. Cmpr originally appr vn or strings in place of fl but now appr only fl.

Symphony on G (begun 1947, compl 1964, rev 1966). See 1964 listing

1948

134. † *Cupid and Psyche*
I cham orch short score **D** Mar. 19, 1948 **S** Unpub **N** Incompl

135. *First Suite for Strings* (replaced by *New First Suite,* 1995)
I str orch **M** (1) Allegro moderato (2) Adagio cantabile (3) Molto moderato (4) Poco lento, affetuoso (5) Allegro **D** 1946–48. Mvt 2: Mar.–Aug. 10, 1947; mvt 3: May 14, 1946 (based on earlier wks; see X-R). Rest of wk begun 1947, compl 1948. Mvt 2 rev 1991 **P** May 21, 1948, Nat Inst of Arts and Letters, N.Y. (now the Am Inst and Acad of Arts and Letters) **S** Peer, 1978 and 1991 **X-R** Mvts 1 and 2: incorp w/o alteration into *New First Suite* (1995). Mvt 3 based on a series of revisions as follows: *Passacaglia* comp 1937; rev vers used in *Canticle #2,* mvt 1 (1942); heavily rev vers, titled *Ground for Strings: Version for two pianos,* May 14, 1946; this *Ground* is a pf vers of *First Suite for Str,* mvt 3. In *New First Suite for Str* (1995), this mvt is abandoned. Mvt 4: expanded from 12 mm to 47 mm for *New First Suite.* Mvt 5: replaced by new mvt in *New First Suite.* **N** Entire wk supplanted by *New First Suite for Str* (1995)

136. *Homage to Milhaud*
I pf **D** Sept. 31, 1948 **S** *PMTCA* **L** .5 min

137. *Suite #2 for Strings*
I str orch (str qt appr by comp) **M** (1) Adagio, molto cantabile (2) Allegro moderato (3) Allegro moderato, tranquillo **D** 1948 **P** Mar. 15, 1949, McMillin Th, Columbia U, N.Y.: Orch of Greenwich House Mus Sch **S** Merrymount Mus Press, 1949 **L** 10.5 min **R** *LP*: Col ML-4491: New Mus Str Qt **N** Comp for Fritz Rikko's Greenwich House ens

1949

138. *The Perilous Chapel*
I fl, vc, hp, 1 perc **M** (1) Prelude: Andante (2) Poco maestoso (3) Barbaro (4) Brilliante (5) Energico (6) Alleluia: Poco adagio **D** 1948–49 (before Jan. 23); rev 1989 **P** Jan. 23, 1949, Hunter Playhouse, N.Y.: Erdman Dance Group **C** Jean Erdman **S** Peer, 1990 **L** 13 min **R** *LP*: Opus 1 #129: Ens Nova; *CD*: NA 055: S.F. Contemp Mus Players

139. *Marriage at the Eiffel Tower*
I (a) cham ens (fl, cl, tpt, vn, vc, cb, pf, 1 perc) (b) suite for orch (2-2-2-2; 0-2-2-0; 1 perc, pf; str) **M** Vers (b): (1) Overture (2) March for the Marriage of Frank and Anne Wigglesworth (3) Waltz (4) Speech by the General (5) Blues for the Trouville Bathing Beauty (6) Funeral of the General (7) Quadrille **D** Summer 1949; rev and orch 1961 **P** (a) July 29, 1949, Reed College, OR: Harrison, cond (b) Oct. 20, 1961, Santa Cruz Sym **C** Bonnie Bird **T** Cocteau, trans Dudley Fitz **S** (b) only: Peters (*Suite from the Marriage at the Eiffel Tower*) **L** 16 min **R** MusicMasters: Brooklyn Philharmonic, D. R. Davies, cond (forthcoming)

140. *The Only Jealousy of Emer*
I fl, vc, cb, tack-pf, cel **M** Incid music for drama: (1) Music for the unfolding of the cloth (2) Eithne Inguba (3) Emer's story; the Evil of Bricriu (4) Emer's

incantation; the Woman of the Sidhe (5) Music for the folding of the cloth **D** Summer 1949 **P** July 29, 1949, Reed College, OR **C** Bonnie Bird **T** Yeats, *Four Plays for Dancers* **S** HBP **L** 28.5 min incl spoken text **R** *LP*: Esoteric ES-506, Harrison, cond

141. *Suite for Cello and Harp*
     I vc, hp (arr for cello and str orch by R. Hughes, 1997) **M** (1) Chorale (2) Pastorale (3) Interlude (4) Aria (5) Chorale reprise **D** Mvt 4: 1947 (for *Sym on G*), rev 1949 for use in *Suite*. Other mvts comp 1949 (after July). Mvt 2 rev July 1994 **P** Apr. 15, 1950, McMillin Th, Columbia U, N.Y.: Seymour Barab, Lucille Lawrence **S** Peer, 1954 **L** 11 min **R** *LP*: Col ML-4491; NewW 281: S. Barab, L. Lawrence **X-R** Mvts 1–2 taken from sketches for a Time/Life film on Lascaux caves wall paintings, which never materialized. Mvt 4 taken from short score for *Sym on G*, mvt 3c ("Song," 1947); rev and orch in 1964 for compl of sym. **N** For S. Barab and L. Lawrence. Mvt 3 orig for vc solo; arr for vc/hp by Barab

142. *Little Suite for Piano*
     I pf **M** (1) Pastorale (2) Quadrille (3) Chorale **D** Nov. 8, 1949 **S** E. B. Marks, *Amer Cmprs of Today*, 1965 **L** 2.5 min **N** For Remy Charlip

1950

143. *Solstice*
     I fl, ob, tpt, 2 vc, cb, tack-pf, cel **M** (1) Garden of the Sun (2) Entrance of the Moon Bull (3) Battle (4) Earth's Invitation (5) Vernal Dance (6) Saturnalia (7) Rekindling of the Fire (8) Turning of the Wheel (9) Blaze of Day **D** 1949–50; compl before Jan. 22, 1950 **P** Jan. 22, 1950, Hunter Playhouse, N.Y.: Erdman dance group **C** Jean Erdman **S** Peer, 1978 **L** 27 min **R** *CD*: MusM 60241X: D. R. Davies, cond; Decca-Argo 455 590-2: Calif Sym (excerpts)

144. ∫ *An Almanac of the Seasons*
     I singer, narr, cham orch (see note) **D** Summer 1950 **P** July 28, 1950, Reed College, OR, Harrison, cond **C** Bonnie Bird **T** Nicolas Breton; song texts by Dell Hymes **X-R** One mvt rev for *Suite for Symph Str*, mvt 8 (1960) **N** Orch personnel listed on Reed Coll prog: str qt, cb, fl, ob, cl, bn, 2 tpt, hp, pf; since program included 3 dance works, it is not possible to determine which instruments performed in *Almanac*.

1951

145. *Chorales for Spring*
     I pf **M** (1) Adjustable Chorale (2) Chorale for Spring **D** "Chorale for Spring": Mar. 22, 1951 **P** Nov. 29, 1951, BMC **C** Katherine Litz **S** Ms, NYPL Litz Coll JPB 86-15 #11 **X-R** "Chorale for Spring" rev and used in *Suite for Symph Str*, mvt 2 (1960)

Vestiunt Silve (sop, fl, 2 vla, hp; begun Apr. 4, 1951, compl July 4, 1994.) See 1994 listing

146. *Io and Prometheus* (orig title: *Prometheus Bound*)
     I (a) pf; (b) cham ens w vocal pts **D** (a): 1951 (before July 9); (b): 1985 **P** (a):

July 9, 1951, U of Colo, Boulder: David Tudor. (b): Sept. 7, 1985, Athens, Greece **C** Jean Erdman **S** HBP **N** Score originally titled *Prometheus Bound*. Vocal pts are variable in perf.

147. † *Portrait of Abby Shahn on her Birthday*
I pf **D** July 31, 1951 **S** Unpub

148. *The Glyph*
I prepared pf, perc **M** 6 untitled mvts **D** Summer 1951 **P** Aug. 24, 1951, BMC **C** Katherine Litz **S** Ms, NYPL Litz Coll JPB 86-15, #12 **L** 7.5 min **N** Part of a cross-disciplinary arts collaboration with Charles Olson, Ben Shahn, Charles Oscar, Harrison, and Litz. Video of Litz's perf, Sept. 4, 1977 (N.Y. Dance Festival) in NYPL dance coll MGZIC 5-419

149. *Seven Pastorales* (original title: *Suite #3*)
I cham orch (2-1-0-1; hp; str) **M** (1) To Remy Charlip: Flowing, a little fast (2) To Ellie and David Decker on their marriage: [Moderato] (3) To Remy Charlip: Poco lento, espressivo, con tenderita (4) To Fritz Rikko: Allegro vigoroso (5) To John Cage: Moderato, tenuto, molto tenderita (6) To my mother: Allegro ecstatico, poco presto, leggiero (7) To my brother: Poco lento, sempre molto sostenuto ed espressivo **D** (1) Mar. 17, 1950; (2) Oct. 4, 1949; (3) Aug. 1950; (4) Mar. 13, 1950; (5) Oct. 1951; (6) July 1, 1951; (7) Aug. 1951 **P** Two mvts (from 1, 2, and 4): Apr. 15, 1950, Cmprs' Forum, N.Y.; entire set: Nov. 25, 1951, Circle-in-the-Square, N.Y.: Collegium Musicum, Fritz Rikko, cond **S** Peer, 1978 **L** 16 min **R** *CD*: MusM 67089-2: Bklyn Phil, D. R. Davies, cond **N** Inspired by Eclogues of Virgil. Tempo of mvt 2 appears on ms but not in pub score.

150. † *Nocturne (Nokturno)*
I (a) 2 vn, tack-pf; (b) strings **M** (1) Untitled (2) Poco allegro **D** Oct. 22–23, 1951 **P** 1958/59 season: Contemp Mus Soc of Houston, L. Stokowski, cond (not verified; info from O. Daniel, *Stokowski*) **S** Unpub **X-R** Mvt 1 rev and used as *Suite for Symph Str*, mvt 9 (1960) **N** For Victor Sprague

151. *New York Waltzes*
I pf **M** (1) Waltz in C (2) Hesitation Waltz (3) Waltz in A **D** (1) Sept. 16, 1945 (2) Fall 1951 (3) Sept. 14, 1944 **P** Oct. 22, 1994, Cabrillo Coll, Aptos: Michael Boriskin **S** HBP **L** 4 min **R** NewpCl NPD-85606: M. Boriskin **N** Waltz 2 is undated, but the autograph is on the same unusual paper used for *Nocturne* (Oct. 23, 1951).

152. *Alma Redemptoris Mater*
I bar, vn, tbn, tack-pf **D** Begun 1949; compl 1951, BMC **P** May 20, 1962, Nepenthe, Big Sur **T** Catholic liturgy **S** Peer, 1962 **L** 1.5 min

153. *Double Canon for Carl Ruggles*
I pf **D** 1951 **S** Unpub **L** 1.5 min **X-R** Rev and used in *Conc for Organ with Perc Orch*, mvt 2 (1973)

154. *Festival Dance*
I 2 pf **D** 1951, rev 1996 **P** Mar. 18, 1997, Cooper Union College, N.Y.: Aki Takahashi, Sarah Cahill **S** HBP

155. † *Group on a Row the Same*
I Mvt 1: keybd; 2: tbn, vibraphone; 3: vo, vla, pf; 4: bn **M** (1) Prelude (2) Poco allegro (3) Veritas Veritatum; (4) Unnumbered, untitled **D** 1–3: 1951, 4: 1960s **S** Unpub **N** Additional sketches for cembalo

Holly and Ivy (ten, cham ens; begun 1951; compl 1962). See 1962 listing
Songs in the Forest (fl, vn, pf, str; begun 1951; compl 1992). See 1992 listing
156. *Suite for Violin, Piano, and Small Orchestra*
     I Solo vn, solo pf, cham orch (2 fl, ob, hp, tack-pf, cel, tam-tam, 2 vc, 2 cb)
     M (1) Overture: Allegro poco maestoso (2) Elegy: Adagio (3) First Gamelan:
     Allegro (4) Aria: Lento espressivo (5) Second Gamelan: Allegro moderato (6)
     Chorale: Andante moderato D 1951 P Jan. 11, 1952, Carnegie Hall, N.Y.:
     Maro and Anahid Ajemian; Harrison, cond S Assoc Mus Pub, 1955; Peters
     1985 L 18.5 min R *LP*: RCA LM-1785; CRI-114: A. and M. Ajemian; L.
     Stokowski, cond; *CD*: NewW 80366-2: L. Stoltzman, K. Jarrett; R. Hughes,
     cond N Comm by Maro and Anahid Ajemian

1952

157. *Fugue for David Tudor*
     I pf D Begun 1947; compl 1952 P Feb. 10, 1952, Cherry Lane Th, N.Y.:
     David Tudor S HBP L 3.5 min X-R Orch for *Suite for Symph Str*, mvt 7 (1960)
158. *Serenade for Guitar* (*Serenado por Gitaro*; *Serenade for Frank Wigglesworth*)
     I guit (hp also appr by cmpr) D Feb. 12, 1952 S *MHp*; *LHGB* L 2 min R *LP*:
     Turnabout TV-34727: D. Starobin, guit; *LP* and *CD*: Desto DC-6478 and Ph
     PHCD-118: B. Bellows, hp; *CD*: NA 055: D. Tanenbaum, guit; Etc KTC 1071:
     J. Schneider, guit; NewpCl 85509: B. Verdery, guit N Written in a letter to
     Frank Wigglesworth
159. *Mass to St. Anthony*
     I chor, tpt, hp, str (orig vers, chor and perc, never completed) M Kyrie, Glo-
     ria, Credo, Sanctus, Agnus Dei D Begun Sept. 1, 1939; compl Mar. 12, 1952
     (perc for Kyrie/Gloria & all vo pts compl 1939) P Jan. 24, 1954, Carl Fischer
     Hall, N.Y.: Collegium Musicum and Cantata Singers, Fritz Rikko, cond T
     Cath mass ordinary S Peer, 1962 and 1974 L 25.5 min R *LP*: Vox SVBX-5354:
     Gregg Smith Singers, Orpheus Ens; Epic LC-3307: N.Y. Conc Choir and Orch,
     M. Hillis, cond; *CD*: Koch 3-7177-2H1: Oregon Rep Singers, G. Seeley, cond
     N Fromm Music Foundation Award, 1955
160. † *Little Gamelon for Katherine Litz to Teach With*
     I pf D Mar. 23, 1952 C Katherine Litz S Ms, NYPL Litz Coll JPB 86-15 #9
161. *Praise(s) for the Beauty of Hummingbirds*
     I fl, 2 vn, cel, perc D Apr. 5, 1952 P 1966, Old Spaghetti Factory, S.F. S Peer
     1975 L 2 min N Title on printed score reads "Praise"; Harrison prefers
     "Praises."
162. † *Praises for Hummingbirds and Hawks* (aka *Suite for Small Orchestra*)
     I cham orch M Set of 5 pieces D 1952 (before Apr. 23) P Apr. 23, 1952,
     Brooklyn H.S. for Homemaking, Brooklyn Mus Stage for Dancers series: stu-
     dents of S. Broughton (info from Harris, *Arts at BMC*) C Shirley Broughton
     S Unpub N Comm by Broughton
163. *Rapunzel*
     I 3 solo singers (sop, alto, bar); cham orch (1-2-1-0; 0-1-1-0; pf–tack-pf–
     cel–hp–tam-tam; 1 vn, 1 vla, 4 vc, 2 cb) M Opera in 6 acts D Short score,
     Aug.–Oct. 1952: Act 1: Aug. 21–23; Act 2: Aug. 31; Act 3: Sept. 4; Act 4:
     Sept. 30; Act 5: Oct. 5; Act 6: Oct. 7. Orchestration compl Apr. 1953. Rev

1996 **P** "Air" (Act 3): Apr. 14, 1954, Rome (Internatl Fest of the Congress for Cultural Freedom): Leontyne Price. Full opera: May 14, 1959, Kaufmann Aud, YM-YWHA, N.Y.: Artists' Company, Newell Jenkins, cond **T** William Morris **S** Peer, 1966 and 1992 **L** 53.5 min **R** *CD*: NA 093: N. Paiement, cond; "Air" only: MHS 513616L: P. Maginnis **X-R** "Air" reorch for Rome competition and pub separately (see *Air from Rapunzel*, 1954)

1953

164. ♩ *The Pool of Sacrifice*
   I chor, soloists, metallophone **M** Music to accompany Seami Motokiyo's Noh drama **D** Summer 1953 **P** Aug. 1953, BMC **N** Date established by letter from Harrison to Wigglesworth, Aug. 26, 1953
165. *Peace Piece 3: Little Song on the Atom Bomb*
   I vo (alto or bar), 2 vn, vla, hp **D** 1953, rev 1968 **P** Aug. 17, 1968, CMF, Aptos **T** L. Harrison **S** HBP; *Soundings* 3/4 (July–Oct. 1972) **L** 2 min

1954

166. *Air from Rapunzel*
   I sop, fl, vn, vla, vc, hp, pf **P** Apr. 14, 1954, Rome: Leontyne Price **T** Wm Morris **S** Peer 1966 **L** 7.5 min **R** *CD*: MHS 513616L: P. Maginnis; N. Paiement, cond **X-R** Act 3 of *Rapunzel* with diff orch. See 1952 listing **N** Prize-winning wk at Internatl Fest of the Congress of Cultural Freedom

1955

167. *Strict Songs*
   I (a) 8 bar (in 2–3 pts), cham orch (2 tbn, pf, hp, perc, str); male chorus appr by cmpr; (b) bar solo, SATB chor, cham orch **M** Four untitled mvts. Text beginnings: (1) Here is Holiness (2) Here is Nourishment (3) Here is Tenderness (4) Here is Splendor **D** (a) Mvt 1: begun 1951, compl 1955; mvt 2: July 13, 1955; mvt 3: undated (1955); mvt 4: June 1, 1955; (b) 1992 **P** (a) Jan. 18, 1956: Louisville Orch, Robert Whitney, cond; (b) Nov. 20, 1992, UCSC: N. Paiement, cond **S** (a) Assoc Mus Pub, 1956 **T** L Harrison, *JP*, 34-35 **L** 19 min **R** *LP*: LOU 58-2: Louisville Orch, R. Whitney, cond; *CD*: MHS 513616L: UCSC Orch and Cham Singers; N. Paiement, cond; LHCAW (mvt. 3 only): UCSC Orch and Cham Singers, N. Paiement, cond **N** Comm by Louisville Orch. Mvt 2 rev of Gloria from an unfinished mass (1951–Mar. 18, 1954). Mvt 3 dedicated to cmpr's father. Choreogr by Mark Morris, 1987
168. † *Recording Piece*
   I 5 perc **M** (1) ca. 108 (2) ca. 120 **D** July 29, 1955 **S** Unpub **N** For multiple perc with instructions about recording and electronic overlay
169. *Simfony in Free Style*
   I Specially constructed plastic flutes in Just Intonation, viols with movable or independent frets, harps, tack-pf, trombones **D** Oct. 8, 1955 **P** Digitally

realized by David Doty, 1992 S Peters, 1977 L 4 min R CD: LHCAW N For Henry Allen Moe and the Guggenheim Foundation

1957

170. *Incidental Music for Corneille's 'Cinna'* (additional title, 1976: *Suite for Tack Piano*)

I tack-pf M (1) Medium fast (2) Slow (3) Fast (4) Medium slow (5) Medium: Grand D 1955–May 1957 P Aug. 4, 1968: Old Spaghetti Factory, S.F.: Donald Pippin S *Xenharmonikon* 3, no. 1 (Spr 1976); *MUSA* L 12 min R CD: LHCAW: Lou Harrison N Sequence of pieces to be perf as prelude, conclusion, and between the acts of Corneille's play. For Henry Allen Moe and the Guggenheim Foundation. Anticipated presentation at Harrison's home puppet theater in Aptos never materialized.

1958

171. *Political Primer* (incomplete)

I Overtures: orch; recits: bar, occasional perc M Mvts completed: 3 overtures (monarchy, republic, democracy) later used in *Third Sym* and *Elegiac Sym*; 4 recits (mvts 1: Dedication; 5: First Comment, with two timely remarks; 9: Second comment; and 13: Last comment with remark and salutation) D Begun 1951; overtures and recits compl. 1958 P Recits only: May 23/24, 1959, U of Buffalo, Herbert Beattie, bar T L. Harrison (alternative texts in English and Esperanto), *Frog Peak Anthology* (Hanover, N.H.: Frog Peak Music, 1992), 77–83 S Unpub ms of recits and overture 1; remainder: sketches only X-R Overtures later rev for use as *Elegiac Sym*, mvt 1 (1975), and *Third Sym*, mvts 1 and 4 (1982). N Choruses never completed; recits in "Free Style"

1959

172. *Concerto for Violin with Percussion Orchestra* (*Konĉerto por la violono kun perkuta orkestro*)

I vn, 5 perc M (1) Allegro maestoso (2) Largo: Cantabile (3) Allegro vigoroso, poco presto D Begun 1940 or 1941 as *Concerto #5* for vn; compl 1959; rev 1974 P Nov. 19, 1959, Carnegie Recital Hall, N.Y.: Anahid Ajemian; Paul Price, cond S Peters 1961 L 20 min R *LP*: Turnabout QTVS-34653: C. Glenn; Eastman Perc Ens, J. Beck, cond; NewW 80382-2: J. Lower; Continuum Perc Qt, R. Brown, cond; *LP* and *CD*: Crys S853 and CD853: E. Shapiro; L.A. Perc Ens, W. Kraft, cond *CD*: Pan Classics 510103: P. Sacher, cond N Comm by Anahid Ajemian

1960

173. *Suite for Symphonic Strings*

I str orch M (1) Estampie (2) Chorale: Et in Arcadia Ego (3) Double Fugue: In Honor of Heracles (4) Ductia: In Honor or Eros (5) Lament (6) Canonic Variations: In Honor of Apollo (7) Little Fugue: Viola's Reward (8) Round: In Honor of Hermes (9) Nocturne **D** Mvts 1, 4, 6: 1960; mvts 2, 3, 5, 7, 8, 9 rev or arr of previous wks (see X-R) **P** Oct. 18, 1961: Louisville Sym, Robert Whitney, cond **S** Peters 1961 **L** 32 min **R** *LP*: LOU-621, Louisville Sym, R. Whitney, cond; *CD*: Argo 444 560-2: Am Comp Orch, D. R. Davies, cond (mvts rearranged and some omitted) **X-R** Mvt 2: rev vers of *Chorale for Spring* (1951; new middle section added); mvt 3: rev vers of *Dbl Fugue* (1936); mvt 5: rev vers of *Triphony* (1945) and *Trio* (1946); mvt 7: orch of *Fugue for David Tudor* (1952); mvt 8: taken from *Almanac of the Seasons* (1950); mvt 9: rev vers of *Nocturne*, mvt 1 (1951) **N** BMI 20th anniversary comm; for Carl Haverlin, pres, BMI

1961

174. *Concerto in Slendro*
    I Solo vn, 2 tack-pf, cel, 2 perc **M** (1) Allegro vivo (2) Molto adagio (3) Allegro, molto vigoroso **D** Apr. 6, 1961; rev 1972 **P** Jan. 21, 1962, Santa Cruz: Zelik Kaufman; R. Hughes, cond **S** Peters 1978 **L** 9.5 min **R** *LP* and *CD*: Desto DC-7144 and CRI CD-613: D. Kobialka; R. Hughes, cond; *CD*: Decca-Argo 455 590-2: Calif Sym, B. Jekowsky, cond; Pan Classics 510103: P. Sacher, cond. **N** For Richard Dee

175. *Moogunkwha, Se Tang Ak* (*Sharonrose, a New Song in the Old Style* or *A New Tang Melody*)
    I Korean court orch (cross-flutes, dbl reeds, viols, psalteries, perc) **D** June 1961 **P** Read-through by students at Korean National Classical Music Institute in Seoul, 1961 or 1962 **S** Unpub

176. *Quintal Taryung*
    I (a) 2 Korean fl, opt changgo (b) alto and ten recorders, opt snareless drum **D** June 1961 **S** Unpub **N** For Robert Hughes

177. *Psalter Sonato* (*Sonata for Psaltery*)
    I great psaltery (or cheng) **D** Oct. 1961, rev 1962 **P** Nov. 12, 1961, Sticky Wicket, Aptos: Lou Harrison **S** HBP **L** 2.5 min **R** *LP* and *CD*: Desto DC-6478 and Ph PHCD-118: L. Harrison **N** For Liang Tsai-Ping

178. *Prelude for Piri and Reed Organ*
    I p'iri, org **D** Between Aug. and Nov. 1961 **P** Nov. 12, 1961, Sticky Wicket, Aptos: L. Harrison **S** Unpub **X-R** Used in *Nova Odo*, mvt 2 (1968), and *Homage to Messaien* (1996)

179. *Nak Yang Chun* (*Spring in Nak Yang;* joint comp with Lee Hye-Ku)
    I chor, 3 fl, 3 tbn, cel, hp, pf, 2 perc, str **D** Late 1961 (or early 1962) **T** Transl in *JP*, 99 **S** Unpub **N** Orig Korean wk from 960 to 1279 A.D.; Korean orch vers survives from notation from the 18th cent and later, but orig chor pts lost. Restoration of chor pts by Harrison and Lee Hye-Ku and arr for orch of Western instr

1962

180. *Holly and Ivy: A Carol*
    I ten, hp, 2 vn, vc, cb (or choral tenors and mezzo-sopranos, hp, str orch) **D**

Begun 1951; compl 1962 **P** Feb. 17, 1963: Sticky Wicket, Aptos **S** HBP **L** 2 min **R** MHS 513616L: B. Staufenbiel (altered orch)

181. *A Joyous Procession, and a Solemn Procession*

I 2-pt chor, 2 tbn, 5 perc (additional tbns may be used) **M** (1) Joyous Procession (2) Solemn Procession **D** 1962 **T** To be supplied by the perf for each occasion. Appropriate texts by Harrison in *JP*, 13 **S** Peters 1963 **L** Variable **R** Audio Tape Productions, Michigan State Univ. **N** For the Sisters at Immaculate Heart Coll, L.A.

1963

Nova Odo (male chor, reciting chor, orch. Pts 1–2: 1963; pt 3: 1968.) See 1968 listing

182. *A Majestic Fanfare*

I 3 tpts, 2 perc **D** Jan. 20, 1963 (2:15–3:00 P.M.) **P** Mar. 7, 1963 **S** HBP **L** variable **N** For the opening of the Art and Music Dept of the S.F. Pub Library. The repeat may be "ignored, observed or multiplied at pleasure."

183. *Jephtha's Daughter*

I fl, perc, other optional instr **M** Theater kit w dramatic readings, 3 melodies for fl, 4 rhythms for perc, drones, theater realization **D** 1st vers: Feb. 26, 1941 (perc, reader, dance); expanded kit: Mar. 1963 (fl pts and other material added; see notes) **P** Mar. 9, 1963, Cabrillo College, Aptos: David Johnson, mus dir **C** Carol Beals **S** HBP **L** variable **N** A kit in which the cmpr appr any combination of fl pieces, perc pieces, drones, chords, colors, etc., interspersed with the dramatic readings

184. *Pacifika Rondo*

I fl, tbn, org, cel, pf, vibraphone, perc, str; p'iris, sheng, psalteries, cheng, kayagùm, pak, jalataranga **M** (1) Family of the Court (2) A Play of Dolphins (3) Lotus (4) In Sequoia's Shade (5) Netzahualcoyotl Builds a Pyramid (Homage to Carlos Chávez) (6) A Hatred of the Filthy Bomb (7) From the Dragon Pool **D** May 1963 **P** May 26, 1963, U of Hawaii **S** Peer; reprinted in Michael Byron, ed., *Pieces: A Second Anthology* (Maple, Canada, 1976) **L** 24 min **R** *LP* and *CD*: Desto DC-6478 and Ph PHCD-118: Oakland Youth Orch, R. Hughes, cond; LHCAW (mvt 6 only): Oakland Youth Orch, R. Hughes, cond **N** Comm by East-West Center, U of Hawaii. Dedic to Calline and Clarence Harrison

185. *At the Tomb of Charles Ives*

I tbn, 2 psalteries, 2 dulcimers, 3 hp, tam-tam, 5 vn, vla, vc, cb **D** Nov. 20, 1963 **P** July 23, 1970, Aspen Mus Fest **S** *Xenharmonikon* 1, no. 2 (Fall 1974); Peer 1978 **L** 4 min **R** *LP*: Gramavision GR-7006: Brooklyn Phil, L. Foss, cond **N** Partly in "Free Style": tuning tape available from pub

John Cage, *Suite for Toy Piano*: orchestrated by Harrison in 1963

1964

186. *Wesak Sonata*

I cheng **M** (1) Grave (2) Allegro **D** Mvt 1: Apr–May 1964; compl June 1964 **P** Nov. 15, 1964, Old Spaghetti Factory, S.F.: Margaret Fabrizio **S** HBP **N** For Wesak day (Apr. 8)

187. *Symphony on G*

   I orch (2-3-3-0; 2-2-2-0; timp–perc–pf–tack-pf–2 hp; str) M (1) Allegro
   deciso (2) Largo (3) Scherzo (a. Waltz; b. Polka; c. Song; d. Rondeau) (4)
   Largo—Molto allegro, vigoroso, poco presto D Begun 1947, compl 1964
   (before Aug.), rev 1966 (new finale). Mvt 1: short score, Dec. 26, 1947.
   Pts of mvts 2 and 3: summer/fall 1947. Mvt 3b: short score, Oct. 9, 1953.
   Compl first vers: 1964. New finale, 1966. P Aug. 23, 1964, CMF, Gerhard
   Samuel, cond. Rev vers, Feb. 8, 1966: Oakland Sym, G. Samuel, cond S
   Peer 1975 L 35 min R *LP* and *CD*: CRI 236 and 715: Royal Phil Orch,
   G. Samuel, cond; LHCAW (mvt 1 only): Royal Phil. Orch, G. Samuel, cond.
   X-R Mvt 3c: short score compl 1947; rev in 1949 as mvt 4 of *Suite for Vc
   and Hp*; rev and orch for compl of sym in 1964. N Mvt 3c for John Cage;
   mvt 3d for Jack Heliker; mvts 3a–b for "Leona" and "Janet," patients at
   Presbyt Hosp

188. † *Elegy for Harpo Marx*

   I short score for orch D Oct. 4, 1964 S Unpub L 2.5 min

189. *The Garden at One and a Quarter Moons*

   I great psaltery (or cheng) D Dec. 21, 1964; rev Nov. 9, 1966 S HBP L 2.5
   min R *LP* and *CD*: Desto DC-6478 and Ph PHCD-118: L. Harrison; LHCAW:
   Lou Harrison N For Robt Hughes

190. *Avalokiteshvara*

   I hp or grand psaltery, perc (guit also appr by cmpr) D Dec. 29, 1964 S *MHp*
   (w/o perc); *LHGB* (guit and perc pts) L 2 min R *LP* and *CD*: Desto DC-6478
   and Ph PHCD-118: B. Bellows, hp; *CD*: NA 055: D. Tanenbaum, guit; Etc
   KTC-1071: J. Schneider, guit

1966

Symphony on G. New finale completed. See 1964 listing

191. *Easter Cantata*

   I Solo contralto, SATB chor, 2 tpt, 2 tbn, glock, chimes, hp, str M (1) Sinfo-
   nia (2) Aubade, Chorale en Rondeau (3) Mary's Song at the Tomb (4) Narrative (5) Alleluia D Begun summer–fall 1943; compl 1966 (before Apr.) P Apr.
   3, 1966, Hartnell College: Vahé Aslanian, cond T Paraphrase of Luke 24 S
   HBP N Comm by Hartnell Coll student body assn

192. ∫ *Reflections in Motion*

   I taped music for bells, gongs, plucked instr, et al. M Three dances: "Mirrors," "Black and White," untitled D 1966 P KQED broadcast, date unknown
   C Lorle Kranzler N 3 tape recordings of improvised music for sliding tones,
   drums, and bells, which Harrison intended to be mixed according to the
   form of the dance

1967

193. *Music for Bill and Me*

   I hp (guit also appr by cmpr) D Begun late 1966, compl 1967 S *MHp*; *LHGB*
   L 3.5 min R *LP* and *CD*: Desto DC-6478 and Ph PHCD-118: B. Bellows, hp;

CD: NA 055: D. Tanenbaum, guit; Etc KTC-1071: J. Schneider, guit **N** Anticipated as one of several wks Harrison and Colvig could perform together.
Other wks incompl

194. *Haiku*
I unis mixed chor, shiao, hp, wind chimes, gong **D** Feb. 7–Mar. 14, 1967
T Kay Davis **S** Unpub **L** 37 measures **N** To Wm Erlendson

195. *Music for Violin with Various Instruments, European, Asian, and African*
I solo vn, reed org in Pyth tuning, 1 perc, psaltery (alt: tack-pf or hpsch),
4 mbiras (alt: hp or marimba) **M** (1) Allegro vigoroso (2) Largo (3) Allegro
moderato **D** 1967 (before May), rev 1969 **P** May 1, 1967, SJSU, Gary
Beswick, vn **S** Peer 1972 **L** 10.5 min **R** *LP* and *CD*: Desto DC-6478 and Ph
PHCD-118: Thomas Halpin, vn **N** For Gary Beswick. Recording erroneously
lists W. Bouton as vn soloist.

196. *Beverly's Troubadour Piece*
I hp, perc (guit also appr by cmpr) **D** Oct. 1967 **S** *MHp*; *LHGB* **L** 1.5 min
R *LP* and *CD*: Desto DC-6478 and Ph PHCD-118: B. Bellows, hp; *CD*: NA
055: D. Tanenbaum, guit; Bridge BCD-9041: J. Schneider, A. Shulman,
G. Sterling

197. *In Memory of Victor Jowers*
I cl (or Eng hn), pf (or hp) **D** Nov. 1967 **P** Nov. 19, 1967, Unitarian Fellowship, Aptos (Jowers memorial service) **L** 3.5 min **S** HBP

1968

198. *Peace Piece 1: Invocation for the Health of all Beings*
I unis chor, cham orch (tbn, 3 perc, 2 hp, reed org, str) **D** Mar. 14, 1968 **P**
Apr. 7, 1968, First Unitarian Ch, Berkeley **T** Buddhist Metta Sutta **S** HBP;
Soundings 3/4 (July–Oct. 1972); *LHR* **L** 6 min **N** To the memory of Martin
Luther King Jr.

199. *Peace Piece 2: Passages 25*
I ten, cham orch (3 perc, 2 hp, str) **D** Mar. 31, 1968 **P** Apr. 7, 1968, First Unitarian Ch, Berkeley **T** Robert Duncan, "Passages 25" **S** HBP; *Soundings* 3/4
(July–Oct. 1972) **L** 6.5 min **R** *CD*: LHCAW: E. Townsend, ten, G. Samuel,
cond

200. *Nova Odo*
I male chor, reciting chor, orch (3-3-3-3; 4-3-3; pf, tack-pf, cel, org, hp, perc
[incl pak]; str), 7 p'iris [alt: Eng hn, saxes, clarinets] **M** (1) quar = ca. 144; (2)
Largo, cantabile, solenel (3) quar = 132–44 **D** Pts 1–2: 1961–63; pt 3: Aug.
10, 1968 **P** Pts 1–2: read-through by Seoul Phil, 1962. Compl wk: Aug. 17,
1968, CMF, Aptos: Gerhard Samuel, cond **T** L. Harrison, English and Esperanto, *JP*, 115–20 **S** HBP **L** 20.5 min **N** To Rockefeller Foundation. For
Cmprs' Wkshop of the S.F. Conserv of Music, the S.F. Sym, and Enrique
Jorda. The "Prelude for P'iri and Reed Organ" (1961) from this piece can be
perf as an independent wk.

201. *Nuptiae*
I 2-pt chor, Filippine kulintang **M** Film score **D** Nov. 27, 1968 **P** May 20–22,
1969 **F** James Broughton **S** Unpub

1969

202. *Orpheus—for the Singer to the Dance*
    I ten solo, SATB chor, 15 perc **M** (1) Sweet tone, vibrant wing (2) Ode (3) Passage thru dreams (4) Fountain of forms (5) Seed (6) The lyre's ablaze (7) In praise of Orpheus (8) Image in the soil **D** 1969 (based on 1941 wk; see X-R) **P** May 22, 1969: SJSU Perc Ens, Anthony Cirone, dir; Robert Buchanan, ten **T** Robert Duncan, "A Set of Romantic Hymns" **S** HBP **L** 38 min **X-R** Expansion of *Labyrinth #3* (1941). Mvt 2 is a rev of *Labyrinth*, mvt 1; mvt 3 is virtually identical to *Labyrinth*, mvt 2; mvt 5 is a rev of *Labyrinth*, mvt 3; mvt 8 loosely based on *Labyrinth*, mvt 4 **N** To Francis Thorne

1971

203. *Young Caesar* (puppet opera version)
    I (a) 5 instrumentalists playing a variety of Asian, European inst, incl AmGam; 5 puppeteers; 5 singers; (b) arr for orch (fl, ob, tpt, org, hp, tack-pf, 5 perc, str) by Kerry Lewis **M** 2 acts, 14 scenes **D** (a) Begun 1970; compl Oct. 1971 (b) Nov. 1977 **P** (a) Nov. 5, 1971, Cal Inst of Tech (excerpts perf prior to this date) **T** Robert Gordon **S** Peer (both versions) **L** 2 hrs **X-R** Rev and transformed into standard opera w chor added; see listing in 1988 **N** Comm by Encounters (Pasadena) and the Judith S. Thomas Foundation

1972

204. *Jahla in the Form of a Ductia to Pleasure Leopold Stokowski on his Ninetieth Birthday*
    I hp, perc (guit also appr by cmpr) **D** Mar. 28, 1972 **S** *MHp*; *LHGB* **L** 2 min **R** *CD*: NA 055: D. Tanenbaum, guit; Bridge BCD-9041: J. Schneider, A. Shulman

205. *La Koro Sutro*
    I (a) SATB chor, small org, hp, AmGam (b) arr for chor and orch (pf, cel, 2 hp, 3 perc, str) by Kerry Lewis **M** (1) Kunsonoro Kaj Gloro (2)–(8) Paragrafo 1–7 (9) Mantro Kaj Kunsonoro **D** (a) July 29, 1972 (b) ca. 1977 **P** Aug. 11, 1972, SFSU, Donald Cobb, cond **T** Esperanto transl of Buddhist "Heart Sutra" by Bruce Kennedy **S** Peer **L** 29 min **R** *CD*: NA 015: P. Brett, cond **N** For Vahé Aslanian

206. † *Festive Movement*
    I fl, cl, vn, vc, pf **D** Begun June 1972; compl Oct. 15, 1972 **P** Nov. 13, 1972, Alice Tully Hall, N.Y.: Aeolian Chamber Players **S** Unpub **L** 10.5 min **N** Premiere was benefit for Francis Thorne Fund

1973

207. *Concerto for Organ with Percussion Orchestra*
    I org, 8 perc, pf, celeste **M** (1) Allegro (2) Andante: Siciliana in the Form of a Double Canon (3) Largo (4) Canons and Choruses (5) Finale: Allegro **D** Mvt 2:

1951, rev 1973. Rest of wk begun 1972, compl 1973. **P** Apr. 30, 1973: SJSU, Philip Simpson, org, Anthony Cirone, dir, perc ens **S** Peer 1978 **L** 23 min **R** *LP* and *CD*: Crys 858 and CD850: D. Craighead; L.A. Perc Ens, W. Kraft, cond **X-R** Mvt 2 is rev vers of *Dbl Canon for Carl Ruggles* (1951) **N** To Gibson Walters, Anthony Cirone, and Philip Simpson

1974

208. *Sonata in Ishartum*

> **I** hp (guit also appr by cmpr) **D** Apr. 14 (Easter Sunday), 1974 **S** *MHp*; *LHGB* **L** 1.5 min **R** *CD*: NA 055: D. Tanenbaum, guit; Etc KTC-1071: J. Schneider, guit; Bridge BCD-9041: J. Schneider, A. Shulman **N** Written in ancient Babylonian mode. For Randall Wong

209. *Suite for Violin and American Gamelan* (joint comp with Richard Dee). Lewis arr titled *Suite for Violin with String Orch*. Davies arr titled *Suite for Violin, Piano, and String Orch*

> **I** (a) solo vn, AmGam (b) arr for vn and orch (pf, cel, 2 hp, str) by Kerry Lewis (c) arr for vn, pf, str orch by Dennis Russell Davies (w/o mvt 3 and the first two sections of mvt 4) **M** (1) Threnody (2) Estampie (3) Air (4) Three Jahlas (Moderato—Allegro poco presto—Adagio) (5) Chaconne **D** (a) Mvt 5: 1972; rest of wk, 1974 (b) 1977 (c) 1997 **P** (a) Mvt 5: Oct. 29, 1972, Hartnell Coll; compl wk, Dec. 9, 1974, Lone Mtn Coll, S.F.: Lauren Jakey, vn (b) July 17, 1993, Pacific Mus Fest, Sapporo, Japan: Chi Yun, vn, Michael Tilson Thomas, cond (c) Apr. 26, 1997, Lincoln Ctr, N.Y.: Dennis Russell Davies, cond **S** Peer (versions a and b) **L** 28 min **R** (a) *CD*: NA 015: D. Abel; J. Bergamo, cond **N** Comm by S.F. Cham Mus Soc, Norman Fromm Cmpr's Award

210. *A Phrase for Arion's Leap*

> **I** 3 ya chengs (bowed psalteries), 2 hp, perc **D** Dec. 15, 1974 **S** *Ear* 1 (Berkeley, ND); *Xenharmonikon* 2, no. 1 (Spr 1975) **L** .5 min **N** In Free Style. For Charles Shere

1975

211. *Elegiac Symphony*

> **I** orch (3-3-3-3; 4-3-3-1; timp—3 perc—pf—tack-pf—2 hp—org—cel—vib; str) **M** (1) Tears of the Angel Israfel (2) Allegro, poco presto (3) Tears of the Angel Israfel 2 (4) Praises for Michael the Archangel (5) The Sweetness of Epicurus **D** Mvt 1 begun 1958; mvts 2 and 5, begun 1942; mvt 4, 1946—47 (see X-R). Sym compl Nov. 15, 1975; rev 1988 **P** Dec. 7, 1975, Paramount Th, Oakland: Oakland Sym Youth Orch, Denis de Coteau, cond **S** Peer 1977, 1988 **L** 33.5 min **R** *LP*: 1750 Arch S-1772: Oakl Youth Orch, D. de Coteau, cond; *CD*: MusM 60204K: Amer Comp Orch, D. R. Davies, cond **X-R** Mvt 1: rev vers of overture 2 or 3 from the *Political Primer* (1958). Mvt 2: rev vers of *Canticle #6*, mvt 1 (1942). Mvt 4: orch and rev of organ wk w same name (1947). Mvt 5: rev vers of *Canticle #6*, mvt 2 (1942) **N** Comm from Koussevitzky Foundation. To memory of Natalie and Serge Koussevitzky

1976

Gending Samuel. See *Music for Kyai Hudan Mas*
Gending Pak Chokro. See *Music for Kyai Hudan Mas*
Bubaran Robert. See *Music for Kyai Hudan Mas*

212. *Music for Kyai Hudan Mas*
I Jav gam (1: pelog; 2–3: slendro), picc tpt (mvt 3 only) M (1) Gending
(later: Lancaran) Samuel (2) Gending Pak Chokro (3) Bubaran Robert
D 1976, before Mar. Mvt 1 rev Feb. 1981 (renamed "Lancaran"). Mvt 3 rev
Feb. 1981; picc tpt pt added Apr. 28, 1981 S Orig vers: *Soundings* 10 (Sum-
mer 1976). Rev vers of (1) and (3): *GGC* (incl tpt pt). (2): *LHR* (3): *MGWI* L
Variable R *LP*: (2) only: Cambridge CRS-2560: Berkeley gam; *CD*: (3) only:
MHS 513382K, MusM 01612-67091-2 X-R Opening section of (1) used in
A Cornish Lancaran (1986) N (1) For Samuel Scripps (owner of gam Kyai
Hudan Mas) (2) for K. R. T. Wasitodipuro (Pak Cokro) (3) for Robert E. Brown
(Am Soc for Eastern Arts); tpt pt for Mary Woods Bennett. N Mvt 3 sub-
sequently choreogr by Mark Morris in "World Power" (premiere: Oct.
27, 1995)

213. *Lancaran Daniel*
I Jav gam (slendro) D July 1976 S HBP; *GGC* L Variable N For Daniel
Schmidt

214. *Lagu Sociseknum*
I Jav gam (slendro) D July 1976 S HBP; *GGC* L Variable N Melody based on
Harrison's social security number

1977

215. † *Binary Variations on "O Sinner Man"*
I Ren instr ens (sop/alto/ten recs and crumhorns; hpsch; sackbut; treble/bass
viol; alto shawm; dulcian) D Begun 1934; compl Jan. 10, 1977 P Feb. 25,
1977, UCSC: independent concert dir by Philip Collins S Unpub L 6 min

216. *Gending Paul*
I Jav gam (slendro) D May–July 1977 S HBP L Variable N For Paul Dresher

217. *Gending Jody*
I Jav gam (slendro) D July 1977 S HBP; *Balungan* 3, no. 1 (Nov. 1987): 32
X-R Used as gam pt of *Scenes from Cavafy*, mvt 2b (1980). L Variable N For
Jody Diamond

218. *Music for the Turning of a Sculpture by Pamela Boden*
I Jav gam (slendro) D July–Aug. 1977 S HBP L Variable

219. *Waltz for Evelyn Hinrichsen*
I pf (hp or guit also appr by cmpr) D Sept. 1977 P Feb. 3, 1979, The
Kitchen, N.Y. S *Waltzes by 25 Contemporary Composers*, Peters 1978 L 2
min R *LP*: Nonesuch D-79011: Y. Mikhashoff, pf; *CD*: NA 055: D.
Tanenbaum, guit; Etc KTC-1071: J. Schneider, guit; Bridge BCD-9041:
J. Schneider, A. Shulman X-R Orch and used as *Third Sym*, mvt 2b
(1982)

Charles Ives, *Christmas Music*: arr for chor/orch by Lou Harrison

1978

220. *Serenade for Guitar with Optional Percussion*
I guit, 1 perc (opt) **M** (1) Round (2) Air (3) Infinite Canon (4) Usul (Little Homage to Sinan) (5) Sonata **D** (1) Jan. 6, 1978 (2) Jan. 6, 1978 (3) Jan. 10, 1978 (4) Jan. 8, 1978 (5) Jan. 10, 1978 **P** Jan. 26, 1979: Amer Cmprs' Forum, Schenectady, N.Y.: Ray Andrews, guit, David Bittner, perc **S** Peer 1981 **L** 11 min **R** *CD*: NA 055: D. Tanenbaum; Etc KTC-1071: J. Schneider **N** First of a planned set of five suites for guit w interchangeable fingerboards in various tunings. For Betty Freeman and Franco Assetto

221. *Main Bersama-sama (Playing Together)*
I hn, Sundanese gam degung **D** 1978 **S** *Balungan* 1, no. 2 (Feb. 1985); *MGWI* **L** 7.5 min **R** *LP* and *CD*: CRI SD-455 and CD-613: S. Hartman, gam Sekar Kembar **X-R** Used in film *BFBM* (1982) **N** For William George, SJSU

222. *Serenade for Betty Freeman and Franco Assetto*
I suling, Sundanese gam degung **D** 1978 **S** HBP **L** 6 min **R** *LP* and *CD*: CRI SD-455 and CD-613: L. Harrison, suling; gam Sekar Kembar; CRI CD-721 (ditto)

223. *Threnody for Carlos Chávez*
I vla, Sundanese gam degung **D** 1978 **P** Aug. 27, 1978, CMF, Santa Cruz, CA **S** HBP; *MGWI* **L** 7 min **R** *LP* and *CD*: CRI SD-455 and CD-613: S. Bates, gam Sekar Kembar **N** Orig title: *Main Bersama-sama II*

1979

224. *String Quartet Set*
I str qt **M** (1) Variations on the "Palestine Song" by Walther von der Vogelweide (2) Plaint (3) Estampie (4) Rondeau (5) Usul **D** (1) Opening sketched in 1940s; compl Jan. 24, 1978 (2) Mar. 24, 1978; (3)–(5) 1978–79 **P** Apr. 28, 1979, U of Toronto: Orford Qt **S** Peer 1980 **L** 26.5 min **R** *LP* and *CD*: CRI SD-455 and CD-613: Kronos Qt. *CD*: CRI CD-721 (mvts 1 and 3 only): Kronos Qt; Guit arr (mvts 1 and 2 only in reverse order): Etc KTC-1071: J. Schneider **N** Comm by Robt Aitken for New Music Concerts. Dedic to Aitken and Canada Council. Guit arr projected as pt of the second of five suites for guit w interchangeable fingerboards in different tunings (suite never compl)

225. *Discovering the Art of Korea*
I variety of East Asian instr, hp, bells, misc perc **M** Film score **D** 1979 **F** David Myers **S** Unpub

1970s

226. † *Air*
I vn, ya cheng, gendèr **D** ND (begun 1940, rev 1970s) **S** Unpub

226A. *Payatamu*
I vocal soloists, chor, rec, fl, vla, hp, perc **M** (1) Prelude and Chant (2) Rainbow Boy's and Payatamu's Entrance (3) Drought Music (4) Dance (5) Rainbow Boy's Grief (6) Rain Dance **D** 1975-79 **T** Elsa Gidlow **S** Unpub

1980

227. *Scenes from Cavafy*
I bar, male chor, hp, Jav gam (slendro and pelog) **M** (1) The Glasses of
Blue and Red and Green (2a) At the Table Next (2b) The Poet Remembers
the Two of Them (3) The Poet Instructs Antony **D** Compl betw Mar. 2
and May 9, 1980 **P** May 9, 1980, SJSU: David Rohrbaugh, Gam Si Betty
T L. Harrison, paraphrase of texts by Constantine Cavafy, *JP* 27 (poem titles:
Coronation; In a Tavern; Antony) **S** HBP **N** The gam pts of this piece may
be perf as separate works, entitled *Gending Cavafy* (mvt 1), *Gending Bill*
(mvt 2a), *Gending Jody* (mvt 2b), and *Gending Ptolemy* (mvt 3). Comp for
Betty Freeman and Franco Assetto. *Gending Bill* for William Colvig; *Gending
Jody* for Jody Diamond

228. † *Double Fanfare* (joint comp w Anthony Cirone)
I 12 perc (two 6-perc orch). **D** Sept. 23, 1980 **P** Nov. 13, 1980: San Jose Civic
Aud **S** HBP **L** 13 min

1981

229. *Gending Alexander*
I Jav gam (pelog) **D** Feb. 23, 1981 **P** Apr. 22–24, 1981: U of Delaware: U of
DE Perc Ens, Harvey Price, cond **S** HBP; *GGC* **L** Variable **R** *CD*: MHS
513382K, MusM 01612-67091-2: Gam Si Betty **N** For Michael Zinn

230. *Ladrang Epikuros*
I Jav gam (pelog) **D** Mar. 3, 1981 **S** HBP; *GGC* **L** Variable **X-R** With addition
of solo vn and vc pts, used in *Dbl Conc for Vn, Vc and Jav Gam*, mvt 1 (1982)

231. *Gending Hephaestus*
I Jav gam (slendro) **D** Mar. 10, 1981 **S** HBP; *GGC* **L** Variable **X-R** With addition of solo vn and vc pts, used in *Dbl Conc for Vn, Vc and Jav Gam*, mvt 3
(1982)

232. *Estampie for Susan Summerfield*
I org **D** May 7, 1981 **P** June 13, 1981, Chico, CA, Am Guild of Org: S. Summerfield **S** HBP **L** 4 min **X-R** Orch for use as *Third Sym*, mvt 2c (1982)

233. *Gending Hermes*
I Jav gam (pelog) **D** Jan.–July 1981 **P** Feb. 18, 1981, Evans Auditorium,
Lewis and Clark Coll, Portland **S** HBP; *GGC* **L** Variable **N** For Vincent McDer-
mott and the "Venerable Showers of Beauty" gamelan at Lewis and Clark
Coll

234. *Gending Demeter*
I Jav gam (pelog) **D** May–July 1981, rev 1983 (after June) **S** HBP **L** Variable
X-R Used in film *BFBM* (1982)

235. *Gending in Honor of the Poet Virgil*
I Jav gam (slendro) **D** Oct. 16, 1981; rev Feb.–Mar. 1985 **S** HBP **L** Variable **R**
CD: LHCAW: Gamelan Si Betty, T. Nielsen, dir. **N** For Trish Nielsen

1982

236. *Gending Claude*

I Jav gam (slendro) D early 1982 S HBP L Variable X-R Used in film *BFBM* (1982) N In honor of Claude Lorraine

237. *Lancaran Molly*

I Jav gam (slendro) D Feb. 21, 1982 S HBP L Variable X-R Used in film *BFBM* (1982) N For Molly Davies

238. *Gending Dennis*

I Jav gam (slendro) D Feb. 24, 1982 S HBP L Variable X-R Used in film *BFBM* (1982) N For Dennis Russell Davies

239. *Gending Pindar*

I Jav gam (pelog) D Feb. 25, 1982 S HBP L Variable X-R Used in film *BFBM* (1982)

240. *Double Concerto for Violin, Cello, and Gamelan*

I Solo vn, solo vc, Jav gam (pelog and slendro) M (1) Ladrang Epikuros (2) Stampede: Allegro molto, vigoroso (3) Gending Hephaestus D Mvts 1 and 3: gam pt, Mar. 3 and 10, 1981; vn/vc pts added before May 1982. Mvt 2: Apr. 1982 P May 10, 1982, MC: Kenneth Goldsmith, vn, Terry King, vc, MC Gam S HBP L 23 min R *LP* and *CD*: TR Records TRC-109 and Music and Arts 635: K. Goldsmith, T. King, W. Winant, drums, MC Gam X-R *Ladrang Epikuros* and *Gending Hephaestus* (separate gam wks, 1981) used as gam pt in mvts 1 and 3 of *Dbl Conc*

241. *Tributes to Charon*

I 3 perc M (1) Passage through Darkness (2) Counterdance in the Spring D (1) May 6, 1982 (2) Mar. 29, 1939 P Mvt 1: May 10, 1982, MC: Wm Winant and ens; mvt 2: May 19, 1939, Cornish School, Seattle: John Cage and ens S *MUSA* L 7 min X-R See 1939 listing for "Counterdance" N Mvt 1 (incl title) envisioned in 1939 but not comp until 1982. "Counterdance" choreogr by Jean Erdman as "Creature on a Journey" (1943)

242. *Beyond the Far Blue Mountains*

I Jav gam M Film score D 1982, before June P June 10, 1982: Centre de Pompidou, Paris F Molly Davies X-R Uses previously composed gam compositions, including: *Gending Demeter, Main Bersama-Sama, Gending Dennis, Gending Pindar, Lancaran Molly, Gending Claude,* and filler material

243. *Third Symphony*

I orch (3-3-3-3; 4-3-3-1; cel–tack-pf–hp–perc; str) M (1) Allegro moderato (2) a. A Reel in Honor of Henry Cowell; b. A Waltz for Evelyn Hinrichsen; c. An Estampie for Susan Summerfield (3) Largo Ostinato (4) Allegro D Aug. 9, 1982, rev 1985 P Aug. 29, 1982: CMF, Aptos: Dennis Russell Davies, cond S Peters 1982 L 33 min R MusM 7073-2-C: CMF Orch, D. R. Davies, cond X-R Mvt 1: rev vers of overture 2 or 3 of the *Pol Primer* (1958; ms sketches in cmpr's archives fail to clarify which mvt). Mvt 2a: rev and orch vers of *Reel: Homage to H. Cowell* (1939). Mvt 2b: orch of *Waltz for E. Hinrichsen* (1977). Mvt 2c: rev and orch vers of *Estampie for S. Summerfield* (1981). Mvt 3: rev and orch vers of *Largo Ostinato* (1937, rev 1970). Mvt 4: rev vers of overture 1 from *Pol Primer* (1958)

244. *Elegy, to the Memory of Calvin Simmons*
I ob, cel, vibr, hp, hn, gong, vn, vla, 2 vc, cb D Aug. 22–24, 1982 P Aug. 26, 1982: CMF, Aptos, CA S HBP L 4.5 min R Decca-Argo 455 590-2: Calif Sym, B. Jekowsky, cond

245. *Gending in Honor of Herakles*
I Jav gam (slendro) D Oct. 11, 1982 S HBP L Variable

246. † *Richard Whittington*
I gam, vo, narr, and puppets M Incid music for narrative D 1980–82 P Dec. 9, 1982, MC T John Masefield (1931) S Unpub N Compilation of gam wks with new vocal pts. Theater design and construction by Harrison and Colvig

1983

247. *Devotions (Gending in Honor of James and Joel)*
I Jav gam (slendro; incl 2 suling) M Film score D May–June 1983 F James Broughton S HBP N For James Broughton and Joel Singer

248. *Lagu Lagu Thomasan*
I Cirebonese gam (pelog) M To Honor Jennifer, To Honor Allen, and For the Children D Aug. 9, 1983 S HBP L Variable

249. *Lagu Cirebon*
I Cirebonese gam (pelog) D 1983 P Sept. 28, 1983: Victoria U of Wellington (New Zealand) S HBP L Variable N For Allen Thomas's gam

250. *Ketawang Wellington*
I Solo vo, Jav gam (pelog) D July–Oct. 1983 T Lou Harrison S *Canzona* (Cmprs Assn of New Zealand), Feb. 1984 L Variable

251. *Lagu Victoria*
I Cirebonese gam (pelog) D Oct. 1983 (Wellington) S HBP L Variable

252. *Foreman's Song Tune*
I Jav gam (slendro) D Latter half of 1983 S *MGWI* L variable X-R "Coyote Stories" text added in 1987 (see reference in 1987); subsequently orch for *Fourth Sym*, mvt 4 (1990)

253. *For the Pleasure of Ovid's Changes*
I Jav gam (slendro) D Aug.–Nov. 1983; rev Dec. 1986 P Dec. 7, 1984, MC gam S HBP L Variable

254. † *Gending in Honor of Sinan*
I Jav gam (pelog) D 1983 S HBP L Variable N Still undergoing revision

255. *Gending in Honor of Palladio*
I Jav gam (slendro) D 1st vers: Feb.–July 1982; rev 1983 and 1984 S HBP L Variable

1984

256. *Lagu Elang Yusuf*
I Cirebonese gam (slendro) D Feb. 29, 1984 S HBP L Variable X-R Used in *Faust* (1985) N For Elang Yusuf Dendabrata (Elang Muhammad Yuwana Yusuf)

257. *Gending Max Beckmann*
    I Jav gam (pelog) D 1984; rev 1991 P July 17/18, 1992, Lick Observatory:
    Gam Si Betty S HBP L Variable
258. *Gending Vincent*
    I Jav gam (slendro) D Dec. 1984 P Feb. 16, 1985, U of Oregon, Eugene
    (program erroneously gives date as 1984) S HBP L Variable N For Vincent
    McDermott

1985

259. *Lagu Pa Undang*
    I Sundanese gam degung D Apr. 6, 1985 S HBP L Variable X-R Used in *Faust*
    (1985)
260. *Faust*
    I Sop, ten, bass soloists; chor; cham orch (4 fl, tpt, 4 perc, pf, 2 hp, org, str),
    Sundanese gam degung M (1) Opening scene in heaven (2) Fire spirit's chant
    (3) Easter music (4) Witch's Song (5) Wine-Love Song (6) Three dances for
    two harps (7) Gretchen's Spinning Song (8) Estampie ("Walpurgisnacht") (9)
    Gam wks: Lagu Pa Undang, Lagu Elang Yusuf; misc perc interludes D 1985
    (before May): mvt 1: Mar. 12; mvts 2, 3, 4, 5, 7: ND; mvt 6: Mar. 19; mvt 9a:
    Apr. 6; mvt 9b: 1984 P May 9, 1985, UCSC T Adaptation of Goethe's text by
    Kathy Foley S Unpub X-R Mvt 7 adapted for *The Clays' Quintet*, mvt 3 (1987;
    same music w diff instr and no text). Mvt 8 heavily rev and used in *Pf
    Conc*, mvt 2 (1985).
261. *Three Songs*
    I male chor, cham orch (pf, org, str, perc) M (1) King David's Lament for
    Jonathan (2) Oh You Whom I Often and Silently Come (3) When I Heard at
    the Close of Day D (1) 1941, rev June 18, 1985; (2) 1946, rev June 1985; (3)
    June 1985 P Sept. 28, 1985: Portland Gay Men's Chor, Gilbert Seeley, cond T
    (1) II Samuel; (2) and (3) Walt Whitman, *Leaves of Grass* ("Calamus") S Peer
    1985 L 10 min R *CD*: LHCAW (mvt 1 only): Portland Gay Men's Chor, G.
    Seeley, cond X-R Mvt 1: rev vers of 1941 wk of same name. Mvt 2: rev vers
    of *Frag from Calamus* (1946)
262. *Piano Concerto with Selected Orchestra*
    I pf, orch (3 tbn, perc, hp, str) M (1) Allegro (2) Stampede: Allegro (3) Largo
    (4) Allegro moderato D Begun May 1983; compl July–Aug. 1985 (mvt 1:
    July 29; mvt 2: July 13; mvt 3: Aug. 5; mvt 4: Aug. 9) P Oct. 20, 1985,
    Carnegie Hall, N.Y.: Keith Jarrett; Am Cmprs Orch, Dennis Russell Davies,
    cond S Peters 1985 L 29.5 min R *CD*: NewW 80366-2: K. Jarrett; New Japan
    Phil, N. Otomo, cond X-R Mvt 2: heavily rev vers of *Faust*, mvt 8 (1985) N
    For Keith Jarrett. Comm by Betty Freeman. Pf in Kirberger #2 tuning

1986

263. † *Gending in Honor of Aphrodite*
    I chor, hp, Jav gam (pelog) D Gam pt: Oct. 11, 1982. Hp pt added June 10,
    1986 T L. Harrison, *JP*, 1 S *MGWI* N Currently under rev

264. *New Moon*
  I fl, cl, tpt, tbn, vn, cb, perc **M** (1) Alabado: largo (2) Usul: moderato (3) Bright call: slow but free (4) Barcarole (5) Stampede: molto allegro (6) Epilogue **D** Begun: May 1986. Mvts 1, 2, 3, 5 compl June 16, 1986; mvt 6 compl Sept. 5, 1986. Mvt 4 compl before Nov. 1989 (replacement for rejected mvt from 1986) **P** Nov. 28, 1989, Joyce Th, N.Y.: Hawkins Dance Co **C** Erick Hawkins **S** HBP **L** 22.5 min **R** *CD*: MHS 513616L: N. Paiement, cond **X-R** Rejected fourth mvt ("Song") used as basis for *Fourth Sym*, mvt 1 (1990)

265. *Ladrang in Honor of Pak Daliyo*
  I Jav gam (slendro) **D** 1st vers (abandoned): Mar. 21–Aug. 8, 1984; new vers 1986 **S** HBP **L** Variable

266. *Mass for St. Cecilia's Day*
  I unis chor; opt drone and/or figuration on org, hp **M** (1) Introitus (2) Kyrie (3) Gloria (4) Graduale (5) Alleluia (6) Offertory (7) Sanctus (8) Agnus Dei (9) Communion (10) Hymn (11) Ite Missa Est **D** Kyrie: Oct. 25, 1983; compl mass, 1986 **P** Introitus, Gloria, Hymn: Nov. 15, 1987, Cal State Sacramento. Compl mass: Nov. 18, 1988, Santa Cruz Cham Players **T** Cath mass ordinary and the proper for the Feast of St. Cecilia (Nov. 22) **S** HBP **L** 22 min **N** Monoph mass in Greg chant style. For Saint Cecilia Soc for the Preservation and Restoration of Gregorian Chant and the Peking Opera of Santa Cruz, CA

267. *A Cornish Lancaran*
  I sop sax, Javanese gam (pelog) **D** Dec. 27, 1986; rev Feb. 1, 1989 **S** HBP; *MGWI* **L** 5.5 min **R** *CD*: MHS 513382K, MusM 01612-67091-2: Gam Si Betty **X-R** Uses opening part of *Gending* (later *Lancaran*) *Samuel* from *Music for Kyai Hudan Mas* (1976, rev 1981) **N** The opening of *Gending Samuel* was renamed *A Cornish Lancaran* in honor of Cornish College; sax pt added for Don Stevens, 1986; rev for Bill Trimble, 1989

1987

268. *Varied Trio*
  I vn, pf, perc (orig vers: w hp, bells) **M** (1) Gending (2) Bowl Bells (3) Elegy (4) Rondeau in Honor of Fragonard (5) Dance **D** Begun 1986; compl Feb. 4, 1987 **P** orig. vers (with Harrison and Colvig on hp and bells): Feb. 28, 1987, Hertz Hall, Berkeley; rev vers: May 14, 1987, MC: both perf by Abel-Steinberg-Winant Trio **S** *MUSA* **L** 15 min **R** *CD*: NA 015 and 036: Abel-Steinberg-Winant Trio

Coyote Stories texts and chant added to *Foreman's Song Tune* (1983) on Mar. 29, 1987. (Vo, gam; four tales, quoted in Bruce Walter Barton, *The Tree at the Center of the World* [Santa Barbara: Ross-Erikson, 1980]. Two of these later orch for *Fourth Sym*, mvt 4 [1990])

269. *Ariadne*
  I fl, 1 perc **M** (1) Ariadne Abandoned (2) The Triumph of Ariadne and Dionysos **D** Mar. 30, 1987 **P** May 14, 1987, MC: Wm Winant, perc, David Colvig, fl, Eva Soltes, dancer **C** Eva Soltes (Barata-natyam dance) **S** HBP **L** variable (ca. 9 minutes or longer) **R** *CD*: MusM 60241X: L. Miller, W. Winant; CRI CD-568: R. Rudich, K. Grossman **N** Mvt 2 is a musical kit: fl and perc lines may be played in any order or any combination.

270. *Concerto for Piano with Javanese Gamelan*
I Solo pf, Jav gam (slendro and pelog) M 3 mvts (no tempi) D Begun 1986;
compl 1987 (before May 14) P May 14, 1987, MC: Belle Bullwinkle, pf; MC
Gam, Jody Diamond, dir S HBP L 23 min R *Leonardo Music Journal*, CD Se-
ries vol 2: Belle Bulwinkle, Bay Area New Gamelan N For Belle Bullwinkle.
The gam parts of mvts 1 and 3 may be played as separate wks, titled "Bull's
Belle" and "Belle's Bull," respectively.

271. *Philemon and Baukis*
I vn, Jav gam (slendro) D Begun 1985, compl 1987 (before May 17) P May
17, 1987: All Saints Episcopal, Watsonville, CA: Dan Kobialka, vn; Gam Si
Betty, Trish Nielson, dir S HBP; *MGWI* L 12.5 min R *CD*: MHS 513382K;
MusM 01612-67091-2: D. Kobialka, Gam Si Betty N For Daniel Kobialka

272. *The Clays' Quintet*
I tpt, hn, mandolin, hp, perc M (1) Song with Canons (2) Song with Dance
(3) Air on a Ground (4) Fanfare with Three Dances D 1987 (before July) P
Aug. 14, 1987, Catskill Conserv, N.Y. S HBP L 22.5 min X-R Mvt 3: rescoring
of Gretchen's Spinning Song from *Faust* (1985) N For Carleton Clay, tpt, and
Julia Hasbrouck, hn

273. *Air for the Poet* (*Air from "Scattered Remains"*)
I (a) metallophone, drum (b) solo inst w 2 ostinati (c) orch M Music for film D
Autumn 1987 F James Broughton and Joel Singer, "The Scattered Remains of
James Broughton" S (b) only: HBP L 3.5 min R *CD*: NA 093: L. Miller, et al.

1988

274. *A Summerfield Set*
I pf or other keybd instr M (1) Sonata (2) Ground (3) Round for the Triumph
of Alexander D Mvt 1: Jan. 1, 1988; mvt 2: Sept. 5, 1936, rev 1970, 1988;
mvt 3: Jan. 12, 1988 P Feb. 28, 1988, MC: Susan Summerfield S HBP L 11
min R *CD*: MusM 60241X: N. Fernández X-R Mvt 2 rev of *Ground in E Minor*
(1936; rev 1970; further rev for *Summerfield Set*) N For Susan Summerfield

275. *Young Caesar* (standard opera vers)
I male and female soloists, male chor, cham orch (fl, ob, tpt, org, hp, tack-pf,
5 perc, str) M 14 scenes D 1988 (before Apr.), currently undergoing rev P
Apr. 9/10, 1988, Portland: Portland Gay Men's Chorus, Virtuosi della Rosa,
Robert Hughes, cond T Robt Gordon S Peer L 2 hrs X-R Heavily rev and ex-
panded vers of the puppet opera (1971), with choral mvts

276. *Grand Duo*
I vn, pf M (1) Prelude: Moderato (2) Stampede: Allegro (3) A Round
(Annabelle and April's): Molto moderato, generally tender (4) Air: Slow and
sometimes rhapsodically (5) Polka D Mvts 1–2: 1988. Mvt 3: begun May
29–31, 1981; compl May 1988. Mvt 4: May 5, 1988. Mvt 5: May 30, 1988 P
July 28, 1988, CMF, Aptos: Romuald Tecco, vn, Dennis Russell Davis, pf S
MUSA L 35 min R *CD*: MusM 7073-2C: R. Tecco, D. R. Davies X-R Opening
motive of mvt 5 related to *Reel: Homage to Henry Cowell* (1939) N Comm by
CMF. Mvts 1, 2, 3, and 5 subsequently chor by Mark Morris (1993)

1989

277. *Pedal Sonata*
I org (pedals only) M (1) Chorale (2) As fast as possible (3) Jahla: Fast D Feb. 1989 P Mar. 17, 1989, Central United Methodist Ch, Stockton: Fred Tulan S HBP L 7 min

New Moon. New fourth mvt compl to replace orig one (before Nov. 1989; see listing in 1986)

278. *A Soedjatmoko Set*
I unis chor, solo vo, Jav gam (pelog) M (1) Untitled (2) Isna's Song (3) Untitled D Dec. 1989 P Jan. 13–14, 1990, Lewis and Clark Coll, Portland: the "Venerable Showers of Beauty" gam S HBP N Comm by Peter J. Poole as an offering to the Soedjatmoko family of Indonesia

279. *Ibu Trish*
I Sundanese gam degung D Begun 1987; compl 1989 S HBP L Variable

1990

280. *Piano Trio*
I vn, vc, pf M (1) Molto moderato (2) Slow (3) a. Dance, b. Rhapsody, c. Song (4) Allegro D Mvt 1: Sept. 3, 1989; mvt 2: Oct. 6, 1989; mvt 3: ND; mvt 4: Feb. 22, 1990 P Apr. 3, 1990, Da Camera Society, Houston: Mirecourt Trio S HBP L 33.5 min R CD: Music and Arts CD687: Mirecourt Trio N Comm by Mirecourt Trio. Mvt 2 dedic to Virgil Thomson. Several mvts subsequently chor by Mark Morris in "Pacific" for the S.F. Ballet

281. *Fourth Symphony (Last Symphony)*
I bar (orig ten), orch (3-3-3-3; 4-3-3-1; 4 perc–tack–pf–cel; str) M (1) Largo (2) Stampede: Poco presto (offered to Wm Colvig) (3) Largo (4) Intro—Coyote's Path—Story I—Coyote's Path—Story II—Coyote's Path—Story III—Finale D Aug. 31, 1990, rev 91, 93, and 95. Mvt 4: orch and expansion of wk from 1983 (see X-R) P Nov. 2, 1990, Brooklyn Acad Opera House: Brooklyn Phil, Dennis Russell Davies, cond, Damon Evans, ten T Mvt 4: stories 1 and 3: trad Amerindian tales (see listing for *Coyote Stories*, 1987); story 2: Daniel-Harry Steward S Peer 1993 L 42 min R Decca-Argo 455 590-2: Calif Sym, B. Jekowsky, cond, Al Jarreau, bar X-R Mvt 1: based on rejected fourth mvt of *New Moon* (1986). Mvt 4: outer pts of the mvt are an orch of the *Foreman's Song Tune* (1983) with two of the *Coyote Stories* (1987); new middle section added N Comm by Brooklyn Phil Orch and Brooklyn Acad of Music. For Dennis Russell Davies. Mvts 2 and 4 previously reversed; listing here reflects latest vers

282. *Threnody for Oliver Daniel*
I hp D Dec. 31, 1990 S HBP L 2.5 min R Bridge BCD-9041: J. Schneider, guit

1991

283. *Homage to Pacifica*
I chor, solo vo, narrator, Jav gam (slendro and pelog), bn, hp, psaltery, 1 perc M (1) Prelude (2) In Honor of the Divine Mr. Handel (3) In Honor of

Mark Twain (4) Interlude (5) Ode (6) Interlude (7) Litany (8) In Honor of Chief Seattle **D** 1991 (before Oct.) **P** Oct. 4, 1991 **T** Mvt 3: Mark Twain, taken from Howard Zinn, *A People's History of the United States*. Mvts 5 and 7: L. Harrison, *JP*, 60 and 63. Mvt 8: attr. to Chief Seattle (Chief Sealth) **S** HBP **L** 37 min **R** *CD*: MHS 513382K, MusM 01612-67091-2: Gam Si Betty, R. Hughes, bn, H. Spiller, hp, M. Williams, declaimer, J. Diamond, vo **N** Comm by Gerbode Foundation for inaug of new bldg of the Pacifica Foundation. Two mvts subsequently choreogr by Mark Morris in "World Power" (premiere: Oct. 27, 1995)

284. *A Round for Jafran Jones*
   I Balinese gam (pelog) **D** 1991 **P** Oct. 5, 1991 **S** HBP **L** Variable

1992

285. † *Now Sleep the Mountains, All*
   I chor, perc, 2 pf **D** Feb.–Mar. 1992 **P** Apr. 6, 1992, SJSU: Charlene Archibeque, dir **T** Fragment 89 from Alkman, transl Andrew Bowman **S** Unpub

286. *Songs in the Forest*
   I fl, vn, pf, vibraphone (w narr) **M** (1) Slowish (2) Fastish (3) Largo **D** Begun 1951, rev and compl 1992 (before Mar. 7) **P** Mar. 7, 1992, De Young Museum, S.F.: Abel-Steinberg-Winant Trio **T** L. Harrison, *JP*, 12 **S** Peer **L** 9.5 min **R** *CD*: NA 093: Ens. Parallèle **N** Rev for BMC reunion, 1992. Spoken text preceding each mvt

287. *White Ashes (Gobunsho)*
   I chor, keybd **D** Mar. 1992 **T** Rennyo Shonin, transl Hiroshi Kashiwagi **S** *Gāthās: Shin Buddhist Service Book* (Buddhist Churches of America, 1994) **L** 2.5 min **R** BCA Records CD1

288. *Tandy's Tango*
   I pf **D** June 1992 **P** Nov. 27, 1992 **C** Tandy Beal **S** *Various Leaves: A Collection of Brief Works for Piano by Contemporary American Composers* (Fallen Leaf Press, Berkeley, 1992) **L** 3.5 min **R** *CD*: NewpCl NPD-85606: M. Boriskin

289. *Suite for Four Haisho*
   I 4 haisho (Japanese panpipes), perc, narr **M** (1) qu = ca. 60 (2) qu = ca. 104 (3) Slow and free **D** Mvts 1–2: Oct.–Nov. 1992; mvt 3: Dec. 22, 1992 **P** Jan. 14, 1993 **T** L. Harrison, "Journeys," *Reed Magazine* (SJSU), 47 (1993) **S** HBP **L** 21 min **N** Mvt 2 is a kit w 10 phrases for haisho and 10 for perc that can be rearr, repeated, or omitted at will. Texts, to be spoken in Noh drama style, inserted between mvts

1993

290. *An Old Times Tune for Merce Cunningham's 75th Birthday*
   I (a) str qt, pf (b) arr. for pf solo by Michael Boriskin **D** Dec. 11, 1993, based on sketches from 1952 **P** (a) Mar. 1, 1994, N.Y. St Th, Lincoln Ctr: White Oak Cham Ens (b) Oct. 22, 1994, Cabrillo Coll, Aptos: Michael Boriskin **S** HBP **L** 2 min **R** *CD*: NewpCl NPD-85606: M. Boriskin (pf solo)

291. *Canticle and Round in Honor of Gerhard Samuel's Birthday*
     I 3 perc (mvt 1 arr by Allen Otte) M (1) Canticle (2) Round D Mvt 1: June
     10, 1942 (see X-R); mvt 2: Dec. 17, 1993 P Apr. 25, 1994, U of Cincinnati:
     Allen Otte, dir S HBP X-R Mvt 1: reduction of *Canticle #5* (1942) from 5
     players to 3

1994

292. † *Gending Moon*
     I Male vo, Jav gam (slendro) D Apr. 1994 P May 15, 1994: Cabrillo College:
     Cabrillo Gamelan Ens T Lou Harrison, *JP*, 65 S Unpub L variable
293. *Vestiunt Silve*
     I Sop, fl, 2 vla, hp D Begun Apr. 4, 1951, compl July 4, 1994 P Aug. 18,
     1994, Dartington Internatl Summer Sch and Fest, Dartington Hall, Totnes,
     Devon, England T "A Summer Song of Birds": Goliardic song from the Cam-
     bridge Songs Ms, ca. 1050. See *The Cambridge Songs*, ed Karl Breul (Cam-
     bridge U Press, 1915); transl in *MUSA* S *MUSA* L 4 min R MusicMasters: R.
     Gola, D. R. Davies (forthcoming) N For Wilfrid Mellers's 80th birthday
294. † *Book Music*
     I Selected gam instr D Oct. 24, 1994 T Lou Harrison S Unpub L variable N
     Music to insert between readings of Harrison's poetry
295. *Lazarus Laughed*
     I fl, ob, tbn, hp, perc, str M Incid music for radio broadcast of O'Neill's play
     D 1994 P Downlinked to PBS in winter 1995 for spring broadcasts on public
     radio stations **Prod/dir** Erik Bauersfeld/Edward Hastings T Eugene O'Neill S
     Unpub

1995

296. *New First Suite for Strings* (supplants *First Suite for Strings*, 1948, rev 1991)
     I str orch M (1) Fantasia (2) Chorale (3) Round-Dance (4) Threnody (5) Cha-
     conne D Mvts 1, 2: from *First Suite for Str* (1948); mvt 3: Feb. 12, 1995 based
     on tune from the 1930s; mvt 4: Nov. 17, 1994 (expansion from 12 to 47 mm
     of mvt 4 of *First Suite for Str*); mvt 5: ca. 1950, rev 1994 P Sept. 8, 1995, Ma-
     jorca: Stuttgart Cham Ens, D. R. Davies, cond S Peer L 16 min R MusicMas-
     ters: Brooklyn Philharmonic, D. R. Davies, cond (forthcoming) X-R heavily
     rev vers of *First Suite for Str* (1948) N Dedic to Mary Woods Bennett
297. *Suite for Cello and Piano*
     I vc, pf (arr for cello and str orch by R. Hughes, 1997) M (1) Moderato (2)
     Elegy (3) Allegro D May 5, 1995 (mvts 1 and 3 based on sketches from
     1947–48) P May 13, 1995, All Saints Episcopal Ch, Watsonville, CA (mem
     service for Robert Korns) S Peer L 8 min X-R Mvt 1 from sketch of a ron-
     deau, ca. 1948; mvt 3 from sketches (1947–48) originally envisioned as part
     of *Air in G minor* N In honor of Robert Korns
298. *A Parade for M.T.T.* (Michael Tilson Thomas)
     I orch (4-4-4-4; 4-4-4-1; 4 or 5 perc–cel–pf–org–hp; str) D June 1, 1995 P
     Sept. 6, 1995, Davies Hall, S.F.: S.F. Sym, Michael Tilson Thomas, cond S Peer
     1995 L 6 min N Comm by the S.F. Sym

1996

Homage to Messaien (organ): arr of *Prelude for Piri and Reed Organ* (1961) with
added text by Harrison

299. *Suite for Sangen*

I shamisen **M** (1) Prelude (2) Estampie (3) Adagio (4) Round **D** Oct. 31, 1996
P Dec. 6, 1996 **S** HBP **L** 18.5 min **N** For Akiko Nishigata

300. *Rhymes with Silver*

I vn, vla, vc, pf, perc **M** (1) Prelude (2) Allegro (3) Scherzo (4) Ductia (5)
Gigue and Musette (6) Chromatic Rhapsody (7) Romantic Waltz (8) Fox Trot
(9) Threnody (10) In Honor of Prince Kantemir (11) 5-Tone Kit (12) Round
Dance **D** Nov. 1996 (mvt 7: Dec. 1995) **P** Mar. 6, 1997, Zellerbach Hall, Berkeley: Yo-Yo Ma, cello, et al. **C** Mark Morris **S** Peer **L** ca. 22 min **X-R** Mvt 5: arr
of *Gigue and Musette* (1943) **N** For Mark Morris and Yo-Yo Ma

1997

Suites for Cello with String Orchestra (arr by Robert Hughes of *Suite for Cello and
Harp*, 1949, and *Suite for Cello and Piano*, 1995)

301. *Concerto for P'i-p'a with String Orchestra*

I p'i-p'a, str orch **M** (1) Allegro moderato (2) Bits and Pieces: a. Troika;
b. Three Sharing; c. Wind and Plum, an Elegy for Liu Tien Hua; d. Neapolitan (3) Threnody to the Memory of Richard Locke (4) Estampie **D** Mar. 3,
1997 **P** Apr. 26, 1997, Lincoln Ctr, N.Y.: Wu Man and the Stuttgart Chamber
Orch, D. R. Davies, cond **S** HBP **L** ca. 18 min

302. *In Honor of Munakata Shiko*

I Jav gam (pelog) **D** Sept. 15, 1997 **S** HBP **L** Variable

Notes

Introduction

1. All interviewees are quoted herein by permission.

2. Quotes in this chapter are taken from interviews listed in appendix 1. Interviews here and elsewhere have been edited for readability.

3. Heidi Von Gunden's analytical monograph, *The Music of Lou Harrison* (Metuchen, N.J.: Scarecrow Press, 1995), overlaps very little with the present volume.

4. Von Gunden and other writers, who relied primarily on interviews, had limited access to archival material, much of which has only recently become available. We do not point out every discrepancy between this work and previous ones but have cross-checked material derived from interviews and cite our sources.

Chapter 1

1. Von Gunden (*Lou Harrison*) says Calline was born in Point No Point, Washington, but in Cal's keepsake "wedding book" she lists her birthplace as Seattle. There is no record of the birth in the King County or Kitsap County, Washington, archives; officials note that births in that era often were not recorded.

2. Information on Charles Silver comes from an obituary published in an unidentified Salem, Ohio, newspaper and reproduced in a compendious volume by Benjamin Stump Silver and Frances Aylette Silver, *Our Silver Heritage* (Gatesville, Tex.: Gatesville Printing Company, 1976), p. 5263. Lou and Bill Harrison were told by their mother that Charles rode at least part of the three hundred miles on a hand-pumped railway car.

3. Harrison interview 11/21/95.

4. Lou and Bill Harrison both recall the surname as "de Nësja," but the family's Norwegian-language Bible, in the possession of Bill Harrison, is engraved "T. H. Nësja."

5. Bill Harrison interview.

6. Von Gunden, *Lou Harrison*, 1, implies that Clarence emigrated from Norway. For the birthdates, birthplaces, and wedding date of Clarence and Calline Harrison, we used information from Lou and Bill Harrison's birth certificates as well as entries by Calline in a keepsake "wedding book."

7. Harrison interview 11/21/95.

8. Ibid.

9. Harrison, personal communication. ("Interviews" are formal sessions, recorded and transcribed. "Personal communications" are informal discussions.)

10. The Silver Manufacturing Company was established in 1890 after splitting off from the Silver and Deming Manufacturing Company. See Dale E. Shaffer, *Salem Stories: A Backward Glance* (Salem, Ohio: 1993), 51ff., 56–57; Thomas R. and Mary B. Howett, eds., *The Salem Story, 1806–1956* (Salem, Ohio: Salem Sesquicentennial Com-

mittee of the Salem Historical Society, 1956), 97–98; and Dale E. Shaffer, *More of the Salem Story . . . with Photographs* (Salem, Ohio: 1992), 48–.

11. Mary died intestate on Nov. 15, 1910, but the estate was not settled until Jan. 1911. A seventh child of Mary and Albert died in infancy.

12. Legal documents from Columbiana County, Ohio, Jan. 18, 1911, provide details of the inheritance. Dollar equivalency is derived from John J. McCusker, *How Much Is That in Real Money? A Historical Price Index for Use as a Deflator of Money Values in the Economy of the United States* (Worcester: American Antiquarian Society, 1992), and from the Consumer Price Index calculation page posted on the Web site of the Federal Reserve Bank of Minneapolis. Lou's recollection that his mother inherited several hundred thousand dollars from her uncle is not correct. The misunderstanding may have arisen because Albert Otis Silver, Calline's uncle, was her trustee. For a genealogical chart, see Silver and Silver, *Our Silver Heritage*, 1976.

13. Felton ended her career in television as Spring Byington's friend in *December Bride,* a CBS network morning series that ran from 1954 to 1961 (Tim Brooks and Earle Marsh, *The Complete Directory to Prime Time Network TV Shows, 1946–Present* [N.Y.: Ballentine, 1979]).

14. "New Bills at the Theaters," *Oregonian,* Feb. 16, 1920, p. 16.

15. Harrison interview 12/29/93. This performance of *Seven Pastorales* took place on Aug. 15, 1976, with John Nelson, conductor.

16. Clarence had three brothers and a sister: Harry O., born Apr. 1, 1880; John C., born Oct. 17, 1884; Stella T., born June 6, 1886; and George W., born July 5, 1893 (information from entries in the Nësja family Bible in the possession of Bill Harrison).

17. Lou's surviving report cards come from Portland (pre-1926), Woodland (1926–27), Stockton (1927–29), Berkeley (1929–30), Redwood City (1931–33), and Burlingame (1934). When they moved to California, Cal and Pop sold the Portland apartment house and made a transitionary investment in a "grand old resort hotel," as Lou puts it, in Astoria. Lou particularly recalls a visit there during which he marveled at the wonderful Bechstein piano in the hotel's ballroom.

18. Harrison interview 11/21/95.

19. Harrison interview 12/29/93.

20. Bill Harrison interview.

21. Metcalf interview. The performance was *Changing World* on May 2, 1937.

22. James Sandoe, "Choral Singers Win Applause in Saturday Concert," unidentified newspaper, Nov. 9, 1931 (preserved by Calline in a scrapbook).

23. The institution was then San Francisco State College. Enrollment dates have been verified by the records office. During the depression years, Lou's father bought and ran an "auto car wash rack" at Tenth and Market in San Francisco, which was highly successful because he cleaned all the vehicles for the Van Ness Avenue car dealers. In the late 1930s Clarence became involved in mining cinnabar (the ore that yields mercury) in McDermitt, Nevada. Later he opened a lumber mill in Arcata, California. Upon retirement he and Cal returned to Redwood City. (Information from interviews with Lou and Bill Harrison.)

24. Cleghorn's *Three Ironies for Piano* were published in the same volume of the *New Music Quarterly* as Harrison's *Saraband* and *Prelude for Grand-piano* (vol. 11, no. 4 [July 1938]).

25. Lou Harrison, "Asian Music and the United States," in *Third Asian Composers' League Conference/Festival Final Report* (Manila: National Music Council of the Philippines, 1976), 87.

26. Cowell taught the course twice, in spring 1935 and spring 1936. He also taught

"Appreciation of Modern Music" through UC Extension. (Source: UC Extension brochures, Bancroft Library, UC Berkeley.)

27. Harrison's composition lessons with Cowell seem to have begun in Sept. 1935; a postcard from Cowell to Harrison (Special Collections, University of California, Santa Cruz) dated Sept. 11, 1935, and addressed to "Mr. Harrison" invites Lou to "come see me" and to bring "anything you'd like me to see."

28. Rita Mead, *Henry Cowell's New Music, 1925–1936: The Society, the Music Editions, and the Recordings* (Ann Arbor, Mich.: UMI Research Press, 1981), appendix 2, 582.

29. The "Ricercare" was later set for strings as the second movement of *Canticle #2*.

30. *Report of the Chief Engineer to the Board of Directors of the Golden Gate Bridge and Highway District,* Sept. 1937 (Reprint: Golden Gate Bridge Highway and Transportation District, 1987), 36. Morrow designed the house of Harry and Olive Cowell and a series of soundproof listening rooms for Wilson's Record Rental Library (Lou Harrison, "Learning from Henry," in *The Whole World of Music: A Henry Cowell Symposium*, ed. David Nicholls [Amsterdam: Harwood Academic Press, forthcoming], 163–64). Morrow also designed a rammed earth building (which first stimulated Harrison's interest in architecture) and gave Harrison a copy of *Green Mansions*, which led to his 1941 composition.

31. Cowell had no formal training in theory or composition before his studies with Seeger. "His parents were 'philosophical anarchists,' and their ideas of complete educational freedom led him to accept readily the many sounds around him as valid musical material" (*New Grove Dictionary of American Music,* s.v. "Cowell, Henry," by Bruce Saylor).

32. Michael Hicks, "Cowell's Clusters," *Musical Quarterly* 77, no. 3 (1993): 434.

33. Harrison, "Learning from Henry," 163.

34. Harrison interview 3/31/94.

35. Ibid.

36. Ibid.

37. Lou Harrison, "Percussion Music and Its Relation to the Modern Dance," *Dance Observer* 7, no. 3 (1940): 32.

38. The concept is discussed at length in Cowell's *New Musical Resources,* part 1.

39. Harrison interview 10/21/94.

40. Harrison interview 3/31/94.

41. Harrison, "Learning from Henry," 164.

42. Ibid., 167, and Harrison interview 2/23/94.

43. The program for the New Music Society concert at Columbia University on May 10, 1951, lists Harrison's *Fugue*, but Arthur Berger's review describes a performance of *Canticle #3* ("New Music Society: 'Imaginary Landscape' No. 4 for 12 Radios Heard," *New York Herald Tribune,* May 12, 1951).

44. Nicolas Slonimsky, "Henry Cowell," in *American Composers on American Music: A Symposium,* ed. Henry Cowell (1933; reprints, New York: Frederick Ungar, 1961), 60.

45. Harrison interview 1/13/94.

46. Cowell had been involved sexually with a number of young men at his Menlo Park home. Though the activities were consensual, some of the men were under eighteen; none, however, was under sixteen, despite some later claims to the contrary. One asked for hush money, which Cowell refused to pay; the parents then reported the activities to the county's juvenile officer. During Cowell's years in San Quentin, he virtually created a prison music school. He rehearsed the prison band, formed an orchestra, taught music courses, performed on the piano and other instruments, and instituted chamber music recitals; he also wrote eleven journal articles and fifty musical compositions and completed a book on the nature of melody. He was released in June 1940 to assume the duties of secretary and research assistant to Percy Grainger in New York. In

1941 the San Quentin Prison Board restored his civil rights, enabling him to work for the federal government on a cultural defense project involving the exchange of music scores among North and South American composers. In Dec. 1941 California governor Culbert Olson granted Cowell unconditional clemency. For details on his imprisonment, see Michael Hicks, "The Imprisonment of Henry Cowell," *Journal of the American Musicological Society* 44, no. 1 (Spring 1991): 92—119.

47. Harrison, personal communication.

48. Harrison interview 3/31/94.

49. The work in question is *Ritual of Wonder*. See William Lichtenwanger, *The Music of Henry Cowell: A Descriptive Catalog* (New York: Institute for Studies in American Music, 1986), 154—55 (#539). Cowell could not hand the score to Harrison in person because prison officials were concerned that it might contain a coded communication.

50. Harrison interview 10/21/94.

51. Letter from Lou Harrison (San Francisco) to Calline Harrison (Portland), postmarked July 2, 1936 (Harrison's personal papers).

52. The event, on Jan. 16, 1942, was part of a series of such luncheons, "organized as a wartime diversion." It was given prominent billing in the San Jose and Los Gatos papers, including publication of the entire guest list. Newspaper references erroneously state that Lou played lute as well.

53. Lou Harrison, notes to the score (New York: Peer International, 1990).

54. Lou Harrison, interview by Virginia Rathbun, quoted in "Lou Harrison and His Music" (M.A. thesis, San Jose State University, 1976), 65.

55. "Lou Harrison's Mass to Be Highlight of Festival," *Santa Cruz County Journal News*, Aug. 12, 1970. For more about Lou Harrison and World War II see chapter 10.

56. Alfred Frankenstein, "Radiana Pazmore [sic] 'Refreshing'" *San Francisco Chronicle*, Nov. 15, 1940, and "Composers' Forum Presents Second Session," ibid., Jan. 15, 1941. The program from the Nov. 14, 1940, premiere identifies Pazmor as a faculty member at the Music and Arts Institute of San Francisco.

57. Alfred Frankenstein, "San Francisco Rejuvenated," *Modern Music* 18, no. 3 (Mar./Apr. 1941).

58. Alexander Fried, "Cushing Works Excel in Composers' Concert: S. F. Museum Hall Jammed for 2nd Forum; Many Standees," *San Francisco Examiner*, Jan. 15, 1941.

59. Harrison-Ives correspondence: originals in the Ives archive, Yale University; copies in Harrison's personal archive.

60. In an undated letter to Ives, Harrison reported on two performances of movements from the second sonata and noted that a third was planned.

61. Letter postmarked Dec. 17, 1936. The cost for these photostats would have been more than trivial. Harrison only recalls writing to Ives once to request scores. Quotations from the Ives collection of letters at Yale are reprinted by permission of the American Academy of Arts and Letters, copyright owner. (All rights reserved.)

62. Ibid.

63. Harrison interview 3/31/94.

64. H. Wiley Hitchcock and Vivian Perlis, eds., *An Ives Celebration* (Urbana and Chicago: University of Illinois Press, 1977), 82.

65. The "war march" was a revision of Ives's World War I song, "He Is There."

66. Cage had previously studied with Cowell in New York.

67. Cage/Harrison panel, Cornish School, Jan. 1992. (Quotations from unpublished material by John Cage are used with the permission of the John Cage Trust; videotape of the Cornish panel by Bob Campbell used by permission. We would like to thank Jarrad Powell for securing a copy of this tape.) Cage apparently condensed the time frame a

bit in telling the anecdote. According to David Revill (*The Roaring Silence: John Cage: A Life* [New York: Arcade, 1992], 50), the Cages had moved out of his parents' home a year earlier to their own lodgings in Los Angeles. He also appears to have engaged in a bit of hyperbole in stating that Lou found him eight jobs; the number he cited to Revill, for instance, was four. Cage left Xenia in Carmel because two of her sisters lived there (Xenia Cage interview; see chapter 4).

68. Mills College summer session brochure, 1938; the summer session ran from June 26 to Aug. 6. See also Karen Bell-Kanner, *Frontiers: The Life and Times of Bonnie Bird, American Modern Dancer and Dance Educator* (Amsterdam: Harwood Academic Books, forthcoming).

69. Cage/Harrison panel, Cornish School, Jan. 1992. Bell-Kanner, *Frontiers*, says that Bird first offered the job to Lou, who declined. Lou does not recall this offer. For more information on Cage, Harrison, and the percussion ensemble, see Leta E. Miller, "The Art of Noise: John Cage, Lou Harrison, and the West Coast Percussion Ensemble," in *Essays in American Music* 3 (forthcoming).

70. "Second percussion concert," May 19, 1939. While Cage was in Seattle, he and Harrison exchanged compositions by mail. Two letters from Cage in the spring of 1939 acknowledge receipt of *Counterdance* and *Fifth Simfony* and describe rehearsals in progress (Harrison, personal papers). The Cornish ensemble also performed *Counterdance* at the University of Idaho, the University of Montana, Whitman College, and Reed College in Jan.–Feb. 1940. (For further information see Miller, ibid.)

71. Some sources state that Lou was hired by Mills in 1936, but surviving documents from the college substantiate employment only from the fall of 1937. Lou is listed as dance accompanist (in the physical education department) beginning in the 1937–38 catalog. (The previous year's catalog lists Ruth Hunt in that position.) The catalog from 1939–40 lists faculty with the year of first employment; Harrison is listed as "1937–." Lou's own curriculum vitae from the early 1950s lists his years at Mills as 1937–40. Evidence suggesting employment in 1936 comprises the following: the date on the bust of Harrison in the Mills College music department, and Harrison's recollection that Cowell had personally introduced him to Mills dance instructor Tina Flade, which necessarily occurred before Cowell's arrest in May 1936. The dates on the bust (1936–39) appear to be wrong: we know from surviving programs and reviews that Harrison worked at Mills through the summer of 1940, and inquiries to college officials confirmed that the 1936 date was based on recollection rather than documentation. Cowell was scheduled to teach at the Mills summer session in 1936 (he is listed in the brochure, dated Feb. 1936), but could not have done so because of his arrest. It is possible that Harrison worked for Mills in a temporary capacity before being hired as regular staff in the fall of 1937. To further investigate this possibility, we sought pay records from the college but were informed that they are lost.

72. Alfred Frankenstein, "A Program of Percussion," *San Francisco Chronicle*, July 28, 1939.

73. Henry Cowell, "Drums along the Pacific," *Modern Music* 18, no. 1 (Nov./Dec. 1940): 46, 49.

74. Although the program lists this performance as the premiere of *Canticle #1*, Van Tuyl's dancers had played it earlier on a tour of southern California. In the summer session brochure for 1940, both Cage and Harrison are listed on the faculty, and they taught courses in percussion and musical composition for dance.

75. Alfred Frankenstein, "A Splendid Performance Opens Red Cross Series," *San Francisco Chronicle*, July 19, 1940; Esther Rosenblatt, "The 1940 Mills College Summer Session in Dance," *Dance Observer* 7, no. 7 (Aug./Sept. 1940): 101.

76. *Elsa, I Come with My Songs* (San Francisco: Booklegger Press, 1986), 296, 364. Gidlow erroneously located the Jackson Street studio above a Chinese laundry.

77. Harrison interview 10/21/94.

78. Published as "Quetzecoatl." Frankenstein's review of the concert says that the composers are not identified; they are, though identification is somewhat difficult due to the program's graphic design.

79. Harrison interview 3/31/94.

80. Cage/Harrison panel, Cornish School, January 1992. Cage also told this story in an interview with Richard Dufallo, published in *Trackings: Composers Speak with Richard Dufallo* (New York: Oxford University Press, 1989), 225, and repeated it to David Revill (*Roaring Silence*, 74). Some years later in New York, Varèse's wife explained that her husband was concerned that his work should not be confused with that of Cage and Harrison. Varèse's article, "Organized Sound for the Sound Film," was published in *The Commonweal* on Dec. 13, 1940.

81. Alfred Frankenstein, "The New Records in Review," *San Francisco Chronicle*, Sept. 28, 1941.

82. Lewitzky interview.

83. Performances were June 9 at Mills and June 10 on Treasure Island (which was constructed by the U.S. Army Corps of Engineers specifically for the exposition). A privately made, off-the-air recording of the *Trojan Women* overture survives in Lou's personal archive; on the reverse side is a processional for recorder and percussion to Aeschylus's *Choephoroe* (The Libation Bearers). *Choephoroe* was performed at Mills in the spring of 1936 with music by Domenico Brescia. The origin of Harrison's "processional" (which appears to date from 1939—40) is unclear; no score has been found.

84. Dorothy James Russell interview.

85. David Doty, "The Lou Harrison Interview," *1/1: The Quarterly Journal of the Just Intonation Network* 3, no. 2 (Spring 1987).

86. Harrison, "Learning from Henry," 164.

87. Several sources give the date of *Canticle #3* as 1941, but Harrison's manuscript is dated Jan.–Feb. 1942.

88. Alfred Frankenstein, "A Recital on Percussion Instruments," *San Francisco Chronicle*, May 8, 1942.

89. For information on this series and the succeeding Monday Evening Concert Series, see Dorothy Crawford, *Evenings On and Off the Roof* (Berkeley and Los Angeles: University of California Press, 1995).

90. Harrison interview 3/31/94, and personal communication, Feb. 6, 1997. (Rudolf von Laban's *Kinetographie Laban* was first published in 1928.)

91. Peter Yates, oral history (UCLA special collections), 123—24.

92. The concerts of 1939, for example, included all-Bartók and all-Ives programs, as well as works by Schoenberg, by composers published in Cowell's *New Music Edition*, and by local composers. Mullen had given recitals at Mills College (Crawford, *Evenings On and Off the Roof*), but Lou did not meet her before he moved to Los Angeles.

93. Peter Yates, "Lou Harrison," *ACA Bulletin* 9, no. 2 (1960): 3.

94. Harrison interview 12/29/93.

95. Cage/Harrison panel, Cornish School, Jan. 1992.

96. Vivian Perlis, *Charles Ives Remembered* (New Haven: Yale University Press, 1974), 199.

97. Harrison, "Homage to Schoenberg: His Late Works," *Modern Music* 21, no. 3 (Mar.–Apr. 1944): 136.

98. Harrison's works appeared in the *New Music Quarterly* 11, no. 4 (July 1938). (For a list of works published in the *NMQ*, see Mead, *Henry Cowell's New Music*, appendix 3.) "I was very embarrassed," Lou added after recounting this story in an interview, 9/30/94.

99. Erwin Stein, ed., *Arnold Schoenberg: Letters*, trans. Eithne Wilkins and Ernst Kaiser (New York: St. Martin's Press, 1964), 234.

100. Peter Yates, "A Trip up the Coast," *Arts and Architecture* 74, no. 12 (Dec. 1957): 10. Lou incorporated the piece into his 1996 *Rhymes with Silver*.

101. Harrison interview 3/31/94.

102. The following Harrison compositions were performed during Evenings on the Roof recitals: *Sanctus* (Dec. 4, 1944); *Six Cembalo Sonatas* (Mullen on piano, Jan. 24, 1944, and Carol Rosenstiel on harpsichord, Feb. 6, 1950); *Gigue and Musette* (May 8, 1944); *Suite for Piano* (May 8, 1944, and Nov. 2, 1953); *String Trio* (Apr. 5, 1948). After the series became the Monday Evening Concerts, these works were programmed: *Song of Quetzalcoatl, Mass to St. Anthony, Dance Chromatique* (an arrangement of *Canticle #3*), and *Concerto for Violin with Percussion Orchestra* (Jan. 18, 1960); *Fifth Simfony* (Nov. 7, 1960); *Concerto in Slendro* (Oct. 1, 1962); *Concerto for Violin with Percussion Orchestra* (Mar. 18, 1974); *Double Concerto for Violin, Cello, and Javanese Gamelan, Gending Pindar* for gamelan, and *Richard Whittington* (a puppet play with selected gamelan works; all on Mar. 7, 1983).

103. Letter from Yates to Houston, Apr. 11–June 1, 1943, Yates Collection, UCSD; quoted in Crawford, *Evenings On and Off the Roof*, 62.

Chapter 2

1. Letter in Harrison's personal papers. His first reviews in *Modern Music* appeared in vol. 21, no. 1 (Nov./Dec. 1943): 34–36.

2. Yates oral history, UCLA Special Collections; confirmed by Harrison (personal communication).

3. Lou's impromptu house concerts were colorfully described by Edward McGowan (interview, 11/6/95).

4. Letter, Lou Harrison to Calline Harrison, July 9, 1943.

5. In his introduction to *Jaime de Angulo*, Harrison notes that Slayback drowned while trying to rescue a relative (Peter Garland, ed., *Jaime de Angulo: The Music of the Indians of Northern California* [Santa Fe: Soundings Press 1988], 6).

6. Excerpted from letter to Bill and Dorothy Harrison, Sept. 1943.

7. Peter Yates, "Lou Harrison," *Arts and Architecture* 61, no. 2 (Feb. 1944): 26.

8. Von Gunden, *Lou Harrison*, states that Harrison wrote fifty-four reviews between Jan. and May 1947. In fact, eighty-one appeared during this period. The error may have arisen from her reliance on an album of clippings Lou's mother collected, which is incomplete. On the other hand, there are reviews in Calline's album that do not appear on microfilms of the *Tribune*. The only explanation we can offer is that the microfilm lacks some editions on particular days, although in most cases both the regular and late editions were filmed. Anthony Tommasini, *Virgil Thomson: Composer on the Aisle* (N.Y.: Norton, 1997), 369, states that Harrison went back to work as a reviewer for the *Tribune* after 1947. We have found no evidence to support this claim nor does Lou recall reviewing after May 1947.

9. Christopher Sawyer-Lauçanno, *An Invisible Spectator: A Biography of Paul Bowles* (New York: Weidenfeld and Nicolson, 1989), 249, states that at the end of 1945 Bowles

decided to restrict his *Tribune* work to a Sunday column only. Harrison remembers Bowles asking him to consider expanding his reviewing to take up the slack, but his recollection that the request was occasioned by Bowles's move to Morocco is incorrect.

10. Lou Harrison, personal communication.

11. Letter to Leta Miller, July 9, 1996. Harrison never completed the second bridge.

12. Harrison interview 10/21/94. The program shows *Lousadzak* as the *second* work on the concert, following the Armenian Rhapsody No. 2 for string orchestra.

13. Ibid.

14. Harrison, "Alan Hovhaness Offers Original Compositions," *New York Herald Tribune*, June 18, 1945.

15. Hovhaness interview.

16. Letter from Harrison to Frank Wigglesworth, Feb. 12, 1952.

17. Harrison, "Music for the Modern Dance," *American Composers' Alliance Bulletin* 2, no. 3 (Oct. 1952), 12.

18. Hovhaness interview.

19. *Modern Music* 21, no. 3 (Mar./Apr. 1944), 134–38; 22, no. 2 (Jan./Feb. 1945), 85–86; and 23, no. 3 (Summer 1946), 166–69. The last is reprinted in Minna Lederman, *The Life and Death of a Small Magazine* (*Modern Music, 1924–1946*), (New York: Institute for Studies in American Music, 1983).

20. Letters to Harrison from Harmony Ives, Apr. 8, 1946, and Ruggles, Dec. 13, 1945. The pamphlet, *About Carl Ruggles* (Yonkers, N.Y.: Oscar Baradinsky, 1946), is reprinted in *The Score and I.M.A. Magazine* 12 (June 1955): 15–26, and in Peter Garland, ed., *A Lou Harrison Reader* (Santa Fe: Soundings Press, 1987), 39–45.

21. Reprinted in Cowell, *American Composers on American Music*, 14–35.

22. Harrison, *About Carl Ruggles*, 6 (Garland, *Lou Harrison Reader*, 39; *Score* 12:15).

23. Ibid.

24. Harrison interview 9/30/94.

25. Harrison, *About Carl Ruggles*, 8 (Garland, *Lou Harrison Reader*, 40; *Score* 12:16).

26. *New Music Quarterly* 21, no. 2 (January 1948). Jack Heliker recalls that Ruggles was similarly supportive of the work of Merton Brown (Heliker interview).

27. Mead, *Henry Cowell's New Music*, 369. Lou's editorial board included John Cage, Elliott Carter, and Kurt List. After Lou's year as editor, Frank Wigglesworth took over.

28. Marilyn J. Ziffrin, *Carl Ruggles: Composer, Painter, and Storyteller* (Urbana and Chicago: University of Illinois Press, 1994), 182. An arrangement of *Organum* for piano by John Kirkpatrick was ultimately published in the *New Music* Quarterly in January 1948. On the order of the four *Evocations*, see Ziffrin, *Carl Ruggles*, 182.

29. Ziffrin, *Carl Ruggles*, 182. Lou has a copy of the guest list among his personal papers.

30. McGowan interview.

31. The phrase *exquisite corpse* refers to a surrealist game in which groups of people constructed sentences or drawings while unaware of the contributions of previous players. The name comes from the first sentence so constructed: The exquisite / corpse / shall drink / the bubbling wine (for further information see Calvin Tomkins, *The World of Marcel Duchamp* [New York: Time-Life Books, 1966]).

32. Harrison, "Barone Conducts Concert by N. Y. Little Symphony," *New York Herald Tribune*, Dec. 2, 1944.

33. The letter from Harmony Ives inviting Lou to lunch is dated Feb. 14, 1947. The date of the *Third Symphony* premiere has frequently been given erroneously as May 5, 1947, stemming from a mistake on the title page of the first published score (Associated Music Publishers, 1964).

34. Harmony Ives to Harrison, Feb. 19, 1946.

35. Harrison, "The Music of Charles Ives," *Listen: The Guide to Good Music* (Nov. 1946): 8.

36. See, for example, the letter from Ives to Harrison after Ives received the Pulitzer Prize (reprinted in Garland, *Lou Harrison Reader*, 23, and in Perlis, *Charles Ives Remembered*, 202). See also Stuart Feder, *Charles Ives: "My Father's Song"* (New Haven: Yale University Press, 1992), 347.

37. Harrison, "Ruggles, Ives, Varese," *View* 5, no. 4 (Nov. 1945): 11.

38. Harrison to Ives, Oct. 23, 1944.

39. Ives to Harrison, Nov. 1944.

40. Letters, Barone to Harrison, Mar. 3, 12, and 16, 1946 (Harrison's personal papers).

41. Letter, Barone to Harrison, Mar. 31, 1946 (Harrison's personal papers).

42. Undated letter, Harrison to Ruggles, shortly after the performance (Harrison's personal papers).

43. Ibid.

44. "New York Little Symphony Offers New Native Works," *Musical America* 66, no. 6 (Apr. 25, 1946): 10 and 13.

45. Noel Straus, "Symphony by Ives in World Premiere: Composer's Third Featured by Little Symphony Here, with Harrison on Podium," *New York Times*, Apr. 6, 1946.

46. Letter to Harrison, June 16, 1946.

47. Draft of letter in the Ives Collection, Yale. Reproduced in Garland, *Lou Harrison Reader*, 23, and in Perlis, *Charles Ives Remembered*, 202.

48. Harrison, "On Quotation," *Modern Music* 23, no. 3 (Summer 1946): 167–68.

49. A letter from Harmony Ives on Jan. 15, 1947, provides some clarification of biographical data.

50. The revised title is "They Are There." The work was recorded on Oct. 18, 1967, and issued on Columbia M32504; it is included on the compact disc *Concise Norton Recorded Anthology of Western Music* (Norton, 0-393-10059-6)

51. Harmony Ives to Harrison, Nov. 1944. See also Feder, *Charles Ives*, 347.

52. Harrison interview 3/31/94.

53. Ibid.

54. Performed in Oklahoma, Dec. 4, 1977, and in New York, Dec. 5, 1977.

55. Walter Blum, "The Bell-like World of Lou Harrison," *San Francisco Chronicle and Examiner: California Literary Magazine*, Apr. 26, 1981.

56. Harrison interview 4/3/95.

57. Hitchcock and Perlis, *Ives Celebration*, 200. Ives composed three pieces for "quarter-tone piano" or two pianos tuned a quarter-tone apart. Lou, too, composed quarter-tone works during his teen years, though inspired more by Hába than by Ives.

58. Letter, Harrison to Harmony Ives, July 24, 1946.

59. Letter, Harrison to Ruggles, Mar. 1, 1945 (Harrison's personal papers).

60. Undated letter, Harrison to Harmony Ives (summer 1946).

61. Letter, Henry Cowell to Harrison, Aug. 6, 1945 (New York Public Library, New Music Edition Papers, folder 43). Cowell notes that he and Sidney were very upset to hear about the doctor's diagnosis of Harrison's ulcer. At the same time, he tries to console Lou by telling him that while the condition is unpleasant, Cowell understands that it is not dangerous providing Lou is careful.

62. Letter, Harrison to Henry Cowell, fall 1945 (New York Public Library, New Music Edition Papers, folder 251). The two composers were Lou and Merton Brown; the divine was Edward McGowan. One of the painters was Jack Heliker. Lou does not recall the identities of the other two painters or the "drone," a "hard worker who did not make much of an intellectual contribution" (personal communication).

63. Letter, Harrison to Riegger, Sept. 28, 1945 (New York Public Library, Wallingford Riegger Papers, series 5, folder 51).

64. Virgil Thomson, *Portraits for Piano Solo*, album 1 (New York: Mercury Music, 1948), 14–15 (dated Dec. 5, 1945). See also Anthony Tommasini, *Virgil Thomson's Musical Portraits* (New York: Pendragon Press, 1986), 159–60.

65. Parmenter interview.

66. Cunningham interview.

67. Heliker interview.

68. Ibid.

69. Letter, John Cage to Charles Ives, postmarked May 13, 1947 (Ives collection, Yale).

70. Cage noted that the bill for the first nine days was $96.42 (ibid).

71. Cage/Harrison panel, Cornish School, 1992.

72. Letter, Cage to Ives, May 13, 1947.

73. Yates, "Trip up the Coast," 10.

74. Harrison, interview by Rathbun ("Lou Harrison and His Music," 87).

75. The five documented performances of the work are: Hunter College, N.Y., Dec. 14, 1947; UCLA, Apr. 1948; Marines' Memorial Theatre, San Francisco, May 1, 1948; Stephens College, Columbia, Mo., May 8, 1948; YM/YWHA, New York, May 14, 1950 (letter from Cunningham Foundation archivist David Vaughan, Nov. 8, 1995).

76. John Cage, *Silence* (Middletown, Conn.: Wesleyan University Press, 1961), 56.

77. Joseph Campbell, *The Hero with a Thousand Faces*, 2d ed. (Princeton: Princeton University Press, 1968).

78. Ibid., 58.

79. Ibid., 59.

80. Harrison interview 3/31/94.

81. Mildred Norton, "Music Review," unidentified Los Angeles paper, ca. Apr. 6, 1948 (Harrison's personal papers). The concert took place on Apr. 5.

82. Harrison interview 10/21/94.

83. Harrison, personal communication, 8/7/95.

84. Lou recently revised the *First Suite for Strings*, now published under the title *New First Suite for Strings*. The new version is dedicated to Mary Woods Bennett, who endowed the professorial chair at Mills that he occupied in the 1980s. The pastorales are dedicated to friends and relatives, including his mother and brother, his companion Remy Charlip, John Cage, conductor Fritz Rikko, and two hospital friends, Ellie and David Decker, on the occasion of their marriage.

85. Virgil Thomson, "Music: Composers' Forum," *New York Herald Tribune*, Apr. 17, 1950.

86. Quotes are from the LP liner notes: Columbia ML-4491; New World 281. The proposed film commission never materialized.

87. The National Institute of Arts and Letters was founded in 1898 and incorporated in 1913. The American Academy of Arts and Letters was founded in 1904 and incorporated in 1916. In 1976, the two organizations were amalgamated.

88. From the brochure and membership directory of the American Institute and Academy of Arts and Letters.

89. Letter, Jean Erdman to Leta Miller, Dec. 1, 1996.

90. Erdman interview. The original mobile was replaced in 1951 by a new one designed by Carlus Dyer. It met with mixed reviews: *Dance Magazine* called it "a ponderous symbolic decor, . . . a huge ring encircling a mass that resembles congealed spaghetti," while the *Dance Observer* reviewer found it "ecstatic visual imagery . . . skele-

tal and cosmic, perfectly scaled to the Hunter stage" (Doris Hering, "Jean Erdman and Dance Company," *Dance Magazine* 25, no. 3 [March 1951]: 43; Nik Krevitsky, "Jean Erdman and Company," *Dance Observer* 18, no. 3 [March 1951]: 42).

91. Erdman interview.

92. *Boulder Daily Camera*, July 11, 1951.

93. The dramatic change in Lou's handwriting has aided significantly in the dating of manuscripts, sketches, writings, and correspondence.

94. Bell-Kanner, *Frontiers*.

95. Harrison interview 3/31/94. Virgil Thomson gave both the performance and the composition high marks in the *Tribune*. Carter Harman in the *Times* was less effusive though still complimentary. Ruggles was his typical curmudgeonly self, calling his work "a jewel in a muck-heap" (letter to John Kirkpatrick, Mar. 8, 1949, quoted in Ziffrin, *Carl Ruggles*, 195). The "muck-heap" was comprised of works by Henry Cowell, Elliott Carter, Vincent Persichetti, Richard Franko Goldman, Ingolf Dahl, David Diamond, and others.

96. Ziffrin, *Carl Ruggles*, dates this meeting on Oct. 27, 1946, but doesn't mention the racist outbursts.

97. Harrison interview 9/30/94.

98. Lou Harrison, "Season's End, May 1944," *Modern Music* 21, no. 4 (May–June 1944): 235–36. The work can be heard on the compact disc *Historic Speech-Music Recordings from the Harry Partch Archives* (Innova 401).

99. Harrison interview 9/30/94.

100. Harrison interview 2/10/94.

101. Judith Malina, *Diaries of Judith Malina* (New York: Grove Press, 1984), 148. The excitement and urgency of their work is apparent even from a cursory reading of the diaries. Malina also records in some detail her short-lived but intense infatuation with Harrison.

102. Malina interview (condensed from a longer discussion).

103. Ibid.

104. *Diaries of Judith Malina*, 157–58. Also discussed in Malina interview and Harrison, personal communications.

105. By this time Rice had left the institution. For detailed information on Black Mountain College, see Martin Duberman, *Black Mountain: An Exploration in Community* (1972; reprint, New York: Norton, 1993), and Mary Emma Harris, *The Arts at Black Mountain College* (Cambridge: MIT Press, 1987). The latter includes extensive photographic reproductions and documentation.

106. Rathbun, "Lou Harrison and His Music," 20. This statement has been misinterpreted by several authors to mean that Lou had two nervous breakdowns.

107. Harrison interview 11/21/98. Both score and painting were restored. The Fiores (who inspired the characters of Rapunzel and the prince in Harrison's opera) barely recall the incident and have fond recollections of Lou from their college days. Duberman (*Black Mountain College*) relates similar incidents.

108. Two undated letters from Harrison to Vladimir Ussachevsky (New York Public Library, New Music Edition Archives, folder 97). Since Harrison finished the third act of *Rapunzel* in Aug. 1952 and the fourth in Sept. 1952, the second letter probably dates from late Aug. or early Sept. 1952.

109. Tudor interview.

110. Huss interview.

111. Letter, Harrison to Wigglesworth (who was in Rome), Feb. 12, 1952 (Wigglesworth's private papers).

112. Undated letter to Peter Oskarson in Bonn on the occasion of the performance of *Rapunzel* in 1993.

113. Robert Commanday, "Aptos Cabrillo Festival: Heartiness, Vitality in Sound," *San Francisco Chronicle*, Aug. 22, 1966.

114. Letter, Harrison to Peggy Glanville-Hicks, Nov. 28, 1956 (New York Public Library, Composers Forum documents, Music-Am [Letters] 83–39, folder 377).

115. First recording, New Albion Records (NA 093), 1997.

116. Fiore interview.

117. Cage, *Silence*, x.

118. Harrison interview 4/3/95. Cage, too, often took himself less seriously than others did. His infectious laughter pervades even his most puzzling and absurd scores, a sense of humor readily apparent in the brief anecdotes in *Silence*.

119. Richard Kostelanetz, ed. *John Cage, Writer: Previously Uncollected Pieces* (New York: Limelight Editions, 1993), 177.

120. Harrison interview 12/29/93. Remy Charlip experimented with a similar idea, which he calls "mail-order dances." He paints images of dancers in various positions on a large sheet. The dancers imitate these positions in any order and devise means of moving between them.

121. Letter, Harrison to Calline and Clarence Harrison, Apr. 14, 1953 (Harrison's personal papers).

122. Letter, Harrison to Charles Ives, July 19, 1952.

123. Harmony Ives to Harrison, July 24, 1952.

124. Harrison conducted *The Perilous Chapel* at the Hunter Playhouse on Jan. 18, 1952. Stokowski's performance of the *Suite* took place at the Museum of Modern Art on Oct. 28, 1952; he thereafter recorded it, taking the liberty of altering Harrison's ending (see chapter 11). The performance of *Canticle #3* occurred on Feb. 22, 1953; Lou wrote ecstatically to his parents about the lavish reception that followed.

125. In a letter to Frank and Anne Wigglesworth (May 29, 1953), Lou wrote: "Virgil offered me a post (regular) on the Tribune, 'for ever.' I declined." Lou has no recollection of this offer.

Chapter 3

1. Letter, Aug. 18, 1953, NYPL (Composers Forum; Music-Am [Letters] 83–39, folder 377).

2. *New York Herald Tribune*, "Roman Prize" (editorial), Apr. 20, 1954. In a letter to his parents from New York on Apr. 14, 1953 (Harrison, personal papers), Lou wrote that he had been selected as one of the contestants and outlined his plan to compose a work for voice and six instruments. On May 12, 1953, Virgil Thomson wrote to ask Lou to prepare his piece for performance by Leontyne Price (letter, Thomson to Harrison, Special Collections, UCSC). The conference was organized by Nicolas Nabokov and included a congress for composers, performers, and critics; the composition contest; and a series of new music concerts. Contestants were provided with full-scale performances of their works, a free trip to Rome, and the rights to the score and orchestral parts, with copying expenses paid by the conference. Details of the competition are given in Allen Hughes, "Rome Conference Selects Prize Scores," *Musical America* 74, no. 7 (May 1954), 3, 20.

3. "R[edwood] C[ity] Man Sole U.S. Winner in Music Fete," *San Mateo Times*, Apr. 16, 1954.

4. Michael Steinberg, "Leontyne Price Soloist in Rome; Offers Setting of Prayer in Chamber Music Category—3 Fragments Heard," *New York Times*, Apr. 15, 1954.

5. Harrison interview 10/21/94.

6. Hughes, "Rome Conference," 3.

7. Announcements appeared in various San Francisco Bay Area papers on May 3, 1954.

8. Correspondence between Partch and Harrison (Special Collections, UCSC) dates from Nov. 1954.

9. Harrison interview 2/10/94.

10. Ibid.

11. In April 1953 the Louisville Philharmonic received a $400,000 grant from the Rockefeller Foundation to commission forty-six compositions during the following four seasons and issue recordings of them through Columbia Records. The project is described in Jeanne Belfy, *The Louisville Orchestra New Music Project* (Louisville: University of Louisville, 1983).

12. Full text in Harrison, *Joys and Perplexities: Selected Poems of Lou Harrison* (Winston-Salem, N.C.: The Jargon Society, the University Library (UCSC), and the Cabrillo Music Festival, 1992), 34–35. A dramatic reading is included on the compact disc *Lou Harrison: A Birthday Celebration* (Musical Heritage Society 513616L, 1994).

13. Dwight Anderson, "Orchestra's Program of Arresting Quality," *Louisville Courier-Journal*, Jan. 19, 1956.

14. Hughes interview 12/12/94.

15. The May 14 program at the YMHA's Kaufmann Concert Hall also included the premiere of Peggy Glanville-Hicks's opera, *Glittering Gate* (Howard Taubman, "Opera: Two Premieres: 'Glittering Gate' and 'Rapunzel' at 'Y,'" *New York Times*, May 15, 1959; Francis D. Perkins, "Two U.S. Operas in Debut at Kaufmann Concert Hall," *New York Herald Tribune*, May 15, 1959).

16. The West Coast premiere took place at a Monday Evening Concert on Jan. 18, 1960, with William Kraft and the Los Angeles Percussion Ensemble and Eudice Shapiro, violin. Shapiro and Kraft recorded the work in 1975, and it has been reissued on compact disc (Crystal Records CD850).

17. Lou Harrison, "The Violin Concerto in the Modern World," *Listen: The Guide to Good Music* (March 1947): 4–6.

18. Letter, Hughes to Harrison, May 1963.

19. Harrison, personal communication.

20. "Sticky wicket" refers to a damp playing field in cricket, which makes the game more difficult. By extension, to "bat on a sticky wicket" means "to contend with great difficulties" (OED).

21. In February 1962 the county zoning board denied the Sticky Wicket's use permit. After a fuller hearing of the complaints, supportive editorials in the newspaper, and numerous letters and petitions (including one from Harrison), the summer season of 1962 was permitted to continue on condition of an 11:30 P.M. closing time and no amplification.

22. Hughes interview 12/12/94.

23. Programs, photos, and clippings were preserved by Sidney Jowers in a scrapbook now in Special Collections, UCSC.

24. Harrison, personal communication.

25. *Music—East and West* (Executive Committee for 1961 Tokyo East-West Music Encounter, 1961), 141–43.

26. Mantle Hood, *The Nuclear Theme as a Determinant of Patet in Javanese Music* (Groningen: J. B. Walters, 1954).

27. Campbell, *Hero*, 72.

28. Lee Hye-Ku, *Essays on Korean Traditional Music* (Seoul: Royal Asiatic Society, 1981), translator's introduction, by Robert Provine, xiii. Much of the information on Lee is drawn from Provine's excellent biographical sketch.

29. Harrison interview 10/21/94.

30. The trips are documented by Lou's passport (arrival in Korea May 4, 1961, departure July 6; second arrival in Korea June 28, 1962, departure for Taiwan in October).

31. The manuscript, in Lou's beautiful calligraphy on folio-size paper, is preserved in his archive, with a copy at UCLA dedicated to Mantle Hood.

32. Liang Tsai-Ping, "A Short Note in Honor of Lou Harrison," in Garland, *Lou Harrison Reader*, 87. (The conference is erroneously dated 1962.) Lou's passport registers arrival in Taiwan Oct. 16, 1962, and departure Nov. 7. See also James Wade, "Lou Harrison: East Meets West," *Musical America* 82, no. 12 (Dec. 1962): 62; reprinted in James Wade, *One Man's Korea: A Miscellany Chosen by the Author* (Seoul: Hollym, 1967), 220.

33. Benton and the Red Gate Players presented Chinese shadow plays at Mills on Oct. 23, 1939. The notes to this program state that the group had been organized in 1932 and comprised Benton and Robert Youmans (animation and dialogue) and William Russell (music). Benton had studied Chinese shadow theater on several trips to rural Chinese regions.

34. Alexander Fried, "'White Snake Lady' a Shadow Fairy Tale," *San Francisco Examiner*, Oct. 5, 1971.

35. Virgil Thomson, "The World of Lou Harrison," *KPFA Folio* 39, no. 5 (May 1987): 7. Reprinted in Garland, *Lou Harrison Reader*, 86.

36. Marc Perlman, ed., *Festival of Indonesia Conference Summaries* (New York: Festival of Indonesia Foundation, 1992), 33. Also Harrison, *Music Primer* (New York: C. F. Peters, 1971), 129.

37. The festival's first year was reviewed by Peter Yates ("Music: Cabrillo Festival at Aptos," *Arts and Architecture* 81, no. 1 [Jan. 1964]: 8–9, 32). Harrison was scheduled to lecture, but since his mother was ill, Yates substituted and talked about current trends in American music.

38. Ibid., 8.

39. Alfred Frankenstein, "Brilliant Bartók Opens Festival," *San Francisco Chronicle*, Aug. 23, 1963.

40. After this premiere Lou rewrote the finale, and Samuel premiered the new version with the Oakland Symphony on Feb. 8, 1966. Several sources erroneously give 1954 as the completion date for the symphony's first version.

41. Davies had conducted *The Perilous Chapel* in Hawaii in 1969 but did not meet Lou before assuming the directorship of the Cabrillo Festival.

42. Lorle Kranzler, "Reflections in Motion—A Photographic Essay," *Impulse* (1966): 34–39.

43. Information on this award from a letter to Leta Miller from Francis Thorne, Dec. 22, 1995. The award was named in honor of Thorne's paternal grandmother, an amateur pianist who impressed him as a child. In a letter of Dec. 20, 1965, Thorne personally informed Lou of the award, which took effect in Jan. 1966.

44. Letters from Harrison to Lieberman in 1966 confirm Lou's departure for Mexico on Sept. 24 of that year.

45. Published in 1971 by C. F. Peters, the *Primer* has recently been reissued in Japanese and English with an appendix containing new material.

46. A typed resume in Lou's files lists him teaching world music theory at Stanford as well, but surviving schedules of classes from the time list only composition

courses. (Albert Cohen, then chair of the music department, also recalls Lou teaching world music.) Harrison taught at USC in 1977, commuting by plane from San Jose to Los Angeles.

47. Colvig interview 4/3/95.

48. John H. Chalmers Jr., *Divisions of the Tetrachord* (Hanover, N.H.: Frog Peak Music, 1993).

49. From the program at the premiere, California Institute of Technology, Nov. 5, 1971.

50. The story is related briefly by Suetonius: "Caesar first saw military service in Asia, where he went as aide-de-camp to Marcus Thermus, the provincial governor. When Thermus sent Caesar to raise a fleet in Bithynia, he wasted so much time at King Nicomedes' court that a homosexual relationship between them was suspected, and suspicion gave place to scandal when, soon after his return to headquarters, he revisited Bithynia: ostensibly collecting a debt incurred there by one of his freedmen" (Gaius Suetonius Tranquillus, *The Twelve Caesars*, trans. Robert Graves [London: Penguin Books, 1957]), 13.

51. Colvig's two-page description of the American gamelan is reproduced in various sources, including Rathbun, "Lou Harrison and His Music," 149–50, and Patrick Grant Gardner, "'La Koro Sutro' by Lou Harrison: Historical Perspective, Analysis and Performance Considerations" (D.M.A. thesis, University of Texas at Austin, 1981), 121–22.

52. The translation was prepared by Bruce Kennedy. For a discussion of Buddhist theological concepts and the Heart Sutra, as well as a detailed explication of the text, see Gardner, "'La Koro Sutro,'" 71–89.

53. Cathy Schulze, letter to Leta Miller, Sept. 30, 1996.

54. This work, for flute and two percussionists, was dedicated to Henry Cowell, who performed one of the percussion parts at the premiere on Aug. 10, 1941, at the Bennington summer institute. Otto Luening played flute, Frank Wigglesworth the second percussion part. (A second performance took place on Aug. 17.) Cowell described the performance in *Modern Music* 19, no. 1. See also postcard from Cowell to Harrison, dated Aug. 21, 1941, reproduced in Garland, *Lou Harrison Reader*, 30, in which Cowell notes that the concerto was performed twice, "last Sunday" and "the Sunday before" (original in Special Collections, UCSC).

55. Yates left Los Angeles for Buffalo in 1968; see Crawford, *Evenings On and Off the Roof*, 233. Lou went to Buffalo with Bill, Richard Dee, and flutist Jain Fletcher.

56. "Multi-Talented Harrison Here for Talks, Concerts," *Buffalo Evening News*, Jan. 26, 1972. (The newspaper is not identified in the clipping preserved in Harrison's files. We are grateful to Robert Hughes for supplying this information.)

57. Tom Johnson, "Gifts from the East," *Village Voice*, Feb. 10, 1972.

58. Schmidt interview.

59. Doty interview.

60. Judith Becker, *Traditional Music in Modern Java: Gamelan in a Changing Society* (Honolulu: University Press of Hawaii, 1980).

61. Mantle Hood, *The Evolution of Javanese Gamelan*, Book 2: *The Legacy of the Roaring Sea* (New York: C. F. Peters, 1984), 125.

62. See, for example, the interview transcripts in Hood, ibid.

63. *The Music of K. R. T. Wasitodiningrat*, CMP CD 300, 1992.

64. From the introduction to the score in *Soundings* 10 (1976), where the three pieces appear under the title "Music for Kyai Hudan Mas."

65. Daniel Schmidt, personal communication.

66. Schmidt interview.

67. Becker, *Traditional Music in Modern Java*, 49.

68. Diamond interview.

69. The concerto was based on two pieces he had written for gamelan in 1981, *Gending Hephaestus* and *Ladrang Epikuros*, the first in slendro and the second in pelog. *Ladrang Epikuros* was transformed into the concerto's first movement, *Gending Hephaestus* into its finale.

70. Oct. 12–18; Harrison's presentation took place on Oct. 15. Essay published in *Third Asian Composers' League Conference/Festival Final Report*.

71. Arthur Bloomfield, "A Mournful but Upbeat Work," *San Francisco Examiner*, Dec. 8, 1975.

72. Paul Hertelendy, "A Harrison Symphony Takes Time and Love," *Oakland Tribune*, Dec. 7, 1975.

73. Scott MacClelland, "Keith Jarrett: Classical Piano Contender," *Monterey Peninsula Herald*, Sept. 1, 1982.

74. Jeff Hudson, "Smash Finish for Cabrillo Music Festival: New Harrison Symphony, Jarrett Piano Steal Show," *Capitola Green Sheet*, Sept. 1, 1982.

75. Paul Hertelendy, "Two Cabrillo Coups for Lou Harrison," *San Jose Mercury*, Aug. 23, 1982.

76. John Rockwell, "A Composer from the West Coast Looks to the Far East for Inspiration," *New York Times*, Nov. 1, 1990.

77. Paul Hertelendy, "The Last Version of the 'Last Symphony,'" *San Jose Mercury News*, Jan. 17, 1995.

78. Ibid. Davies used a tenor instead of a baritone for the Brooklyn premiere.

79. An article in the *San Jose Mercury* erroneously reported that he broke his nose and right wrist (Paul Hertelendy, "Composer Harrison Recuperating after Auto Accident," *San Jose Mercury*, Jan. 22, 1982).

80. Scholz played in the Mills College gamelan for the premiere of Harrison's *Concerto for Piano with Javanese Gamelan* in 1987.

81. Documents from the Office of the Dean at Mills confirm his employment from Sept. 2, 1980 to Dec. 23, 1980, as the Milhaud Professor of Music and from spring 1981 through the end of the 1982–83 academic year as Mary Woods Bennett Professor. The catalogue lists him as teaching in the music department in 1982–83 and 1983–84. It is not clear whether he continued to teach at Mills during the 1983–84 year or whether the catalog information is erroneous. The impetus for the honorary degree came from Larry Polansky.

82. Winant interview.

83. Harrison interview 3/8/94.

84. Freeman interview.

85. E. Ruth Anderson, *Contemporary American Composers: A Biographical Dictionary* (Boston: G. K. Hall, 1982), 490.

86. Freeman interview.

87. McDermott interview.

88. Ibid.

89. ASKI stands for Akademi Seni Karawitan Indonesia (Indonesian Academy of the Arts); STSI stands for Sekolah Tinggi Seni Indonesia (Indonesian College of the Arts).

90. Brown interview.

91. "'Young Ceasar' Fails," *Oregonian*, Apr. 10, 1988.

Chapter 4

1. Carl Philipp Emanuel Bach, *Versuch über die wahre Art das Clavier zu spielen* (Berlin, 1753 and 1762), ii, 325—26 (translated by Leta Miller).

2. Harrison, "Society, Musician, Dancer, Machine—a Set of Opinions Entirely Attributable to Lou Harrison, in 1966," *Impulse: Annual of Contemporary Dance* (1966): 41.

3. Harrison interview, 12/2/93.

4. Cited in Yates, oral history (UCLA Special Collections), 124, and in Crawford, *Evenings On and Off the Roof*, 61.

5. Harrison interview, 12/29/93.

6. Lewitzky interview.

7. Ibid.

8. Harrison, "Society, Musician, Dancer, Machine," 41.

9. Erdman interview.

10. Ibid.

11. By Broughton and Joel Singer (available on *The Films of James Broughton*, vol. 4).

12. In a version of this piece prepared in 1987, Lou made several changes including the number of repetitions of each part of the ostinato. The revised version is included on the compact disc *Lou Harrison: Rapunzel and Other Works* (New Albion, NA 093).

13. Erdman interview.

14. Lewitzky interview (condensed from a longer discussion).

15. Cunningham interview.

16. Harrison interview, 12/29/93.

17. Larry Simon, "Interview with Lou Harrison," *Ear Magazine of New Music* 9, no. 5 (Fall 1985): 18.

18. Harrison interview 1/13/94.

19. Information derived from the Dance Council's Festival Souvenir Program, May 17, 1936; from the Beals interview; and from Dorothy Walker, "Three Girls Pool Dance Ideas to Prepare Modern Ballet Fete," *San Francisco News*, Aug. 21, 1941. Beals studied with Graham in 1933—34, then returned to San Francisco and taught at the Peters-Wright School. For further information, see Miller, "The Art of Noise."

20. Harrison interview 12/29/93.

21. Beals interview.

22. Alfred Frankenstein, "Oakland Composer's Opera, 'Ming-Yi,' Presented Here," *San Francisco Chronicle*, Apr. 27, 1938. Frankenstein reported that there were two more acts following his departure, but the opera was in three acts, not four (program in Special Collections, UCSC).

23. Alfred Frankenstein, "'Park' Ballet: The Emphasis Is on the Modern Side," *San Francisco Chronicle*, Aug. 25, 1941. By spring 1942 Beals, Genkel, and Innes were advertising themselves as the "Modern Ballet Theater of San Francisco," with choreography by the three women and musical direction by Lou Harrison. (An advertisement on the back of the program for the May 7, 1942, percussion concert at the Holloway Playhouse announces that the group is "now booking for the coming season.")

24. For information on the strike, see *San Francisco: The Bay and Its Cities*. Compiled by Workers of the Writers' Program of the Work Projects Administration in Northern California (New York: Hastings House, 1947); Felix Riesenberg Jr., *Golden Gate: The Story of San Francisco Harbor* (New York: Knopf, 1940); and especially Mike Quin, *The Big Strike* (Olema, Calif.: Olema Publishing Company, 1949). Quin was a columnist, pamphleteer, and radio newscaster who witnessed or participated in the events he described. He completed his book soon after the strike, but it was not published until thirteen years later.

25. *San Francisco: The Bay and Its Cities*, 125.

26. The name was changed from Levy out of fear of anti-Semitism. Harrison dedicated a violin suite to him; see catalog, #90.14.

27. Beals later instructed Bridges's daughter in dance. For years after the strike, government officials vainly sought Bridges's deportation by trying to prove his Communist Party membership. Charles P. Larrowe, *Harry Bridges: The Rise and Fall of Radical Labor in the United States* (New York: Lawrence Hill, 1972); Estolv E. Ward, *Harry Bridges on Trial* (Honolulu: ILWU, 1940).

28. Harrison interview 12/29/93.

29. Dance Council Festival program, May 17, 1936. On Oct. 29, workers voted for a second strike that lasted ninety-nine days and ultimately resulted in the granting of most of their demands.

30. Dorothy James Russell interview.

31. Ibid.

32. Alfred Frankenstein, "Dancers Present Modernist Cycle," *San Francisco Examiner*, May 3, 1937.

33. Alfred Frankenstein, "Dance Recital Draws Throngs to Playhouse," *San Francisco Chronicle*, Nov. 17, 1937. The program, which took place at the Community Playhouse on Nov. 16, 1937, also included Van Gelder's "Dance toward Depth" and "Prelude, 1937," choreographed by Tina Flade and later published in the *New Music Quarterly* as *Prelude for Grandpiano* (see catalog #56).

34. On conflicting information regarding the dates of Lou's employment at Mills, see chapter 1. Harrison does not recall whether Cowell directly introduced him to Flade or whether he met her at one of Olive Cowell's house concerts.

35. Lewitzky interview.

36. Sali Ann Kriegsman, *Modern Dance in America: The Bennington Years* (Boston: G.K. Hall, 1981), 317–18.

37. Harrison interview 12/29/93.

38. On Herrmann, the daughter-in-law of photographer Edward Weston, see Bell-Kanner, *Frontiers*.

39. Course descriptions from the Mills College summer session brochure. See also "San Francisco Notes," *Dance Observer* 5, no. 2 (Feb. 1938): 29.

40. Anthony Tommasini, *Virgil Thomson: Composer on the Aisle* (New York: Norton, 1997), 368.

41. Larry Warren, *Lester Horton: Modern Dance Pioneer* (New York: Marcel Dekker, 1977), 70.

42. Ibid., 87.

43. Ibid., 72.

44. Harrison interview 10/21/94. *Conquest* was performed on Aug. 5, 1938 at Lisser Hall, Mills College. Horton later renamed the work *Tierra y Libertad* (the title of the last section). He performed it in Los Angeles with music by Gerhard Dorn, according to a review in the *Los Angeles Herald and Express*, Nov. 4, 1939.

45. Alfred Frankenstein, "At Mills—Strip Tease!" *San Francisco Chronicle*, July 8, 1940. This article does not appear on the *Chronicle* microfilm (not every edition of the paper was filmed). A copy of the review was graciously made available to us by Bella Lewitzky and her husband, Newell Reynolds.

46. "Horton Dance Group Takes Life Seriously," *Redlands Facts*, Aug. 31, 1940.

47. Frankenstein, "At Mills—Strip Tease!"

48. The Bennington School of Dance in Vermont operated from 1934 to 1942; only

one summer session took place at Mills. For a history of the school, see Kriegsman, *Modern Dance in America*.

49. Alfred Frankenstein, "A Program of Percussion," *San Francisco Chronicle*, July 28, 1939.

50. A review in the *Dance Observer* noted instrumentation of double bass, xylophone, drums, bells, and an amplified zither. See Esther Rosenblatt, "The 1940 Mills College Summer Session in Dance," *Dance Observer* 7, no. 7 (Aug./Sept. 1940): 100. Lou does not recall the amplified zither; nor does he have a score to this work, even though it was fully composed, not improvised.

51. Harrison interview 12/29/93.

52. Xenia Cage interview. Ricketts was the model for Doc in Steinbeck's *Cannery Row*. For detailed information on Campbell, see Stephen and Robin Larsen, *A Fire in the Mind: The Life of Joseph Campbell* (New York: Doubleday, 1991). See also *The Log from the* Sea of Cortez, by Steinbeck and E. F. Ricketts (N.Y.: Viking, 1951), particularly Steinbeck's foreward, "About Ed Ricketts."

53. Erdman interview. Revill, *Roaring Silence*, states that the Cages lived in the apartment along with the Campbells.

54. From videotape titled *Dance and Myth: The World of Jean Erdman*.

55. Von Gunden, *Lou Harrison*, lists "Creature on a Journey" as an independent work. The MOMA concert, sponsored by the League of Composers on Feb. 7, also included *Canticle #1*.

56. Erdman interview. Erdman continued to perform the dance frequently; some documented performances: Dec. 29, 1954, Honolulu Community Theatre; June 30, 1955, University of Colorado, Boulder; Feb. 1955, New Delhi and Baroda, India; Apr. 13, 1956, Davidson College, N.C.; May 3, 1956, State Teachers College, Towson, Md.; Jan. 4, 1957, Shorter College, Ga.; Oct. 23, 1957, Xavier University; Feb. 27, 1958, Skidmore College; July 21, 1959, University of British Columbia; June 24, 1960, Portland; March 15, 1971, Bronxville School.

57. Harrison, personal communication.

58. Letter, Jean Erdman to Leta Miller, Dec. 1, 1996.

59. Rorem interview. Lou doubts that he ever secured any money "down" but does recall deciding with Cage on a standard "per minute" fee. See Calvin Tomkins, *The Bride and the Bachelors* (New York: Penguin Books, 1962), 96.

60. Barab interview.

61. The *New York Times* announced the formation of her company on Dec. 19, 1948. Dancers in *The Perilous Chapel* were Erdman, Tao Strong, Billie Kirpich, Jacqueline Hairston, Rickie Fields, and Lillian Chasnoff.

62. Erdman's teaching methods are described in Doris Hering, "Jean Erdman Finds a New Approach to Dance," *Dance Magazine* (May 1950).

63. Harrison, interview by Rathbun ("Lou Harrison and His Music," 134).

64. The original score resulted from a Juilliard commissioning project that paired young choreographers with young composers, according to Erdman's assistant, Nancy Allison (personal communication).

65. Doris Hering, "Jean Erdman and Dance Company," *Dance Magazine* 25, no. 3 (March 1951): 43.

66. Erdman, personal communication.

67. From liner notes by Leta Miller to the compact disc recording of *Solstice* (MusicMasters MMD 60241X).

68. The title page of the score shows the word "Bound" crossed out and "Io and"

added above the word "Prometheus." (Von Gunden lists *Prometheus Bound* and *Io and Prometheus* as separate works.)

69. Harrison interview 12/29/93.

70. Hilmar Grondahl, "Summer Festival at Reed Opened by Dance Section," *Oregonian*, July 30, 1949.

71. Lou transformed the original chamber music version into an orchestral suite that was premiered by the Santa Cruz Symphony in 1961 ("SC Symphony Will Present Aptos Composer's Work," *Santa Cruz Sentinel,* Sept. 26, 1961).

72. Harold Schonberg, "Concert in Honor of Composers: Group Marks 40 Years with 3 Premieres on Program," *New York Times*, Feb. 8, 1977. (The concert celebrated the fortieth anniversary of the American Composers' Alliance.)

73. Hilmar Grondahl, "Reed Dances Prove Merit," *Oregonian*, July 29, 1950.

74. Erdman interview.

75. Harrison interview 12/29/93.

76. There is a fuller description in Harris, *Arts at Black Mountain College*, 210.

77. The video can be viewed at the New York Public Library dance collection: MGZIC 5-419.

78. *Musical America* 72, no. 2 (Jan. 15, 1952): 13.

79. Quotations in this paragraph from Tudor interview.

80. Quotations in this paragraph from Huss interview.

81. Harrison interview, 12/29/93.

82. Kranzler, "Reflections in Motion," 34.

83. Harrison, "Society, Musician, Dancer, Machine," 40.

84. Harrison, personal communication.

85. Harrison interview 12/29/93. Hawkins's performance was panned by Beatrice Gottlieb in *Dance News* 20, no. 3 (March 1952): 7: "Erick Hawkins' solo performance used every possible means of avoiding dance. . . . Hawkins is not a bad performer, but he surrounds himself with such a thick wall of pretentiousness it is very hard to get at what he is trying to do."

86. Harrison interview 12/29/93.

87. *New Grove Dictionary of Music and Musicians*, s.v. "India."

88. Soltes interview.

89. Quotes in the following paragraphs are from Morris interview.

90. For information on Morris and a works list, see Joan Acocella, *Mark Morris* (New York: Farrar, Straus and Giroux, 1993).

91. Lou took the text from Howard Zinn, *A People's History of the United States* (New York: Harper and Row, 1980). For further information on *Homage to Pacifica*, see chapter 9.

92. Morris interview.

93. Allan Ulrich, "Rare Collaboration Makes a Special Evening," *San Francisco Examiner*, Mar. 7, 1997.

94. Lewitzky interview.

95. Asked about this hypothesis, Lou responded that though it had not previously occurred to him, it might well be true (personal communication).

96. Harrison interview 1/13/94.

97. Ibid.

Chapter 5

1. A "pure" interval is beatless: the shared overtones of the two pitches vibrate at the same frequencies.

2. For a concise summary of intervals and interval theory, see the *New Harvard Dictionary of Music*, s.v. "Interval."

3. The Chinese acoustician Ching Fang (first century B.C.), using a ten-foot-long monochord, divided the octave into 60 pitches based on pure 3:2 fifths. By the fifth century A.D. Ch'ien Yüeh-chih had developed a system with 360 unique pitches within the octave. Additional experiments were made in China, including compromises with more or less effective temperament systems, leading eventually to an Equal Temperament by Prince Chu Tsai-yü in the late sixteenth century, later borrowed by Western theorists.

4. The "blues seventh," though it may approach a similar pitch, is an unstable expressive device arising from pitch bending rather than from the overtone series.

5. Although the tuning is described in many sources, Lou recommends as a practical guide G. C. Klop, *Harpsichord Tuning* (Garderen, Holland: Werkplaats voor Clavecimbelou, 1974, 22–23), where it is called "Kirnberger II" (Kirnberger I is not described). In practical terms, Kirnberger II and its cognates are relatively easy to tune in comparison to Equal Temperament. For further discussion, see Owen H. Jorgensen, *Tuning* (East Lansing: Michigan State University Press, 1991), chaps. 75–79.

6. Doty, "Lou Harrison Interview," 15. The article gives Kirnberger's system and instructions on how to tune it.

7. Oppens interview.

8. Harrison, personal communication.

9. Partch admitted prime numbers through eleven and their multiples, a somewhat arbitrary limit.

10. Albert Cohen, *Music in the French Royal Academy of Sciences: A Study in the Evolution of Musical Thought* (Princeton: Princeton University Press, 1981), 28.

11. Nicola Vicentino, *L'antica musica ridotta alla moderna prattica* (1555; facsimile ed., Kassel: Bärenreiter, 1959). Vicentino built both an arcicembalo and an arciorgano.

12. Salmon's demonstrations, on June 27 and July 3, 1705, are recorded in the *Journal Book* of the Royal Society, 10: 110–11. His paper describing the viol (with a detailed diagram) was published by the society: "The Theory of Musick Reduced to Arithmetical and Geometrical Proportions," *Philosophical Transactions of the Royal Society of London* 24, no. 302 (Aug. 1705): seven nonconsecutively numbered pages: 2072, 2069, 2041, 2080, 2076, 2073, 2077. See Leta E. Miller and Albert Cohen, *Music in the Royal Society of London, 1660–1806*, Detroit Studies in Music Bibliography 56 (Detroit: Information Coordinators, 1987).

13. Harrison, personal communication.

14. Harrison, *Music Primer*, 110–17.

15. Harrison interview 1/13/94.

16. Doty, "Lou Harrison Interview," 2.

17. Ibid.

18. Harrison interview 2/10/94. (Alain Daniélou's book was published in London in 1943.)

19. Ajemian interview.

20. Wigglesworth interview.

21. This data follows Chalmers, *Divisions of the Tetrachord*, 8–9.

22. Lou also used tetrachords as a basic compositional parameter in the *Suite for Cello and Harp*. See Rathbun, "Lou Harrison and His Music," 110–11.

23. Lou Harrison, "Blessed Be Translators, for They Give Us Worlds," *1/1: The Journal of the Just Intonation Network* 7, no. 1 (Sept. 1991): 4 (reprinted in *Music Primer*, 2d ed., 136).

24. 8/7 x 7/6 = 4/3; 4/3 x 9/8 x 4/3 = 2/1. Harrison describes this tuning in Doty, "Lou Harrison Interview," and in "Blessed Be Translators."

25. Harrison, *Music Primer* (2d. ed.), 141.

26. The manifesto, preserved in the Virgil Thomson archives at Yale, is printed in its entirety in Von Gunden, *Lou Harrison*, 162–65.

27. Chalmers, *Tetrachord*, xiii.

28. Wilson has patented two non-twelve-tone keyboards and done extensive theoretical work on keyboard design (John Chalmers, personal communication 7/22/96).

29. Harrison interview 2/10/94.

30. Harrison, *Music Primer* (2d. ed.), 143; reprinted in Chalmers, *Tetrachord*, x.

31. Harrison, foreword to Chalmers, *Tetrachord*.

32. The difference between Free Style and Strict Style is described by Larry Polansky, "Item: Lou Harrison's Role as a Speculative Theorist," in Garland, *Lou Harrison Reader*, 92.

33. Harrison, Introduction to the score of *Simfony* (New York: C. F. Peters, 1977).

34. Since there is no industrywide standard, each synthesizer requires recalculating the same basic tuning data into its own format.

35. Doty interview.

36. Ibid.

37. Introductory notes to the manuscript score of the *Political Primer* recitatives.

38. Harrison interview 2/10/94.

39. Subsequently published in *Xenharmonikon* and *Ear* (see catalog #210)

40. Lou Harrison, interview by Rathbun ("Lou Harrison and His Music," 62).

41. Harrison interview 2/10/94. The curriculum of the medieval university was comprised of seven courses, divided into three literary subjects, the trivium (grammar, rhetoric, and logic) and four scientific subjects, the quadrivium (arithmetic, geometry, music, and astronomy.)

42. The tuning is described by Bill Colvig in Rathbun, "Lou Harrison and His Music," 149–50, and Gardner, "La Koro Sutro," 121.

43. Harrison interview 1/31/94. Lou tells the same story and describes the tunings in Doty, "Lou Harrison Interview."

44. Harrison interview 1/31/94.

45. Harrison interview 2/10/94.

46. Actually, only thirty-eight measures in the last section of the slow movement are in harmonics.

47. Harrison interview 2/10/94. According to legend, Pythagoras first discovered the proportional ratios of perfect intervals.

48. Lou Harrison, videotape of lecture at the University of Utah, Nov. 1993.

49. Harrison interview 2/10/94.

50. Wilfrid Mellers, *Percy Grainger* (Oxford: Oxford University Press, 1992), 153.

Chapter 6

1. Kraft interview.

2. David Chadwick, *Thank You and OK!: An American Zen Failure in Japan* (New York: Penguin, 1994), 111.

3. Bells are instruments with vibrating rims or lips, suspended from or resting on a

nonvibrating center. Gongs, by contrast, vibrate most in the center, and may rest on or be suspended from edges or rims.

4. Colvig interview 5/20/95.

5. There are a few exceptions, such as the orchestral transcriptions of *La Koro Sutro* and the *Suite for Violin and American Gamelan*.

6. Harrison interview 1/13/94.

7. Harrison interview 10/21/94.

8. Heuwell Tircuit,"A Bacchanal Bravo for 'Labyrinth No. 3,'" *San Francisco Chronicle*, Aug. 29, 1967.

9. Rathbun, "Lou Harrison and His Music," 50.

10. Don Baker's analysis of *Labyrinth* shows that the ninety-four instruments of the ensemble are nearly equally divided between what he calls "wet" and "dry" sounds ("The Percussion Ensemble Music of Lou Harrison, 1939–1942," D.M.A. thesis, University of Illinois, 1985, 86).

11. Harrison interview 5/20/95.

12. Alfred Frankenstein, "Music: A Recital on Percussion Instruments," *San Francisco Chronicle*, May 8, 1942.

13. Hughes interview 1/14/96.

14. Dennison subsequently taught in the dance department at Mills College for many years.

15. Dennison interview.

16. Harrison, "Percussion Music and Its Relation to the Modern Dance," 32.

17. Harrison interview 1/13/94.

18. Harrison, interview by Rathbun ("Lou Harrison and His Music," 30).

19. Remarks to the audience preceding performance of *Canticle #3* by the San Francisco Symphony, Feb. 1996.

20. Harrison interview 1/13/94.

21. Oliver Daniel, *Stokowski: A Counterpoint of View* (New York: Dodd, Mead, 1982), 578.

22. Tom Johnson, "First Chair Sweet Potato," *Village Voice*, Nov. 22, 1973; John Kraglund, "Array Concert Sheds Light on New Music," June 1980; Benjamin Permick, review of recording of *Canticle #3* et al., *Fanfare*, Sept./Oct. 1990; Thomas Albright, "The Weird and Wonderful in Classical Music," *San Francisco Chronicle*, Feb. 9, 1958.

23. Score in Fleisher Music Collection, Free Library of Philadelphia.

24. Harrison interview 10/21/94.

25. Cowell, "Drums along the Pacific," 47.

26. Xenia Cage interview.

27. Cowell, "Drums along the Pacific."

28. Alfred Frankenstein, "Music and Art in New York," *San Francisco Chronicle*, Nov. 29, 1959.

29. Thomas, personal communication.

30. Harrison interview 1/13/94.

31. Frank Wilson, "Home Entertainment: His Is a Rare Classical Tune," *Philadelphia Inquirer*, May 14, 1992.

32. Kraft interview.

33. "Make Music with Pipes, Pots, Cans," *Watsonville Register-Pajaronian*. Aug. 19, 1965.

34. Soltes interview.

35. San Francisco Symphony, Feb. 1996; Harrison, personal communication.

36. Notes to the recording by the Oakland Youth Orchestra, Robert Hughes, conductor (Phoenix 118).

37. Lou was working out this solution at the time of his interviews with Rathbun in 1973 (Rathbun, "Lou Harrison and His Music," 48–49).

38. Patrice Maginnis, personal communication.

39. Letter dated Jan. 17, 1953 (Wigglesworth personal papers).

40. Kathleen Schlesinger, *The Greek Aulos* (London: Methuen, 1939).

41. Letter, Harrison to Wigglesworth, May 29, 1953.

42. Letter, Harrison to Charles Fahs, Library of Congress Music Division, ML95.H289.

43. Colvig interview 4/19/94.

44. Colvig interview 5/16/94.

45. Many of Colvig's instruments are described in Sasha Bogdanowitsch, "Instruments by Bill Colvig," *Experimental Musical Instruments* 9, no. 4 (June 1994): 16–20; excellent photographs are included.

46. Garland, *Lou Harrison Reader*, 66–68.

Chapter 7

1. Harrison interview 5/16/94.

2. Ibid.

3. Ibid.

4. Lou Harrison, class lecture at San Jose State University (undated tape in Harrison's archive).

5. Harrison interview 5/16/94.

6. Ibid.

7. We would like to thank Robert Provine for providing details about the Confucian ceremonies (personal communication to Fred Lieberman, Dec. 1996).

8. Robert Provine, translator's introduction to Lee Hye-Ku, *Essays on Korean Traditional Music*, xiii.

9. The quotation is complete as given and is a typical Asian literary device: an elliptical reference that the reader must complete ("What's in a name? That which we call a rose / By any other name would smell as sweet": Shakespeare, *Romeo and Juliet*, II,ii,43). Actually, the Koreans have all the various names sorted out. There's the elegant name and the popular name, plus all the names assigned in various contexts for various purposes. (Robert Provine, personal communication, Dec. 1996.)

10. Liang Ming-yüeh, *Music of the Billion: An Introduction to Chinese Musical Culture* (New York: Hinrichshofen, 1985), 163.

11. R. H. van Gulik, "Brief Note on the Cheng, the Chinese Small Cither," *Journal of the Society for Research in Asiatic Music* 9 (Mar. 1951): 10–25. Long out of print, the *Ni Cheng Pu* was included in a photographic reprint as an appendix to the eleventh edition (1986) of Liang's *Music of the Cheng*.

12. "Liang on the Ku-Cheng," *Time*, Apr. 1, 1946.

13. Printed in Liang Tsai-Ping, ed., *On Chinese Music* (Taipei: Chinese Classical Music Association, 1964), n.p.

14. The cheng may have originated in the larger zither called *se*. Some legends tell of two sisters whose quarrel over an instrument prompted their father to cut it in two, thus creating the smaller version of the instrument, one with about sixteen strings.

15. Harrison interview 5/16/94.

16. Old Spaghetti Factory, Nov. 15, 1964.

17. Harrison interview 5/16/94.

18. Note the differing spellings, *Pacifika Rondo* versus *Homage to Pacifica*. The first is Lou's preferred Esperanto; the second refers to the Pacifica Foundation, for which this work was composed.

19. Harrison interview 5/16/94.

20. Dee interview.

21. Harrison interview 5/16/94.

22. Ibid.

23. Ming-yüeh's performance is recorded on Lyrichord LL 92.

24. Dee interview.

25. Harrison interview 5/16/94.

26. Dee interview.

27. Harrison, personal communication 5/30/97.

28. Harrison interview 5/16/94.

29. May 1963 festival program.

30. Harrison interview 5/16/94.

Chapter 8

1. Harrison interview 3/8/94.

2. For more information, see Claire Holt, *Art in Indonesia: Continuities and Change* (Ithaca: Cornell University Press, 1967).

3. Sumarsam, *Gamelan: Cultural Interaction and Musical Development in Central Java* (Chicago: University of Chicago Press, 1995), 2.

4. Ibid., 131.

5. See, for example, Neil Sorrell, *A Guide to the Gamelan* (London: Faber and Faber, 1990); Paul Griffiths, ed., *The Thames and Hudson Encyclopaedia of 20th-Century Music* (N.Y.: Thames and Hudson, 1986); and Robert Johnson, *Messiaen* (Berkeley: University of California Press, 1975).

6. Schmidt built and directed the Berkeley Gamelan; Benary directs the New York-based Gamelan Son of Lion, which included many composers among its regular members (e.g., Dika Newlin, Larry Polansky, Philip Corner). Newlin wrote "Machine Shop," a short jeux d'esprit that brings to mind one of Luigi Russolo's futurist "noise" pieces, "suggested by the sounds of presses, paper-punchers, electric staplers, and electric comb binders in the print shop of Beneficial Management, Morristown, N.J." (*Gamelan in the New World*, vols. 1 and 2 [Folkways FTS 31312 and 31313, 1979 and 1982], liner notes). Totally non-Indonesian, but fun for both performers and audience, it is one of the more frequently performed works in the American gamelan repertory. Is it chance that Newlin and Harrison, the two young composers Arnold Schoenberg singled out in his 1945 letter to Roy Harris as America's most promising, should eventually write experimental works for gamelan? John Cage also wrote for gamelan in *Haiki*, where he calls for bowed bonang pots and other extended techniques.

7. "Nano S" is short for Nano Suratno (liner notes to *New Music Indonesia*, Vol. 1, Lyrichord, LYRCD 7415).

8. Becker, *Traditional Music in Modern Java*, 102.

9. Harrison interview 3/8/94. We have not been able to pinpoint who these visiting Indonesians were.

10. Ibid.

11. Ibid.

12. His formal name is Elang Muhammad Yuwana Yusuf.

13. Diamond interview.

14. *Colotomy* is a term coined by Jaap Kunst to describe a procedure in which sections are delineated by rhythmic punctuation.

15. This departure may also affect perception of *pathet* (discussed later), which some theorists link to kinetic factors on single octave instruments as well as to other aural factors.

16. Harrison interview 3/8/94.

17. On this aspect of gamelan performance, see Benjamin Brinner, *Knowing Music, Making Music: Javanese Gamelan and the Theory of Musical Competence and Interaction* (Chicago: University of Chicago Press, 1995), 213–17.

18. Diamond interview.

19. Polansky interview.

20. "Gamelan Builders' Notes from Lou Harrison and William Colvig," *Ear* 8, no. 4 (1983): 26.

21. Ibid.

22. Harrison interview 3/8/94. Although the current spelling is "gendhing," Lou uses the older form, which we maintain in his titles.

23. Ibid.

24. *Nibani* and *mlaku* are the corresponding Solonese terms.

25. Sorrell, *Guide to the Gamelan*, 68.

26. Harrison interview 3/8/94.

27. Sorrell, *Guide to the Gamelan*, 58.

28. Sumarsam, *Gamelan*, 135.

29. McDermott interview.

30. Harrison, personal communication.

31. Sorrell, *Guide to the Gamelan*, 134.

32. Unique "treatments" of tempo, rhythmic development, and irama level negotiation are found in gamelan music from Semarang, one of Harrison's interests. See R. Anderson Sutton, *Traditions of Gamelan Music in Java: Musical Pluralism and Regional Identity* (Cambridge: Cambridge University Press, 1991).

33. Sumarsam, *Gamelan*, 233.

34. Diamond interview.

35. Thomson, "World of Lou Harrison," 7.

36. McDermott interview.

37. Harrison interview 3/8/94.

Chapter 9

1. Lin Yutang, trans. and ed., *The Wisdom of Confucius* (New York: Random House, 1938), ch. 10, "On Music," 252 (selection from the music chapter of the "Book of Rites" [*Li Chi*]).

2. Ibid., 254

3. Plato, *Timaeus* 47; trans. Desmond Lee

4. Plato, *Laws* 2: 654, and 669b-c, trans. A. E. Taylor.

5. Lester del Rey's *Nerves* first appeared in *Astounding* in September 1942 (Paul Brians, *Nuclear Holocausts: Atomic War in Fiction, 1895–1984* [Kent, Ohio: Kent State University Press, 1987], 8).

6. David L. Brunner, "Cultural Diversity in the Choral Music of Lou Harrison," *Choral Journal* (May 1992): 20; confirmed by Harrison, personal communication.

7. Harrison interviews 2/10/94 and 10/21/94.

8. Harrison interview 4/3/95.

9. *Souvenir History of Salem, Ohio, 1806–1906*, quoted in Silver and Silver, *Our Silver Heritage*, 5201.

10. For a discussion of this work (as well as the score), see Leta E. Miller, ed. *Lou Harrison: Keyboard and Chamber Music, 1937–1994*, in *Music in the United States of America* (Madison, WI: A-R Editions, forthcoming).

11. Beals interview; Lenore Peters Job, *Looking Back While Surging Forward* (San Francisco: Peters Wright Creative Dance, 1984), especially pp. 89–99.

12. McGowan interview.

13. Malina interview.

14. Rathbun, "Lou Harrison and His Music," 65. The bell accompaniment for the Gloria survives in a notebook; the percussion accompaniment for the Kyrie has not yet been found.

15. Ibid., 143–44.

16. Lou Harrison, lecture at the University of Utah, November 1993.

17. Harrison, Introduction to the *Political Primer*, in *Frog Peak Anthology* (Hanover, N.H.: Frog Peak Music, 1992), 78.

18. Ibid., 81. Harrison envisioned the musical composition as having three sections, one for each form of government, each comprising an overture with recitatives and choruses. He completed the three overtures, which were later incorporated into his *Elegiac* and *Third Symphonies*, and the recitatives, which were performed in 1959 in Buffalo. The choruses were never written.

19. Hughes interview 12/12/94.

20. Ralph Engelman, *Public Radio and Television in America: A Political History* (Thousand Oaks, Calif.: Sage Publications, 1996), 44–45. The Pacifica Foundation was incorporated in 1946, and KPFA went on the air in 1949.

21. Transcribed from a tape of the lecture in Harrison's archive.

22. Quoted in full in Von Gunden, *Lou Harrison*, 162–65.

23. Harrison took the text from a letter to the *San Francisco Chronicle* by Cindy Weaver.

24. Harrison interview 10/21/94. Lou composed *In Memory of Victor Jowers* for clarinet and piano, and it was performed at the Unitarian Fellowship memorial service on Nov. 19, 1967.

25. *Peace Pieces 1* and *2* had been premiered at the First Unitarian Church of Berkeley on Apr. 7, 1968, in a concert of "Music and Words of War." Also on the program was Ives's "He Is There," which Lou had edited in New York (chapter 2). *Peace Piece 3* ("Little Song on the Atom Bomb") was composed in 1953 and incorporated into the trilogy for the Cabrillo Festival performance.

26. The text is from the Metta Sutta, and the work is dedicated to Martin Luther King Jr.

27. Robert Duncan, "Up Rising, Passages 25," in *Bending the Bow* (1968). See Robert J. Bertholf, ed., *Robert Duncan: Selected Poems* (New York: New Directions Books, 1993), 92–94. (By permission of the literary estate of Robert Duncan.)

28. Arthur Bloomfield, "Doves Win Music Festival Decibel Poll," *San Francisco Examiner*, Aug. 20, 1968.

29. Ibid. We would like to thank Robert Hughes, who was a member of the orchestra, for clarifying the source of the comment.

30. Robert Commanday, "Harrison 'Peace Pieces' Stir Cabrillo Festival," *San Francisco Chronicle*, Aug. 20, 1968.

31. Titles respectively from: *Oakland Tribune*, Aug. 19, 1968 (Paul Hertelendy); *San*

Francisco Chronicle, Aug. 20, 1968 (Robert Commanday); *San Jose Mercury*, Aug. 19, 1968 (unsigned); *Watsonville Register-Pajaronian*, Aug. 23, 1968 (Bob Levy); *Santa Cruz Sentinel*, Aug. 19, 1968 (Dale Jarvis); *San Francisco Examiner*, Aug. 20, 1968 (Arthur Bloomfield).

32. Paul Hertelendy, "Festival Recital," *Oakland Tribune*, Aug. 19, 1968.

33. Harrison, introductory notes to the published score of *Suite for Symphonic Strings* (New York: C. F. Peters, 1961).

34. Harrison, "From: Lou Harrison's Bureau for the Consideration of Pathetic Complaints: A Prospectus for Musicians (Department of Utopian Fantasy)," *American Composers' Alliance Bulletin* 6, no. 2 (1957): 14, 22. Harrison also discusses the problem of the artist's lack of ownership of his/her work in "Society, Musician, Dancer, Machine," 40.

35. Lecture, University of Utah, Nov. 1993.

36. Harrison interview 1/13/94.

37. Harrison, "Society, Musician, Dancer, Machine," 40.

38. Dorothy Walker, "Three Girls Pool Dance Ideas to Prepare Modern Ballet Fete," *San Francisco News*, Aug. 21, 1941, 10.

39. Harrison's "Letter to a Critic" (responding to Commanday's article, "Western Confusion of Asian Music," *San Francisco Chronicle*, Apr. 7) appeared in the *Sunday Examiner and Chronicle* on Apr. 28, 1968, along with Commanday's response, "Enrichment from Another Stream."

40. The excerpt is not from Seattle's famous speech to territorial governor Isaac Stevens but from an 1854 letter to President Franklin Pierce, most likely written by Dr. Henry Smith, though purportedly conveying Seattle's words. See David M. Buerge, "The Man We Call Seattle," in *Washingtonians: A Biographical Portrait of the State*, ed. David Brewster and David Buerge (Seattle: Sasquatch Books, 1988): 97–114.

Chapter 10

1. Mark Levine, "Annals of Composing: The Outsider: Lou Harrison Comes In from the Fringe," *New Yorker*, Aug. 26/Sept. 2, 1996, 155.

2. Harrison, personal communication.

3. H. G. Wells, *The Outline of History*, chap. 40.

4. Lawrence Mass, "A Conversation with Ned Rorem," in Philip Brett, Elizabeth Wood, and Gary C. Thomas, eds., *Queering the Pitch* (New York: Routledge, 1994), 110.

5. Lewitzky interview.

6. Among recent significant books, we might highlight Brett et al., *Queering the Pitch*; Ruth A. Solie, ed., *Musicology and Difference: Gender and Sexuality in Music Scholarship* (Berkeley and Los Angeles: University of California Press, 1993); Susan McClary, *Feminine Endings: Music, Gender, and Sexuality* (Minneapolis: University of Minnesota Press, 1991); Corinne E. Blackmer and Patricia Juliana Smith, *En Travesti: Women, Gender Subversion, Opera* (New York: Columbia University Press, 1995); John Gill, *Queer Noises: Male and Female Homosexuality in Twentieth-Century Music* (London: Cassell, 1995); and Jeffrey Kallberg, *Chopin at the Boundaries: Sex, History, and Musical Genre* (Cambridge: Harvard University Press, 1996).

7. Philip Brett, "Eros and Orientalism in Britten's Operas," in Brett et al., *Queering the Pitch*, 235–56. For more on the connotations of "Orientalism," see Edward W. Said, *Orientalism* (New York: Pantheon, 1978).

8. Stuart Norman, "Profiles/Interviews: Lou Harrison and William Colvig," *RFD: A Journal for Gay Men Everywhere* (Winter 1987–88): 60.

9. Harrison interview 4/19/94.

10. Ibid. For a discussion of camp, see Susan Sontag, "Notes on 'Camp,'" in *Against Interpretation and Other Essays* (New York: Farrar, Straus and Giroux, 1966), 275—92. Among the recent articles on Schubert, we should particularly cite Susan McClary's provocative essay "Constructions of Subjectivity in Schubert's Music," in Brett et al., *Queering the Pitch*, 205—34, and several articles by Maynard Solomon: "Franz Schubert's 'My Dream,'" *American Imago* 38, no. 2 (Summer 1981): 137—54, reprinted in Wayne R. Dynes and Stephen Donaldson, eds., *Homosexuality and Homosexuals in the Arts* (New York: Garland, 1992), 285—302; and "Franz Schubert and the Peacocks of Benvenuto Cellini," *19th-Century Music* 12, no. 3 (Spring 1989): 193—206. Additional sources are cited in McClary, "Constructions of Subjectivity."

11. Rorem interview.

12. Ibid.

13. Harrison, personal communication, 5/30/97.

14. For a recent study of the issue, see Kallberg, *Chopin at the Boundaries*.

15. Eve Kosofsky Sedgwick, *Epistemology of the Closet* (Berkeley and Los Angeles: University of California Press, 1990), 87. She contrasts it with the equally prevalent model of separatism.

16. Robert Helps, quoted in liner notes to the recording *Gay American Composers* (CRI 721), 1996.

17. J. Michele Edwards, personal communication.

18. For example, Sedgwick, *Epistemology of the Closet*, 91—130; and Robert K. Martin, *Hero, Captain, and Stranger: Male Friendship, Social Critique, and Literary Form in the Sea Novels of Herman Melville* (Chapel Hill: University of North Carolina Press, 1986).

19. Sedgwick, *Epistemology of the Closet*, 96.

20. Giteck interview.

21. See, for instance, Jennifer Rycenga, "Lesbian Compositional Process: One Lover-Composer's Perspective," in Brett et al., *Queering the Pitch*, 275—96, but also the critique of this essay by Ruth Solie in the *Journal of the American Musicological Society* 48, no. 2 (Summer 1995): 311—23.

22. Rorem interview.

23. Davies interview.

24. Harrison, "Literature: All about Music," *View* 6, no. 1 (Feb. 1946): 17.

25. Harrison, personal communication.

26. Malina interview.

27. Letter, Lou Harrison to Bill Harrison, Sept. 1943 (composer's personal papers).

28. Harrison, personal communication 5/30/97.

29. Harrison interview 4/19/94.

30. Rhonda Rivera, "Homosexuality and the Law," in *Homosexuality: Social, Psychological, and Biological Issues*, ed. William Paul, James D. Weinrich, John C. Gonsiorek, and Mary E. Hotvedt (Beverly Hills, Calif: Sage Publications, 1982), 324. The Model Penal Code was adopted by the Illinois legislature in 1961, effective Jan. 1, 1962.

31. David J. Thomas, "San Francisco's 1979 White Night Riot: Injustice, Vengeance, and Beyond," in Paul et al., *Homosexuality: Social, Psychological, and Biological Issues*, 337.

32. For a history of this period, see John D'Emilio, "Gay Politics, Gay Community: San Francisco's Experience," *Socialist Review* 11 (1981): 77—104; reprinted in Wayne R. Dynes and Stephen Donaldson, *History of Homosexuality in Europe and America* (New York: Garland, 1992), 85—104; and Susan Stryker and Jim Van Buskirk, *Gay by the Bay: A History of Queer Culture in the San Francisco Bay Area* (San Francisco: Chronicle Books, 1996).

33. D'Emilio, "Gay Politics, Gay Community," 89.

34. Ibid.

35. See *The Challenge and Progress of Homosexual Law Reform* (San Francisco: The Council on Religion and the Homosexual, the Daughters of Bilitis, the Society for Individual Rights, and the Tavern Guild of San Francisco, 1968).

36. Norman, "Profiles/Interviews," 67.

37. Harrison, personal communication.

38. Harrison interview 4/19/94.

39. Robert Duncan, "The Homosexual in Society," *Politics* 1 (Aug. 1944): 209-11.

40. Robert J. Bertholf, ed., *Robert Duncan: A Selected Prose* (New York: New Directions Books, 1995), 43.

41. Ibid., 38.

42. A case can be, and has been, made for the homoerotic content of several operas by Benjamin Britten, especially *Billy Budd* and *Death in Venice* (1973). The latter, in any case, postdates *Young Caesar*. See Brett, "Eros and Orientalism in Britten's Operas." For another treatment of gender issues in operatic history, see Blackmer and Smith, *En Travesti*.

43. Harrison, personal communication.

44. Although the San Francisco chorus was the first to use the word *gay* in its name, it was not the first gay chorus in the nation. Matthew W. Wise, in a forthcoming article, "Choruses and Marching Bands" (*Garland Encyclopedia of Homosexuality*, 2d ed., vol. 2: *Gay Histories and Cultures*, ed. George Haggerty) mentions two New York groups, "Women Like Me" (a lesbian chorus) and the "Gotham Male Chorus," which was founded in late 1977 and became (after inviting women to join in 1980) "the nation's first lesbian and gay chorus, the Stonewall Chorale." Wise also mentions "Anna Crusis" in Philadelphia (founded by a lesbian), an "early feminist choir." We are indebted to Philip Brett for bringing this information to our attention.

45. Brown interview.

46. Ibid.

47. Letter, Harrison to Brown, June 16, 1985.

48. Letter, Harrison to Brown, Apr. 20, 1988.

49. Brown interview.

50. David Stabler, "'Young Caesar' Fails Despite Noble Narrator, Dancers," *Oregonian*, Apr. 10, 1988.

51. Letter, Gay Men's Chorus to Lou Harrison, Apr. 20, 1988 (courtesy of Richard Brown).

52. "New Rose and Gay Men's Chorus Roll the Dice with Two Daring Productions," *The Downtowner* (a mainstream weekly), Apr. 16, 1988; Harold Moore, "Great Queers of History: With the Stretch to *Young Caesar* the Portland Gay Men's Chorus Establishes Itself as a Performance Vehicle Beyond Expectations," *Just Out*, May 1988; Dr. Tantalus, "Bithynia or Bust: Musical Growth Is Accomplished Not by Treading Familiar Paths, but by Venturing in the Unknown," *Just Out*, May 1988; "Lou Harrison's Gay Opera, *Young Caesar,* Is a Sensuous Masterwork about Love and Loss," *The Advocate*, Sept. 13, 1988.

53. Norman, "Profiles/Interviews," 67 (date erroneously given as 1977). The initiative, Proposition 6, was sponsored by state senator John Briggs (R-Fullerton). It appeared on the California ballot on Nov. 7, 1978, but was defeated by 58 percent of those voting.

54. Ibid., 66. Lou and Bill were also grand marshals of a gay pride parade in 1992.

55. Letter, Lou Harrison to the editor of *Ka Leo O Hawaii*, May 10, 1963 (private collection of Fredric Lieberman).

Chapter 11

1. Harrison, *Music Primer* 117–18, 121–22.

2. Thomson, "World of Lou Harrison," 7; also in Garland, *Lou Harrison Reader*, 86.

3. Hughes interview 1/14/96 (condensed from a longer discussion).

4. Harrison, *Music Primer*, 100.

5. Marta Morgan, "Composer Puts a 'Sense of Play' in His Music," *San Jose Mercury News*, Aug. 2, 1976.

6. Rorem interview.

7. Daniel Cariaga, "Bay Area Trio Closes Monday Concerts' 50th Season," *Los Angeles Times*, May 4, 1988.

8. Rathbun, "Lou Harrison and His Music," 86.

9. The movement is a revision of the "Song" from the *Symphony on G*.

10. Davies interview.

11. Donald Fuller, "Russian and American Season, 1945," *Modern Music* 22, no. 4 (May–June 1945): 257; Mildred Norton, "Music Review," unidentified Los Angeles paper, April 1948 (Harrison's personal papers).

12. Virgil Thomson, "Music," *New York Herald Tribune*, Jan. 27 and 28, 1947.

13. Harrison interview 4/3/95.

14. Quotations in this paragraph are from Harrison, *About Carl Ruggles*. For more information on Ruggles's compositional procedures, see Ziffrin, *Carl Ruggles*, and Charles Seeger's article in Cowell, *American Composers on American Music*.

15. Copland's *Piano Quartet* of 1950, based on an eleven-tone row, is commonly credited as his first serial work.

16. Giteck interview.

17. Heinrich Christoph Koch, *Versuch einer Anleitung zur Composition* (Leipzig: Adam Friedrich Böhme, 1787).

18. C. P. E. Bach, *Versuch über die wahre Art das Clavier zu spielen*, final chapter of part 2 (1762).

19. Harrison interview 5/26/94.

20. Doty interview.

21. Hughes interview 12/12/94. John Cage taught his students by similar methods, assigning them, for instance, an exercise to create an extended composition using only two notes as the melodic material (Cage, personal communication to Lieberman). Most likely both Cage and Harrison followed the pedagogical example of Henry Cowell.

22. Harrison, *About Carl Ruggles*, 8 (Garland, *Lou Harrison Reader*, 40; *Score* 12:16)

23. Harrison, *Music Primer*, 96.

24. Lou Harrison and William Winant, personal communication.

25. CD recording: New Albion Records 093.

26. Harrison, personal communication. He discusses jhālā in the *Music Primer*, 123.

27. Harrison, "Alan Hovhaness Offers Original Compositions," *New York Herald Tribune*, June 18, 1945.

28. Hovhaness interview.

29. Harrison interview 10/21/94.

30. Harrison, "Music for the Modern Dance," *American Composers' Alliance Bulletin* 2, no. 3 (1952): 11–12.

31. Harrison, "Creative Ideas in Classical Korean Music," *Korea Journal* 2, no. 11 (1962): 34.

32. Frank Wilson, "Home Entertainment: His Is a Rare Classical Tune," *Philadelphia Inquirer*, May 14, 1992.

33. Letter, Cowell to Harrison, Dec. 16, 1953. Cowell and Frank Wigglesworth played percussion in the 1941 premiere.

34. Tim Page, "Concert: New Music Consort," *New York Times*, Jan. 20, 1984.

35. Harrison, interview by Rathbun ("Lou Harrison and His Music," 130).

36. Harrison interview 5/26/94.

37. Alan Rich, "Philharmonic Cleans Up with a Washtub Concerto," *Los Angeles Herald Examiner*, Mar. 9, 1988.

38. Harrison interview 10/21/94.

39. The *conductus* appears in the *Suite for Piano* (1943); the *ductia* (a short estampie) in the *Suite for Symphonic Strings* (1960), *Rhymes with Silver* (1996), and *Jahla in the Form of a Ductia to Pleasure Leopold Stokowski on his Ninetieth Birthday* (1972). Variation forms appear in numerous works.

40. Lewis Turco, *The Book of Forms* (New York: Dutton, 1968); rev. ed., *The New Book of Forms* (Hanover, N.H.: University Press of New England, 1986).

41. Terza rima form in the fourth movement of *Labyrinth #3* (1941) is discussed in Baker, "Percussion Ensemble Music of Lou Harrison."

42. For example, in Harrison, *Music Primer*, 105.

43. Ibid., 106.

44. Harrison, unpublished interview with Mary E. Harris, Jan. 5, 1972, quoted in Rathbun, "Lou Harrison and His Music," 147.

45. For a fuller discussion, see Miller, "The Art of Noise."

46. Richard Dyer, "Composer Lou Harrison Brings a Diverse Background to His Music," *Boston Globe*, Oct. 16, 1988.

47. RCA LM-1785; CRI-114: Anahid and Maro Ajemian; Leopold Stokowski, cond.

48. Hughes interview 12/12/94.

49. Davies interview.

50. Interview, United Airlines in-flight audio program, Nov. 1988.

51. Alexander Fried, "Lou Harrison's Aptos Triumph," *San Francisco Examiner*, Aug. 25, 1964. In 1966, the symphony was strengthened by a new sonata-rondo finale, a product of Lou's stay in Mexico.

52. Paul Hertelendy, "The Time of His Life: Composer Harrison Notes Birthday with His Music," *San Jose Mercury News*, May 9, 1982.

53. Giteck interview.

54. Harrison, personal communication.

55. Daniel L. Farber, "Dennis Russell Davies Comes to the BSO," *The Jewish Advocate*, Oct. 27, 1988.

Chapter 12

1. Quotations in this paragraph from Harrison interview 9/30/94.

2. Parmenter interview.

3. Olin Downes, "Stokowski Conducts Final Concert of WNYC's Annual Music Festival," *New York Times*, Feb. 23, 1953. Thomson review quoted in Oliver Daniel, "Alchemy by Stokowski," *American Composers' Alliance Bulletin* 3, no. 1 (Spring 1953): 6–7.

4. Parmenter interview.

5. Ibid.

6. Ibid.

7. Harrison interview 9/30/94. He doesn't recall which review led to this episode.

8. He reviewed the same group performing the same work a year earlier (Mar. 28,

1945) and similarly remarked about the "gigantic" chorus, which "was well unified and clear, though some old fuddy-duds, including this reporter, would question the use of so splendiferous an aggregate of music makers in the rendition of the work." At this point in his career, however, he complimented the use of the tack-piano, finding it preferable to the modern piano.

9. Letter, Lou Harrison to Calline Harrison, July 15, 1935 (composer's personal archive).

10. The book in question was probably James Legge's *Sacred Books of China* (Oxford: Clarendon Press, 1899–1926). The chapter on music, Yueh-chi, is in the *Li Chi* ("Classic of Rites"), vols. 3–4 of Legge's translation. Lou now uses the translation by Lin cited in chapter 9.

11. Harrison interview 2/23/94.

12. Poetic quotations in this chapter are from Harrison, *Joys and Perplexities*.

13. Harrison interview 12/29/93. Lou learned of their friendship from a biography of Crapsey, probably Mary Elizabeth Osborn, *Adelaide Crapsey* (Boston: Bruce Humphries, 1933). Webster wrote the preface to a posthumous collection of Crapsey's verse (Edward Butscher, *Adelaide Crapsey* [Boston: Twayne, 1979], 120).

14. Osborn, *Adelaide Crapsey*, 89–90.

15. Harrison interview 2/23/94.

16. Information on the type fonts and their models is from Scholz interview.

17. Unidentified newspaper article from 1933 preserved in Calline Harrison's scrapbook.

18. Harrison interview 6/10/94.

Conclusion

1. Lou Harrison, "Kensley Rosen, Violinist, Heard in His Debut Here," *New York Herald Tribune*, Nov. 26, 1946.

2. Giteck interview.

3. Lewitzky interview.

4. K. Robert Schwarz, "Continuum: Robert Erickson and Lou Harrison Retrospective," *Musical America*, July 1985, 31–32.

5. Will Crutchfield, "Music: By Continuum, California Retrospective," *New York Times*, Mar. 11, 1985.

6. Andrew Imbrie, personal communication.

7. Lewitzky interview.

8. Hughes interview 12/12/94.

9. Alan Rich, "Land of the Giants," *California Magazine*, Aug. 1987, 42.

10. Hughes interview 12/12/94.

11. "Wally Trabing's Mostly about People: Five-Year-Old Soup," *Santa Cruz Sentinel*, Mar. 22, 1973.

12. Amirkhanian interview.

13. Postconcert public interview with Leta Miller, Lick Observatory, May 20, 1995.

Selected Bibliography

We have not attempted a comprehensive listing of Harrison's writings. For articles in *Modern Music*, for example, we have included the "think pieces" but not the reviews. The hundreds of newspaper reviews we have consulted are not listed; full citations are provided in footnotes for any direct quotations. For a list of interviews, see appendix 1.

Acocella, Joan. *Mark Morris*. New York: Farrar, Straus,and Giroux, 1993.

Anderson, E. Ruth. *Contemporary American Composers: A Biographical Dictionary.* Boston: G. K. Hall, 1982.

Bach, Carl Philipp Emanuel. *Versuch über die wahre Art das Clavier zu spielen.* Berlin: part 1, 1753; part 2, 1762.

Baker, Don. "The Percussion Ensemble Music of Lou Harrison, 1939–1942." D.M.A. thesis, University of Illinois, 1985.

Becker, Judith. *Traditional Music in Modern Java: Gamelan in a Changing Society.* Honolulu: University Press of Hawaii, 1980.

Belfy, Jeanne. *The Louisville Orchestra New Music Project*. Louisville: University of Louisville, 1983.

Bell-Kanner, Karen. *Frontiers: The Life and Times of Bonnie Bird, American Modern Dancer and Dance Educator*. Amsterdam: Harwood Academic Books, forthcoming.

Blackmer, Corinne E., and Patricia Juliana Smith. *En Travesti: Women, Gender Subversion, Opera*. New York: Columbia University Press, 1995.

Blackwood, Michael. *Musical Outsiders: An American Legacy*. Videocassette. Michael Blackwood Productions, 1995.

Bogdanowitsch, Sasha. "Instruments by Bill Colvig." *Experimental Musical Instruments* 9, no. 4 (June 1994): 16–20.

Brett, Philip. "Eros and Orientalism in Britten's Operas." In Brett et al., *Queering the Pitch*, 235–56.

Brett, Philip, Elizabeth Wood, and Gary C. Thomas, eds. *Queering the Pitch*. New York: Routledge, 1994.

Brinner, Benjamin. *Knowing Music, Making Music: Javanese Gamelan and the Theory of Musical Competence and Interaction*. Chicago: University of Chicago Press, 1995.

Broughton, James. *Coming Unbuttoned: A Memoir*. San Francisco: City Lights, 1993.

Brunner, David Lee. "The Choral Music of Lou Harrison." D.M.A. thesis, University of Illinois, 1989.

————. "Cultural Diversity in the Choral Music of Lou Harrison." *Choral Journal* 32, no. 10 (May 1992): 17–28.

Buerge, David M. "The Man We Call Seattle." In *Washingtonians: A Biographical Portrait of the State*, ed. David Brewster and David M. Buerge. Seattle: Sasquatch Books, 1988.

Butscher, Edward. *Adelaide Crapsey*. Boston: Twayne, 1979.

Cage, John. *Silence*. Middletown, Conn.: Wesleyan University Press, 1961.

Campbell, Joseph. *The Hero with a Thousand Faces*. 2d ed. New York: Princeton University Press, 1968.

————. *Myths to Live By*. Toronto: Bantam Books, 1972.

Carey, David. "Double Music: A Historico-Analytic Study." M.A. thesis, University of California, San Diego, 1978.

Celso, Lynnette V. "A Study and Catalogue of Lou Harrison's Utilization of Keyboard Instruments in His Solo and Ensemble Works." M.A. thesis, San Jose State University, 1979.

Chadwick, David. *Thank You and OK!: An American Zen Failure in Japan*. New York: Penguin, 1994.

The Challenge and Progress of Homosexual Law Reform. San Francisco: The Council on Religion and the Homosexual, the Daughters of Bilitis, the Society for Individual Rights, and the Tavern Guild of San Francisco, 1968.

Chalmers, John H., Jr. *Divisions of the Tetrachord*. Hanover, N.H.: Frog Peak Music, 1993.

Chase, Gilbert. *America's Music from the Pilgrims to the Present*. Urbana and Chicago: University of Illinois Press.

Cohen, Albert. *Music in the French Royal Academy of Sciences: A Study in the Evolution of Musical Thought*. Princeton: Princeton University Press, 1981.

Colvig, William. "Colvig Metallophones." *Experimental Musical Instruments* 10, no. 2 (Dec. 1994): 24–25.

Cowell, Henry. "Drums along the Pacific." *Modern Music* 18, no. 1 (Nov./Dec. 1940): 46–49.

————. *New Musical Resources*, ed. David Nicholls. Cambridge: Cambridge University Press, 1996.

————. "Oriental Influence on Western Music." In *Music East and West*. Tokyo: Executive Committee for the 1961 Tokyo East-West Music Encounter, 1962.

————, ed. *American Composers on American Music: A Symposium*. 1933. Reprint, New York: Frederick Ungar, 1962.

Cowell, Henry, and Sidney Cowell. *Charles Ives and His Music*. New York: Oxford University Press, 1955.

Crawford, Dorothy. *Evenings On and Off the Roof*. Berkeley and Los Angeles: University of California Press, 1995.

Daniel, Oliver. "Alchemy by Stokowski." *American Composers' Alliance Bulletin* 3, no. 1 (Spring 1953): 6–7.

————. "New Recordings." *American Composers' Alliance Bulletin* 3, no. 1 (Spring 1953): 15–16.

————. *Stokowski: A Counterpoint of View*. New York: Dodd, Mead, 1982.

D'Emilio, John. "Gay Politics, Gay Community: San Francisco's Experience." *Socialist Review* 11 (1981): 77–104. Reprinted in Dynes and Donaldson, *History of Homosexuality in Europe and America*.

Diamond, Jody. "'In the Beginning Was the Melody': The Gamelan Music of Lou Harrison." In Garland, *A Lou Harrison Reader.*

————. "Making Choices: American Gamelan in Composition and Education (from the Java Jive to 'Eine Kleine Gamelan Music')." In *Essays on Southeast Asian Performing Arts: Local Manifestations and Cross-Cultural Implications*, ed. Kathy Foley. Berkeley: Centers for South and Southeast Asia Studies, 1992.

Doty, David. *The Just Intonation Primer.* 2d ed. San Francisco: Just Intonation Network, 1994.

————. "The Lou Harrison Interview." *1/1: The Quarterly Journal of the Just Intonation Network* 3, no. 2 (Spring 1987): 1–16.

Dresher, Paul. "Looking West to the East." In Garland, *A Lou Harrison Reader.*

Duberman, Martin. *Black Mountain: An Exploration in Community.* 1972. Reprint, New York: Norton, 1993.

Dufallo, Richard. *Trackings: Composers Speak with Richard Dufallo.* New York: Oxford University Press, 1989.

Duncan, Robert. "The Homosexual in Society." In *Robert Duncan: A Selected Prose,* ed. Robert J. Bertholf. New York: New Directions Books, 1995.

————. "Up Rising, Passages 25." In *Robert Duncan: Selected Poems,* ed. Robert J. Bertholf. New York: New Directions Books, 1993.

Dynes, Wayne R., and Stephen Donaldson. *History of Homosexuality in Europe and America.* New York: Garland, 1992.

————, eds. *Homosexuality and Homosexuals in the Arts.* New York: Garland, 1992.

Engelman, Ralph. *Public Radio and Television in America: A Political History.* Thousand Oaks, Calif.: Sage Publications, 1996.

Feder, Stuart. *Charles Ives: "My Father's Song."* New Haven: Yale University Press, 1992.

Gagne, Cole. *Soundpieces 2: Interviews with American Composers.* Metuchen, N.J.: Scarecrow Press, 1993.

Gardner, Patrick Grant. "'La Koro Sutro' by Lou Harrison: Historical Perspective, Analysis and Performance Considerations." D.M.A. thesis, University of Texas at Austin, 1981.

Garland, Peter. *Americas: Essays on American Music and Culture, 1973–80.* Santa Fe: Soundings Press, 1982.

————. "James Tenney: Some Historical Perspectives." In *A Celebration of American Music: Words and Music in Honor of H. Wiley Hitchcock,* ed. Richard Crawford, R. Allen Lott, and Carol J. Oja. Ann Arbor: University of Michigan Press, 1990.

————, ed. *Jaime de Angulo: The Music of the Indians of Northern California.* Santa Fe: Soundings Press, 1988.

————, ed. *A Lou Harrison Reader.* Santa Fe: Soundings Press, 1987.

Gidlow, Elsa. *Elsa, I Come with My Songs.* San Francisco: Booklegger Press, 1986.

Goss, Madeleine. *Modern Music-Makers: Contemporary American Composers.* New York: E. P. Dutton, 1952.

Harris, Mary Emma. *The Arts at Black Mountain College.* Cambridge: MIT Press, 1987.

Harrison, Lou. *About Carl Ruggles.* Yonkers, N.Y.: Oscar Baradinsky, 1946. Reprinted in *The Score and I.M.A. Magazine* 12 (June 1955), 15–26, and in Garland, *A Lou Harrison Reader.*

————. "Asian Music and the United States." In *Third Asian Composers' League Conference/Festival Final Report*. Manila: National Music Council of the Philippines, 1976.

————. "Blessed Be Translators, for They Give Us Worlds." *1/1: The Journal of the Just Intonation Network* 7, no. 1 (Sept. 1991): 4–5. Reprinted in Harrison, *Music Primer*, 2d. ed., 136.

————. "Couples, Souls and Prosceniums: A Note on Dance and Music." *Listen: The Guide to Good Music* (Aug. 1945): 6–8.

————. "Creative Ideas in Classical Korean Music." *Korea Journal* 2, no. 11 (1962): 34–36.

————. "English-Speaking Gamelan." *Ear* 8, no. 4 (Sept.–Nov. 1983).

————. "Five Poems." In *Frog Peak Anthology*, 9–16. Hanover, N.H.: Frog Peak Music, 1992.

————. "From: Lou Harrison's Bureau for the Consideration of Pathetic Complaints. A Prospectus for Musicians (Department of Utopean Fantasy)." *American Composers' Alliance Bulletin* 6, no. 2 (1957): 14, 22.

————. "Homage to Schoenberg: His Late Works." *Modern Music* 21, no. 3 (Mar.–Apr. 1944): 134–38.

————. "Item: Five-Tone, Six-Tone, and Seven-Tone Modal Forms within the Traditional Matrix of Two Tetrachords Separated by a Nine to Eight." *Xenharmonikon* (Fall 1975): 6 pp.

————. *Joys and Perplexities: Selected Poems of Lou Harrison*. Winston-Salem, N.C.: The Jargon Society, the University Library (UCSC), and the Cabrillo Music Festival, 1992.

————. *Korean Music*. Unpublished incomplete book manuscript. Copy at Ethnomusicology Archive, University of California, Los Angeles. 46 pp.

————. "Learning from Henry." In *The Whole World of Music: A Henry Cowell Symposium*, ed. David Nicholls. Amsterdam: Harwood Academic Press, forthcoming.

————. "Literature: All about Music." *View* 6, no. 1 (Feb. 1946): 17.

————. "A Little Narrative with Several 'Off-ramps.'" *1/1: The Quarterly Journal of the Just Intonation Network* 5, no. 2 (Spring 1989): 1–2, 14–15.

————. "Music for the Modern Dance." *American Composers' Alliance Bulletin* 2, no. 3 (Oct. 1952): 11–12.

————. "The Music of Charles Ives." *Listen: The Guide to Good Music* (Nov. 1946): 7–9.

————. *Music Primer*. New York: C. F. Peters, 1971. Reprint with appendix and Japanese trans., 1993.

————. "On the Choros of Villa Lobos." *Modern Music* 22, no. 2 (Jan.–Feb. 1945): 85–86.

————. "On Quotation." *Modern Music* 23, no. 3 (Summer 1946): 166–69. Reprinted in Lederman, *The Life and Death of a Small Magazine*.

————. "Percussion Music and Its Relation to the Modern Dance." *Dance Observer* 7, no. 3 (1940): 32.

————. "Political Primer." In *Frog Peak Anthology*, 77–83. Hanover, N.H.: Frog Peak Music, 1992.

————. "Recent Records and Concerts." *View* 5, no. 5 (Dec. 1945): 21–22.

―――. "Refreshing the Auditory Perception." In *Music—East and West,* 141–43. Executive Committee for 1961 Tokyo East-West Music Encounter, 1961.

―――. "Ruggles, Ives, Varese." *View* 5, no. 4 (Nov. 1945): 11. Reprinted in *Soundings,* 1974.

―――. "Society, Musician, Dancer, Machine—a Set of Opinions Entirely Attributable to Lou Harrison, in 1966." *Impulse: Annual of Contemporary Dance* (1966): 40–41.

―――. "Some Notes on the Music of Mouth-Organs." In *Essays in Ethnomusicology: A Birthday Offering for Lee Hye-Ku.* Seoul: Korean Musicological Society, 1969.

―――. "Summer Music." *View* 3 (Oct. 1945): 21.

―――. "Thoughts about 'Slippery Slendro.'" *Selected Reports in Ethnomusicology* 6 (1985): 111–17.

―――. "The Violin Concerto in the Modern World." *Listen: The Guide to Good Music* (Mar. 1947): 4–6.

Harrison, Lou, and William Colvig. "Gamelan Builders' Notes from Lou Harrison and William Colvig." *Ear* 8, no. 4 (Sept.–Nov. 1983): 26.

Harrison, Lou, and Trish Neilson, eds. *Gending-Gending California,* 1981.

Hicks, Michael. "Cowell's Clusters." *Musical Quarterly* 77, no. 3 (1993): 428–58.

―――. "The Imprisonment of Henry Cowell." *Journal of the American Musicological Society* 44, no. 1 (Spring 1991): 92–119.

Hitchcock, H. Wiley, and Vivian Perlis, eds. *An Ives Celebration.* Urbana and Chicago: University of Illinois Press, 1977.

Hood, Mantle. *The Evolution of Javanese Gamelan.* Book 1: *Music of the Roaring Sea.* New York: C. F. Peters, 1980.

―――. *The Evolution of Javanese Gamelan.* Book 2: *The Legacy of the Roaring Sea.* New York: C. F. Peters, 1984.

―――. *The Nuclear Theme as a Determinant of Patet in Javanese Music.* Groningen: J. B. Walters, 1954.

Horton, James, and LuAnne Daly. "'To a Gnat's Eyebrow': Lou Harrison." *Ear* (West) 6, no. 2 (Mar./Apr. 1978): 6–7, and 6, no. 3 (May/June 1978): 5, 9.

Howett, Thomas R., and Mary B. Howett, eds. *The Salem Story, 1806–1956.* Salem, Ohio: Salem Sequicentennial Committee of the Salem Historical Society, 1956.

Job, Lenore Peters. *Looking Back While Surging Forward.* San Francisco: Peters Wright Creative Dance, 1984.

Jorgensen, Owen H. *Tuning.* East Lansing: Michigan State University Press, 1991.

Jurgrau, Robert. "A New Work by Lou Harrison." *Pitch: For the International Microtonalist* 1, no. 1 (Fall 1986): 3.

Kakinuma, Toshie, and Mamoru Fujieda. "'I Am One of Mr. Ives' Legal Heirs': An Interview with Lou Harrison." *Sonus* 9, no. 2 (Spring 1989): 46–58.

Kallberg, Jeffrey. *Chopin at the Boundaries: Sex, History, and Musical Genre.* Cambridge: Harvard University Press, 1996.

Keezer, Ronald. "A Study of Selected Percussion Ensemble Music of the Twentieth Century." *Percussionist* 8, no. 1 (Oct. 1970): 11–23.

Keislar, Douglas. "Six American Composers on Nonstandard Tunings." *Perspectives of New Music* 29, no. 1 (Winter 1991): 176–211.

Kluger, Richard. *The Paper: The Life and Death of the New York Herald Tribune.* New York: Knopf, 1986.

Koch, Heinrich Christoph. *Versuch einer Anleitung zur Composition*. Leipzig: Adam Friedrich Böhme, 1787.

Kostelanetz, Richard. "A Conversation in Eleven-minus-one Parts, with Lou Harrison about Music/Theater." *Musical Quarterly* 76, no. 3 (1992): 383–409.

———. "Interview on Poetry with Composer Lou Harrison." *Reed Magazine* 47 (Spring 1993).

———, ed. *John Cage*. New York: Praeger, 1968.

———, ed. *John Cage, Writer: Previously Uncollected Pieces*. New York: Limelight Editions, 1993.

———, ed. *Writings about John Cage*. Ann Arbor: University of Michigan Press, 1993.

Kranzler, Lorle. "Reflections in Motion—A Photographic Essay." *Impulse* (1966): 34–39.

Kriegsman, Sali Ann. *Modern Dance in America: The Bennington Years*. Boston: G. K. Hall, 1981.

Lane, Mervin, ed. *Black Mountain College: Sprouted Seeds: An Anthology of Personal Accounts*. Knoxville: University of Tennessee Press, 1990.

Larrowe, Charles P. *Harry Bridges: The Rise and Fall of Radical Labor in the United States*. New York: Lawrence Hill, 1972.

Larsen, Stephen, and Robin Larsen. *A Fire in the Mind: The Life of Joseph Campbell*. New York: Doubleday, 1991.

Lasar, Matthew. "From Dialogue to Dissent: The Pacifica Foundation and the Cold War, 1942–1964." Ph.D. dissertation, Claremont Graduate School, 1996.

Lederman, Minna. *The Life and Death of a Small Magazine (Modern Music, 1924–1946)*. New York: Institute for Studies in American Music, 1983.

Lee Hye-Ku. *Essays on Korean Traditional Music*. Seoul: Royal Asiatic Society, 1981.

Levine, Mark. "Annals of Composing: The Outsider: Lou Harrison Comes In from the Fringe." *New Yorker*, Aug. 26/Sept. 2, 1996, 150–59.

Leyland, Winston. "Lou Harrison." In *Gay Sunshine Interviews* 1. San Francisco: Gay Sunshine Press, 1978. Reprinted in Garland, *A Lou Harrison Reader*.

Liang Ming-yüeh. *Music of the Billion: An Introduction to Chinese Musical Culture*. New York: Hinrichshofen, 1985.

Liang Tsai-Ping. "A Short Note in Honor of Lou Harrison." In Garland, *A Lou Harrison Reader*.

———, ed. *On Chinese Music*. Taipei: Chinese Classical Music Association, 1964.

Lin Yutang, trans. and ed. *The Wisdom of Confucius*. New York: Random House, 1938.

Malina, Judith. *The Diaries of Judith Malina*. New York: Grove Press, 1984.

Martin, Robert K. *Hero, Captain, and Stranger: Male Friendship, Social Critique, and Literary Form in the Sea Novels of Herman Melville*. Chapel Hill: University of North Carolina Press, 1986.

McClary, Susan. *Feminine Endings: Music, Gender, and Sexuality*. Minneapolis: University of Minnesota Press, 1991.

McDermott, Vincent. "Gamelans and New Music." *Musical Quarterly* 72, no. 1 (1986): 16–27.

Mead, Rita. *Henry Cowell's New Music, 1925–1936: The Society, the Music Editions, and the Recordings*. Ann Arbor, Mich.: UMI Research Press, 1981.

Mellers, Wilfrid. *Percy Grainger.* Oxford: Oxford University Press, 1992.

Miller, Leta E. "The Art of Noise: John Cage, Lou Harrison, and the West Coast Percussion Ensemble." In *Essays in American Music* 3 (forthcoming).

———. *Lou Harrison: Keyboard and Chamber Music, 1937–94.* In *Music in the United States of America.* Madison, WI: A-R Editions, forthcoming.

Miller, Leta E., and Albert Cohen. *Music in the Royal Society of London, 1660–1806.* Detroit Studies in Music Bibliography 56. Detroit: Information Coordinators, 1987.

Morton, Brian, and Pamela Collins, eds. *Contemporary Composers.* Chicago: St. James Press, 1992.

Nicholls, David. *American Experimental Music, 1890–1940.* Cambridge: Cambridge University Press, 1990.

———, ed. *The Whole World of Music: A Henry Cowell Symposium.* Amsterdam: Harwood Academic Publishers, forthcoming.

Norman, Stuart. "Profiles/Interviews: Lou Harrison and William Colvig." *RFD: A Journal for Gay Men Everywhere* (Winter 1987–88): 56–67.

Oja, Carol. *American Music Recordings: A Discography of 20th-Century U.S. Composers.* Brooklyn, N.Y.: Institute for Studies in American Music, 1982.

———. "The Writings of Lou Harrison: A Salute at Seventy." *Newsletter of the Institute for Studies in American Music* 16, no. 2 (1987): 1–2.

Osborn, Mary Elizabeth. *Adelaide Crapsey.* Boston: Bruce Humphries, 1933.

Partch, Harry. *Genesis of a Music.* Madison: University of Wisconsin Press, 1949. 2d ed., enl. New York: Da Capo Press, 1974.

Paul, William, James D. Weinrich, John C. Gonsiorek, and Mary E. Hotvedt, eds. *Homosexuality: Social, Psychological, and Biological Issues.* Beverly Hills, Calif.: Sage Publications, 1982.

Pavlakis, Christopher. *The American Music Handbook.* New York: Free Press, 1974.

Perlis, Vivian. *Charles Ives Remembered.* New Haven: Yale University Press, 1974.

Perlman, Marc, ed. *Festival of Indonesia Conference Summaries.* New York: Festival of Indonesia Foundation, 1992.

Polansky, Larry. "Item: Lou Harrison's Role as a Speculative Theorist." In Garland, *A Lou Harrison Reader.*

Quin, Mike. *The Big Strike.* Olema, Calif.: Olema Publishing Company, 1949.

Rathbun, Virginia Madison. "Lou Harrison and His Music." M.A. thesis, San Jose State University, 1976.

Reis, Claire. *Composers, Conductors, and Critics.* New York: Oxford University Press, 1955.

Revill, David. *The Roaring Silence: John Cage: A Life.* New York: Arcade, 1992.

Riesenberg, Felix, Jr. *Golden Gate: The Story of San Francisco Harbor.* New York: Knopf, 1940.

Rivera, Rhonda. "Homosexuality and the Law." In *Homosexuality: Social, Psychological, and Biological Issues,* ed. William Paul, James D. Weinrich, John C. Gonsiorek, and Mary E. Hotvedt. Beverly Hills, Calif.: Sage Publications, 1982.

Rockefeller Foundation Annual Report, 1961.

Rubin, Nathan. *John Cage and the Twenty-Six Pianos of Mills College: Forces in American Music from 1940 to 1990: A History.* Moraga, Calif.: Sarah's Books, 1994.

Rutman, Neil. "The Solo Piano Works of Lou Harrison." D.M.A. thesis, Peabody Conservatory, 1982.

Said, Edward W. *Orientalism*. New York: Pantheon, 1978.

San Francisco: The Bay and Its Cities. Compiled by Workers of the Writers' Program of the Work Projects Administration in Northern California. New York: Hastings House, 1947.

Sawyer-Lauçanno, Christopher. *An Invisible Spectator: A Biography of Paul Bowles*. New York: Weidenfeld and Nicolson, 1989.

Schlesinger, Kathleen. *The Greek Aulos*. London: Methuen, 1939.

Sedgwick, Eve Kosofsky. *Epistemology of the Closet*. Berkeley and Los Angeles: University of California Press, 1990.

Shaffer, Dale E. *More of the Salem Story . . . with Photographs*. Salem, Ohio, 1992.

————. *Salem Stories: A Backward Glance*. Salem, Ohio, 1993.

Shaffer, Richard. "A Cross-Cultural Eclectic: Lou Harrison and His Music." *Percussive Notes* 29, no. 2 (1990): 43–47.

Silver, Benjamin Stump, and Frances Aylette Silver. *Our Silver Heritage*. Gatesville, Tex.: Gatesville Printing Company, 1976.

Simon, Larry. "Interview with Lou Harrison." *Ear Magazine of New Music* 9, no. 5 (Fall 1985): 18, 36–37.

Smith, Geoff, and Nicola Walker Smith, eds. *New Voices*. Portland: Amadeus Press, 1995.

Smith, Stuart. "Lou Harrison's Fugue for Percussion." *Percussionist* 16, no. 2 (Winter 1979): 47–56.

Solie, Ruth A., ed. *Musicology and Difference: Gender and Sexuality in Music Scholarship*. Berkeley and Los Angeles: University of California Press, 1993.

Solomon, Maynard. "Franz Schubert and the Peacocks of Benvenuto Cellini." *19th-Century Music* 12, no. 3 (Spring 1989): 193–206.

————. "Franz Schubert's 'My Dream.'" *American Imago* 38, no. 2 (Summer 1981): 137–54. Reprinted in Dynes and Donaldson, *Homosexuality and Homosexuals in the Arts*.

Sontag, Susan. *Against Interpretation and Other Essays*. New York: Farrar, Straus, and Giroux, 1966.

Sorrell, Neil. *A Guide to the Gamelan*. London: Faber and Faber, 1990.

Steeh, Judith. *History of Ballet and Modern Dance*. London: Hamlyn, 1982.

Stein, Erwin, ed. *Arnold Schoenberg: Letters*. Trans. Eithne Wilkins and Ernst Kaiser. New York: St. Martin's Press, 1964.

Stryker, Susan, and Jim Van Buskirk. *Gay by the Bay: A History of Queer Culture in the San Francisco Bay Area*. San Francisco: Chronicle Books, 1996.

Sumarsam. *Gamelan: Cultural Interaction and Musical Development in Central Java*. Chicago: University of Chicago Press, 1995.

Sutton, R. Anderson. *Traditions of Gamelan Music in Java: Musical Pluralism and Regional Identity*. Cambridge: Cambridge University Press, 1991.

Thomas, Allan. "Skip, Skip, Skip to My Lou." *Canzona* 5, no. 17 (1984): 4–13.

Thomas, David J. "San Francisco's 1979 White Night Riot: Injustice, Vengeance, and Beyond." In Paul et al., *Homosexuality: Social, Psychological, and Biological Issues*.

Thomson, Virgil. *American Music since 1910*. New York: Holt, Rinehart and Winston, 1970.

————. "A Note Regarding Lou Harrison." In Garland, *A Lou Harrison Reader*.

————. "The World of Lou Harrison." *KPFA Folio* 39, no. 5 (May 1987): 7. Reprinted in Garland, *A Lou Harrison Reader*.

Tomkins, Calvin. *The World of Marcel Duchamp*. New York: Time-Life Books, 1966.

Tommasini, Anthony. *Virgil Thomson: Composer on the Aisle*. New York: W.W. Norton, 1997.

————. *Virgil Thomson's Musical Portraits*. New York: Pendragon Press, 1986.

Turco, Lewis. *The Book of Forms*. New York: Dutton, 1968. Rev. ed., *The New Book of Forms*. Hanover, N.H.: University Press of New England, 1986.

Van Gulik, R. H. "Brief Note on the Cheng, the Chinese Small Cither." *Journal of the Society for Research in Asiatic Music* 9 (Mar. 1951): 10–25.

Vanlandingham, Larry. "The Percussion Ensemble 1930–1945." *Percussionist* 10, no. 1 (Fall 1972): 11–25.

Vicentino, Nicola. *L'antica musica ridotta alla moderna prattica*. 1555. Facsimile ed. Kassel, Germany: Bärenreiter, 1959.

Von Gunden, Heidi. *The Music of Lou Harrison*. Metuchen, N.J.: Scarecrow Press, 1995.

Wade, James. *One Man's Korea: A Miscellany Chosen by the Author*. Seoul: Hollym, 1967.

————. *West Meets East*. Pomso Publishers, 1975.

Waley, Arthur. *The Analects of Confucius*. New York: Random House, 1938.

Ward, Estolv E. *Harry Bridges on Trial*. Honolulu: ILWU, 1940.

Warren, Larry. *Lester Horton: Modern Dance Pioneer*. New York: Marcel Dekker, 1977.

Wen-Chung, Chou. "Asian Concepts and Twentieth-Century Composers." *Musical Quarterly* 57, no. 2 (Apr. 1971): 211–29.

Wiecki, Ronald V. "Relieving '12-Tone Paralysis': Harry Partch in Madison, Wisconsin, 1944–1947." *American Music* 9, no. 1 (Spring 1991): 43–66.

Wright, Irma-Louise. "The *Koncherto for Violin with Percussion Orchestra* by Lou Harrison." D.M. thesis, Florida State University, 1994.

Yates, Peter. "A Collage of American Composers." *Arts and Architecture* 75, no. 12 (Dec. 1958), and 76, no. 2 (Feb. 1959).

————. "Lou Harrison." *Arts and Architecture* 61, no. 2 (Feb. 1944): 26, 37.

————. "Lou Harrison." *American Composers' Alliance Bulletin* 9, no. 2 (1960): 2–7.

————. "A Trip up the Coast." *Arts and Architecture* 74, no. 12 (Dec. 1957): 4, 6–7, 10, 33–34.

————. *Twentieth-Century Music: Its Evolution from the End of the Harmonic Era into the Present Era of Sound*. New York: Random House, 1967.

Ziffrin, Marilyn J. *Carl Ruggles: Composer, Painter, and Storyteller*. Urbana and Chicago: University of Illinois Press, 1994.

Zinn, Howard. *A People's History of the United States*. New York: Harper and Row, 1980.

Lou Harrison:
A World Composed

Compact Disc Contents

*1. Simfony #13 (1941) 9:06
UC Santa Cruz Percussion Ensemble (Kristine Carelli, Emerson Dubois, Jaime Hailpern, Anne Yoshikawa), directed by William Winant. Recorded 1997 by Richard Karst and Fredric Lieberman. Edited by June Millington, Janelle Burdell, and Fredric Lieberman at IMA Studios, Bodega, CA. By permission of the artists and Hermes Beard Press. [Text reference: p. 19]

*2–3. Two improvisations in Greek tunings (early 1970s) 5:49
Lou Harrison and Richard Dee, harp. From a monaural home recording, 1970s. Reproduced by permission. [Text reference: pp. 113 and 115]

> 2. Archytas's enharmonic: two tetrachords with unequal quarter tones and a pure major third (28:27, 36:35, 5:4), separated by a whole tone **3:02**

> 3. Didymos's chromatic: two tetrachords with unequal minor seconds and a pure minor third (16:15, 25:24, 6:5), separated by a whole tone **2:47**

*4–9. Cinna (Suite for Tack Piano; 1957) 15:59
Lou Harrison, tack piano. Monaural home recording, ca. 1957. Sonic restoration: Gordon Mumma. By permission of Lou Harrison and Hermes Beard Press. [Text reference: p. 113]

> 4. Lou Harrison introduces the tuning system **3:59**
> 5. Movement 1: Medium Fast **2:00**
> 6. Movement 2: Slow **2:52**
> 7. Movement 3: Fast **1:50**
> 8. Movement 4: Medium Slow **2:41**
> 9. Movement 5: Medium; Grand **2:37**

10. Strict Songs (1955; revised 1992), mvt. 3: Here is Tenderness 3:04
> SATB choir. UCSC Orchestra and Chamber Singers; Nicole Paiement, conductor. Musical Heritage 513616L. Reproduced by permission. [Text reference and tuning, p. 114 and example 5-3]
> *Here is Tenderness—Of the redwood tree, which is immortal.*
> *Here is Tenderness—Of the fantail goldfish trailing double tails.*

* = First Recording

Here is Tenderness—Of the tree, the fish, and moon Ganymede encircling third, the largest planet.
Here is Tenderness—Of the tourmaline showing Flamingo light. (text by Lou Harrison)

*11. Simfony in Free Style (1955) 4:08
Electronic realization by David Doty. By kind permission C.F. Peters Corp. and Lou Harrison. [Text reference: p. 117]

*12. Hyi Mun (Hùimun; Korea, 15th century) 3:36
Transcribed and realized by Lou Harrison. Lou Harrison, p'iri; Richard Dee, bowed zither; William Colvig, pak and bells. Live performance, Pomona College, Nov. 15, 1970. By permission of Lou Harrison. [Text reference: p. 143]

13. The Garden at One and a Quarter Moons (1964; revised 1966) 2:33
Lou Harrison, cheng. Phoenix PHCD-118. Courtesy of Phoenix Records and Hermes Beard Press. [Text reference: p. 148]

*14. Gending in Honor of the Poet Virgil (1981; revised 1985) 9:30
Javanese gamelan (slendro) with the addition, for this performance, of a pesindhèn (vocal) part. Gamelan Si Betty, directed by Trish Nielsen. Live performance at the San Francisco Conservatory of Music's "Celebrating Lou Harrison!" festival, Feb. 15, 1997. Recorded by Mikako Endo. Used by permission. (Members of Gamelan Si Betty: Colleen Donovan, Daniel Kelley, Trish Neilsen, Henry Spiller, George Tredick, Peter Huboi, Laura McColm, Richard Newell, Rae Ann Stahl, Mickey Helms, Kenneth Miller, Bill van Osdol, Michael Strunk.) [Text reference: p. 161]
Lord of Language/Thou that singest wheat and woodland,
Tilth and vineyard, hive and horse and herd;/All the charm of all the Muses
Often flowering in a lovely word. (text: Alfred Lord Tennyson)

15. Pacifika Rondo (1963), mvt. 6: A Hatred of the Filthy Bomb 2:50
Oakland Youth Orchestra, Robert Hughes, conductor. Phoenix PHCD-118. Courtesy of Phoenix Records and Peer International Corp. (BMI). [Text reference: p. 182]

*16. Peace Piece 2: Passages 25 (1968) 7:02
Erik Townsend, tenor; Cabrillo Music Festival Orchestra, Gerhard Samuel, conductor. Live performance, Aug. 17, 1968. By permission of composer, artists, and the literary estate of Robert Duncan. [Text reference: p. 183]
    Text: "Up Rising, Passages 25." Full text in Robert J. Bertholf, ed. *Robert Duncan: Selected Poems.* New York: New Directions, 1993.

*17. Three Songs (1985), mvt. 1: King David's Lament for Jonathan 3:21
Commissioned and performed by the Portland Gay Men's Chorus. Live performance, Sept. 28-29, 1985, Gilbert Seeley, guest conductor. Re-

corded and edited by Frank Stearns and Gene Lysinger for Oregon Public Broadcasting. Used by permission of the performers and Peer International Corp. (BMI). [Text reference: p. 200]

Text: II Samuel: 1.26, three simultaneous versions: King James, Revised Standard, Hebrew

Now I grieve for you, my brother Jonathan./Dear and delightful you were to me.
Your love was wonderful, surpassing the love of woman.

Now I am sore distressed, for thee my brother Jonathan./Very pleasant hast thou been unto me.
Thy love was wonderful, passing the love of woman.

Tzar li, alecha achi Jonatan,
Naam'ta li m'od,/Nif'l'ata ahavat'cha li, mei'ahavat nashim (II Samuel: 1.26)

18. Symphony on G (1947-64), mvt. 1 6:07

Royal Philharmonic Orchestra, Gerhard Samuel, conductor. CRI CD 715. Courtesy of Composers Recordings, Inc. and Peer International Corp. (BMI). [Text reference: p. 196].

The works on this CD vary widely in audio quality due to the condition of the original sources. Some sonic restoration was applied to reduce extraneous noise and the ravages of time. The works included here were chosen primarily for their musical quality and interest, their value in illustrating the written text, and their contribution to the recorded repertory of works by Lou Harrison.

Producer and editor: Fredric Lieberman

Mastering: David Gans, Truth and Fun, Inc., Oakland CA (tnf@well.com)

Supported in part by the Eyes of Chaos Foundation, a tax-exempt organization supporting the composition, recording, and performance of new music (484 Lake Park Ave. #102, Oakland, CA 94610-2730).

Total time: 73:49

Index